MEDIA POWER IN POLITICS

Sixth Edition

Edited by
Doris A. Graber

University of Illinois at Chicago

CQ PRESS

A Division of SAGE
Washington, D.C.

CQ Press
2300 N Street, NW, Suite 800
Washington, DC 20037

Phone: 202–729–1900; toll-free, 1–866–4CQ-PRESS (1–866–427–7737)

Web: www.cqpress.com

Cover design: Paula Goldstein
Composition: C&M Digitals (P) Ltd.

♾ The paper used in this publication exceeds the requirements of the
American National Standard for Information Sciences—Permanence of
Paper for Printed Library Materials, ANSI Z39.48–1992.

Printed and bound in the United States of America

14   13   12   2   3   4   5

Library of Congress Cataloging-in-Publication Data

Media power in politics / Doris A. Graber, editor.—6th ed.
    p. cm.
  Includes bibliographical references and index.
  ISBN 978-1-60426-610-8 (pbk. : alk. paper) 1. Mass media—Political
aspects—United States. 2. Mass media—Social aspects—United States.
I. Graber, Doris A. (Doris Appel), 1923-

  HN90.M3M43 2011
  302.23—dc22
                          2010021643

*For Tom, whose indomitable
courage conquers adversity
and inspires hope*

CONTENTS

PREFACE

How powerful are the news media? On a scale of 0 to 100, ratings have run the full gamut. Intuitively a "minimal effects" rating seems too low, and an "all powerful" evaluation sounds excessively high. What is the real tipping point, and how much does it vary depending on the circumstances? Overall, has media power been waning in the twenty-first century because the Internet enables so many new voices to join the media chorus, or has there merely been a power transfer from old media to new media?

The authors whose writings are featured in this book present impressive evidence pertaining to these questions, but their findings are quite contradictory for several reasons. News media effects are very complex, difficult to measure precisely because their influence is intertwined with the effects of other social forces, and hard to specify because the impact varies for different stakeholders.

The sixth edition of *Media Power in Politics* guides readers through the maze of recent literature and older landmark studies that explore major controversies about news media influence. Answers to questions about news media impact continue to shift as new developments occur. It is important to record these shifts in up-to-date editions of the book while still remaining in touch with the past and anticipating future developments. As always, *Media Power in Politics* is designed to familiarize political communication students with policy-relevant, cutting-edge research presented in a wide-ranging yet clearly focused collection of essays that illuminate important points. The book is designed as primary reading for courses on mass media and politics, mass media and society, political communication, and public opinion. It can also serve as supplementary reading in American government courses that highlight the impact of news media and in courses that focus on public policy formation. The selections in the book span several social science disciplines, encouraging students to view problems from interdisciplinary perspectives. Besides social scientists who represent diverse areas of expertise, contributors include media practitioners who are familiar with a variety of print and electronic venues. In fact, some of the academic authors have also worked for media organizations in the past; their theories, analyses, and recommendations are therefore tempered by the realism that comes from practical experience.

Media Power in Politics is divided into six parts. Each begins with an introduction that delineates a particular sphere of media impact. A brief editorial note then introduces each selection. Each note identifies the selection's author or authors and highlights its principal contributions to understanding news media influence in that particular sphere. The articles reproduce the original texts except for clearly marked deletions, editorial inserts, and corrections of factual errors in dates and misspelled names. Notes have been renumbered when necessary to maintain unbroken sequences, but note styles have been retained with minor exceptions.

The thirty-six selections reprinted in this book represent the work of fifty-nine authors. Many of them are nationally and internationally recognized scholars; others have just embarked on promising careers. I thank all of them for the contributions they have made to understanding media power in politics, and I am grateful for the authors' and copyright holders' willingness to allow me to include their work in this new book. For guidance in choosing essays that accomplish the goals set for this book, I am deeply indebted to the many colleagues who suggested what to include and what to leave out. Had I followed all of their recommendations, this book would have tripled in length. If your favorite study seems to be missing, take heart! You will most likely find it cited in the many references sprinkled throughout the chapters, indicating that its findings are part of the knowledge displayed in these pages.

Preparation of a book of readings entails many tasks beyond selecting and editing the contents and writing introductory comments. As always, I am grateful to the staff at CQ Press for handling these tasks ably, expeditiously, and courteously. Special thanks are due to Charisse Kiino for overseeing the editorial process with the help of her assistant, Nancy Loh. Production editor Allyson Rudolph took extraordinary care in shepherding the manuscript through its final stages. Copy editor Barbara Corrigan took charge of polishing the various editorial notes and chasing out error gremlins. Nancy Loh took care of permissions. Amy Schoenecker, my research assistant at the University of Illinois at Chicago, contributed in major ways to the successful completion of the book. Her keen eye for detail saved me from errors of commission and omission. It is a pleasure to work with her. I would also like to thank reviewers of the previous edition for their detailed critiques and their suggestions for changes in the new edition: Whitney Franklin (Ohio Wesleyan University), Leif Hoffmann (University of Oregon), Michael David Kanner (University of Colorado, Boulder), Joe Lyons, Vaughn May (Belmont University), and Emily Renaud (Rutgers University). Last but not least, I owe a heap of thanks to my family for their unfailing support for all I do. They keep me going during these challenging times.

Doris A. Graber

INTRODUCTION

How powerful are American mass media in shaping politics during a volatile era when the ranks of news professionals are thinning and the numbers of lay news and opinion providers are exploding? No definitive answers are in sight, despite a great deal of research and informed speculation. The full scope of many factors and circumstances that make media power wax and wane remains elusive. Nonetheless, research continues to shed light on some major factors that explain various aspects of media, providing clues about when, where, and why media power is likely to peak or plunge. The literature exploring media power is voluminous and continues to expand rapidly, making it difficult for newcomers to the field to gain an overview of what is currently known and where the research frontiers are. *Media Power in Politics* simplifies the task. In this sixth edition, the new selections introduce readers to cutting-edge research targets.

The new edition of this book analyzes mass media effects on the political system in general as well as on its formal and informal components, such as Congress, the presidency, public opinion, and pressure groups at the national, state, and local levels. The interactions of the mass media with political institutions have influenced the conduct of American politics and shaped political outcomes in diverse ways. The magnitude of these media effects raises profound questions about the roles that private individuals and various types of small and large organizations do play and should play in the government and politics of a democratic society.

Each of the six parts into which the essays have been grouped illustrates the influence of mass media on an important facet of U.S. politics. Part I deals with mass media effects in general. The selections in parts II through V explore the influence of mass media on political opinions and preferences, on presidential and congressional elections, on participants within and outside the political power structure, and on the formation and implementation of domestic and foreign public policies. Part VI examines private and public efforts in the United States and abroad to control media offerings so that they meet the public's needs.

The essays assembled in this book were chosen primarily because they represent high-quality research designed to shed light on diverse aspects of media power. To introduce readers to the intellectual origins of this type of research and to contemporary milestones in the field, many essays feature the work of leading political communication scholars from several social science disciplines. The mix includes old-timers and newcomers with and without extensive experience as practicing journalists. Clarity of presentation, ease of reading, and diversity of research methods also were important selection criteria.

Twenty-one of the thirty-six essays in the current volume are first-timers in this edition. The new selections reflect the major transformations that have occurred and keep occurring on the media scene. The essays continue to cover traditional media because they remain extremely important. But much of the attention now focuses on the impact of new media and on the process of intertwining familiar practices and conventions with new ways of collecting and presenting news. This thoroughly revised sixth edition therefore alerts readers to the latest developments in a rapidly growing, interdisciplinary area of study.

Readers should keep in mind that the excerpts were chosen with a specific purpose in mind: to illustrate and assess the dimensions and scope of media power in politics in a variety of contemporary arenas. This was not necessarily the primary purpose of each of the authors. Therefore, the precise thrust of the unabridged work cannot always be judged from the thrust of the excerpts presented here. The extent of editing varies greatly, with some essays edited only lightly and others cut substantially. To keep essays fairly brief, many tables, footnotes, and endnotes had to be eliminated. Interesting methodological and factual details and arguments were shortened or fell entirely by the wayside. That is the price that must be paid when lengthy discussions are condensed to accentuate particular arguments and whatever lacks pertinence is excised. The reward is a more succinct presentation of relevant information that allows the main arguments to emerge with greater force and clarity. Readers who want the full accounts should read the original sources; they are fully identified for each selection. Readers should always use the original version of an edited selection when quoting from it.

Instead of the six broad categories into which these essays have been divided, other groupings are possible. Guided by the index, readers may wish to focus on essays that illustrate research methods, such as quantitative and qualitative content analysis or small- and large-scale surveys that use cross-sectional or panel approaches. Other research techniques described in the book are intensive interviews and experimental studies. In addition, the footnotes and bibliographies in most selections provide ample leads to methodological explanations and communication theories.

The essays also can be used to examine various aspects of the news-making process. All selections are relevant, but several address the topic explicitly. The study of news making raises questions about the effects of the Internet age on American democracy. New technologies and new forms of interactive communication have brought changes in public opinion formation, the conduct of elections, and the nature and activities of pressure groups. Readers may wish to cluster the essays around particular topics. For example, the media's role in crises is explored repeatedly, suggesting interesting comparisons. Also, several essays refer to media uses in different political settings that involve a diverse array of political actors. These essays allow readers to assess message flows at sites other than the national government of the United States.

The boundaries between the six parts of the book are porous. For example, essays in part I, which addresses how media effects are studied, can be supplemented by relevant illustrations in selections in several other parts. For instance, the role that news media play in setting the agenda for political discussion and action surfaces throughout the book, either explicitly or implicitly. Insights into campaigning via mass media are enriched by comparing the essays about election campaigns in part III with the lobbying campaigns featured in part V. Similarly, discussion of media impact on public policies is not limited to part V. Articles in other parts raise policy issues concerning the stigmatizing of criminals, the regulation of the Internet, and issues of censorship in times of crisis. Part VI, which discusses efforts to control media output, also sheds light on the reciprocal influence of the media and the executive branch, Congress, and pressure groups covered in part IV. Collectively, these selections broaden the picture sketched out in individual parts of the book.

The flexibility of *Media Power in Politics* springs from its rich content and from the variety of disciplinary viewpoints that are represented. Many brilliant scholars have been attracted to the field because of the importance of the issues that it encompasses and the fascination of exploring them while major transformations are happening. You are invited to sample their works in whatever order best suits your purposes.

Part I

PUTTING MASS MEDIA EFFECTS IN PERSPECTIVE

Doris Graber

This section puts research on mass media effects into historical and contextual perspective. Where have we been? Where are we going? In the first selection, Bruce Bimber discusses how the nature of information transmission technologies shapes political institutions in democratic societies. When technologies change, societies undergo far-reaching transformations. The United States has experienced four major media revolutions in its history. It has now entered the age of news abundance. Access to all sorts of information is universal and cheap. The number of suppliers of news for the mass public is mushrooming, and government control over news is ebbing.

The next essay, by Jonathan McDonald Ladd and Gabriel S. Lenz, cautions readers about the difficulties facing investigators who attempt to track media effects. The authors demonstrate that these obstacles are surmountable, using a case in Britain, where newspaper endorsements frequently sway the choices of British voters. When newspapers switch their endorsements, even late in the election, their readers follow suit. Similar individuals who do not read these newspapers stay the course. While the case deals with British politics, the findings about the reality of media power are relevant everywhere.

An essay by sociologist Michael Schudson follows. It offers a surprising twist on the foremost criticisms heaped on the overall performance of the news media. Schudson provides a full account of media misbehaviors that rile the critics most. He concedes that the criticisms are well taken, but then, like a medieval alchemist, he turns lead into gold. The features of American journalism that are damned most frequently—subservience to official sources; shallow, often cynical, accounts of daily happenings; an emphasis on conflicts, scandals, and crimes; a rigid application of journalistic norms—are really blessings in disguise that serve democratic ideals. An unlovable press is an independent press, beholden to no one, free to praise and criticize at will.

Next Michael Gurevitch, Stephen Coleman, and Jay G. Blumler present an overview of the main forces that are currently battling over control of the public's political information supply. The authors discuss the influence of mainstream media, especially television in the past, before these media were seriously challenged by their new Internet-spawned rivals. Gurevitch, Coleman, and Blumler then explore the changes that have ensued and project the likely trajectory of future changes. Their discussion is broadly gauged, covering challenges facing news producers, politicians, and citizens. Obviously, a revolution is in progress, and it may ultimately lead to more democratic systems of news production and distribution that satisfy a broader range of citizens' political needs.

Alex S. Jones's views about the likely future of news are much less optimistic. Viewing the scene from the perspective of a highly experienced Pulitzer Prize–winning journalist, he fears that the quality of news in the future will be a pale shadow of the heights that it was able to reach in the past. Jones uses the label "iron core" of news when he refers to fact-based news about politics that permits citizens to hold their governments accountable. He documents that this iron core has shriveled substantially and continues to crumble. In tandem, the vigor of U.S. democracy has been eroding because citizens lack the essential information that they need to make sound political judgments. Although the public continues to lose solid news, there is still hope that these trends can—and will—be reversed.

In the final selection, two sets of authors examine the shape of news in international affairs reporting, which is the area of news wherein iron core reporting by professional journalists has diminished most sharply. Steven Livingston focuses on the ways in which control over foreign news reporting is shifting from professional journalists to hordes of amateur news providers. The new, easily mastered, inexpensive technologies, such as cell phone cameras and handheld recording devices, empower them to report stories far more effectively than has been possible in the past. If greater diversity of news sources and more extensive audio-visual coverage are desirable developments, then foreign news reporting may actually be improving, rather than worsening. Next, Kaye Sweetser Trammell and David D. Perlmutter offer a case study that illustrates how interesting new types of content are emerging. They tell the story of one Iraqi citizen who blogged to his friends about daily life in war-torn Iraq. The blogs gained wide attention in the United States and elsewhere because they provided fresh, hitherto unavailable, insights about the impact of war on average citizens. The fact that the narrator was an amateur rather than a professional reporter made the story more credible rather than diminished its authenticity.

1

HOW INFORMATION SHAPES POLITICAL INSTITUTIONS

Bruce Bimber

Editor's Note

Bruce Bimber's essay highlights the crucial role that information transmission plays in structuring politics in democratic societies. He points out how changes in the structure, costs, and accessibility of information alter the political system. The United States has moved through four major communications revolutions in its history, mostly fueled by technological developments. Currently, the Internet and other new media have created an era of information abundance, fracturing the communication monopoly of old-style organizations and allowing many resource-poor new voices to be heard. These developments are changing the political landscape in ways that remain as yet unpredictable.

Bimber was the director of the Center for Information Technology and Society and a professor of political science and communication at the University of California, Santa Barbara, when his book was published. He had coauthored *Campaigning Online: The Internet in U.S. Elections* (2003), which won the McGannon Communication Policy Award for social and ethical relevance in communication policy research. He had also written numerous articles dealing with technology and politics. The following selection is from *Information and American Democracy: Technology in the Evolution of Political Power* (2003), which won the Don K. Price Award for best book about science, technology, and politics.

Defining "Information" and "Communication"

Knowledge about facts, subjects, or events is inextricably bound to virtually every aspect of democracy. Such knowledge may concern the interests, concerns, preferences, or intentions of citizens as individuals or collectives. It may also concern the economic or social state of communities or society, or the actions and intentions of government officials and candidates for office. In what follows, political information constitutes any knowledge relevant to the working of democratic processes.

In his classic *The Nature and Origins of Mass Opinion,* John Zaller observes that the content of elite discourse, such as claims about the state of the world from party leaders and editorial positions of newspapers, contains information, but it is not "just information." Because political discourse is the product of values and selectivity as much as verifiably "objective" observations, it comprises a mix of information and other factors. For my purposes this definition too narrowly constrains the concept of information by associating it with "truth" and "objectivity."[1] I assume that when a political actor communicates a personal statement about the world containing a mix of facts and values, that actor is simply communicating a package of information, some of it dealing with "facts" and some of it with his or her values and predispositions. Some "facts" may even be wrong, but they can be communicated nonetheless and they constitute information.[2]

"Information" need not stand in opposition to opinions, stories, rhetoric, or signals about value structures. Information might be a "fact" about the rate of inflation published by the Bureau of Economic Analysis just as well as a political official's statement about the need to control inflation. A candidate's promise on a web site or broadcast advertisement "to protect Social Security" conveys certain political information, just as a Congressional Budget Office report on Social Security fund solvency conveys other information of a different and perhaps more satisfyingly "objective" sort. Information is simply something that can be known or communicated.

. . . [I]t is useful not to bind the definition of information too tightly to the human acts of perception and knowing. I assume that information can exist independently of its perception and understanding by any particular political actor. It is important, however, to observe the intimacy of the connection between "communication" and "information." . . . I use "communication" to mean simply the transfer or exchange of information. Certainly, different forms of communication may convey different quantities of information in different ways, but I do not attempt to isolate the two concepts.

My definition of information therefore extends well beyond facts, and my definition of communication well beyond a quantitative transmission model. My conception of information is consistent with Inguun Hagen's interpretation of the process of television news-watching by citizens, which may involve not only becoming informed in a narrow sense, but also diversion, habit or ritual, and fulfillment of a sense of duty or obligation.[3] Information defined this way permeates human activity, and in principle the complete range of human meaning can be conveyed by communication.

Defined this broadly, information becomes vital to democracy in myriad ways: in the processes by which citizen preferences are formed and aggregated, in the behaviors of citizens and elites, in formal procedures of representation, in acts of governmental decision making, in the administration of laws and regulations, and in the mechanisms of accountability that freshen democracy and sustain its legitimacy. None of these elements of the democratic process can operate apart from the exchange and flow of information among citizens and their associations and organizations, among citizens and government, and within government itself.

More to the point, the *structure* of information in America at the outset of the twenty-first century is very different from that at the outset of the twentieth century, just as its structure then differed from that in the age of Jefferson. Not only the volume of political information available in society, but also its distribution and cost, have varied from one age to another. . . . How do historically changing properties of political information affect the evolution of democracy? What patterns might exist in the evolving nature of information and its relationship to politics? To what extent can the character of democracy be traced to causes rooted in the informational characteristics of a particular age? To pose these questions is to situate modern technology and applied questions about the contemporary information revolution in the larger sweep of American political development.

Overview of the Theory

. . . How can the relationship between information and political change be approached theoretically? My perspective is based on the observation that many features of social and economic structure were derived from the characteristics of information during the period in which they arose. Throughout most of the twentieth century, for example, the information necessary for economic transactions, education, social interaction, and many other facets of modernity had certain properties. It was hierarchically organized, costly to obtain and difficult to manage, and in most settings asymmetrically distributed. French social theorist Pierre Levy refers to these properties as a "communications ecology," the basic features of information and communication to which human institutions and organizations are adapted.[4] Vertically integrated firms, retail stores, administrative organizations, and even universities are in part adaptations to a communications ecology in which information is costly and asymmetric.

From this perspective, the contemporary information revolution involves deep changes in the communications ecology, with potential consequences for institutions and processes whose structures are in substantial ways adapted to older communications arrangements. This revolution is not simply an increase in the volume of information. . . . It is also qualitative, as information of all kinds becomes cheaper, its structure ever more complex and nonlinear, and its distribution far more symmetric than at any time in the past.

In principle, such developments could have structural consequences that are far-reaching. Indeed, it is already apparent that economic structure is sensitive to such changes, as economic transactions are transformed on a large scale, new methods of retailing visibly overtake the commercial world, and old business relationships and structures give way to new, information-intensive arrangements. Perhaps less abruptly but no less profoundly, other institutions sensitive to features of information and communication may change as well. Education may be altered for better or worse (or both) as printed matter grows less central to the transmission of knowledge, meaningful engagement with others at a distance becomes more readily possible, and the kinds of skills relevant to economic and personal well-being change. The fabrics of social association, cultures, even private lives may be rewoven, insofar as these depend upon the nature and accessibility of information. And so it may be for democracy, to the extent that its structures represent adaptations to particular informational circumstances.

. . . I believe that there are good but underappreciated reasons that scholars have noticed the relevance of information technology at what are arguably the two most important historical turning points in American political development: the rise of party-based majoritarian politics and the evolution of group-based political pluralism. My aim is to explore what integration might be possible between those two developmental milestones and the present, using information as the nexus. I should add that in so doing, it is not my primary aim to predict the *future* of the information revolution and American politics, a risky temptation to which a number of writers have succumbed. I restrict myself instead to analyzing the nature and causes of changes under way in American democracy *at present*. I intend this . . . to be an argument for conceptualizing the evolution of information as an important contributor to political change at the largest scale—not information defined narrowly as the quantifiable messages exchanged by rational agents in signaling games and the like, but as a universally important ingredient in political processes.

Much of my thesis is based on the observation that elites exercise a powerful influence on the organization of democracy, through their capacity to influence public opinion, set agendas, mobilize citizens into collective action, make decisions, and implement policies. The identity and structure of elites is neither fixed across time nor random in its changes. Many factors affect the identity and structure of elites, and the state of information is one of them. Exogenous changes in the accessibility or structure of information cause changes in the structure of elite organizations that dominate political activity, and these in turn affect the broad character of democracy.

Information Regimes and Revolutions

I develop this theoretical claim in two steps, one historical and one contemporary. First, I reinterpret parts of American political history in informational terms. I argue that information regimes exist in American political history as periods of stable relationships among information, organizations, and democratic structure. The features of an information regime are: (1) a set of dominant properties of political information, such as high cost; (2) a set of opportunities and constraints on the management of political information that these properties create; and (3) the appearance of characteristic political organizations and structures adapted to those opportunities and constraints. Information regimes in the United States have been interrupted by information revolutions, which involve changes in the structure or accessibility of information. These revolutions may be initiated by technological developments, institutional change, or economic outcomes. An information revolution disrupts a prior information regime by creating new opportunities for political communication and the organization of collective action. These changes create advantages for some forms of organization and structure and disadvantages for others, leading to adaptations and change in the world of political organizations and intermediaries. This is to say that democratic power tends to be biased toward those with the best command of political information at any particular stage in history.

The first information regime in the United States emerged from an information revolution during the Jacksonian democratization. It was facilitated by the creation of the first national-scale system for communicating political information, namely, the remarkable U.S. Postal Service and the equally remarkable American newspaper industry. . . . National flow of political information was largely impossible in the decades after the founding. Its absence had blocked the development of new parties prior to the 1830s. Those parties that arose in the mid-nineteenth century were the final component of this information regime, an adaptation in part to the opportunities and constraints for the flow of information created by the postal service and newspaper systems. Beneath America's majoritarian politics of the nineteenth century was a distinguishing set of arrangements for the distribution of political information. These arrangements would eventually be superseded by others; but for a half to three-quarters of a century, they defined the majority of possibilities for large-scale political communication and civic engagement in the United States.

The second American information revolution led to an information regime that lasted into the middle of the twentieth century. That revolution was a product of the industrial revolution and the growing American state, which transformed the landscape of political information requisite to politics.

Information became enormously complex and highly differentiated between about 1880 and 1920 because the number of policy issues on the national agenda multiplied, as did the number of private and public actors engaged in the exchange of information. Such complexity favored a new form of organization adapted to the management and flow of specialized and increasingly costly information: the organized interest group. Though this new form of organization would eventually rise to prominence after the New Deal, interest-group politics of the twentieth century reflected and rested upon the new set of informational characteristics that emerged at the turn of the century. Interest groups can be understood as information specialists that prevailed over generalists (the parties) in some of the central communication functions in politics.

The pluralism connected with the second information regime persisted throughout the twentieth century, but was affected by a third, transitional revolution during the period of the 1950s–1970s involving broadcasting. The broadcast information revolution had two distinct phases. In the first, the mass audience for communication tended to weaken party organizations as central players in campaigning and at the same time create new possibilities for mass politics—a trend counter to the group-based politics of the second information regime. However, in the later stage of this information revolution, the rise of cable television and the multiplication of channels began a process of fragmentation and division of communication and information. These developments set the stage for the contemporary information revolution involving the Internet and associated technologies.

It should be clear that an information revolution is not simply an abrupt change in the technology of communication. A set of technological changes becomes revolutionary when new opportunities or constraints associated with political intermediation make possible altered distributions of power. These new capacities and possibilities are a function of the political and social context in which technology evolves. Moreover, an information revolution need not necessarily be driven by communication technology at all. My approach to analyzing political history has not been to draw up a list of technologies—telegraph, steamboat, railroad, telephone, radio, television, and so on—and ask how each affected politics. I have approached the problem orthogonally, by asking when, if ever, the properties of information and communication have changed abruptly, and then inquiring how such changes influenced politics. This approach implicates some technological innovations in abrupt information revolutions but not others. It identifies sources of informational change that would not make most lists of interesting technologies, such as the postal service. It also includes socioeconomic developments involving technologies but which are not, strictly speaking, technologies at all, such as the industrial revolution.

The Current Information Regime

. . . The second large step in my theory of information and democracy deals with contemporary political change, and involves applying lessons from the history of information in American politics to the present situation. The information-regime model of American politics and insights from the study of interest groups and political participation provide the means to investigate how contemporary information technology affects democracy. In the current period, as in the Jacksonian age and era of industrialization, the properties of information are again changing. Technology is increasing the complexity and specialization of information while at the same time decreasing its cost, thereby making abundant political information and communication available to anyone with the motivation to acquire it, provided they have access to information technology. In a general sense, the information regime model predicts that such a large-scale change in the cost of information should lead to political change, through its effects on the identity and structure of political intermediaries.

. . . [A]mong the most important trends predicted from theory are a decreasing association between the distribution of traditional political resources and the capacity to organize political action. . . . This phenomenon involves the substitution of information infrastructure for organizational infrastructure. It suggests the rise of new ad hoc political associations and groups, as well as altered strategies and commitments of resources on the part of traditional organizations. It entails increasing attention in the policy process toward "outside" lobbying and public opinion, as well as increasing orientation toward issues and events, rather than more stable interests and long-term political agendas.

My main thesis about contemporary political developments is that *technological change in the contemporary period should contribute toward information abundance, which in turn contributes toward postbureaucratic forms of politics.* This process involves chiefly private political institutions and organizations such as civic associations, as well as interest groups, rather than formal governmental institutions rooted in law or the Constitution. To the extent that the central functions of these private institutions involve the collection, management, or distribution of information under circumstances where information has been costly and asymmetrically distributed, the contemporary information revolution has the capacity to alter organizational structures. The result is a diminished role on many fronts for traditional organizations in politics. The pluralism of the 1950s and 1960s was a politics of bargaining among institutionalized interests. That changed in the 1970s and 1980s to a pluralism of more atomistic issue groups, less inclined and able at elite bargaining and more tightly focused on so-called single issues.

The accelerated pluralism of the 1990s and 2000s increasingly involves situations in which the structure of group politics is organized around not interests or issues, but rather events and the intensive flow of information surrounding them.

This progression from interest groups to issue groups to event groups does not imply that the former organizational form is displaced entirely. It should involve, rather, the loosening of certain organizational boundaries and structures and an increasing heterogeneity of forms working alongside one another. . . . As in previous information regimes, political influence in the fourth regime should remain biased toward those with the best command of political information. The contemporary information revolution should make traditional, bureaucratically structured organizations of all kinds less able to dominate political information—this is the central motor of political change.

In this way, it is possible to array contemporary developments with historical ones. The first information revolution made national-scale political information available for the first time, which contributed to centralized, hierarchical organizations serving as the basis for collective action in politics. In the second information revolution, national-scale political information, grew complex and costly, which led to the rise of decentralized, specialized, and bureaucratized organizations as the basis for collective action. The third information revolution created a modern tension between mass politics and pluralism, but left major, highly institutionalized organizational forms in a position of dominance. In the contemporary revolution, national-scale information is growing abundant, but no less complex than ever. The result should be a weakening of the organizational structures of the previous regimes. This sequence is summarized in Figure 1–1.

One of the major problems facing social scientists concerned with American democracy is the state of citizenship and levels of civic engagement. By many traditional measures, these are in decline, as the literatures on social capital, public opinion, voting participation, and the public sphere indicate. On the other hand, critics of declinist arguments have posited alternative interpretations of the data, based on new forms of engagement and changes in the meaning of citizenship. Many have suggested that participation in affinity groups, youth soccer leagues, support groups, interest organizations, and other novel associations may be replacing memberships in venerable but outdated groups such as Elks Clubs, Rotaries, and Boy Scouts. If so, the research indicating a decline in social capital may be due to a combination of inadequate conceptualization and measurement of the wrong activities.[5] Likewise, in influencing explicitly political engagement, new forms of "lifestyle" politics, political consumerism, and other novel ways of being "political" may be displacing the traditional political actions that scholars have measured.[6] Therefore, to the extent that political and civic identity and

Figure 1-1   Summary of the Four Political Information Revolutions in the
United States

First Information Revolution: 1820s–1830s

Technological and institutional developments lead to:
The first possibilities for mass flows of political information.

These contribute to an information regime with:
A centralized, simple system of political organizations (parties) serving as
the dominant influence on policy-making and collective action.

Second Information Revolution: 1880s–1910s

Socio-economic development leads to:
National-scale political information growing costly, specialized, and
complex.

This contributes to an information regime with:
A decentralized, complex system of specialized and resource-
dependent organizations (interest groups) serving as the dominant
influence on policy-making and collective action.

Third Information Revolution: 1950s–1970s

Technological development leads to:
Possibilities for commanding the attention of a
national-scale mass audience.

This contributes to an information regime with:
A centralized, extremely resource-dependent system of market-
driven organizations capable of influencing policy-making and some
forms of collective action, along with the specialized political
organizations of the previous information regime.

Fourth Information Revolution: 1990s–present

Technological development leads to:
A condition of information abundance.

This contributes to possibilities for an information regime with:
Post-bureaucratic political organizations as the basis for policymaking and collective action.

modes of action are changing, civic engagement may also simply be changing shape rather than decaying.

This debate will benefit substantially from the passage of time, as historical perspective sharpens assessments of stability and change and as new survey evidence differentiates long-term from short-term trends. The debate is relevant here, nonetheless, because of the possible role of information technology in it. One of the most persistent speculations about "the Internet and politics" has been that cheap, ubiquitous information and communication will expand possibilities for engagement and fuel a rise in overall levels of citizen involvement with their communities and political system. It is clear that the contemporary information revolution is making the individual's political *environment* far more information-rich. It is also clear from research on political behavior and public opinion that political knowledge—information that has been assimilated by individuals—is connected with political action. In other words, more knowledgeable citizens are indeed more engaged. But the link between changes in citizens' informational environment and changes in their internal political knowledge is far less clear. It seems intuitive that exposure to more information should lead to the internalization of more information and to changes in behavior. Some rational theories of political behavior formalize that link, interpreting the cost of information as an important regulator of its "consumption" and of the action that follows. Decrease the cost of a desired good, such as information, and more will be acquired by citizens, up until the point where marginal costs match marginal value. Empirical verification of this apparently straightforward model has been highly problematic, however, especially when it is framed in terms of longitudinal variation in citizens' information environments.

It is important that a theoretical account of information and political change take up this problem as a counterpart to organizational-level matters. My approach involves a psychological perspective on political information that stands in contrast to instrumental conceptions of information as a rationally consumed good. Following work in political psychology, I posit that the informed citizen in the age of the Internet is not a rational actor, nor necessarily even one who pursues shortcuts and satisficing strategies in lieu of exhaustive and thorough information-gathering. Instead, informed citizenship involves the information-rich growing even richer as the cost of information falls, while those poor in information remain so. In practice, people should acquire information in so-called biased ways that support existing beliefs rather than reducing uncertainty. Most important, their consumption of information should occur in ways that are highly contingent on context and the stimulus provided by elites and organizations.

This view leads to the hypothesis that in the cycle of information revolutions and regimes, including contemporary developments, changes in the nature of political information should typically exert little direct influence on levels of citizen engagement. As a force in democracy, therefore, information should work somewhat differently at the level of organizations and the level of individuals. Information revolutions, including the present one, should have profound and direct consequences for organizations and political structure, but only indirect, less tangible consequences for politics at the level of individual political engagement. The effects of changes in information, I argue, are concentrated on *political form* through an increasing independence of political structure from traditional economic and social structures.

Notes

1. John Zaller, *The Nature and Origins of Mass Opinion* (Cambridge, Eng.: Cambridge University Press, 1991), p. 13.
2. That a recipient of communication may have difficulty distinguishing the facts and values in a message or may be unable to verify truth claims does not change the fact that information in a broad sense has been transmitted, perhaps with a high level of uncertainty associated with it. How much "true" information recipients extract from a message is a function of their own sophistication and their knowledge of the person communicating. Imagine, for instance, a situation where a candidate for office broadcasts a factually false message that his opponent is a communist, or an opponent of civil rights, or an adulterer. If a voter, believing the message, abandons her support for the accused candidate and votes instead for the accuser, there can be no doubt that communication has occurred and that information—albeit containing a false claim—has been transmitted. Whether the information in a message is "true" or "objective," and whether in this case the accuser sincerely believes his propaganda, is a separate question from the existence of information and communication.
3. Inguun Hagen, "Communicating to an Ideal Audience: News and the Notion of an 'Informed Citizen,'" *Political Communication* 14, no. 4 (1997): 405–419.
4. Pierre Levy, *Collective Intelligence: Mankind's Emerging World in Cyberspace* (Cambridge, Mass.: Perseus, 1997).
5. Theda Skocpol, "Unravelling from Above," in Robert Kuttner, ed., *Ticking Time Bombs: The New Conservative Assault on Democracy* (New York: New Press, 1996), pp. 292–301; Michael Schudson, "What If Civic Life Didn't Die?" in Kuttner, ed., *Ticking Time Bombs*, pp. 286–291; Nicholas Lemann, "Kicking in Groups," *The Atlantic Monthly* 277, no. 4 (1996): 22–26.
6. For a discussion, see W. Lance Bennett, "The UnCivic Culture: Communication, Identity, and the Rise of Lifestyle Politics," *PS: Political Science and Politics* 31, no. 4 (1998): 741–761.

2

DOCUMENTING THE PERSUASIVE POWER OF THE NEWS MEDIA

Jonathan McDonald Ladd and Gabriel S. Lenz

Editor's Note

News media operate in complex environments where political events are influenced by interactions among many different factors. Media researchers face multiple methodological pitfalls when they try to single out the potency of the media factor. Jonathan Ladd and Gabriel Lenz were able to surmount these hurdles thanks to a fortuitous set of circumstances. Their essay illustrates the major obstacles that confront media-effects research. To keep the essay sufficiently brief, most of the sophisticated statistical analyses and related footnotes have been omitted.

When the original article was published, Jonathan McDonald Ladd was an assistant professor of government and public policy at Georgetown University, and Gabriel S. Lenz was an assistant professor of political science at the Massachusetts Institute of Technology. The authors had collaborated on several projects that detail the forces that shape political behaviors.

... The Challenges of Documenting Media Persuasion

Research on news media persuasion—and media effects more generally—faces four major obstacles that have frustrated scholars as they try to reach consensus. The first two obstacles prevent the detection of media effects, while the latter two are alternative explanations for evidence that is uncovered. The first is lack of variation in message. For instance, based on the relative short-term stability of aggregate public opinion (Converse 1990; Page and Shapiro 1992), even in the face of fierce political campaigns (Finkel 1993), some researchers infer that campaigns (and news coverage of them) leave little imprint on public opinion. Others, however, note that we should only expect

---

Source: Jonathan McDonald Ladd and Gabriel S. Lenz, "Exploiting a Rare Communication Shift to Document the Persuasive Power of the News Media," in *American Journal of Political Science,* 53:2 (April 2009): 394-410. Reprinted by permission of John Wiley and Sons.

opinion movement when the balance of persuasive messages varies (Erikson 1976; Zaller 1996), a surprisingly rare occurrence. They point out that rival campaign messages tend to offset each other, making aggregate opinion stability unsurprising (Bartels 1992, 2006). In the case of news outlets, the balance of persuasive messages rarely varies because each outlet usually maintains a similar political stance over long periods. The *New York Times,* for instance, has generally supported Democratic candidates for almost 40 years (Ansolabehere, Lessem, and Snyder 2006).

The second obstacle preventing the detection of campaign and news media effects is that measures of exposure tend to be poor. To measure exposure, researchers often must use error-prone variables such as whether a respondent lives in a county in which a newspaper has high circulation (e.g., Erikson 1976), general political knowledge (e.g., Price and Zaller 1993; Zaller 1992), or self-reported campaign attention or media usage (e.g., Barker 2002; but see Bartels 1993; Hetherington 1996). These error-prone variables introduce biases of potentially substantial magnitude and unpredictable direction (Achen 1983). Combined, the lack of variation in the balance of messages and difficulties measuring exposure are major obstacles to detecting media effects and may have led to the "minimal effects" paradigm that once dominated media effects scholarship (Klapper 1960; McGuire 1986).

Despite these difficulties, some studies find evidence consistent with campaign or news media persuasion. When they do find such evidence, however, researchers face two additional obstacles to demonstrating these effects convincingly. These obstacles take the form of alternative explanations that are difficult to rule out. First, individuals may choose media outlets that share their politics (self-selection), creating the appearance of persuasion. Second, media outlets may follow, not lead, their audiences' politics, which also could be mistaken for persuasion. Thus, although many studies find individual-level associations between survey reports of exposure to certain news outlets and political opinions (Barker 1999, 2002; Barker and Lawrence 2006; Dalton, Beck, and Huckfeldt 1998; Druckman and Parkin 2005; Kahn and Kenney 2002; Lawson and McCann 2004; Newton and Brynin 2001; Project for Excellence in Journalism 2007), these associations could arise either because of media persuasion or because of these two alternatives.

Research on media persuasion has employed several strategies to address these four obstacles. For example, Erikson (1976) finds variation in news media messages by exploiting the 1964 shift to Democratic Party endorsements by many newspapers. DellaVigna and Kaplan (2007) find variation by examining the entry of the Fox News Channel onto cable systems in the late 1990s. Several studies develop better measures of exposure by using survey data to directly tie individuals to the newspapers they read, radio programs they listen to, or television shows they watch (Barker 1999, 2002; Barker and

Lawrence 2006; Druckman and Parkin 2005; Lawson and McCann 2004; Newton and Brynin 2001). Laboratory experiments (e.g., Ansolabehere and Iyengar 1995; Berinsky and Kinder 2006; Gilliam and Iyengar 2000; Iyengar and Kinder 1987) can avoid many inferential pitfalls, but face concerns over external validity. Field experiments greatly reduce concerns about external validity, but, so far, are rare (but see Gerber, Karlan, and Bergan 2006).

However, few studies directly examining news media persuasion convincingly surmount all four obstacles. Some studies that come closest to surmounting the obstacles find large media effects (Veblen 1975; Zaller 1996). Yet, these only examine outcomes such as policy opinions or primary election votes, not votes in national elections, which may be more difficult to shift. A few recent persuasion studies use approaches surmounting these obstacles and find evidence of large television advertising effects (e.g., Huber and Arceneaux 2007; Johnston, Hagen, and Jamieson 2004) and substantial elite influence on public opinion (e.g., Gabel and Scheve 2007; Zaller 1992), but do not examine news media persuasion. In sum, formidable methodological obstacles and the tendency of the most convincing studies to focus on other types of media effects have left the question of whether major news outlets can readily shift national-level, major party vote choice largely unanswered.

The 1997 UK Election . . .

In this article, we examine the effect of newspaper endorsements and slant in the 1997 UK general election. It presents a rare opportunity to study media persuasion because it provides the elements necessary to overcome the aforementioned obstacles. First, this election has variation in media messages: a shift in the editorial stance and tone of coverage of some newspapers but not others. Soon after the 1992 election, in response to the United Kingdom's ejection from the European Exchange Rate Mechanism, a recession, and Conservative Party leadership squabbles and scandals, most British newspapers became less enthusiastic about the Conservative government, including longtime supporters like the *Times* and *Daily Mail* (McNair 2003, 159–60; Norris 1998; Seymour-Ure 1997; Tunstall 1996, 254–55). Although most papers merely dampened their Conservative support, several papers eventually went further, suddenly breaking with their past behavior by endorsing the Labour Party during the 1997 election campaign.

In particular, the *Sun,* which had the largest circulation in Great Britain, broke with its strident support for the Conservatives and swung its support to Labour (McNair 2003; Norris 1998; Seymour-Ure 1997). The *Sun* announced its shift with a front-page endorsement of Tony Blair on the second day of the official 1997 campaign (McNair 2003). It labeled Blair a "strong, dynamic, purposeful leader" whom Britain was "crying out for" (Scammell and Harrop 1997, 160) and finished the campaign with an election-day cover photo of Blair and a banner headline proclaiming, "IT MUST BE YOU" [caps in original] (179). According to published accounts, the *Sun*'s owner, Rupert Murdoch, dictated the *Sun*'s shift (Cassidy 2006; Scammell and Harrop 1997). He reportedly did so in part because Blair made policy concessions, including assuring Murdoch of his moderate views on European integration and offering Murdoch a friendly regulatory environment (Cassidy 2006; McGuire and McKinney 1997; Smith 2006). Besides the *Sun*, three smaller newspapers switched from no endorsement in 1992 to a Labour endorsement in the 1997 election. These were the *Daily Star, Independent,* and *Financial Times. . . .*

While most British newspapers became critical of the Conservative government during its 1992–97 term and positive toward Blair personally, these papers' endorsements of Labour were surprising. These "switching" papers had no recent histories of supporting Labour and did not leak their endorsements in advance. Of all traditional Conservative Party papers, the *Times* had had the earliest and often most serious criticisms of John Major's government (McNair 2003), yet did not endorse Labour in 1997. Scammell and Harrop (1997, 160) recount the *Sun*'s switch this way:

> Until the [*Sun*] declared for Labour, with deadly timing on the day after Major announced the election, it had been careful to distinguish between the admirable Blair and his dubious party. Now, on the instructions of Rupert Murdoch, the *Sun* threw its weight behind Labour, to the obvious discomfort of some correspondents, including its political editor, Trevor Kavanagh.

The *Sun*'s campaign coverage emphasized Blair's leadership abilities and Major's ineptitude. Unsurprisingly for a tabloid, it did not delve into the policy issues at stake in the election (Seymour-Ure 1997). By providing a rare case of over-time variation in communication flows, the unexpected switch in partisan slant by these four newspapers during the 1997 campaign provides an opportunity to estimate the persuasive effect of news media outlets on voting behavior.

In exploiting changes by these papers, we capture both the effects of the editorial endorsement and changed slant in news coverage. In a media environment in which papers endorse on the front page, the line between editorials and news is blurry. While distinct in theory, these are too confounded to differentiate here.

This case is also unusually well suited for studying media persuasion because the British media environment facilitates more accurate measurement of individuals' exposure to press messages (Newton and Brynin 2001), overcoming the second major obstacle faced by media effect studies. In the United States, for instance, connecting survey respondents with the endorsement of their newspapers is difficult because most people read local papers, and respondents in national samples thus read hundreds of different papers. In Britain, however, the major daily newspapers have national distribution, so one can more easily connect respondents in national surveys with the contents of the paper each one reads.

To examine the effect of these editorial and slant shifts, we use the British Election Panel Study 1992–97 (BEPS), which interviewed the same national sample four times before the endorsement shifts (in 1992, 1994, 1995, and 1996) and once afterwards (following the 1997 election). This panel survey provides at least four elements that aid causal inference. First, it allows us to rule out self-selection because we can measure which papers respondents read before the endorsement shifts. While other tests of media persuasion with panel data remain vulnerable to self-selection bias,[1] the suddenness of these shifts makes the prospect of self-selection remote. Among voters in the BEPS sample, 211 read one of the slant-switching papers in 1996 (the last wave before the endorsement shifts), which, using terms suitable for a quasi-experiment, we refer to as receiving the *Treatment*. We refer to the 1,382 panelists who either read papers whose partisan slants were constant or who did not read a paper as the control or untreated group. To rule out the possibility that readers in 1996 sensed future endorsement shifts, we also use readership in the first wave (1992) to instrument the treatment. Second, the BEPS enables us to address concerns about measurement error by constructing an additional, more demanding, measure of the treatment: habitual readership. We code individuals as habitual readers when they read one of the switching papers in every wave in which they were interviewed before the endorsement shifts. Third, the multiple panel waves enable us to measure many other characteristics that might differ between the treatment and control individuals, and to do so before the papers switched (pretreatment). Moreover, the large number of control subjects (1,382) allows us to correct for bias from spurious covariates that vary across treatment and control groups using parametric models and matching techniques. Finally, the multiple pretreatment interviews also permit us to conduct placebo tests (or falsification tests), which help to further rule out omitted variable bias and reverse causation. . . .

Analysis

Estimating the Treatment Effect While Accounting for Nonrandom Selection on Observables

Did the change in partisan endorsements and news slant by the *Sun, Daily Star, Independent,* and *Financial Times* persuade readers to vote differently than they would have otherwise? The evidence suggests that it did. . . .

. . . Among those who did, it rises considerably more: 19.4 points, from 38.9 to 58.3%. Consequently, switching paper readers were 6.6% more likely to vote for Labour in 1992 and 15.2% more likely to do so in 1997. Thus, reading a switching paper corresponds with an (15.2 – 6.6 =) 8.6 point greater increase in the likelihood of voting for Labour. This statistically significant estimate of the bivariate treatment effect . . . suggests that the shifts in newspaper slant were indeed persuasive.

Of course, readers of the switching papers potentially differ from control individuals on a myriad of attributes, and these differences, rather than reading a paper that switched, could be inflating this bivariate relationship. By design, we reduce the possibility that such differences result from self-selection by measuring readership before these papers unexpectedly switched to

Figure 2-1   Persuasive Effect of Endorsement Changes on Labour Vote Choice between 1992 and 1997

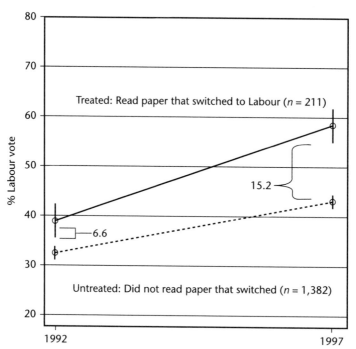

This figure shows that reading a paper that switched to Labour is associated with an (15.2–6.6 =) 8.6 percentage point shift to Labour between the 1992 and 1997 UK elections. Paper readership is measured in the 1996 wave, before the papers switched, or, if no 1996 interview was conducted, in an earlier wave. Confidence intervals show one standard error.

Labour. Nevertheless, differences could still exist. As is evident in Figure 2–1, for instance, switching paper readers were more likely to vote for Labour in 1992, which may also be indicative of a greater predisposition among these readers toward switching to Labour in the future.

To address the possibility that differences on other attributes, not the slant changes, caused switching paper readers' greater shift to Labour, we condition on a large number of potentially confounding variables. We searched the literature and conducted our own analysis to determine what other variables are associated with shifting to a Labour vote. In all cases, we measure these control (or conditioning) variables before the endorsement shifts to avoid bias that can result from measuring control variables after the treatment (post-treatment bias). Unless otherwise specified, these are measured in the 1992 panel wave. Based on our analysis, the best predictor of shifting to Labour is, not surprisingly, respondents' prior evaluations of the Labour Party. . . . Respondents who did not vote for Labour in 1992, but who rated Labour favorably, are much more likely than are others to shift their votes to Labour in 1997. To account for any differences in evaluations of Labour, we include *Prior Labour Party Support* as well as *Prior Conservative Party Support* as controls. We also include indicator variables for *Prior Labour Vote, Prior Conservative Vote, Prior Liberal Vote, Prior Labour Party Identification, Prior Conservative Party Identification, Prior Liberal Party Identification,* and whether their *Parents Voted Labour.*

In addition to support for the parties, we find that a six-item scale of *Prior Ideology* (Heath, Evans, and Martin 1994; Heath et al. 1999) proves a good predictor of switching to a Labour vote. Given the housing market crash earlier in John Major's term (Butler and Kavanagh 1997, 247), we expect that a self-reported measure of respondents' *Prior Coping with Mortgage* might explain vote shifts. We are also concerned that the tabloid format of the *Sun* and *Daily Star* might attract readers of a lower socioeconomic status—Labour's traditional base. One might expect these readers to return to the reinvigorated Labour Party, which had been out of favor for two decades. To account for such differences, we include *Prior Education, Prior Income, Prior Working Class Identification,* whether a respondent is a *Prior Trade Union Member,* whether he or she identifies as *White,* a six-item scale of *Prior Authoritarianism* (Heath, Evans, and Martin 1994; Heath et al. 1999), as well as *Prior Profession* and *Prior Region.* We also account for differences in *Age* and *Gender,* both of which Butler and Kavanagh (1997, 247) find to be associated with switching one's vote to Labour in 1997. Finally, to account for further differences between the treated and untreated groups on variables that might moderate persuasion, we also include *Prior Political Knowledge* and whether the respondent is a *Prior Television Viewer* or a *Prior Daily Newspaper Reader.* Finally, given that Blair positioned himself as a centrist, moderates may have shifted to Blair at higher rates, so we also include a measure of *Prior Ideological Moderation* created by folding over the six-item ideology scale. . . .

Does the evidence of persuasion hold after controlling for these differences? . . .

. . . In summary, the persuasive effect observed in Figure 2–1 does not appear to be an artifact of differences on the observed covariates. Reading one of the papers that switched to Labour appears to have persuaded people to vote for Labour.

Accounting for Possible Nonrandom Selection on Unobservables . . .

While the persuasive effect does not appear to result from differences between the treated and untreated groups on the variables discussed above, it could arise from differences on variables we have failed to incorporate in the analysis, that is, from nonrandom selection into treatment and control groups on *un*observed characteristics. To address this concern, we conduct two placebo tests and a sensitivity analysis. . . .

. . . [T]wo placebo tests and a sensitivity analysis assuage concerns about bias from differences on unobservables.

Did Newspapers Follow Their Readers?

Another alternative explanation for our finding is that switching papers may have shifted to Labour between 1992 and 1997 because they observed their readers shifting to Labour and then followed them (McNair 2003). To address this concern, we conduct a third placebo test by checking that readers of these papers do not begin shifting to Labour before the 1997 campaign. . . . As expected, the treatment effect is absent before the 1997 wave, reducing concerns that the endorsement shifts were responses to already changing voting preferences among readers of these papers.

In summary, the treated group's shift to Labour did not occur before the endorsement shifts, but afterwards. Of course, treated readers could have shifted after the 1996 interviews but before the 1997 endorsement announcements. Although we cannot rule this out, treated and untreated groups are so similar on covariates that it seems unlikely the treated [group] shifted suddenly to Labour in this short interval, long after the Conservative government had become deeply unpopular.

Treatment Group and Panel Attrition

Another remaining concern is that Conservative readers may have self-selected away from reading switching papers before the 1996 panel wave. Many previously pro-Conservative papers, including switching papers like the *Sun, Daily Star,* and *Financial Times,* became critical of Major's government after the 1992 election. This coverage could have provoked Conservative supporters to drop these papers and Labour supporters to read them, leaving switching paper readers potentially more vulnerable to persuasion.

Although plausible, we find little evidence consistent with this account. In the previous section, we showed that readers of switching papers did not become more predisposed to Labour between 1992 and 1996 (compared to others), indicating no net tendency by Conservative supporters to stop reading switching papers before they switched. To address this concern further, we examine newspaper readership across the panel, but find little evidence of self-selection by readers between the 1992 and the 1996 waves. The defection rate from switching papers to other papers or no paper between 1992 and 1996 was identical for 1992 Labour and Conservative voters: 36.6 and 36.5%, respectively. Additionally, slightly more 1992 Labour voters left switching papers for Labour papers than 1992 Conservative voters left the switching papers for Conservative papers: 11 versus 9%. Similar patterns emerge when we examine 1992 partisan identification instead of 1992 vote choice. For instance, 1992 Labour identifiers abandoned switching papers for Labour papers at about the same rate as 1992 Conservative identifiers abandoned the switching papers for Conservative papers: 8.6%. Thus, there is little evidence of self-selection between the 1992 wave and the 1996 wave (when we measure readership).

Although Conservative supporters generally do not drop out of the treatment group at higher rates, they may be more likely to drop out of the panel all together. Panel attrition could be higher for them if they dislike speaking with an interviewer about the seemingly dismal prospects of their party. To ensure that these difficult-to-persuade individuals do not drop out of the panel at higher rates, we check the attrition rates for various groups, but find no cause for concern. In fact, a higher percentage of 1992 Labour voters drop out of the panel between 1992 and 1997 than do Conservative voters, 47 versus 44%, respectively. Similarly, those who strongly support Labour (on the Labour Support variable) drop out of the panel at a higher rate than those who strongly oppose Labour, 50 versus 43%, respectively.

Conclusion

Using panel data and matching techniques, we exploit a rare change in news slant and find strong evidence of news media persuasion. By comparing readers of newspapers that switched to similar individuals who did not read these newspapers, we estimate that these papers persuaded a considerable share of their readers to vote for Labour. We emphasize again the unusual confluence that permits us to estimate this persuasive effect while avoiding many of the methodological problems that plague previous studies. First, we have an uncharacteristic change in the partisan slant of newspapers. Second, we can measure individuals' exposure to these news outlets before the shift occurs. Third, the large sample size of the BEPS allows us to address omitted variable bias by matching similar exposed and unexposed respondents in addition to the standard parametric techniques. Finally, the many pretreatment panel waves in the BEPS allow us to address various other potential sources of bias and conduct several placebo tests. To our knowledge, no other observational media persuasion study combines these attributes.

Depending on the statistical approach, our point estimates of the persuasive effect of news endorsements and slant vary from about 10% to as high as 25% of readers. If, in the 1997 UK election, the *Sun*'s endorsement was in exchange for a friendly regulatory environment for Murdoch, the concession may have bought Blair between 8 and 20% of his 3.9 million-vote margin over the Conservatives. The magnitude of this effect is not just larger than those found in previous press endorsement studies, which usually find persuasion effects between 1 and 5% (Erikson 1976; Krebs 1998; Lessem 2003), but also suggests that the influence of media endorsements and slant on vote choice is large relative to other well-documented effects on voting. For example, it is larger than the incumbency advantage in U.S. House elections, one of the most studied effects in political science, which has averaged about five percentage points in recent decades (for a review, see Ansolabehere et al. 2006).

At the outset, we posed Zaller's (1996) question of whether democratic stability is the product of citizen or elite behavior. Our results offer no solace for those who worry that the public is too easily swayed by the power of mass communication. They indicate that stable elite communication flows, rather than any inherent durability of public preferences, are the likely source of the consistency and relative moderation found in many democracies.

In summary, our analysis provides rare evidence that the news media exert a strong influence on mass political behavior. Consequently, the previous consensus that media messages are minor factors in shaping election outcomes may not just need to be revised, as it already has been, but reversed. Based on these findings, news media messages can be one of the most powerful influences on voting documented by political scientists.

Notes

1. When a news outlet maintains a consistent slant throughout a panel survey, those who choose to expose themselves to it may do so because they share its politics and are therefore predisposed to accept its messages, even after controlling for observable differences.

References

Achen, Christopher H. 1982. *Interpreting and Using Regression.* Beverly Hills, CA: Sage.
Achen, Christopher H. 1983. "Toward Theories of Data." In *Political Science: The State of the Discipline,* ed. Ada W. Finifter. Washington, DC: American Political Science Association, 69–93.

Achen, Christopher H. 2002. "Toward a New Political Methodology." *Annual Review of Political Science* 5: 423–50.

Angrist, Joshua D., and Alan B. Krueger. 1999. "Empirical Strategies in Labor Economics." In *Handbook of Labor Economics Volume 3a,* ed. Orley Ashenfelter and David Card. Amsterdam: Elsevier, 1277–1366.

Ansolabehere, Stephen, John Mark Hansen, Shigeo Hirano, and James M. Snyder Jr. 2006. "The Incumbency Advantage in U.S. Primary Elections." Typescript. Massachusetts Institute of Technology.

Ansolabehere, Stephen, and Shanto Iyengar. 1995. *Going Negative.* New York: Free Press.

Ansolabehere, Stephen, Rebecca Lessem, and James M. Snyder, Jr. 2006. "The Orientation of Newspaper Endorsements in U.S. Elections, 1940–2002." *Quarterly Journal of Political Science* 1(4): 393–404.

Athey, Susan, and Guido W. Imbens. 2006. "Identification and Inference in Nonlinear Difference-in-Differences Models." *Econometrica* 74(2): 431–97.

Barker, David C. 1999. "Rushed Decisions." *Journal of Politics* 61(2): 527–39.

Barker, David C. 2002. *Rushed to Judgment.* New York: Columbia University Press.

Barker, David C., and Adam B. Lawrence. 2006. "Media Favoritism and Presidential Nominations." *Political Communication* 23(1): 41–59.

Bartels, Larry M. 1992. "The Impact of Electioneering in the United States." In *Electioneering,* ed. David Butler and Austin Ranney. New York: Clarendon Press and Oxford University Press, 244–77.

Bartels, Larry M. 1993. "Messages Received." *American Political Science Review* 87(2): 267–85.

Bartels, Larry M. 2006. "Priming and Persuasion in Presidential Campaigns." In *Capturing Campaign Effects,* ed. Henry E. Brady and Richard Johnston. Ann Arbor: University of Michigan Press, 78–112.

Berelson, Bernard, Paul F. Lazarsfeld, and William N. McPhee. 1954. *Voting.* Chicago: University of Chicago Press.

Berinsky, Adam J., and Donald R. Kinder. 2006. "Making Sense of Issues through Media Frames." *Journal of Politics* 68(3): 640–56.

Bullock, Charles S., III. 1984. "Racial Crossover Voting and the Election of Black Officials." *Journal of Politics* 46(1): 238–51.

Butler, David, and Dennis Kavanagh. 1997. *The British Election of 1997.* New York: St. Martin's Press.

Cassidy, John. 2006. "Murdoch's Game." *New Yorker,* Oct. 16, pp. 68–85.

Converse, Philip E. 1990. "Popular Representation and the Distribution of Information." In *Information and Democratic Processes,* ed. John A. Ferejohn and James H. Kuklinski. Urbana: University of Illinois Press, 369–88.

Curtice, John. 1999. "Was It the *Sun* Wot Won It Again?" Typescript. Centre for Research into Elections and Social Trends, Oxford University.

Dalton, Russell J., Paul A. Beck, and Robert Huckfeldt. 1998. "Partisan Cues and the Media." *American Political Science Review* 92(1): 111–26.

DellaVigna, Stefano, and Ethan Kaplan. 2007. "The Fox News Effect." *Quarterly Journal of Economics* 122 (August): 1187–1234.

Diamond, Alexis, and Jasjeet S. Sekhon. 2005. "Genetic Matching for Estimating Causal Effects: A General Multivariate Matching Method for Achieving Balance in Observational Studies." Typescript. University of California, Berkeley.

Druckman, James N., and Michael Parkin. 2005. "The Impact of Media Bias: How Editorial Slant Affects Voters." *Journal of Politics* 67(4): 1030–1142.

Erikson, Robert S. 1976. "Influence of Newspaper Endorsements in Presidential Elections." *American Journal of Political Science* 20(2): 207–33.

Finkel, Steven E. 1993. "Reexamining the 'Minimal Effects' Model in Recent Presidential Campaigns." *Journal of Politics* 55(1): 1–21.

Gabel, Matthew, and Kenneth Scheve. 2007. "Estimating the Effect of Elite Communications on Public Opinion Using Instrumental Variables." *American Journal of Political Science* 51(4): 1013–28.

Gavin, Neil T., and David Sanders. 2003. "The Press and Political Attitudes under New Labour." *Political Studies* 51(3): 573–91.

Gerber, Alan, Dean Karlan, and Daniel Bergan. 2006. "Does the Media Matter?" Typescript. Yale University.

Gilliam, Franklin D., Jr., and Shanto Iyengar. 2000. "Prime Suspects." *American Journal of Political Science* 44(3): 560–73.

Gordon, Sanford C., and Gregory A. Huber. 2007. "The Effect of Electoral Competitiveness on Incumbent Behavior." *Quarterly Journal of Political Science* 2(2): 107–38.

Heath, Anthony, Geoffrey Evans, and Jean Martin. 1994. "The Measurement of Core Beliefs and Values." *British Journal of Political Science* 24(1): 115–32.

Heath, Anthony, Bridget Taylor, Lindsay Brook, and Alison Park. 1999. "British National Sentiment." *British Journal of Political Science* 29(1): 155–75.

Hetherington, Marc J. 1996. "The Media's Role in Forming Voters' National Economic Evaluations in 1992." *American Journal of Political Science* 40(2): 372–95.

Ho, Daniel E., Kosuke Imai, Gary King, and Elizabeth A. Stuart. 2007. "Matching as Nonparametric Preprocessing for Reducing Model Dependence in Parametric Causal Inference." *Political Analysis* 15(3): 199–236.

Huber, Gregory A., and Kevin Arceneaux. 2007. "Identifying the Persuasive Effects of Presidential Advertising." *American Journal of Political Science* 51(4): 957–77.

Hughes, Sallie, and Chappell Lawson. 2004. "Propaganda and Crony Capitalism: Partisan Bias in Mexican Television News." *Latin American Research Review* 39(3): 81–105.

Imai, Kosuke. 2005. "Do Get-Out-the-Vote Calls Reduce Turnout?" *American Political Science Review* 99(2): 283–300.

Iyengar, Shanto, and Donald Kinder. 1987. *News That Matters.* Chicago: University of Chicago Press.

Johnston, Richard, Michael Gray Hagen, and Kathleen Hall Jamieson. 2004. *The 2000 Presidential Election and the Foundations of Party Politics.* New York: Cambridge University Press.

Kahn, Kim Fridkin, and Patrick J. Kenney. 2002. "The Slant of the News." *American Political Science Review* 96(2): 381–94.

Kinder, Donald R. 1998. "Opinion and Action in the Realm of Politics." In *The Handbook of Social Psychology,* ed. Daniel Todd Gilbert, Susan T. Fiske, and Gardner Lindzey. New York: McGraw-Hill, 778–866.

Kinder, Donald R. 2003. "Communication and Politics in the Age of Information." In *The Oxford Handbook of Political Psychology,* ed. David O. Sears, Leonie Huddy, and Robert Jervis. New York: Oxford University Press, 357–93.

King, Gary. 1991. "'Truth' Is Stranger Than Prediction, More Questionable Than Causal Inference." *American Journal of Political Science* 35(4): 1047–53.

King, Gary, James Honaker, Anne Joseph, and Kenneth Scheve. 2001. "Analyzing Incomplete Political Science Data." *American Political Science Review* 95(1): 49–69.

Klapper, Joseph. 1960. *The Effects of Mass Communication.* Glencoe, IL: Free Press.

Krebs, Timothy B. 1998. "The Determinants of Candidates' Vote Share and the Advantages of Incumbency in City Council Elections." *American Journal of Political Science* 42(3): 921–35.

Lawson, Chappell H. 2002. *Building the Fourth Estate: Democratization and the Rise of a Free Press in Mexico.* Berkeley: University of California Press.

Lawson, Chappell, and James A. McCann. 2004. "Television News, Mexico's 2000 Elections and Media Effects in Emerging Democracies." *British Journal of Political Science* 35(1): 1–30.

Lazarsfeld, Paul F., Bernard Berelson, and Hazel Gaudet. 1948. *The People's Choice.* New York: Columbia University Press.

Lessem, Rebecca. 2003. "The Impact of Newspaper Endorsements on Voting." Typescript. Massachusetts Institute of Technology.

Lieske, Joel. 1989. "The Political Dynamics of Urban Voting Behavior." *American Journal of Political Science* 33(1): 150–74.

MacKuen, Michael, and Steven Lane Coombs. 1981. *More Than News: Media Power in Public Affairs.* Beverly Hills, CA: Sage.

McGuire, Stryker, and Perri Colley McKinney. 1997. "How Tony Blair Won." *Newsweek,* May 12, p. 36.

McGuire, William J. 1986. "The Myth of Massive Media Impact." In *Public Communication and Behavior,* ed. George Comstock. New York: Academic Press, 173–257.

McNair, Brian. 2003. *News and Journalism in the U.K.* 4th ed. London: Routledge.

Newton, Kenneth, and Malcolm Brynin. 2001. "The National Press and Party Voting in the U.K." *Political Studies* 49(2): 265–85.

Norris, Pippa. 1998. "The Battle for the Campaign Agenda." In *New Labour Triumphs: Britain at the Polls,* ed. Anthony King, David Denver, Iain McLean, Pippa Norris, Philip Norton, David Sanders, and Patrick Seyd. Chatham, NJ: Chatham House, 113–44.

Norris, Pippa, John Curtice, David Sanders, Margaret Scammell, and Holli Semetko. 1999. *On Message: Communicating the Campaign.* London: Sage.

Page, Benjamin I., and Robert Y. Shapiro. 1992. *The Rational Public.* Chicago: University of Chicago Press.

Price, Vincent, and John Zaller. 1993. "Who Gets the News?" *Public Opinion Quarterly* 57(2): 133–64.

Project for Excellence in Journalism. 2007. "The State of the News Media: An Annual Report on American Journalism." Washington, DC.

Robinson, John P. 1974. "The Press as King Maker." *Journalism Quarterly* 51(4): 587–94.

Robinson, John P. 1976. "Interpersonal Influence in Election Campaigns." *Public Opinion Quarterly* 40(3): 304–19.

Rosenbaum, Paul R. 2002. *Observational Studies*. 2nd ed. New York: Springer-Verlag.

Scammell, Margaret, and Martin Harrop. 1997. "The Press." In *The British Election of 1997*, ed. David Butler and Dennis Kavanagh. New York: St. Martin's Press, 156–85.

Sekhon, Jasjeet S. 2007. "Matching." Version 4.3–1. University of California, Berkeley. http://sekhon.berkeley.edu.

Sekhon, Jasjeet S. n.d. "Multivariate and Propensity Score Matching Software with Automated Balance Optimization." *Journal of Statistical Software*. Forthcoming.

Seymour-Ure, Colin. 1997. "Editorial Opinion in the National Press." *Parliamentary Affairs* 50(4): 586–608.

Shadish, William R., Thomas D. Cook, and Donald T. Campbell. 2002. *Experimental and Quasi-Experimental Designs for Generalized Causal Inference*. Boston: Houghton Mifflin.

Simmons, Beth A., and Daniel J. Hopkins. 2005. "The Constraining Power of International Treaties." *American Political Science Review* 99(4): 623–31.

Smith, Ben. 2006. "Post Election." *The New Republic*, January 16, p. 13.

Tunstall, Jeremy. 1996. *Newspaper Power*. Oxford: Clarendon.

Veblen, Eric P. 1975. *The Manchester Union Leader in New Hampshire Elections*. Hanover, NH: University Press of New England.

Wooldridge, Jeffrey M. 2003. *Introductory Econometrics: A Modern Approach*. 2nd ed. Cincinnati, OH: South-Western College Publishing.

Zaller, John R. 1992. *The Nature and Origins of Mass Opinion*. New York: Cambridge University Press.

Zaller, John R. 1996. "The Myth of Massive Media Impact Revived." In *Political Persuasion and Attitude Change*, ed. Diana C. Mutz, Paul M. Sniderman, and Richard A. Brody. Ann Arbor: University of Michigan Press, 17–78.

3

WHY DEMOCRACIES NEED AN UNLOVABLE PRESS

Michael Schudson

Editor's Note

Criticism of the press abounds in this volume. The press, its critics say, relies too much on official sources; it abides by outdated, constraining norms; it keeps its nose too close to daily events and conventional wisdom and revels in conflicts and cynicism. All true, concedes sociologist Michael Schudson. But in a surprising twist, he shows that these vices may actually be virtues. To understand why unlovable features of the press are vital for democracy, imagine a press without these flaws, a press that avoided official sources and conflicts, abandoned the restraints of journalistic norms, and shied away from reporting the day's events in favor of erudite analyses that never hint at politicians' ulterior motives. Would that be a lovely dream or an awful nightmare?

At the time of writing, Michael Schudson was a professor of communication and adjunct professor of sociology at the University of California. He was the author or editor of eight books, including *The Sociology of News* (2003) and *The Good Citizen: A History of American Civic Life* (1998). Schudson is one of the foremost students of the history and sociology of the American news media. He also studies advertising and popular culture.

Alexis de Tocqueville, widely cited for his view that the American press is a necessary and vital institution for American democracy, did not actually have much affection for it. He objected to its violence and vulgarity. He saw it as a virtue of the American system that newspapers were widely dispersed around the country rather than concentrated in a capital city—they could

Source: Michael Schudson, "Why Democracies Need an Unlovable Press," in *Freeing the Presses: The First Amendment in Action,* ed. Timothy E. Cook, Baton Rouge: Louisiana State University Press, 2005, 73–86. Copyright © 2005 by Louisiana State University Press. Reprinted by permission of Louisiana State University Press.

do less harm this way. He confessed, "I admit that I do not feel toward freedom of the press that complete and instantaneous love which one accords to things by their nature supremely good. I love it more from considering the evils it prevents than on account of the good it does."[1]

It may well be, taking a leaf from Tocqueville, that today's efforts to make journalism more serious, more responsible, and, generally speaking, nicer, are misplaced. I want to propose that most critics of journalism, in and outside journalism itself, have attacked just those features of the press that, for all their defects, best protect robust public discussion and promote democracy. The focus of the news media on events, rather than trends and structures; the fixation of the press on conflict whenever and wherever it erupts; the cynicism of journalists with respect to politics and politicians; and the alienation of journalists from the communities they cover make the media hard for people to love but hard for democracies to do without. These are the features that most regularly enable the press to maintain a capacity for subverting established power.

This is not to suggest that there is anything wrong with in-depth reporting of the sort that Pulitzer juries and media critics applaud and I greatly admire. Nor do I mean to suggest that the dialogue of democracy should jettison editorial writers, op-ed columnists, investigative reporters, and expert analysts who can produce gems of explanatory journalism. That would be absurd. But I do mean to suggest that the power of the press to afflict the comfortable derives more often than not from the journalistic equivalent of ambulance chasing. Just as the ambulance-chasing trial lawyer sees another person's tragedy as a million-dollar opportunity, the newshound reporter sees it as an attention-grabbing, career-advancing, front-page sensation. I want to explore here the ways the most narrow and unlovable features of news may make the most vital of contributions to democracy.

The Press as an Establishment Institution

The press is presumably the bastion of free expression in a democracy, but too often it has been one of the institutions that limits the range of expression, especially expression that is critical of leading centers of power in society. Almost all social scientific studies of the news reveal that journalists themselves, of their own volition, limit the range of opinion present in the news. There are at least three significant ways this happens. First, there is source-dependence. Reporters rely on and reproduce the views of their primary sources, and these tend to be high government officials. Second, reporters and editors operate according to a set of professional norms that are themselves constraints on expression. Third, journalists operate within conventional bounds of opinion, opinions common among a largely secular, college-educated, upper middle class. All of this has been abundantly documented. . . . I will quickly review this literature, but only as a preface to arguing that this account of the compliant press has been overdrawn.

Dependence on Official Sources

Media scholars have consistently found that official sources dominate the news. This is invariably presented as a criticism of the media. If the media were to fulfill their democratic role, they would offer a wide variety of opinions and perspectives and would encourage citizens to choose among them in considering public policies. If the media allow politicians to set the public agenda, they may unduly narrow public discussion and so diminish democracy. This is the argument made, for instance, by W. Lance Bennett in his account of the "indexing" function of the press. For Bennett, the media "tend to 'index' the range of voices and viewpoints in both news and editorials according to the range of views expressed in mainstream government debate about a given topic." Bennett argues that this helps perpetuate a "world in which governments are able to define their own publics and where 'democracy' becomes whatever the government ends up doing."[2]

Sociologist Herbert Gans makes an argument about official sources related to Bennett's. For him, the routines of daily journalism undermine democracy. If supporting democracy means encouraging citizens to be active, informed, and critical, then the standard operating procedures of mainstream journalism subvert their own best intentions. Since most news is "top down," relaying the views of high government officials over lower government officials, all government officials over unofficial groups and oppositional groups, and groups of any sort over unorganized citizens, it diminishes the standing and efficacy of individual citizens.[3]

Whether the normative implications of journalism's favoring high government officials are as dire as Gans fears may be doubted, but it is indisputable that news media coverage emphasizes the views and actions of leading politicians and other top government officials. It is likewise indisputable that this limits the range of opinion to which the general public is exposed.

The Constraints of Professional Culture

Journalists favor high government officials—but why? The answer is that they work within a professional culture or a set of professional values that holds that a journalist's obligation is to report government affairs to serve the informational functions that make democracy work. . . . That is, in the work of political reporting, journalists emphasize "players, policies, and predictions of what will happen next."[4] So even when the press goes to outside experts rather than inside government officials, they seek people with experience in government, access to and knowledge of the chief players in government, and a ready willingness to speak in the terms of government officials, interpreting and predicting unfolding events. . . .

The Constraints of Conventional Wisdom

Journalists swim in conventional wisdom. They are wrapped up in daily events, and it would be disconcerting for them and for their readers if they took a long view. It might also be disconcerting for them to take a comparative (non-American) view. It would certainly be disconcerting for them to spend too much time with academics or others removed from the daily fray of political life. It is in relation to the conventional wisdom that journalists know how to identify "a story." Individual journalists may take issue with convention. Some journalists who work for publications with nonconventional audiences may write with unconventional assumptions and unusual points of departure. But the mainstream journalist writing for a standard news institution is likely to be ignorant of, or, if informed, dismissive of opinions outside the fold.

In Washington, in state capitals, and even more in smaller countries, journalists pick up conventional wisdom through lives intertwined with the lives of politicians. In France, for instance, Thomas Ferenczi, associate editor of *Le Monde,* complains that journalists and politicians—and it does not matter if they are left-wing or right-wing—belong to the same "microcosm": "when they are young they go to the same schools, later they live in the same areas, go to the same holiday resorts, and so on." Ferenczi warns, "There is real danger for democracy here: namely, that, journalists and politicians, because they are so closely linked, have their own, narrow, idea of what the media should cover . . . and ignore the interests of the people."[5] This is less of a problem in the more pluralistic United States than it is in France. In the United States, there is a more widely dispersed journalistic elite—at least across two cities, New York and Washington, and with important pockets of opinion shapers in Los Angeles, Chicago, and Cambridge-Boston, rather than concentrated in one—and it is much more diverse in social and educational background. However, the same general phenomenon occurs.

Other factors also limit the range of opinion in the American media, vitally important factors, although they lie outside the news media as such. For instance, the American political system generally offers a narrower political spectrum, and one less accommodating of minorities, than most other democratic systems. Ralph Nader complained bitterly after the 2000 election that he had not been well covered in the press. Why, he asked, when he was raising real issues, did he get no coverage while Al Gore and George W. Bush, the Tweedle-dum and Tweedle-dee of American politics, were covered every time they blew their noses?[6] The answer seemed pretty straightforward: Ralph Nader was not going to be elected president of the United

States in 2000. Either Al Gore or George W. Bush would. The press—as part of its conventional wisdom—believed its job was to follow what the American political system had tossed up for it. It was not the job of the press to offer the public a wide range of issues but to cover, analyze, and discuss the issues the two viable candidates were presenting. Imagine, however, if Ralph Nader had been running for president in Germany. Would the German press have shown greater interest in his ideas? Yes, but not because the German press is better or more democratic, but because Germany has a parliamentary political system. It is because if Ralph Nader received 5 percent of the vote in Germany, his party would receive 5 percent of the seats in Parliament and would be a force, potentially a decisive force, in forming a government. If Ralph Nader received 5 percent of the vote in the United States, he would get no seats in Congress.

So there are many reasons why media discourse in the United States fails to approximate an ideal of robust and wide-open discussion. Even so, journalism as it functions today is still a practice that offends powerful groups, speaks truth to power, and provides access for a diversity of opinion. How and why does this happen despite all that constrains it? The standard sociological analysis of news places it in so airless a box that exceptional journalistic forays are not readily explained. They are the exceptions that prove the rule. They are the ones that got away from the powers of constraint and co-optation and routine. But these "exceptions" happen every year, every week, at some level every day. How can we explain that?

Strategic Opportunities for Free Expression
Eventfulness

There is a fundamental truth about journalism that all journalists recognize but almost all social scientists do not: things happen. Not only do things happen, but, as the bumper sticker says, shit happens. That is what provides a supply of occurrences for journalists to work with. Shit even happens to the rich and powerful, and it makes for a great story when it does.

Because shit happens, journalists gain some freedom from official opinion, professional routines, and conventional wisdom. Journalism is an event-centered discourse, more responsive to accidents and explosions in the external world than to fashions in ideas among cultural elites. The journalists' sense of themselves as street-smart, nose-to-the-ground adventurers in places where people do not want them has an element of truth to it, and it is very much linked to event-centeredness.

News, like bread or sausage, is something people make. Scholars emphasize the manufacturing process. Journalists emphasize the raw material their work brings them to; they insist that their jobs recurrently place them before novel, unprecedented, and unanticipated events. While sociologists observe how this world of surprises is tamed, journalists typically emphasize that the effort at domestication falls short.[7]

The journalists have a point. Sometimes something happens that is not accounted for in any sociology or media studies. Take President Bill Clinton's efforts to create a system of national service. This was part of his 1992 campaign, and he mentioned it as one of the priorities of his administration the day after his election. He appointed a friend, Eli Segal, to run a new Office of National Service, and Segal set to work to get appropriate legislation through Congress. The administration's efforts led to passage of the National and Community Service Trust Act, which Clinton signed into law in September 1993. One year later, AmeriCorps would be officially launched. Segal took charge of orchestrating a major public relations event that would feature President Clinton swearing in nine thousand AmeriCorps volunteers at sixteen sites around the country by satellite hook-up. Every detail was checked, every contingency plan was rehearsed. Segal looked forward to a triumphant day on the South Lawn of the White House followed by extensive, favorable news coverage. At 4:30 a.m. on the morning of the ceremony, Segal's phone rang. The event as planned would have to be scrapped. Why? Because at that hour a deranged pilot crashed his Cessna aircraft into the back of the White House precisely on the spot where the ceremony was to be staged. The news media predictably went gaga over this bizarre and unprecedented event and could scarcely be bothered by the launching of AmeriCorps—no doubt more important than the plane crash, but infinitely more routine.[8]

Social scientists insist that most news is produced by Eli Segals, not deranged pilots. Quantitatively, they are right; the vast majority of daily news items on television or in print come from planned, intentional events, press releases, press conferences, and scheduled interviews. Even so, journalists find their joy and their identity in the adrenaline rush that comes only from deranged pilots, hurricanes, upset victories in baseball or politics, triumphs against all odds, tragedy or scandal in the lap of luxury, and other unplanned and unanticipated scandals, accidents, mishaps, gaffes, embarrassments, and wonders. The scholars delight in revealing how much of news is produced by the best laid plans of government officials who maneuver news to their own purposes; the journalists enjoy being first to the scene when the best laid plans go awry.

On September 13, 1994, the *New York Times'* lead story, and two related stories, covered the plane crash at the White House. Other news was swamped. The story on AmeriCorps ran on page seventeen. Even there it seemed to be folded into the big story of the day. The third paragraph read: "Some 850 were inducted as more than 2,000 dignitaries and supporters took part in the ceremony on the North Lawn of the White House. They

were kept sweltering there for more than two hours, and an elaborately syn-
chronized satellite television transmission was thrown awry because of the
crash of a light plane early this morning on the South Lawn where the event
was supposed to have taken place."

Journalists make their own stories, but not from materials they have personally selected. Materials are thrust upon them. It can even be argued, as
Regina Lawrence has contended, that in recent years news has become more
event-driven and less institution-driven. Moreover, the news media take events
not as ends in themselves but as "jumping-off points for thematic exploration
of social issues." Content analysis of news over the past one hundred years
indicates that journalists pay increasing attention to context, to reporting
events in detail especially when they serve as "invitations for the news media
to grapple, however gracefully or clumsily, with political and social issues."[9]
This preoccupation with unpredictable events keeps something uncontrol-
lable at the forefront of journalism. The archetypal news story, the kind that
makes a career, the sort every reporter longs for, is one that is unroutinized
and unrehearsed. It gives journalism its recurrent anarchic potential. And it
is built into the very bloodstream of news organizations, it is the circulatory
system that keeps the enterprise oxygenated.

Conflict

Almost all journalists relish conflict. Almost all media criticism attacks
journalists for emphasizing conflict. But conflict, like events, provides a
recurrent resource for embarrassing the powerful.

Consider a story by Randal C. Archibold that appeared in the *New York
Times* on January 11, 2003, with the headline "Nuclear Plant Disaster Plan Is
Inadequate, Report Says." To summarize, New York governor George Pataki
had commissioned a report on safety at the Indian Point nuclear power plant
just thirty-five miles away from midtown Manhattan. The report was produced by a consulting group the governor hired, Witt Associates. James Lee
Witt, its chief executive, was formerly the director of the Federal Emergency
Management Agency. So journalists knew the report was being written, knew
its chief author was a high-ranking former federal official, and knew roughly
when it would appear. This sounds like the kind of government-centered
"official" news story critics complain about.

But was it? Why did Governor Pataki commission the report? Clearly, he
commissioned it after the September 11 terrorist attack made more urgent
the concerns that citizens and citizens' groups had already expressed about
the safety of the Indian Point nuclear reactor. . . . The Witt report, whose
conclusion could not have been fully anticipated by the governor or anyone
else if it was to have legitimacy, declared that the disaster preparedness plan
was inadequate for protecting people from unacceptable levels of radiation

in case of a release at the plant. The elected executive of Westchester County, Andrew J. Spano, commented, "the bottom line is the plant shouldn't be here." The reporter made it clear that Witt Associates did not remark on whether the plant should be shut down but, at the same time, noted that the report's view of the emergency plans for the plant "largely reflected complaints voiced for years by opponents of Indian Point."

The Witt report became news not because the governor's office generated it, but because the governor acted in the face of raging controversy. The continuing controversy made the story news and made the news story interesting. In the end, the report obviously gave support to the environmentalists and others who have urged that Indian Point be shut down. The news story helped keep opponents of government policy alert, encouraged, and legitimated.

Cynicism

Political reporters in the past generation have increasingly made it a point not only to report the statements and actions of leading public officials but to report on the motives behind the actions as best as they can. They report not only the show and the dazzle that the politician wants foregrounded, but the efforts that go into the show and the calculations behind them. They may not intend to undercut the politicians, but they do intend not to be manipulated. The result is a portrait of politicians as self-interested, cynically manipulative, and contemptuous of the general public.

Take, for instance, the *New York Times*' April 16, 2003, front-page story on the proposed Bush tax cut, "In a Concession, Bush Lowers Goal of Tax Cut Plan." The story began by curtly observing that President Bush lowered his target for a tax cut in a tacit admission that his original package was "dead." Then reporter Elisabeth Bumiller cited White House advisers who said "that they were now on a war footing with Capitol Hill" to pass the biggest tax cut they could. They, along with other Republican strategists, said "it was imperative for Mr. Bush to be seen as fighting hard for the economy to avoid the fate of his father, who lost the White House after his victory in the 1991 Persian Gulf war in large part because voters viewed him as disengaged from domestic concerns." The orientation of the story was to the timing and style of the president's speech on the economy, not to its substance. The background—strategy and image—is the foreground. This kind of a story, once exceptional, has become standard.[10]

At the end of September 2003, Laura Bush went to Paris as part of the ceremonies signaling the American reentry to UNESCO after a boycott of nearly two decades. The First Lady's trip was, of course, a well-planned public relations gesture. Would anyone have suspected otherwise? But Elaine Sciolino, the *Times*' veteran foreign correspondent and chief Paris correspondent, made a point of it, noting that Mrs. Bush did not face the American flag as the American national anthem was sung. "Instead, she stood perpendicular to it, enabling photographers to capture her in profile, with the flag and the Eiffel Tower behind. The scene was carefully planned for days by a White House advance team, much to the amusement of long-time UNESCO employees."[11]

. . . This kind of reporting may not be a sign of a press that motivates or mobilizes or turns people into good citizens. It may do more to reinforce political apathy than to refurbish political will. But it may be just what democracy requires of the press.

Outsider News

Why is Trent Lott no longer majority leader of the U.S. Senate? The answer is that on December 5, 2002, he made remarks at Senator Strom Thurmond's one hundredth birthday party that suggested we would all be better off if Senator Thurmond, running on a segregationist platform for the presidency in 1948, had won the election. The room apparently was full of politicians and journalists, none of whom immediately caught the significance of the remark. . . .

But if no one at the party recognized Lott's remarks as a story, how did it become news and force Lott's resignation from his leadership post? The first part of the answer is that several practitioners of the still novel "blogs," or personal Web sites of a kind of highly individualized public diary, took note of Lott's remarks, including several prominent and widely read bloggers. . . . Although mainstream press outlets, both print and broadcast, noted the remarks (and C-SPAN had aired them), the bloggers pressed the fact that Thurmond ran as a segregationist and that Lott had taken many conservative stands through the years, including speaking before white supremacist groups and voting against the Civil Rights Act of 1990. Matt Drudge, in his online report, even found that Senator Lott had made an almost identical statement in praise of Thurmond in 1980.

Thanks to the "blogosphere," the party that Senator Lott and nearly everyone else present regarded as an insider event was available for outsider news. Moreover, as Heather Gorgura argues, the bloggers succeeded in getting the "dump Lott" bandwagon moving not simply by pointing out an indiscreet remark, but, in documenting Senator Lott's long and consistent history of association with organizations and policies offensive to African Americans, by persuading mainstream journalists that Lott's remarks were not casual and thoughtless but representative of a racism Lott had repeatedly expressed and acted upon.[12]

. . . The cyber-pamphleteers today can attract broad attention, including the attention of the old media. They do so, I might point out, by name-calling sensationalism. The most prominent and most consequential cases are that of Matt Drudge breaking the Monica Lewinsky story—"The president is an adulterer"—and the bloggers who cried, "The senator is a racist." An unlovable press, indeed, but perhaps just what democracy requires.

Outsiders are always troublemakers. The news media are supposed to be institutionalized outsiders even though they have in fact become institutionalized insiders. There is much more that might be done to keep journalists at arm's length from their sources. This is something that journalism education could orient itself to more conscientiously—for instance, insisting that journalism students take a course in comparative politics or a course on the politics and culture of some society besides the United States. A serious U.S. history course would also help. The idea would be to disorient rather than orient the prospective journalist. Disorientation—and ultimately alienation of journalists—helps the press to be free.

Social scientists regularly observe how much reporters have become insiders, socializing with their sources, flattered by their intimacy with the rich and powerful, dependent on intimacy for the leaks and leads officialdom can provide. All of this is true, but it is all the more reason to observe carefully and nurture those ways in which journalists remain outsiders. Bloggers in the Trent Lott case, although journalists, took up outposts on journalism's frontier. But even standard issue journalists are outsiders to the conventional opinions of government officials in several respects. For one, they advance the journalistic agenda of finding something novel that will set tongues a-flutter across a million living rooms, breakfast tables, bars, lunchrooms, and lines at Starbucks. Second, journalists have access to and professional interest in nonofficial sources of news. Most important of these nonofficial sources is public opinion as measured by polls or by informal journalistic "taking of the pulse" of public opinion. The American press in particular has a populist streak that inclines it toward a sampling of civilian views. A front-page story in the April 24, 2003, *Chicago Tribune,* for instance, by Jill Zuckman, the *Tribune*'s chief congressional correspondent, and datelined Northfield, Wisconsin, was based on both national opinion polls and local interviewing of people who objected to the USA Patriot Act.

. . . [People] had a surprising amount to say about their fears for domestic civil liberties. So the topic Zuckman wrote about was not what she intended to cover, but her populist instinct made it possible to report on a phenomenon that elites did not anticipate and that the administration could not have found comforting.[13]

Conclusion

Journalists are not free agents. They are constrained by a set of complex institutional relations that lead them to reproduce day after day the opinions and views of establishment figures, especially high government officials. They are constrained by broad conventional wisdom that they are not particularly well located nor well enough educated to buck and they are powerfully constrained by the conventions and routines of their own professionalism. At the same time, they are not without some resources for expanding the range of expression in the news. What structures do or could preserve their capacity to speak freely and to expand the range of voices and views they represent in their reporting? What journalistic predispositions do or could enable them to take advantage of their limited but real autonomy to fulfill the potential of a free press for vigorous, robust discussion of public issues? I am defending, somewhat to my surprise, what is usually attacked as the worst features of the American press—a preoccupation with events, a morbid sports-minded fascination with gladiatorial combat, a deep, anti-political cynicism, and a strong alienation of journalists from the communities they cover.

I hasten to add that the journalists I most admire get behind and beneath events, illuminate trends and structures and moods and not just conflicts, believe in the virtues and values of political life and the hopes it inspires, and feel connected and committed to their communities—global, national, or local. The journalists of greatest imagination discover the nonevents that conceal their drama so well. They recognize the story in conflicts that never arose because of strong leadership or a stroke of luck, or the conflict that was resolved peacefully over a painstakingly long time without sparking a front-page "event." But I propose, nonetheless, that some of the greatest service the media provide for democracy lies in characteristics that few people regard as very nice or ennobling about the press. These features of journalism—and perhaps these features more than others—make news a valuable force in a democratic society, and this means that—if all goes well—we are saddled with a necessary institution we are not likely ever to love.

Notes

1. Alexis de Tocqueville, *Democracy in America,* edited by J. P. Mayer (Garden City, N.Y.: Doubleday, 1969), 180.
2. W. Lance Bennett, "Toward a Theory of Press-State Relations in the United States." *Journal of Communication* 40 (spring 1990): 103–25, quotes at 106, 125.
3. Herbert Gans, *Democracy and the News* (New York: Oxford Univ. Press, 2003). Gans and Bennett, like many other contemporary theorists, both presume that the press at its best should not only report the doings of government but that it should do so in a way to encourage and provide for the participation of ordinary citizens, informing them in advance of governmental decisions so that they can make their voices heard. This is by no means an undisputed assumption. As John Zaller has argued, the job of the press in a mass democracy may be to help people evaluate leaders, not policies. The press should try to make it possible

for the public to evaluate leaders after they have acted, not policies before they have been put in place. See John Zaller, "Elite Leadership of Mass Opinion: New Evidence from the Gulf War," in *Taken by Storm: The Media, Public Opinion, and U.S. Foreign Policy in the Gulf War,* edited by W. Lance Bennett and David L. Paletz (Chicago: Univ. of Chicago Press, 1994), 201–2.

4. Janet Steele, "Experts and the Operational Bias of Television News: The Case of the Persian Gulf War," *Journalism and Mass Communication Quarterly* 72 (1995): 799–812, quote at 799.

5. Thomas Ferenczi, "The Media and Democracy," *CSD Bulletin,* 8 no. 1 (winter 2000–2001): 1–2.

6. Ralph Nader, "My Untold Story," *Brill's Content* (February 2001), 100–3, 153–4.

7. Scholars . . . have provided important explanations for this autonomy. Daniel Hallin sees autonomy provided structurally by divisions among elites. See Daniel C. Hallin, *"The Uncensored War": The Media and Vietnam* (New York: Oxford Univ. Press, 1986). Laws that make it tough to sue for libel also enhance autonomy. These explanations direct attention to structural opportunities for aggressive reporting, but they do not provide journalists with a motive to pursue challenge and critique.

8. Steven Waldman, *The Bill* (New York: Viking, 1995), 240.

9. Regina Lawrence, *The Politics of Force* (Berkeley: Univ. of California Press, 2000), 188.

10. This is not to mention background stories that are exclusively focused on stagecraft. See, for instance, Elisabeth Bumiller, "Keepers of Bush Image Lift Stagecraft to New Heights," *New York Times,* May 16, 2003, p. 1.

11. *New York Times,* September 30, 2003, A4.

12. Heather E. Gorgura, "Lott Gets a Blogging: Did the Amateur Journalists of the Blogosphere Bring Down Trent Lott?" (unpublished paper, University of Washington, March 2003). This student paper is extremely thoughtful and well documented.

13. Email to the author from Jill Zuckman, September 20, 2003.

4

POLITICAL COMMUNICATION: OLD AND NEW MEDIA RELATIONSHIPS

Michael Gurevitch, Stephen Coleman, and Jay G. Blumler

Editor's Note

The environment in which political communication operates is in turmoil. Established media are battling to retain as much of their influence over news production as possible. They are merging well-seasoned practices of the past with new ways of news dissemination made possible by evolving communications technologies. Meanwhile, professional and lay competition for audiences for political news is escalating. The future of news broadcasting is murky. Current structures may not survive. Gurevitch, Coleman, and Blumler shed much-needed light on the moving scene, explaining the role of televised news in the past, the ongoing changes, and the implications for democratic politics in the twenty-first century.

When this essay was written, Michael Gurevitch was an emeritus professor at the Phillip Merrill College of Journalism of the University of Maryland, Stephen Coleman was a professor of political communication and the codirector of the Centre for Digital Citizenship at the Institute for Communications Studies at the University of Leeds, and Jay G. Blumler was an emeritus professor of public communication at the University of Leeds and an emeritus professor of journalism at the University of Maryland. Gurevitch and Blumler are among the leading, internationally recognized founders of the political communication field. All three authors have published numerous important studies about the mass media's political influence.

. . . But as the new medium became settled, ubiquitous, and seemingly invulnerable, it came to seem as if politics in electoral democracies—a game

Source: Excerpts from Michael Gurevitch, Stephen Coleman and Jay G. Blumler, "Political Communication: Old and New Media Relationships," in *The Annals of the American Academy of Political and Social Science,* 625:1 (September 2009): 164–181. Copyright © 2009 by American Academy of Political and Social Science. Reprinted by Permission of SAGE Publications, Inc.

of power, persuasion, mobilizing support for policies and politicians, and aggregating votes—could not take place without or beyond the mediating gaze of television. Thus, television and politics became indeed complementary institutions, existing in a state of mutual dependence. Politics provided the raw materials and television packaged it, subtly reconstructed it, and delivered it to audiences. The rules of the journalistic game precluded any major repackaging of political messages and hence allowed the political sources fairly wide latitude if not full control of their messages. But over time, the rules of the game began to gradually shift. A series of historical events (e.g., the Vietnam War, Watergate) as well as political and technological changes moved television reporters, editors, and executives to adopt more skeptical, less deferential, and often more adversarial stances toward politics and politicians and hence a more actively interventionist role in the presentation of political issues and stories. The balance of power between the two began to shift gradually toward a more even situation.

The changing rules of the game had some significant consequences, both for the political players as well as for the terrain of television's coverage of politics. It thus had several long-range effects on the political processes and their outcomes. First, television moved into the center of the political stage, assuming a "coproducer" role of political messages instead of the earlier journalistically sanctioned "reporter" role, that is, that of transmitting and relating political events to the audience as if from outside the events. Television gradually moved from the role of observer of events and provider of accounts (stories) and emerged as definer and constructor of political reality. Without necessarily breaching journalistic norms, television came to have an impact upon the events it covered.

Second, while television became an integral part of the political process, it ironically contributed to its depoliticization. The accusation that television has shifted the focus of the political discourse from issues to personalities is by now quite familiar. Policy issues and concerns are more often associated with the faces of political leaders rather than with their political, ideological, and philosophical underpinnings. The educational value of election campaigns, which was once regarded as a key benefit of televised politics, was allegedly diminished by this focus on spectacle rather than ideas. It is, perhaps, an inevitable product of the visual character of the medium, in which faces are more easily recognizable by and accessible to mass audiences than abstract arguments about policies. The democratic ideal of conducting election campaigns as platforms for national debates, as an opportunity for societies to discuss their present and future directions (and indeed to examine their past), has been replaced by the familiar notion of the campaign as a horse race or political beauty contest.

Third, television transferred politics to the living room. Since, by definition, politics takes place in the public domain, involving societies in discussions, negotiations, and struggles over public issues and concerns, its natural locus must be in the public arena. Yet, television imported it into the living room and turned it into a parlor game played by small and quasi-intimate circles. The societal aspect of politics was thus diminished and the bonding effects of public debates attenuated. The public/private, outdoor/indoor dualities of the conduct of politics had ironically contradictory consequences. On one hand, by bringing politics into the home, television undoubtedly contributed to the expansion of the audience for politics. It incorporated into the political process individuals and groups in society that in pretelevision times did not regard themselves as participants in the political process, since their exposure to it was at best minimal and marginal. At the same time, the multiplication of television and other media outlets offering diverse contents has allowed viewers to escape from political content into a vast range of diversionary offerings.

Next, while changes in the scope and composition of television audiences require further documentation, the conventional wisdom is that one of the effects of television's forays into politics has been a dilution of the level of partisanship among audience members. The argument hinges on the assumption that changes in the formats of political television, first among them the introduction of televised debates between political leaders, have limited the ability of viewers to exercise selective exposure to political messages. The familiar format of side-by-side presentation of partisan positions, designed, among other things, to display and preserve the medium's claim for balance and impartiality, resulted in "forced exposure" of viewers to both sides (occasionally three or more sides) of political arguments.

Finally, television's entry into the political domain inevitably led to the formation of professional cadres working for the political parties, designed to fashion the parties' messages and the public personae of political actors in ways that are compatible with the medium. Thus, the communicative activities on both sides of the political-media relationship were handed over and conducted by professionals working within and deploying the same set of professional journalistic practices. The professionalization of politics thus constitutes a response and an adaptation to the challenges of professionalized political media.

New Media: Displacement or Reconfiguration?

Does "the end of television" as we know it imply that the intimate relationship between television and politics that has dominated the past half century is fading away? There are some indications that this might indeed be the case.

The most significant change has been the encroachment of the Internet on the terrain hitherto dominated by television. Audiences for television, as well as for other mass media, are on a downward trend. Newspapers are losing readers and the main television outlets are losing viewers. While this is the case for mass media use generally, it is strikingly visible in the figures for audiences relying on television for political news. . . .

> . . . Pew researchers note that "while mainstream news sources still dominate the online news and information gathering by campaign internet users, a majority of them now get political material from blogs, comedy sites, government web-sites, candidate sites or alternative sites." Moreover, the survey data show that younger people are more heavily represented among new media users, suggesting that the trend will accelerate (Pew 2008).

Rather than seeing these changes as a process of displacement, with new, digital media becoming dominant as analogue, print-broadcast media atrophy, they may be interpreted as evidence of an ecological reconfiguration, recasting roles and relationships within an evolving media landscape. As citizens gain access to inexpensive communication technologies through which they can interact with the media, generate their own content, and create alternative networks of information dissemination, the gate-keeping monopoly once enjoyed by editors and broadcasters is waning. While never merely passive recipients of television's account of political reality, audiences are increasingly becoming active participants in public communication, as senders as well as addressees of mass-circulating messages. This profound role change is taking place alongside the continued presence of professional media production aimed at traditional mass audiences. But everywhere, from interactive news Web sites that receive tens of thousands of comments from the public each day to YouTube videos challenging government policy, it is apparent that media producers can no longer expect to operate within an exclusive, professionalized enclave. Media audiences are now able to intervene in political stories with a degree of effectiveness that would have been unthinkable ten or twenty years ago.

Politicians have also become aware of these altered roles and, ever sensitive to shifts in their audiences' media use, have adapted the channels of their message delivery to connect with Internet users wherever they may surf. Already twenty or so years ago, political operatives attempted to reach voters directly by mailing video cassettes containing political messages, thus attempting to supersede the mediation of television. Now they see the Internet as offering a new way of detouring the mass media. In the United States, Barack Obama's presidential campaign relied considerably upon the viral capabilities of social networking sites as a way of overcoming perceived mass-media obstacles. . . .

As well as destabilizing the traditional roles of analogue political communication, digital technologies have modified the communicative balance of power by reconfiguring "access to people, services, information and technology in ways that substantially alter social, organizational and economic relationships across geographical and time boundaries" (Dutton et al. 2004, 32). As access broadens to provide an extensive choice of media platforms, channels, and content, and unprecedented opportunities to store and retrieve media content, new patterns of media use are emerging with distinct sociocultural advantages for some groups. For example, the young, the housebound, and diasporic minorities are three groups that have in many cases benefited from the reconfigured social connections that the Internet affords. In the context of political democracy, voters who go online to seek information, interact with campaigns, and share their views with other citizens are likely to feel better informed, more politically efficacious, and more willing to participate in the democratic process (Shah, Kwak, and Holbert 2001; Johnson and Kaye 2003; Kenski and Stroud 2006; Xenos and Moy 2007; Shah et al. 2007).

However, traditional forms of political communication persist. Television remains dominant as the most highly resourced and far-reaching medium of mass communication; it thus continues to be the locus for "media events" (Dayan and Katz 1992) and the main source of political information for most people (Graber 1990; Chaffee and Frank 1996; Sanders and Gavin 2004; Jerit, Barabas, and Bolsen 2006). But the media ecology that surrounds television is being radically reconfigured with major consequences for the norms and practices of political communication. What exactly has changed?

Channel Multiplication; Audience Fragmentation

The mass television audience is in decline. Viewers are faced with more choices than ever before about what to watch, when to watch it, and how to receive it. . . . The collapsing centrality of terrestrial-based television channels coincides with significant changes in the spatial arrangement of domestic viewing (most homes now have several sets) and growing technological convergence between television and other, once separate technologies, such as telephones and computers. Watching television is a much less distinctive cultural activity than it was in the days when families gathered around the box to watch the same programs as most of their neighbors. As Livingstone (2004a, 76) has observed, "The activity of viewing . . . is converging with reading, shopping, voting, playing, researching, writing, chatting. Media are now used anyhow, anyplace, anytime." In the face of intensified competition for public attention and information, political news and analysis that might in the past have reached most people in the course of a week's viewing can be easily missed.

Channel choices and time-shifting options lead not only to fragmentation of the mass audience but to the emergence of distinct issue publics: people who only want to be addressed on their own terms in relation to issues that matter to them. For example, MTV or Sky Sport viewers might not want to hear about crises in the global economy or the causes of international tensions; they can exclude themselves from exposure to issues and forms of address that they find unappealing, disturbing, or bewildering. Television's role as a public sphere is diminished by these easy opt-outs, and democracy suffers from the absence of socially cross-cutting exchanges of experience, knowledge, and comment.

"Publicness" Transformed

Television emerged as a mass medium at a time when cultural boundaries between public and private life were unambiguous. Constituting a new kind of communicative space in which the debates, dramas, and decisions of politics could be played out daily, television brought the vibrancy of the public sphere to the domestic intimacy of millions of private homes. At the same time, it made public hitherto private lifeworlds through documentaries, plays, and dramatized serials that allowed the public to witness its own multidimensionality. . . .

. . . [T]here is a sense in which other public spaces are now encroaching upon television's historic management of public visibility. It is no longer only television cameras, studios, and formats that politicians need to focus upon as they seek to promote their messages and control their images. The viral energy of the blogosphere, social network sites, and wikis constitutes a new flow of incessantly circulating publicity in which reputations are enhanced and destroyed, messages debated and discarded, rumors floated and tested. From Senator Trent Lott's incautiously disparaging remarks about the civil rights movement at what he thought was a private gathering, to Senator George Allen's offensive mockery of an Indian opponent at a campaign rally, the slips, gaffes, indelicacies, insults, and errors that were once confined to relative invisibility are now captured and circulated through online media in ways that can disrupt elite agendas and ruin political reputations. The ubiquity of media technologies, from mobile phone cameras and pocket recorders to always-on Internet connections, are eradicating traditional barriers between public and private. As Meyrowitz (1985, 271) has observed, "When actors lose part of their rehearsal time, their performances naturally move toward the extemporaneous." As a consequence, mediated publicity has become a 24/7 presence; from reality TV (in which the private is publicized) to political interviews (in which the impersonal is increasingly personalized), the contours of the public sphere are being reshaped in ways to which political actors must learn to adjust.

Interactivity and Remixing

Television is the quintessential broadcast medium: it transmits messages to a mass audience expected to receive or reject what it is offered. The inherent feedback path of digital media subverts this transmission ethos by allowing message receivers to act upon media content. The digital text is never complete; the fluidity of bits and bytes makes digital communication radically different from broadcasting. In the context of political communication, this has entailed a profound shift in the process of message circulation. Whereas political actors were once concerned to produce polished, finished performances for public consumption, contemporary politicians are compelled to think about interactive audiences and their capacity to question, challenge, redistribute, and modify the messages that they receive. In the era of digital interactivity, the production of political messages and images is much more vulnerable to disruption at the point of reception. . . .

The Internet has expanded the range of political sources. On one hand, agenda setting is no longer a politician-journalist duopoly; on the other, the commentariat is no longer an exclusive club. This has led to a radical expansion of the political realm to include aspects of the mundane and the popular, such as celebrity behavior, football management, domestic relationships, and reality TV conflicts. Beyond the subject matter, the style of public interest content has tended to depart from the professional forms that once dominated "high politics." And yet it cannot be ignored by political elites, who are increasingly engaged in efforts to monitor the blogosphere, control the content of wikis, and make their presence felt in unfamiliar environments such as Facebook and YouTube.

As well as the need to respond to the buzz of media interactivity, political actors must consider the possibility that their messages will be modified once they are launched into mediaspace. The digital media environment does not respect the integrity of information; once it has been published online, others are at liberty to remix content, in much the same way as music fans are able to reorder and reconstruct beats, melodies, and lyrics. . . .

Television and Politics—A More Ambivalent Relationship

In the digital era, the relationship between television and politics has become less clear-cut and more ambivalent. While television remains the principal constructor and coproducer of political messages, the systemic entanglement between journalistic and political elites is threatened by new players in the media game. This "fifth estate" (Dutton 2007) sees itself much more in the position of the eighteenth-century fourth estate: reporting, scrutinizing, and commenting from a critical distance, rather than entering into the portals of institutional power. In contrast, broadcast journalists, having become political insiders capable of shaping agendas, find themselves handicapped by their closeness to power.

At the same time, television's emphasis upon political personalization continues unabated. Political leaders who do not look right on television and do not understand its implicit grammar face major disadvantages. In the new media ecology, political actors are under greater pressure than ever to construct rounded media images, not only on television and in the press, but across a range of outlets. In doing so, however, they have to compete with many others who are in search of public attention, on far more equal terms than previously. In Italy, the radical comedian Beppe Grillo has established the country's most popular blog, attracting far more public comments than those sent to the major political parties. Politicians, parties, and governments cannot expect to attract public attention simply because of the legitimacy of their positions; authority within the new media ecology has to be earned by demonstrating commitments to interactive and networked communication that do not come easily to elite political actors.

While television continues to be the principal conduit between the home and the public sphere, both of these spaces have changed since the heyday of broadcasting. Television remains central to the routines and securities of everyday life (Silverstone 1994), but domestic spaces have become more fragmented, as families disperse within and beyond them. Grand televisual events still bring people together, but the experience of media access is now much more individualized, as particularly younger people spend more time using personalized, hybrid forms of public-privatized media technologies. A negative effect of family breakdown has been the reduction of the inter-personal communication about politics that has traditionally been a key force for socializing political participation. The public sphere, as mediated through television and newer communication technologies, has taken an anti-institutional turn, focusing more earnestly upon forms of informal, communitarian, and networked public presence. In many respects, the digital media networks are more sensitive to this circulatory public sphere than television, with its *centralized* distance from the grassroots, is capable of being.

And whereas televised coverage of politics diminished partisanship by reducing possibilities for selective exposure, the new media ecology makes it easier to establish partisan patterns of media access by creating more scope for selectivity and more opportunities for group herding and opinion polarization (Sunstein 2001; Mutz 2006; Feldman and Price 2008). The absence of an online equivalent to the public service broadcasting ethos raises profound risks for democracy. Television production might have been industrially top-heavy, unaccountable, and often authoritarian, but it was susceptible to regulation likely to generate some semblance of balanced political coverage.

In the new media ecology, communication strategists need to work harder than ever to cover the expanded media landscape and to adopt new styles in order not to seem contrived, insincere, and heavy-handed. Vast spin operations have turned political marketing from a means of conveying policies and images to a means of determining them. An emphasis upon generating apparently spontaneous discussion is now preferred to didactic declarations about policy. The cultural appeal of the media amateur, posting spontaneously, sporadically, and incompletely contrasts with the clinical efficiency of the party war room. In an age when politicians do not benefit from seeming to be politicians, affected unprofessionalism may well hold the key to successful communication. Explicitly or otherwise, politicians probably remain yet more dependent upon professional campaign and image management and under pressure to find novel ways of presenting themselves within the ever-expanding spaces of the media.

The future of this ambivalent relationship between television and politics, and of political communication more generally, entails normative policy choices. Contrary to the forceful rhetoric of technological determinism, new means of producing, distributing, receiving, and acting upon information do not in themselves shape or reshape the media ecology. Unanticipated and misunderstood, technological innovations not only disrupt settled cultural arrangements but also appear to possess teleological propensities of their own. In the early days of television—and before it, radio and the printing press—many commentators assumed that culture could not withstand their inherent effects. But this is a mistake: technologies are culturally shaped as well as shaping. In these first years of the twenty-first century, policies to shape the new media ecology in a democratic direction are still in their infancy. It is high time for such a policy to be devised, debated, and implemented. . . .

References

Bimber, B. 2003. *Information and American democracy: Technology in the evolution of political power.* New York: Cambridge University Press.

Blumler, J. G. 1970. The Effects of Political Television. In *The Effects of Television,* ed. J. D. Halloran. London: Panther.

Blumler, J. G., and S. Coleman. 2001. *Realising democracy online: A civic commons in cyberspace.* London: Institute of Public Policy Research.

Blumler, J. G., and D. McQuail. 1968. *Television in politics: Its uses and influence.* London: Faber and Faber.

Bucy, E., and A. Gregson. 2001. Media participation: A legitimizing mechanism of mass democracy. *New Media & Society* 3(3): 357–80.

Cappella, J., and K. H. Jamieson. 1997. *Spiral of cynicism: The press and the public good*. Oxford: Oxford University Press.

Chaffee, S., and S. Frank. 1996. How Americans get political information: Print versus broadcast news. *The Annals of the American Academy of Political and Social Science* 546: 48–58.

Coleman, S., and J. G. Blumler. 2008. *The Internet and democratic citizenship: Theory, practice and policy*. Cambridge: Cambridge University Press.

Coleman, S., and G. Moss. 2008. Governing at a distance—Politicians in the blogosphere. *Information Polity* 13 (1/2): 7–20.

Coleman, S., D. Morrison, and M. Svennevig. 2008. New media and political efficacy. *International Journal of Communication* 2: 771–91.

Coleman, S., and K. Ross. 2009. *Them and us: How the media frame the public*. Oxford, UK: Blackwell.

Couldry, N., and A. Langer. 2005. Media consumption and public connection: Toward a typology of the dispersed citizen. *Communication Review* 8 (2): 237–57.

Dayan, D., and E. Katz. 1992. *Media events: The live broadcasting of history*. Cambridge, MA: Harvard University Press.

Dunleavy, P., H. Margetts, P. Bartholomeou, S. Bastow, T. Escher, O. Pearce, J. Tinkler, and H. Broughton, 2007. *Government on the Internet: Progress in delivering information and services online*. London: National Audit Office.

Dutton, W. 2007. *Through the network (of networks)—The fifth estate*. Inaugural lecture, University of Oxford Examination Halls, October 15.

Dutton, W., S. E. Gillett, L. W. McKnight, and M. Peltu. 2004. Bridging broadband Internet divides: Reconfiguring access to enhance communicative power. *Journal of Information Technology* 19: 28–38.

Dutton, W., and A. Shepherd. 2006. Trust in the Internet as an experience technology. *Information, Communication & Society* 9 (4): 433–51.

Entman, R. 1989. *Democracy without citizens: Media and the decay of American politics*. New York: Oxford University Press.

Feldman, L., and V. Price 2008. Confusion or enlightenment? How exposure to disagreement moderates the effects of political discussion and media use on candidate knowledge. *Communication Research* 35 (1): 61–87.

Graber, D. 1990. Seeing is remembering: How visuals contribute to learning from television news. *Journal of Communication* 40 (3): 134–56.

Groombridge, B. 1972. *Television and the people: A programme for democratic participation*. Penguin: Harmondsworth.

Jamieson, K. H. 1993. *Dirty politics: Deception, distraction and democracy*. Oxford: Oxford University Press.

Jerit, J., J. Barabas, and T. Bolsen. 2006. Citizens, knowledge, and the information environment. *American Journal of Political Science* 50 (2): 266–82.

Johnson, T., and B. Kaye. 2003. A boost or bust for democracy? How the Web influenced political attitudes and behaviors in the 1996 and 2000 presidential elections. *Harvard International Journal of Press Politics* 8 (3): 9–34.

Kenski, K., and N. Stroud. 2006. Connections between Internet use and political efficacy, knowledge, and participation. *Journal of Broadcasting and Electronic Media* 50 (2): 173–92.

Livingstone, S. 2004a. The challenge of changing audiences. *European Journal of Communication* 19 (1): 75–86.

———. 2004b. Media literacy and the challenge of new information and communication technologies. *Communication Review* 7 (1): 3–14.

Lowrey, W. 2006. Mapping the journalism-blogging relationship. *Journalism* 7 (4): 477–500.

Meyrowitz, J. 1985. *No sense of place: The impact of electronic media on social behavior.* New York: Oxford University Press.

Moy, P., and M. Pfau. 2000. *Malice toward all? The media and public confidence in democratic institutions.* Westport, CT: Greenwood.

Muhlberger, P. 2003. Political values, political attitudes, and attitude polarization in Internet political discussion: Political transformation or politics as usual? *Communications* 28 (2): 107–34.

Mutz, D. C. 2006. *Hearing the other side: Deliberative versus participatory democracy.* New York: Cambridge University Press.

Pattie, C., P. Seyd, and P. Whiteley. 2003. Civic attitudes and engagement in modern Britain. *Parliamentary Affairs* 56 (4): 616–33.

Pew Research Center for People and the Press. 2008. *Internet now major source of campaign news: Continuing partisan divide in cable TV news audiences.* October 31. http://pewresearch.org/pubs/1017/internet-now-major-source-of-campaign-news.

Reith, J. 1949. *Into the wind.* London: Hodder and Stoughton.

Sanders, D., and N. Gavin. 2004. Television news, economic perceptions and political preferences in Britain, 1997–2001. *Journal of Politics* 66 (4): 1245–66.

Scannell, P. 2000. For anyone-as-someone structures. *Media, Culture & Society* 22 (1): 5–24.

Scupham, J. 1967. *Broadcasting and the community London; New Thinker's Library.* London: C. A. Watts.

Shah, D., J. Cho, W. Eveland, and N. Kwak. 2005. Information and expression in a digital age: Modeling Internet effects on civic participation. *Communication Research* 32 (5): 531–65.

Shah, D., N. Kwak, and L. Holbert. 2001. Connecting and disconnecting with civic life: Patterns of Internet use and the production of social capital. *Political Communication* 18:141–62.

Shah, D., D. McLeod, L. Friedland, and M. Nelson. 2007. The politics of consumption/the consumption of politics. *The Annals of the American Academy of Political and Social Science* 611 (1): 6–15.

Silverstone, R. 1994. *Television and everyday life.* London: Routledge.

Smith, A. 1979. *Television and political life: Studies in six European countries.* London: Macmillan.

Sunstein, C. 2001. *Republic.com.* Princeton, NJ: Princeton University Press.

Syvertsen, T. 2004. Citizens, audiences, customers and players: A conceptual discussion of the relationship between broadcasters and their publics. *European Journal of Cultural Studies* 7 (3): 363–80.

Trenaman, J., and D. McQuail. 1961. *Television and the political image.* London: Methuen.

Uslaner, E. 2004. Trust, civic engagement and the Internet. *Political Communication* 21 (2): 223–42.

Welch, E., C. Hinnant, and M. Moon. 2005. Linking citizen satisfaction with e-government and trust in government. *Journal of Public Administration Research and Theory* 15 (3): 371–91.

Xenos, M., and P. Moy. 2007. Direct and differential effects of the Internet on political and civic engagement. *Journal of Communication* 57 (4): 704–18.

5

LOSING THE NEWS: THE FUTURE OF THE NEWS THAT FEEDS DEMOCRACY

Alex S. Jones

Editor's Note

Alex S. Jones is a renowned news professional who is passionate about the quality of news. He has practiced all kinds of journalism at small newspapers and big metropolitan papers such as the *New York Times*. He has worked in radio and television, including its Web versions, and he has written books and articles. The excellence of his work has been recognized with a Pulitzer Prize. As the director of Harvard University's Shorenstein Center on the Press, Politics, and Public Policy, he can view and assess news developments from exceptionally deep and broad perspectives.

Jones worries that the vigor of American democracy is declining because fact-based professional news reporting is shriveling. Citizens lack essential information that they need to make sound political judgments. The Web spews out flood tides of information in a variety of formats each day, but much of it is unidentifiable and unverifiable opinion. It fails to perform the essential functions of the free press, which is the "Fourth Branch" of American government at all levels. High-quality news alerts the public about crucial political events, putting them into meaningful contexts. The press informs government about public opinions and holds officials accountable by investigating and assessing their policies and behaviors. Without this type of news, democracy withers.

. . . I believe that journalism is important. That it matters. For over a century, Americans have had as a birthright a remarkably good—though far from perfect—core of reported news that is as essential to our freedom

Source: Excerpted from Alex Jones, *Losing the News: The Future of the News that Feeds Democracy,* New York: Oxford University Press, 2009, Prologue and Chapter 1. Copyright © 2009 by the Oxford University Press, Inc. Reprinted by permission of the Oxford University Press, Inc.

as the Constitution itself. But the times we live in trigger an unsettling cascade of questions about journalism and news. If taken seriously, these are difficult questions. Some are moral or ethical ones. Others are thorny for other reasons. What, indeed, is *happening* to the news at this time of tumultuous technological change? Does it matter that newspapers seem to be in free fall? Is objectivity the best model for American journalism in a new era that prizes the individual voice? Is media concentration a menace or a red herring? Is traditional journalism *really* essential to democracy? What exactly *is* honorable journalism? Such questions are at the center of this book, which is an effort to explain the curious story of news, a tale that has come down laced with mythology and misconceptions. The book's focus is the values of journalism at a time when those values are increasingly viewed as obsolete or unaffordable in a media world turned upside down by digital technology. My purpose is also to try to see over the horizon to where news might go from here, or at least to ponder our choices.

The book is not intended for people seeking fresh ammunition with which to bash the press from the left or from the right. News is like government itself—endlessly subject to criticism, and with few defenders. But also like government, news can be good and bad; it can do its job well or let us down. And usually, like government, it does some of both. This is not a book about media bias, but about the uncertain fate of serious news itself.

News—or something that looks like it—will exist in the future, of course. There will be, through the Web, a torrent of news and opinion. But high-quality news is expensive to produce, and in ever shorter supply. One hopes that the *New York Times* and the *Washington Post* will endure, but two great general interest news organizations are not enough. The best reporting before the Iraq War is widely viewed to have been not by the *Times* or the *Post,* but by what was then the Knight Ridder Washington bureau.

The profit squeeze has wreaked havoc on newsrooms and especially decimated the Washington-based press corps covering government on behalf of citizens back home. For instance, in 2006 Washington-based reporters for the *San Diego Union-Tribune* won a Pulitzer Prize for exposing the corruption of Congressman Randal "Duke" Cunningham—a story that would almost certainly not have come to light without their investigation. Now that bureau has been shuttered, along with a host of others. The future promises an abundance of what might be considered *commodity news,* which is to say plain vanilla news that is generated by a few news companies and sold cheap, like mass-produced fast food. Far less certain is whether *high-quality* news will be part of the daily life of any but the wealthy and the powerful—especially when it comes to local and state coverage. An analysis in 2009 of reporting strength in the nation's state legislatures by *Governing* magazine detailed the wholesale abandonment of statehouse reporting by the nation's news organizations. Government at the state level often has the most impact on people's lives, and it is also where corruption flourishes without a watchdog press.

The word "crisis" is hackneyed in journalism and should be treated with great skepticism—a reporter's virtue. Nevertheless, to my mind there *is* a genuine crisis. It is not one of press bias, though that is how most people seem to view it. Rather, it is a crisis of diminishing quantity and quality, of morale and sense of mission, of values and leadership. And it is taking place in a maelstrom of technological and economic change. The Internet and digital technology have sent the news business into a frenzy of rethinking, an upheaval of historic proportions whose outcome is much in doubt. Things that are precious may well be lost or terribly damaged, and new things that are marvelous will certainly emerge. What is sure is that the old media world is being transformed—collapsing, in some respects—and the new media world will be different, for better and worse. The chips that had been in orderly piles in front of a few players are now scattered all over the floor, and everyone in the casino is scrambling to grab a handful. Tom Brokaw likens it to "the second big bang," a stupendous media explosion in which some things are burning up and no one knows which of the swirling fragments will ultimately support life.

Optimists about the future of news are dazzled by the glories of the digital age and a democratization of news fueled by the Internet. They generally view those who express concern as self-interested sentimentalists clinging desperately to a disappearing media environment or as Luddites who are too old-fashioned to plunge into an exciting new world.

Pessimists see a frightening new order in which serious professional news reporting will be replaced by talk, advocacy, spin, trivia, and out-and-out propaganda. They see a world in which the news diet for most of the nation will be comparable to living on potato chips and beer, and a typical news story will be what fits on a cell phone screen. Despite the thrilling innovations in news taking place, they are alarmed by the dispiriting erosion of what has been the kind of news that made the press an institution of American democracy.

I like to think of myself as a realist, but not a cynic or a doomsayer. An inchoate free-floating anxiety about the news is abroad in our nation, and I certainly share that. Many people are worried, but aren't sure what they should be worried about. The issues are bewildering, the values involved are often contradictory, and the technological landscape seems to change by the hour. This book aspires to clarify what is happening to news and why, to look frankly at news values, and to lay out the important choices that will shape the future. One thing is certain: the revolution in news now taking place will be critical to defining what kind of a nation we become in the years ahead.

The Iron Core

. . . Imagine a sphere of pitted iron, grey and imperfect like a large cannonball. Think of this dense, heavy ball as the total mass of each day's serious reported news, the iron core of information that is at the center of a functioning democracy. This iron core is big and unwieldy, reflecting each day's combined output of all the professional journalism done by news organizations—newspapers, radio and television news, news services such as the Associated Press and Reuters, and a few magazines. Some of its content is now created by new media, nonprofits, and even, occasionally, the supermarket tabloids, but the overwhelming majority still comes from the traditional news media.

This iron core does not include Paris Hilton's latest escapade or an account of the Yankees game or the U.S. Open. It has no comics or crossword puzzle. No ads. It has no stories of puppies or weekend getaways or recipes for cooking great chili. Nor does it include advice on buying real estate, investing in an IRA, movie reviews, or diet tips. There is nothing wrong with any of these things. Indeed, pleasant and diverting stories are far more appealing to most people than the contents of the core, which some find grim, boring, or riddled with bias.

It has no editorials and does not include the opinions of columnists or op-ed writers or political bloggers. These things are *derived* from the core. They are made possible because there *is* a core. Their point of departure is almost always information gleaned from the reporting that gives the core its weight, and they serve to spread awareness of the information that is in the core, to analyze it and interpret it and challenge it. Opinion writers pick and choose among what the core provides to find facts that will further an argument or advance a policy agenda. But they are outside the core, because they almost always offer commentary and personal observation, not original reporting.

Inside the core is news from abroad, from coverage of the war in Iraq to articles describing the effort to save national parks in Mozambique. There is news of politics, from the White House to the mayor's office. There is an account of a public hearing on a proposal to build new ball fields and an explanation of a regional zoning concept that might affect property values. There is policy news about Medicare reform and science news about global warming. There is news of business, both innovation and scandal, and even sporting news of such things as the abuse of steroids. An account of the battle within the local school board about dress codes is there, along with the debate in the state legislature over whether intelligent design should be taught as science. The iron sphere is given extra weight by investigative reports ranging from revelations that prisoners at the county jail are being used to paint the sheriff's house to the disclosure that the government is tapping phones without warrants as part of the war on terror.

What goes into this cannonball is the daily aggregation of what is sometimes called "accountability news," because it is the form of news whose purpose is to hold government and those with power accountable. This is fact-based news, sometimes called the "news of verification" as opposed to the "news of assertion" that is mostly on display these days in prime time on cable news channels and in blogs.

Traditional journalists have long believed that this form of fact-based accountability news is the essential food supply of democracy and that without enough of this healthy nourishment, democracy will weaken, sicken, or even fail.

For more than a century, this core of reported news has been the starting place for a raucous national conversation about who we are as a people and a country. Just as the Earth is surrounded by a blanket of atmosphere, so too is this core enveloped by a thick layer of talk and opinion. The conversation—which seems more like an endless family squabble—takes place on editorial pages and in letters to the editor, in opinion columns and on Sunday morning talk shows, on *The O'Reilly Factor* and the radio programs of Rush Limbaugh and Don Imus, in blogs on the Internet and press releases, over dining-room tables, beside water coolers and in barrooms, in political cartoons and on *The Daily Show with Jon Stewart*.

And in jokes. In his first ten years as host of *The Tonight Show,* Jay Leno told over 18,000 political jokes, almost 4,000 of them about Bill Clinton. But for each of Leno's political jokes, the starting point was something from the core. The core also feeds the entertainment industry, which has its own powerful voice in the national conversation. The quasi-news programs on television, such as *Today* and *20/20,* look to the core for ideas and inspiration. Some pure entertainment programs, such as *The West Wing,* come directly from the core, and even the silliest of sitcoms and nastiest of hip-hop lyrics are often linked to it in some murky way. No matter where the conversation about public affairs takes place, it is almost always an outgrowth of that daily iron cannonball.

The biggest worry of those concerned about news is that this iron core is in jeopardy, largely because of the troubles plaguing the newspaper business. It is the nation's newspapers that provide the vast majority of iron core news. My own estimate is that 85 percent of professionally reported accountability news comes from newspapers, but I have heard guesses from credible sources that go as high as 95 percent. While people may *think* they get their news from television or the Web, when it comes to this kind of news, it is almost always newspapers that have done the actual reporting. Everything else is usually just a delivery system, and while resources for television news have plunged and news on commercial radio has all but disappeared, the real impact on iron core news has been from the economic ravaging of newspapers.

Until now, the iron core of news has been somewhat sheltered by an economic model that was able to provide extra resources beyond what readers—and advertisers—would financially support. This kind of news is expensive to produce, especially investigative reporting. And there are indications that a lot of people aren't really interested. In the media economy of the future, cold metrics will largely determine what is spent on news. The size and quality of the iron core will be a direct reflection of what the audience for it will economically support. Demand will rule, and that may well mean that, as a nation, we will be losing a lot of news. There will be a bounty of talk—the news of assertion—but serious news, reported by professional journalists, is running scared.

Inside the core, there is a hierarchy of news, each type important in its own way. The first tier could be thought of as bearing witness. This is no small service to democracy, and is the meat and potatoes of accountability news in that it lets citizens know the fundamentals of what is happening in their world and in the corridors of power. Much of the headline news, both of the White House and around the world, is the act of journalists bearing witness to events. Firsthand coverage of disasters such as Hurricane Katrina and of wars in Afghanistan and Iraq are examples of this kind of bearing-witness journalism at its most challenging. Similarly, the reporter who tells you what happened at the mayor's press conference or at the school board meeting is bearing witness. Being a reliable surrogate for the public—the nation's eyes and ears—is most of what goes into the core, and it is also the most straightforward form of journalism. The burden for the reporter is to tell it straight and get as much of the truth as is possible.

But bearing witness is frequently not enough—indeed, not nearly enough for important issues. It opens the door to the second tier of core journalism, which can be thought of as "following up." Good journalists rarely stop with bearing witness. That is the point of departure for the second step of finding out what more is to be known and answering the all-important question "why?"—seeking reasons that often are not apparent at the moment of bearing witness. This is the journalism that requires being able to stay with a story rather than simply visit it and then move on to the next thing. It means listening to the mayor's press conference and then finding out what was behind the decision or policy that was announced. It is staying with the war rather than parachuting in, doing a quick report, and leaving on the next plane. It is sometimes simply being able to confirm what seemed to be the truth at the moment of bearing witness, but may have been a selective representation. It requires time to follow up, and it demands—and in turn creates—expertise and sophistication about what is being reported.

Next up the hierarchy of core news is what might be called "explanatory journalism," which takes even more time and expertise. This is the product of boring deeply into a subject, speaking to sources, unearthing data, gathering facts, and mastering complexity. It is the kind of reporting that compares the confusing options for older Americans as they try to choose between prescription plans and that examines—without prejudice—the evidence for and against the reality of global warming and presents the result in a form that is illuminatingly fair-minded. It could be thought of as following up on steroids, and if following up takes effort and dogged curiosity, explanatory journalism takes deeper knowledge and expertise, and even more time.

Finally, at the top of the reporting chain, is investigative reporting. This is the toughest kind of journalism because it not only takes time and great expertise, it must be done in the face of efforts to keep information secret. Inherent in the concept of investigative reporting is that it is news that someone with power does not want the public to know. Often, it starts with a reporter simply bearing witness. In perhaps the most celebrated example, in 1972 Bob Woodward was a low-level metro reporter at the *Washington Post,* on the job for only nine months, when five men broke into the Democratic National Headquarters in the Watergate complex and got caught wearing rubber surgical gloves and carrying fancy bugging equipment and $2,300 in cash. Both Woodward and another metro reporter, Carl Bernstein, worked on the first-day page-one story, along with eight other *Post* reporters, and they didn't even get a byline. But they then attacked the story like wolverines, and the *Post* won a Pulitzer Prize for Public Service for its coverage of the Watergate scandal. As Alicia Shepard points out in her article "The Myth of Watergate, Woodward and Bernstein," the story released a deluge of reportorial energy as the nation's best news organizations competed for scoops. The *Los Angeles Times* was first to get one of the burglars on the record in a hard-hitting interview. In his book *Richard Nixon, Watergate and the Press,* Louis Liebovich said that within six months of the break-in the *Post* had produced 201 staff-written stories, but the *New York Times* had published 99 and the *Los Angeles Times* 45. Important investigative work was also done by the *Washington Star, Time, Newsweek,* and CBS. The aggregate of their work was the fruit of thousands of man-hours by talented reporters, and it took every bit of that commitment by news organizations to finally force the truth to emerge. . . .

. . . [I]t was the prospect of doing serious news that drew most of the best reporters and editors to journalism. Reporting accountability news carried the most prestige. It was the most expensive to produce, took the most time, often got the biggest play, and required the greatest expertise. Much of the other content was provided by syndicates and services or reporters lower in the pecking order. But serious news required employing an experienced news staff that expected raises and vacations, health insurance and pensions, and took themselves increasingly seriously as professionals.

It is this kind of news that is recognized in prizes and awards, which in turn validate the newspaper's inevitable claim to be fulfilling not just a commercial but a societal role. It was this kind of news that was thought important enough to be protected by the First Amendment—though what the amendment actually protected was free expression rather than high-quality news. Even so, in the 20th century, the public service of publishing iron core news was what gave newspaper owners a mantle of honor and respectability that went nicely with their growing profits.

. . . As the audience declines and advertisers experiment with new media, newspaper advertising and circulation revenues are under enormous pressure and are declining at many papers. To make things worse, the costs of labor and newsprint—a newspaper's two highest expenses—have spiraled up. Contractual agreements are making increased salaries unavoidable, and the cost of newsprint has increased dramatically in the past few years. Profit levels of over 20 percent had become commonplace at newspapers, and the squeeze between declining revenues and unavoidable cost increases has sent newspapers into a tailspin. In many cases, the newspaper companies have huge debt obligations from buying other papers in more optimistic times, only to see the revenues dwindle that are needed to pay interest and principal. The reaction at many newspapers has been to cut news staffs—including people who create the type of news that much of the audience considers boring and is expensive, requiring the best, most experienced reporters, who also command the highest salaries. Increasingly, this kind of news is viewed more as a luxury than an essential, and even a turnoff to readers who prefer to know what's up with Hollywood.

As a result, the iron core is in trouble.

A case can be made that the core will not only survive, but grow more weighty through new forms of news media, such as Web-based citizen journalism and journalistic bloggers. Traditional media are trying to find new ways to report news that will appeal to a younger, Web-savvy audience, and creating new publications and Web sites in response to reader tastes. Perhaps that is what will happen. But so far, we appear to be losing this important kind of news far faster than we are replacing it.

Even worse, the sense of social responsibility that has long existed at traditional news organizations is in retreat. This has been true for some time, but a gradual slackening in commitment to news as a social responsibility has become a headlong rout because of the panicky scramble to shore up profit margins. News and business have always been linked in the United States, and traditional news organizations have been commercial enterprises that had profit as a priority. But there was also the parallel priority of social stewardship.

This stewardship was at best uneven, especially in times of financial crunch. It would, of course, be ridiculous to idealize journalism. There was no Golden Age in which the typical publisher was a self-sacrificing paragon, eager to demonstrate his rectitude by trading profits for high ideals. There were a few of those, but they were always the exceptions. Nor was there an Arcadia when news was not sometimes compromised by laziness, human error, greed, and bias. Journalism is a human endeavor, with all the attendant weaknesses.

But it would be just as wrong to suggest that nothing has shifted in the values of the news business, and that the overwhelming power of market thinking has not had a corrosive impact on those values. . . .

. . . Part of the news crisis is finding a solution that will pay the significant costs of generating the accountability news that is essential to our democracy and still allow an acceptable profit. This is a riddle that has yet to be solved, and so the iron cannonball of accountability news continues to grow lighter and shrink. But if within the traditional media a commitment to a social steward-ship becomes mere window dressing and an empty boast, the loss will be terrible indeed. . . .

6

WHAT AMATEUR JOURNALISM MEANS FOR INTERNATIONAL AFFAIRS

Steven Livingston; Kaye Sweetser Trammell and
David D. Perlmutter

Editor's Note

Amateurs are invading the turf of professional journalism, including the hallowed grounds of foreign affairs reporting. They broadcast eyewitness reports, illustrated with their often blurry cell phone pictures. Bloggers use news stories reported by professional journalists and spin them in ways that reshape meanings. What are the effects of these changes? Do they transform the impact of foreign news? Do they affect U.S. foreign policies? Do they mold public opinions? These are the questions that the authors of this essay try to answer in separate chapters of a book that traces foreign news coverage from the days of carrier pigeons to the age of the Internet.

The selection starts with Livingston's analysis of major changes produced by amateur journalism. It concludes with Trammell and Perlmutter's presentation of one memorable blogging incident and its consequences. At the time of writing, Steven Livingston was a professor of political communication at George Washington University, holding appointments in the School of Media and Public Affairs and the Elliott School of International Affairs. Kaye Sweetser Trammell was an assistant professor at the Manship School of Mass Communication at Louisiana State University. David D. Perlmutter was an associate professor, also at the Manship School.

Source: Excerpted from Steven Livingston, "The Nokia Effect: The Reemergence of Amateur Journalism and What It Means for International Affairs," and Kaye Sweetser Trammell and David D. Perlmutter, "Bloggers as the New 'Foreign' Correspondents: Personal Publishing as Public Affairs," in *From Pigeons to News Portals*, ed. David D. Perlmutter and John Maxwell Hamilton, Baton Rouge: Louisiana State University Press, 2007, chapters 3 and 4. Copyright © 2007. Reprinted by permission of Louisiana State University Press.

Steven Livingston: "The Nokia Effect"

. . . This chapter considers how new information technology affects contemporary journalism. It also considers questions about how event-driven news—the sort of news favored by new technology—undermines the public's ability to hold policy makers accountable while increasing the likelihood of supporting a more bellicose foreign policy.

New Technology and News Gathering

Several new information technologies are pulling viewers and readers away from traditional news media. As a recent report by the Carnegie Corporation noted, "Through Internet portal sites, handheld devices, blogs and instant messaging, we are accessing and processing information in ways that challenge the historic function of the news business and raise fundamental questions about the future of the news field."[1] Those with concerns about the future of journalism would find additional discomfort in the declining numbers of newspaper readers in the United States, the creaky status of the network evening news programs (including the apparent demise of the star anchor system), and recent public opinion survey results revealing that Americans trust the news media less than every other major institution in American life. With these trends and public attitudes as backdrop, it is perhaps not surprising that American news consumers are turning to alternatives offered by new technologies.[2]

Ironically, many of the same technologies that threaten traditional news consumption habits dramatically expand the ability to gather and distribute socially relevant information. Often, this enhanced information gathering capability is used by traditional news organizations when reporting news. Examples of this include personal camcorder images used by television news to report natural disasters, plane crashes, or other events caught on camera. On other occasions, traditional media are bypassed altogether, such as when text messaging was used by Chinese citizens to spread news of the SARS epidemic at a time when official state-controlled media ignored it as a matter of official editorial policy. . . .

. . . What implications do these and many other possible examples have for the practice of journalism and the conduct of international affairs? Dan Gillmor, founder of Grassroots Media, an organization that promotes what he calls "citizen journalism," said witnesses' photos and online accounts would reshape the role of traditional news media over time.[3] London, the Indian Ocean tsunami, and many other recent events suggest he may be correct. But the question that emerges from Gillmor's assertion is: Would a reshaped role of traditional news media be good for the prospects of democratic self-governance?[4] Secondly, how does new technology affect the nature of journalism? We will next take up this second question and then turn our attention to the question of its effects on democratic self-governance.

The Further Evolution of Journalism

Philip Seib has written an important book about the ways speed and immediacy—made possible by new technologies—have undermined traditional journalism norms and practices.[5] My additional point to Seib's contribution centers on a historical perspective that puts recent changes in context. Modern journalism, though still dominated by large bureaucratic organizations, is developing a parallel structure that, in important respects, looks remarkably like journalism as practiced two hundred years ago. If it is understood properly as journalism at all, it is best described as amateur journalism.

For well over a century, American journalism has been characterized by the activities of a cadre of professional reporters working for large, bureaucratic organizations. News gathering typically involves the assignment of reporters to beats where they interact with government officials working in even larger bureaucracies. In 1973, Leon Sigal found that the overwhelming majority of the news in the *Washington Post* and the *New York Times* had its origins in the various interactions of reporters and officials. Indeed, about 90 percent of the news originated from a news conference, official press release, interview, or some other means of officials communicating with the press. News was what officials said it was. Conversely, less than 2 percent of the news, according to Sigal's findings, concerned spontaneous events.[6] Tom Fenton has made the same point more recently in his devastating critique of U.S. international news coverage. Fenton remarks, "Most of the time, in truth, most of the media take their cues from the government in deciding which foreign stories to cover."[7] While Fenton is no doubt correct, the close bond between official agendas and news agendas is evolving, at least in part because technology has freed news organizations from their dependence on official handouts.

In a 2003 article, Lance Bennett and I reported that the nature and origins of CNN international news coverage changed over the course of the 1990s.[8] As heavy, cumbersome, and operationally demanding analog equipment was replaced by smaller, more mobile, and operationally simplified digital equipment, remote broadcasts of breaking news became commonplace. Indeed, by the late 1990s, as the Inmarsat videophone (operated by a single technician) replaced or supplemented C-band or Ku-band mobile satellite uplinks (operated by up to a half dozen technicians), event-driven news overtook institutional news in frequency.

In 1994, at the cusp of the convergence from analog to digital technology, event-driven news with some sort of official response actually exceeded institutional news, though not by much. Institutional news, consisting of press conferences, interviews of officials, and background briefings, actually became more common over the course of the next few years. By the late 1990s, however, a clear trend toward event-driven news became evident. By 1998–1999, event-driven news, typically live coverage of breaking events from somewhere around the globe, overtook institutionally sourced news. There is no reason to believe that since 2001, with the enormous amount of videophone coverage of the wars in Afghanistan and Iraq, that this trend has abated.

In 2005, Douglas Van Belle and I reported that from the mid-1960s to the mid-1990s, news of disasters from remote locations was more commonly found in the *New York Times* and on American broadcast network news. We attributed our findings to advances in technology.[9] Although predictability of supply, one of the prime motivators for institutionally based news, remains important in determining news content, the ability to meet competing news values—including drama, the desire for compelling visuals, and immediacy—is facilitated by advances in technology.

There are, no doubt, a variety of explanations for the recent trend toward event-driven news. In the 2003 study mentioned above, Bennett and I found a sharp increase in event-driven news in the late 1990s. Much of the event-driven news in 1999 came in the form of coverage of the NATO bombing campaign against Serbian targets. Then new Ku-band uplinks mounted on trucks ringed the perimeter of Kosovo and offered a steady stream of live event news coverage. News of Kosovo was filled with harrowing images of the aftermath of errant bombs, such as when a NATO aircraft bombed a column of refugees in the belief it was a convoy of Serbian military vehicles, and of refugees streaming into Macedonia. The preponderance of coverage of Kosovo originated from the region and centered on events (errant bombs, targets hit and missed, people killed or saved) and not, at least proportionately, from the corridors of power in Washington and Brussels. News was more likely to be about what happened, rather than what an official said happened. To be sure, officials got their turn—*after* the event. Their role was less as agenda setters and more as reactors.[10]

In 1999, CNN first used a videophone to cover an earthquake in Turkey. But it wasn't until the spring of 2001 that the videophone came into its own. In April 2001, CNN used a videophone to broadcast the departure of the crew of a downed American EP-3 surveillance plane from a restricted Chinese airbase. It was thought to be the first ever unauthorized television transmission from Communist-controlled China. After that, the videophone become a standard technology used by news organizations around the world to cover breaking events live.[11] By the fall of 2001, scores of videophones were used by war correspondents in Afghanistan. Unlike those who relied on the military to transport copy from the battlefield during the 1990–91 Persian Gulf War, correspondents in Afghanistan transmitted live (text, jpegs, and video) using the Inmarsat satellite system.[12]

Is event-driven news, particularly news that is driven by the availability of amateur photographs, properly understood as news at all? In the view of some, journalism is defined by an editorial process that is lacking in amateur information gathering, and even in live-broadcast television: News professionals exercise judgment concerning the importance or relevance of events and processes. Journalism is something more than an unfiltered flow of raw information. Seib articulates this position well in this volume when he draws a distinction between seeing and understanding.

That distinction gets to the heart of the challenge facing journalism in the real-time era. Simply seeing can be accomplished with extraordinary breadth and precision: technology ensures that. But to help the public *understand* is far more difficult, and it will require the news media to occasionally take their feet off the accelerator as they provide information.[13]

The obsession with immediacy and live pictures gets in the way of actual reporting. Abdullah S. Schleifer, founder of the Adham Center for Television Journalism at the American University in Cairo, notes that reporters have no time to "sit down and write a script that provides a coherent story . . . four intelligent hours after an explosive event, and not just an ignorant five minutes after the event."[14] The raw immediacy of some information delivery systems (including live television) lacks the qualities that define news: a thoughtful, vetted, edited presentation of information that has benefited from the experience of news professionals. In this view, amateurs telling stories or posting pictures on the Internet is not journalism.

Yet it is important to remember that this understanding of journalism is, in the long view, quite recent. The modern era of journalism began in the nineteenth century as a "one-man-band undertaking." As historian and sociologist Michael Schudson explains, in the early nineteenth century "one man acted as printer, advertising agent, editor, and reporter."[15] Amateurs assisted him on occasion; friends and relatives described in letters home what they saw in their travels. News of distant places and events was the product of the voluntary actions of amateurs. Today, the new forces of change in journalism are the one-man-band bloggers and other amateurs who, armed with cameras and cell phones, create a steady stream of content for a new type of journalism.

In the 1830s, industrial production techniques enabled newspapers to provide news to a growing urban middle class, giving rise to the first large-scale institutionally based form of journalism: the penny press. Urbanization cut the cost of newspaper distribution while facilitating inducements to literacy. All of these factors were necessary for the establishment of a new understanding of news, one less rooted in the post–Revolutionary War–era emphasis on party-driven political polemics, occasionally salted with commercial information and amateur accounts of distant events. Instead, the penny press emphasized sensational scandals and political intrigue. By the mid-nineteenth century, editors had begun to rely less on informal contacts and more on paid freelance reporters. By the 1880s and 1890s, the steady rise of reporters' income and the growing acceptance (and eventual expectation) of a college degree for such journalists both indicated and helped solidify the new professional status of journalism. It is exactly this trend toward professionalization and bureaucratization of news that has reached its zenith and is now challenged by one-man bands and amateurs. Journalism has come full circle. It remains to be seen whether this new form of an older standard of journalism will replace or simply continue to supplement institutional journalism.

Whether there is a return to amateur journalism or not does not address the question of the political consequences of event-driven, episodic journalism. What are the effects of modern journalism's fascination with dramatic events often brought to light by new technologies?

Information Without Context

The proliferation of highly mobile digital devices such as cell phones, cameras, camcorders, and the many other means of collecting information—raw events—accentuates what Shanto Iyengar has called "episodic frames." According to Iyengar, framing refers to "subtle alterations in the statement or presentation of judgment and choice problems, and the term 'framing effects' refers to changes in decision outcomes resulting from these alternatives." Iyengar further specifies two framing subtypes: *Thematic framing* places issues in a broader or more general context. History, culture, and thick descriptions of politics constitute the essence of thematic framing. *Episodic framing*, on the other hand, "takes the form of event-oriented reports and depicts public issues in terms of concrete instances." As noted by Iyengar speaking of television news at the beginning of the 1990s, most television news reports focus on "concrete acts and breaking events."[16] Quoting David Altheide, Iyengar underscores the importance of framing to political outcomes: "Television reports that rely on visuals of an event will be more entertaining to an audience, yet provide little useful narrative interpretation to understand the broader issue. As long as more dramatic visuals are associated with the tactics and aftermath of terrorism, these aspects will be stressed over the larger issues of history, goals, and rationale."[17]

In a series of experiments designed to test this supposition, Iyengar found that episodic framing encouraged a tendency to attribute responsibility for political outcomes to individual rather than more general or societal causes. For example, when stories about politically motivated violence were contextualized by information about local politics, history, and social and economic conditions, subjects tended to attribute responsibility for the violence to those conditions. Conversely, when violence was reported as an isolated act or event, subjects tended to attribute responsibility to the individual perpetrators of the violence. The causal attribution is to "evildoers" rather than more complex social, historical, or political explanations.

In content analyzing some eleven hundred American broadcast network news stories about crime and some two thousand about terrorism in the 1980s, Iyengar found that both topics were "almost exclusively in episodic terms."[18] What are the consequences of episodic news? As Iyengar summarized, "The dominant episodic frame in network coverage encouraged viewers to attribute causal responsibility for terrorism to the personal qualities of terrorists and to the inadequacy of sanctions. Episodic framing also made viewers more likely to consider punitive measures rather than social or political reform as the appropriate treatment for terrorism."[19]

Iyengar concludes that his findings suggest that episodic news coverage tends to encourage public support for a more bellicose foreign policy, one that addresses problems with military might intended to physically eliminate evildoers rather than addressing complex political conditions. As the pace of event-driven news increases, as surely it must with the growing capability to cover events live from around the world, viewers' ability to think through more complex arguments behind or at the core of events erodes. In this way, event-driven news and political sophistication may be inversely related. If more gadgets lead to an increased tendency to report event-driven news, prospects for critical involvement from citizens seem dim. Even before the proliferation of smaller, mobile, and nearly ubiquitous devices that enable the capture of events, television news tended to emphasize episodic frames. Recent advances in technology might exacerbate this tendency.

Notes

1. Merrill Brown, "Abandoning the News," *Carnegie Reporter* 3, no. 2 (Spring 2005): 3.
2. Ariana Eunjung Cha, "Do-It-Yourself Journalism Spreads; Web Sites Let People Take News into Their Own Hands," *Washington Post,* July 17, 2005.
3. Ibid.
4. W. Lance Bennett, "The Burglar Alarm That Just Keeps Ringing: A Response to Zaller," *Political Communication* 20, no. 2 (April–June 2003): 131–38. A fundamental premise of this essay is that the principal role of a free press, the very reason it is free, as in free of government or other limiting restraints, is that it serves the purposes of maintaining democratic rule. The press must be free to monitor malfeasance, corruption, and other forms of abuse by government and business. Of course, other theories of the press exist, though they are not applied here.

5. Philip Seib, *Going Live: Getting the News Right in a Real-Time, Online Work* (Lanham, MD: Rowman and Littlefield, 2000).

6. Leon V. Sigal, *Reporters and Officials: The Organization and Politics of News-making* (Lexington, MA: Heath, 1973), 121.

7. Tom Fenton, *Bad News: The Decline of Reporting, the Business of News, and the Danger to Us All* (New York: Regan Books, 2005), 76.

8. Steven Livingston and W. Lance Bennett, "Gatekeeping, Indexing, and Live-Event News: Is Technology Altering the Construction of News?" *Political Communication* 20, no. 4 (October–December 2003): 363–80.

9. Steven Livingston and Douglas Van Belle, "The Effects of New Satellite News-gathering Technology on Newsgathering from Remote Locations," *Political Communication* 22, no. 1 (January–March 2005): 45–62.

10. Steven Livingston, "Media Coverage of the War: An Empirical Assessment," in *Kosovo and the Challenge of Humanitarian Intervention,* ed. Albrecht Schnabel and Ramesh Thakur (Tokyo: United Nations University Press, 2001), 360–84.

11. Lisa de Moraes, "Only CNN Gets the Picture," *Washington Post,* April 12, 2001.

12. For a classic description of the frustrations and anger that resulted from the necessity of relying on the U.S. military to transport video and other news to a satellite transmission facility during the Persian Gulf War, see John J. Fialka, *Hotel Warriors: Covering the Gulf War* (Washington, DC: Woodrow Wilson Center, 1992).

13. Philip Seib in David D. Perlmutter and John Maxwell Hamilton, eds., *From Pigeons to News Portals.* Baton Rouge: Louisiana State University Press. 2007.

14. Quoted in Alvin Snyder, "Journalism: A Risky Profession," USC Center on Public Diplomacy Web site, July 21, 2005, http://www.ebu.ch/CMSimages/en/USC%20Center%200n%20Public%20.Diplomacy%20_%20HEST_tcm6-43172.pdf.

15. Michael Schudson, *Discovering the News: A Social History of American News-papers* (New York: Basic Books, 1978), 16.

16. Shanto Iyengar, *Is Anyone Responsible? How Television Frames Political Issues* (Chicago: University of Chicago Press, 1991), 11.

17. Quoted in Iyengar, 28.

18. Iyengar, 27.

19. Ibid., 45.

Kaye Sweetser Trammell and David D. Perlmutter: "Bloggers as Foreign Correspondents"

. . . [T]he definition of "foreign correspondent" is increasingly confounded by new media technology and practices. Heretofore, the term evoked a picture of a ruffled "old China (or Moscow, or Paris, or Beirut) hand" whose baggage trail included a Remington typewriter, a whisky flask, and an expense account book from a major print publication or syndicate. In other words, the traditional source of foreign affairs coverage for most Americans was an American employee of a large American news organization . . .

. . . In the entire history of mass media and journalism, it was the norm for Americans to hear the voices of other peoples by listening to, reading, or watching media created and transmitted by the government or by the mainstream U.S.-based press. Foreigners—unless they were leaders, diplomats, or prominent dissidents—tended to be quoted only as human interest filler or exemplars of larger issues: e.g., "Ahmed the fisherman does not know what to make of the political upheaval in Cairo. . . ." The onset of the commercial Internet in the 1990s promised to bypass these traditional channels: people could access news of foreign lands via (a) the Web sites of their newspapers or governments, (b) independent media that in many cases challenged official points of view and mainstream media consensus, and (c) more rarely, the personal Web sites of the citizens of other countries. Then, beginning in the late 1990s and building to a tidal wave of popularity and power by 2004, a new genre of Web literature took front stage as a source of foreign affairs information. The phenomenon is the blog, short for *Weblog:* as most commonly defined, an online compendium of news, opinion, and debate by individuals.

Here we examine foreign independent blogs that have become extensions of, sources for, or replacements of traditional foreign affairs reporting. Their creators and contributors have the ability to talk to us directly, as the common phrase goes, "from ground zero," from Berlin to Beijing to the Congo. Perhaps more important, we the home-front audience can post comments, ask questions—that is, interact—with the stranger in a strange land, even if we are at war with her or his country. So to read a story about events in Baghdad, we no longer need CBS or the Associated Press; we have Salam Pax and his ordinary Iraqi's personal perspective describing the bombs falling outside his front door. Or to catch up on breaking news about the "Tulip Revolution" in Kyrgyzstan we can turn to an instantly created blog, Akaevu .net, and get the "scoop" while the traditional networks' correspondents are still on the plane from Moscow. In short, while in the past there have been times when the reporter becomes a part of the story,[1] this chapter explores how blogs allow the citizen reporter to become *the story.* . . .

Cases: Blogs From Abroad

The blogs discussed here are those that have been seen as more than just journals; these are blogs that, while they may contain personalized viewpoints, report comprehensively on terrorist activity, strategic military bombing, and genocide—all occurring just outside the bloggers' front steps. They are not necessarily the "top blogs" of the regions they represent; rather, they exemplify changes in the sources, form, styles, and distribution channels through which American audiences (including journalists) receive information from foreign lands.

Salam Pax's "Dear Raed"

In a study of the interplay of blogs with foreign affairs, Daniel W. Drezner and Henry Farrell noted,

> It was March 21, 2003—two days after the United States began its "shock and awe" campaign against Iraq—and the story dominating TV networks was the rumor (later proven false) that Saddam Hussein's infamous cousin, Ali Hassan al-Majid ("Chemical Ali"), had been killed in an airstrike. But, for thousands of other people around the world who switched on their computers rather than their television sets, the lead story was the sudden and worrisome disappearance of Salam Pax.[2]

Indeed, Pax—one young Iraqi's pseudonym—introduced the world public to viewing bloggers as foreign correspondents. His dispatches from Baghdad were seen daily leading up to and throughout the war. Because the blog was run on a free service, many questioned the genuineness of the so-called Baghdad Blogger, as blogs had already seen high-profile hoaxes.

Regardless, many felt that the realism and spirit in the writing proved the blog's authenticity. Beyond the major buzz created by the blog as it gained readers, journalists such as Peter Maass, a foreign correspondent writing for *Slate* magazine, praised the blog: "His [Pax's] lively and acerbic blog was far better than the stuff pumped out by the army of foreign correspondents in the country."[3] Maass was not the only traditional journalist to take note, as the *Guardian* observed: "It was the great irony of the war. While the world's leading newspapers and television networks poured millions of pounds into their coverage of the war in Iraq, it was the Internet musings of a witty young Iraqi living in a two-story house in a Baghdad suburb that scooped them all to deliver the most compelling description of life during the war.[4]

Despite this praise from the mainstream media and an international audience of readers on his blog, Salam Pax's agenda didn't begin with grand aspirations. The blog launched as many American blogs do: it was intended to keep friends (in this case, specifically a friend name Raed who rarely used e-mail and found blogs a more convenient way to keep in touch) up-to-date on Salam Pax's life. After the blogging began, Pax perceived that many Iraqi blogs focused on religion and that few were in English. At that point, Pax decided to identify himself as an Iraqi and—on the off chance that someone from outside his world found the blog—show what the real life of an Iraqi was like. Considering that there are only approximately fifty known blogs published from Iraq,[5] the celebrity of this blog carries even more weight.

Even after the war began and Salam Pax lost the technological means to "file" his stories with his growing list of readers, he kept writing. He wrote because "there will be excellent, amazing, very important stories to be told by lots of people. We, sitting in Baghdad in our protected four walls, were never going to be these stories. There are people who went through much more."[6]

From Web diarist to foreign correspondent, Salam Pax was able to engage and inform the world about what was happening at his doorstep through firsthand accounts. The entries mixed the tenets of journalism (who, what, when, where) with a unique perspective explaining the "why" as only someone whose home had become a war zone could. Furthermore, the humanity of the personal accounts and intermittent insertion of details (e.g., watching the movie *The American President* because Pax was sick of the news or cleaning up the house all day after a fierce sandstorm) created an environment in which readers could form parasocial relationships with the blogger. The rich details of his daily life experiences and feelings allowed readers to feel as if they personally knew Salam Pax or that he was their virtual friend.[7]

Posts from the blog received the most media attention when the *Guardian* began running excerpts, seemingly treating the posts as reports from a foreign correspondent. Eventually, the blogger who transformed the idea of foreign correspondence was himself transformed into a more traditional foreign correspondent, as he began writing for the *Guardian* and turned his blog posts into a book. This blog is noted as a turning point in the popularity of personal publishing and the political power blogs can wield by personalizing a military conflict thousands of miles away. . . .

Conclusion

In looking at the blogs and corresponding phenomena described here, it is clear that untrained (or "citizen") journalists are coming to the Internet, blogging, and adding to the information and understanding about certain world events. What, then, is the mark of success? Must these blogs be read by international leaders and then spur policy changes? Is it enough that these blogs are perused by the world's citizens and that those who read them are touched? Such at least might be a baseline for weighing the alleged powers of the foreign blogger. As stated in the "manifesto" of the Harvard-based Global Voices project, "We believe in the power of direct connection. The bond between individuals from different worlds is personal, political and powerful. We believe conversation across boundaries is essential to a future that is free, fair, prosperous and sustainable—for all citizens of this planet."[8] Blogs enable all of us—if we have access to them despite economic or political obstacles—to engage in such "conversations" for our own edification and, we believe, to the enrichment of both democracy and foreign affairs coverage.

But in weighing the "power" of the press, simple dialogue is often not considered enough added value. Let us examine the Salam Pax case as a benchmark for measuring the "success" of a blogger turned foreign corre-spondent. Was U.S. president George W. Bush or his generals who were run-ning the war reading Pax's blog as the military campaign evolved?

Probably not. Did the blog unequivocally result in changes in foreign policy or presence in Iraq? No. Yet the blog—and others discussed here—are seen as successful ventures in publicizing and at times reporting news *from* abroad. We argue here that these blogs provided a human-scale view of important world events. No longer is the enemy or the oppressed a faceless foreigner: he is someone with a family, someone we can receive updates from every day, someone the reader grows to care for and worry about.

Blogs may also develop into agents of what might be called citizen diplo-macy. This phenomenon was not unknown in foreign affairs. Famously, for example, President Nixon's landmark trip to China in 1972 was paved by the travels of an American table tennis team in 1971. The message of simply seeing ordinary people "getting along" is a powerful one in any context and any age. Some preliminary research on blogging suggests that extra-national communities can be created. One study found:

> Bloggers on the whole perceive a shared sense of community in the blogo-sphere. Notwithstanding the social, political, and economic differences between the regional cultures of our participants, bloggers painted a remark-able picture of congruity in their experiences with activism, reputation, social connectedness and identity. Thus, we can posit that bloggers themselves represent a unique culture that permeates through regional boundaries.[9]

Such linkages may assist the easing of international conflicts at the all-important street level. We may ask, for instance, what happens when a critical number of Israeli and Palestinian bloggers contact each other? As we have seen, the outcome may be flame wars and partisanship, but it could equally be a humanizing and contextual understanding less likely to occur as a result of coverage from national media.

In sum, we do not argue that foreign blogs will replace foreign correspon-dents, but we predict that they will enrich the information the world receives about important events. Specifically, these personalized posts dispatched from the front lines provide an insight and tell a story that an American deployed to the event cannot. Citizens abroad and policy makers alike can read the accounts on blogs from within a nation and expose themselves to alternative viewpoints. Journalists can broaden their sources. Furthermore, the world can get a glimpse into a community and gauge its way of thinking. The one-sided view of a foreigner traveling across the globe to tell a story can be improved by tapping into these bloggers serving as foreign correspondents in their own land.

That said, the foreign blog is ripe for further examination; news researchers and professionals would be unwise to ignore their future developments. Scholars interested in the news gathering and gate keeping process should examine the differences between traditional foreign correspondents and bloggers through in-depth analyses of the process each goes through in producing a news item for publication. Questions about source credibility and information quality should be posed. Finally, scholars should investigate the amount of attention these personalized reports are getting at various levels of government. Are policy makers reading these blogs? Are governments monitoring them and considering information published in them as a form of intelligence? Will these blogs ever have a direct impact on foreign policy or public opinion? The future is unwritten, but it will likely be blogged.

Notes

1. Andrew Paul Williams, "Media Narcissism and Self-Reflexive Reporting: Meta communication in Televised News Broadcasts and Web Coverage of Operation Iraqi Freedom" (Ph.D. diss., University of Florida, 2004).
2. Daniel W. Drezner and Henry Farrell, "Web of Influence," *Foreign Policy* November–December 2004: 32.
3. Peter Maass, "Salam Pax Is Real," *Slate,* June 2, 2003, http://slate.msn.com/id/2083847/.
4. "Salam's Story," *Guardian* Web site, May 30, 2003, http://www.guardian.co.uk/Iraq/Story/o,2763,966819,oo.html.
5. Claude Salhani, "Politics and Policies: The Other Mideast Revolt," *United Press International,* March 2, 2005.
6. "Salam's Story."
7. Kaye D. Trammell, "Celebrity Blogs: Investigation in the Persuasive Nature of Two-Way Communication Regarding Politics" (Ph.D. diss., University of Florida, 2004).
8. "Global Voices Draft Manifesto," http://cyber.law.harvard.edu/globalvoices/wiki/index.php/Global_Voices_Draft_Manifesto.
9. Norman M. Su, "A Bosom Buddy Afar Brings a Distant Land Near: Are Bloggers a Global Community?" paper, Second International Conference on Communities and Technologies (C&T 2005).

Part II

SHAPING THE POLITICAL AGENDA AND PUBLIC OPINION

Doris Graber

Media effects research diminished sharply in the 1960s in the wake of the book *The Effects of Mass Communication* by sociologist Joseph T. Klapper. Klapper examined the findings of communication researchers between 1940 and 1960 and concluded that media effects on political life were minimal. Research was reinvigorated a dozen years later in 1972 with the publication of a seminal article by Maxwell McCombs and Donald Shaw in *Public Opinion Quarterly*. The article examined agenda setting— the ability of the media to focus public attention on a set of issues—rather than the ability of the media to generate specific opinions. The study sparked a spate of empirical research that has demonstrated that the media are powerful transmitters of political information and that this information arouses the public's concerns and shapes politicians' agenda.

Examples of this scholarship are presented in the opening essay by Benjamin I. Page, Robert Y. Shapiro, and Glenn R. Dempsey. The authors discuss the important role played by the media in shaping public opinion about a broad array of public policies. They examine changes in policy preferences expressed in public opinion polls covering eighty issues over fifteen years. Their sample of polls demonstrates convincingly that the intervening television news stories affected the public's policy preferences. Like other scholars, the authors point out that contextual factors determine the degree and direction of news impact. The Page-Shapiro-Dempsey study illustrates how a major research venture, simultaneously involving many issues over an extended period of time, can reveal trends and patterns when other, less comprehensive studies fail to produce conclusive findings.

The next chapter focuses on public attitudes about the press. Do people trust the news media that inform them about politics, or do they take the news about politics with the proverbial grain of salt? If skepticism is the rule, it would sap media influence. Paul Gronke and Timothy Cook investigated trust in news media by charting public opinion trends from 1973 to 2004. They found that trust in news media had declined sharply. But this overall finding masked many important variations, such as continuing trust in the specific news outlets that each respondent had personally used. The research also shows that the same political indicators that led to higher confidence in political institutions in general drove down confidence in the press. The press, it seems, is a unique political force.

But the press is a many-splendored thing. On which sources do average people actually rely when they construct their opinions and make policy assessments? The conventional view has been that the regular print and electronic news media are the public's main information sources. That view produced a panic reaction among public opinion analysts when it became clear in recent decades that audiences for the conventional news media were declining steadily. A dangerous lowering of the civic IQ seemed inevitable. That spirit of doom was relieved somewhat by the discovery that the info-tainment programming—also called "soft news"—that combines entertainment and information, as well as many outright entertainment offerings on television and radio, contained substantial amounts of "hard," serious, factual news. Matthew A. Baum's painstaking research on what Americans learn about important political issues when the information is embedded in soft news shows that they learn quite a bit. This holds true for unlikely learners—people who lack an interest in politics—and for topics deemed unattractive to average Americans, namely, foreign policies. The entertainment format's sugarcoating makes serious news palatable when it would be shunned otherwise.

Frank D. Gilliam Jr. and Shanto Iyengar also found a strong link between the thrust of news stories and the opinions and policy preferences of news audiences. But in addition, they were able to demonstrate that the predispositions of audience members mattered a great deal. When the authors used experimental designs that allowed them to expose selected individuals to various versions of crime stories, they discovered that prior beliefs about demographic characteristics of frequent offenders came to the fore in interpreting and reacting to the seriousness of the crime threat. The research demonstrates that assessing audience predispositions is an essential part of media effects research. The essay is also notable for its step-by-step description of the design and execution of experimental research. Experiments have become a fruitful addition to the media research tool kit.

When news stories present newsworthy events from a variety of perspectives, which perspective, if any, dominates public opinions? What are the consequences for peoples' views about these events and their preferences for particular policies, and what are the public policy outcomes? Jill A. Edy and Patrick C. Meirick offer answers, drawing on public opinion polls conducted immediately after the attack on the United States on September 11, 2001. News media were framing the event as either a crime or an act of war. The mixing of these diverse information streams turned out to be a complex process that yielded a variety of results. People combined the various news story perspectives to accord with their personal preferences and then developed compatible policy choices. Media frames were important, but other influences substantially enhanced or diminished their effect.

In the final essay, Markus Prior assesses the likely impact of media-based public opinions on public policies. He contends that the proliferation of news sources is dividing the public into news buffs and entertainment buffs. The entertainment buffs become political dropouts in the formation and expression of political opinions. The news buffs, who feast on the rich flow of news, shape the public opinion currents that drive political processes. The dropout phenomenon makes American democracy less representative and less effective because the pool of informed citizens who participate in politics is much smaller than it should be. Moreover, news buffs' opinions tend toward the extreme ends of the political spectrum. That turns bridgeable political cleavages into unbridgeable political chasms.

7

WHAT MOVES PUBLIC OPINION?

Benjamin I. Page, Robert Y. Shapiro, and
Glenn R. Dempsey

Editor's Note

Benjamin I. Page, Robert Y. Shapiro, and Glenn R. Dempsey contend that shortcomings in research design explain why many studies of media impact on public opinion do not detect substantial agenda-setting effects. The authors note that most research designs focus on first-impression opinion formation about single events or classes of events rather than on opinions produced over longer periods of time by a multiplicity of media stimuli. Investigators seldom develop baselines that would allow them to assess opinions prior to news exposure, and they usually fail to analyze the intrinsic appeal of stories and the attractiveness of the actors who are involved in it.

Choosing a more realistic design, Page, Shapiro, and Dempsey examine media impact on a variety of opinions about public policy issues before and after audiences have been exposed to a wide range of news stories. Their findings demonstrate clearly that television news affects citizens' opinions about public policy issues. The influence varies, depending on who is advocating particular policies. Well-liked sources are more influential than disliked ones.

At the time of writing Page was the Frank C. Erwin Jr. Centennial Professor of Political Science at the University of Texas at Austin; he had written about elections and about the presidency. Shapiro was an assistant professor of political science at Columbia University. His writings had focused on public opinion. Dempsey was a graduate student in political science at the University of Chicago.

Source: Benjamin I. Page, Robert Y. Shapiro, and Glenn R. Dempsey, "What Moves Public Opinion?" in *American Political Science Review,* 81:1 (March 1987): 23–43. Copyright © 1987 by the American Political Science Association. Reprinted with the permission of Cambridge University Press.

Rational Citizens and the Mass Media

. . . [N]ew information that modifies relevant beliefs can change the expected utility of policies for citizens. This should occur if five conditions are met: if the information is (1) actually received, (2) understood, (3) clearly relevant to evaluating policies, (4) discrepant with past beliefs, and (5) credible. (For related views of attitude change, see Jaccard 1981; Zaller 1985.)

When these conditions are met to a sufficient extent, new information should alter an individual's preferences and choices among policies. Further, if the conditions are met in the same way for many individuals, there may be a change in collective public opinion that shows up in opinion polls. For example, if many citizens' policy preferences depend critically on the same belief (e.g., "We must spend more on national defense because the Russians are overtaking us") and if highly credible, well publicized new information challenges that belief (e.g., U.S. military spending is reported to rise sharply and a CIA study concludes that Soviet spending has changed little since 1976), then enthusiasm for increased military spending may drop.

Since most people have little reason to invest time or effort learning the ins and outs of alternative policies (Downs 1957), we would not expect new information ordinarily to produce large or quick changes in public opinion. Indeed the evidence indicates that aggregate public opinion about policy is usually quite stable (Page and Shapiro 1982).

By the same token, however, for whatever they do learn about politics, most people must rely heavily upon the cheapest and most accessible sources: newspapers, radio, and television, especially network TV news. When news in the media reaches large audiences and meets our five conditions for many individuals, we would expect public opinion to change.

Television news often meets the exposure condition. Most U.S. families own television sets, and most tune in to network news broadcasts from time to time. Viewers may wander in and out; they may eat or talk or be distracted by children; but every day millions of U.S. citizens catch at least a glimpse of the major stories on TV news. Others see the same stories in newspaper headlines or get the gist of the news from family and friends. Over a period of weeks and months many bits and pieces of information accumulate.

The conditions of comprehension and relevance, too, are often met. The media work hard to ensure that their audiences can understand. They shorten, sharpen, and simplify stories, and present pictures with strong visual impact so that a reasonably alert grade-schooler can get the point. Often stories bear directly upon beliefs central to the evaluation of public policies.

Credibility is a more complicated matter. Rational citizens must sometimes delegate the analysis or evaluation of information to like-minded, trusted agents (Downs 1957, 203–34). The media report the policy-relevant statements and actions of a wide variety of actors, from popular presidents and respected commentators, to discredited politicians or self-serving interest groups. News from such different *sources* is likely to have quite a range of salience and credibility, and therefore quite a range of impact on the public (see Hovland and Weiss 1951–52). The analysis of effects on opinion should allow for such variation.

News may also vary greatly in the extent to which it is or is not discrepant with past beliefs. If it closely resembles what has been communicated for many months or years, if it simply reinforces prevalent beliefs and opinions, we would not expect it to produce change. If, on the other hand, credible new information calls into question key beliefs and opinions held by many people, we would expect changes in public opinion. The extent of discrepancy with past news and past opinions must be taken into account.

We are, of course, aware of the curious notion that the contents of the mass media have only minimal effects (Chaffee 1975; Klapper 1960; Kraus and Davis 1976; McGuire 1986 but cf. Graber 1984; Noelle-Neumann 1973, 1980, 1984; Wagner 1983). This notion seems to have persisted despite findings of agenda-setting effects upon perceptions of what are important problems (Cook, Tyler, Goetz, Gordon, Protess, Leff, and Molotch 1983; Erbring, Goldenberg, and Miller 1980; Funkhauser 1973; Iyengar, Peters, and Kinder 1982; McCombs and Shaw 1972; MacKuen 1981, 1984).

We believe that the minimal effects idea is not correct with respect to policy preferences, either. It has probably escaped refutation because of the failure of researchers to examine collective opinion over substantial periods of time in natural settings and to distinguish among news sources. One-shot quasi-experimental studies (e.g., of presidential debates) understandably fail to find large, quick effects. Cross-sectional studies seek contrasts between media attenders and media "nonattenders" that hardly exist: nearly everyone is exposed either directly or indirectly to what the media broadcast (see Page, Shapiro, and Dempsey 1985a, 2–4). A more appropriate research design yields different results.

Data and Methods

Taking advantage of a unique data set in our possession, we have carried out a quasi-experimental study that overcomes several of the limitations of previous research. The design involved collecting data from many pairs of identically repeated policy preference questions that were asked of national survey samples of U.S. citizens; coding TV news content from broadcasts aired in between (and just before) each pair of surveys; and predicting or explaining variations in the extent and direction of opinion change by variations in media content.

Our design facilitated causal inferences and permitted comparison across types of issues and historical periods. The use of natural settings meant that all real world processes could come into play, including major events and actions, the interpretation of news by commentators and others, and the dissemination of information through two-step or multiple-step flows and social networks (cf. Katz and Lazarsfeld 1965). The examination of moderately long time periods (several weeks or months) allowed enough time for these natural processes to work and for us to observe even slow cumulative opinion changes. In addition, our measurement scheme permitted us to distinguish among different sources of news and to take into account the extent of news story relevance to policy questions, the degree of discrepancy between current and previous media content, and the credibility of news sources.

As part of our ongoing research project on public opinion and democracy, we have assembled a comprehensive collection of survey data on U.S. citizens' policy preferences. It includes the marginal frequencies of responses to thousands of different policy questions asked by various survey organizations since 1935. Among these data we have identified several hundred questions that were asked two or more times with identical (verbatim) wordings, by the same survey organization. (For a partial description, see Page and Shapiro 1982, 1983a.)

For the present research we selected 80 pairs of policy questions from the last 15 years (for which TV news data are readily available) that were repeated within moderate time intervals averaging about three months.

These 80 cases are not, strictly speaking, a sample from the universe of policy issues or poll questions but (with a small number of exceptions) constitute either a random sample of the available eligible survey questions and time points for a given survey organization or all the available cases from an organization. They are very diverse, covering many different kinds of foreign and defense ($n = 532$) and domestic ($n = 548$) policies. In nearly half the cases public opinion changed significantly ($p < .05$; 6 percentage points or more), and in a little more than half, it did not—nearly the same proportion as in our full data set of several hundred repeated items. A list of cases and a more detailed methodological discussion is available in Page, Shapiro, and Dempsey (1985a, b).

The dependent variable for each case is simply the level of public opinion at the time of the second survey (T2), that is, the percentage of the survey sample, excluding "don't know" and "no opinion" responses, that endorsed the most prominent (generally the first) policy alternative mentioned in the survey question. As will be seen, our method of using T2 level of opinion as the dependent variable and including first survey (T1) opinion as a predictor yields nearly identical estimates of media effects as does using a difference score—the magnitude and direction of opinion change—as the dependent variable.

For each of the 80 cases, we and our research assistants coded the daily television network news from one randomly selected network (in a few low-salience cases, *all* networks) each day, using the summaries found in the *Television News Index* and Abstracts of the Vanderbilt Television News Archive. These summaries, while rather brief and not intended for such purposes, were generally satisfactory in providing the fairly straightforward information we sought, especially since they were aggregated over several weeks or months. We coded all news stories that were at least minimally relevant to the wording of each opinion item, beginning two months before the T1 survey—in order to allow for lagged effects and for discrepancies or changes in media content—and continuing with every day up to T1 and through to the date of the T2 survey.

Being interested in the effects of particular actors or sources—particular providers of information, or Downsian "agents" of analysis and evaluation—whose rhetoric and actions are reported in the media, we distinguished among the original sources found in each news story. We used 10 exhaustive and mutually exclusive categories: the president; fellow partisans and members of his administration; members of the opposing party; interest groups and individuals not fitting clearly into any of the other categories; experts; network commentators or reporters themselves; friendly (or neutral) foreign nations or individuals; unfriendly foreign states or individuals; courts and judges; and objective conditions or events without clearly identifiable human actors (e.g., unemployment statistics, natural disasters, unattributed terrorist acts).

Our independent variables characterize *reported statements or actions by a specified source.* Each such *source story,* or "message," constitutes a unit of analysis in measuring aggregate media content over the time interval of a particular case. For each reported statement or action by a particular source—each source story—we coded the following: 1) its degree of *relevance* to the policy question (indirectly relevant, relevant, or highly relevant); 2) its *salience* in the broadcast (its inclusion in the first story or not, its proximity to the beginning of the broadcast, its duration in seconds); 3) the pro-con *direction* of intended impact of the reported statement or action in relation to the most prominent policy alternative mentioned in the opinion item; 4) the president's popularity (measured by the standard Gallup question) as an indication of his *credibility* as news source at the time of his statement or action; and 5) some judgments—not used in this paper—concerning the quality of the information conveyed, including its logic, factuality, and degree of truth or falsehood.

The most important part of the coding effort concerned the directional thrust of reported statements and actions in relation to each opinion question. Proceeding a little differently from the method of our earlier work on newspapers (Page and Shapiro 1983b, 1984), we measured directional thrust in terms of the intentions or advocated positions of the speakers or actors themselves. We took considerable care in training and supervising coders and in checking the reliability of their work. We prepared detailed written instructions and held frequent group discussions of coding rules and the treatment of problematic cases. All pro-con coding decisions, and those on other variables central to our analysis, were validated by a second coder and also by one of the present authors, who made the final coding decisions.[1] We masked the public opinion data so that coders would not be affected in any way by knowledge of whether or how policy preferences changed; we gave them only the exact wording of each opinion item and the time periods to be examined, not the responses to the questions.

As a result of these efforts we are confident that very high quality data were produced. It proved rather easy to code reported statements and actions on a five-point directional scale with categories "clearly pro," "probably pro," "uncertain or neutral," "probably con," and "clearly con" in relation to the main policy alternative outlined in each opinion question.

For each type of news source in each opinion case, we summed and averaged all the numerical values of pro-con codes (ranging from 12 to 22, with 0 for neutral) in order to compute measures of total and average directional thrust of the news from each source. The sums and averages of directional codes for television news content prior to T1 and between T1 and T2—for all messages coming from all sources combined and for messages coming separately from each distinct source—constitute our main independent variables. Most of our analysis is based on measures restricted to "relevant" or "highly relevant" source stories because we found that inclusion of less relevant source stories weakened the observed relationships.

Our principal mode of analysis was ordinary least squares regression analysis, in which we estimated the impact of each news source (or all sources taken together) along with opinion levels at T1, upon the level of public opinion at T2. We analyzed all cases together and also each of our two independently selected subsets of 40 cases, as well as subsets of cases involving different kinds of issues (e.g., foreign versus domestic policies), different time periods, and different levels of source credibility (popular versus unpopular presidents).

After testing hypotheses and exploring the aggregate data, we closely examined individual cases of public opinion change, scrutinizing media-reported statements and actions and the precise sequence of events. This served two purposes. First, it helped us with causal inference, shedding light on possibilities of spuriousness or reciprocal influence. Second, it enabled us to generate some new hypotheses about effects on opinion by certain sets of actors not clearly differentiated in our aggregate data.

Findings

. . . News commentary (from the anchorperson, reporters in the field, or special commentators) between the T1 and T2 surveys is estimated to have the most dramatic impact. A single "probably pro" commentary is associated with more than four percentage points of opinion change! This is a startling finding, one that we would hesitate to believe except that something similar has now appeared in three separate sets of cases we have analyzed. It was true of editorial columns in our earlier analysis of 56 two-point opinion series using the *New York Times* as our media source (Page and Shapiro 1983b), in the first 40 TV news cases we collected (Page, Shapiro, and Dempsey 1984), and in the 40 new TV cases, which we analyzed separately before doing all 80 cases together.

We are not convinced that commentators' remarks in and of themselves have such great potency, however. They may serve as indicators of elite or public consensus (Hallin 1984; McClosky and Zaller 1984; Noelle-Neumann 1973, 1980). Or the commentaries may—if in basic agreement with official network sentiment or the attitudes of reporters (perhaps providing cues for reporters . . .)—indicate slants or biases in media coverage that are transmitted to citizens in ways that supplement the statements of the commentators. These could include the selection of news sources and quotes, the choice of visual footage, the questions asked in interviews, camera angles, and so forth.

Certain other estimated effects on opinion are probably important even though some do not reach the .05 level of statistical significance according to a conservative two-tailed test. . . .

Most notably—and clearly significantly—a single "probably pro" story about experts or research studies is estimated to produce about three percentage points of opinion change, a very substantial amount. Presidents are estimated to have a more modest impact of about three-tenths of a percentage point per "probably pro" story, and stories about opposition party statements and actions may also have a positive effect.

There are indications, on the other hand, that interest groups and perhaps the courts (in recent years) actually have negative effects. That is, when their statements and actions push in one direction (e.g., when corporations demand subsidies or a federal court orders school integration through busing) public opinion tends to move in the opposite direction. We are not certain about the negative effect of courts, however, because of the instability of coefficients across data sets.

Certain kinds of news appear on the average to have no direct effect at all upon opinion, or less impact than might be expected. The president's fellow partisans, when acting independently of the president himself, do not appreciably affect opinion. Events may move public opinion indirectly, but they do not speak strongly for themselves. They presumably have their effects mainly through the interpretations and reactions of other news sources. The same applies to statements and actions from foreign countries or individuals, whether friends or foes. U.S. citizens apparently do not listen to foreigners directly but only through interpretations by U.S. opinion leaders.

The marked distinctions among types of news fits well with our idea that information from different sources has different degrees of credibility. It is quite plausible, for example, that the public tends to place considerable trust in the positions taken by network commentators and (ostensibly) nonpartisan experts. Some other sources may be considered irrelevant. Still others, like certain interest groups that presumably pursue narrowly selfish aims, may serve as negative reference points on public issues (see Schattschneider 1960, 52–53). Similarly, the federal courts may have served as negative referents in the 1970s and the early 1980s because of their unpopular actions on such issues as busing and capital punishment. In any case, it is clearly important to distinguish among sources of news. . . .

When presidents are popular, they tend (though the estimate falls short of statistical significance) to have a small positive effect on public opinion. Each "probably pro" statement or action is estimated to produce more than half a percentage point of opinion change. Part of the effect is undoubtedly temporary and part reciprocal. The impact presumably could not be multiplied indefinitely by talkative presidents because of potential saturation and overexposure of the reporters' and editors' desires for fresh topics to cover. Still, this constitutes some evidence that a popular president does indeed stand at a "bully pulpit." On an issue of great importance to him he can hammer away with repeated speeches and statements and can reasonably expect to achieve a 5 or 10 percentage point change in public opinion over the course of several months (see Page and Shapiro 1984).

Unpopular presidents, in contrast, apparently have no positive effect on opinion at all. They may try—like Glendower in *Henry IV*—to call spirits from the vasty deep, but none will come.

There are some indications that the effects of other news sources interact with presidential popularity. . . . [C]ommentaries may have their strongest effects when presidents are unpopular. Perhaps news commentators substitute for a respected leader, challenging the one that is out of favor. In addition, administration officials and the president's fellow partisans in Congress and elsewhere, when acting independently of a popular president, appear to have a slightly negative impact on opinion, whereas they may have positive effects when presidents are unpopular. The opposition party, rather strangely, seems especially potent when presidents are popular. In short, there may be some substantial differences in the dynamics of opinion change depending upon whether the president in office at a particular time is popular or not.

Discussion

Our examination of a number of specific cases of opinion change has bolstered our general confidence in the aggregate findings. . . .

News Commentary

The most dramatic finding . . . is the strong estimated impact of news commentary. Our examination of specific cases provides a number of instances in which the statements of news commentators and reporters clearly parallel opinion change. Examples include Howard K. Smith's praise for Nixon's policies and his criticism of calls for unilateral withdrawal from Vietnam in 1969; various newsmen's support for continued slow withdrawal from Vietnam during 1969–70; commentary favoring conservation and increased production rather than stopping military aid to Israel in order to get cheap oil during 1974–75; Smith's and others' support for more attention to the Arabs during 1974–75 and during 1977–78; Eric Severeid's, David Brinkley's, and Smith's advocacy of campaign contribution limits in 1973; Brinkley's and Smith's backing of stricter wage and price controls during 1972–73; John Chancellor's editorializing on the importance of fighting unemployment (versus inflation) in 1976; Smith's support for federal work projects in 1976; and commentaries in the spring of 1981 that Reagan's proposed tax cuts would benefit the wealthy.

. . . We would not claim that individual news commentators like Howard K. Smith—for all the esteem in which they are held—are, in themselves, the biggest sources of opinion change (but cf. Freeman, Weeks, and Wertheimer 1955). We do not believe that Walter Cronkite single-handedly ended the Vietnam War with his famous soul-searching broadcast in 1968.

Instead, the commentary we have examined may reflect the positions of many journalists or other elites who communicate through additional channels besides TV news or even a widespread elite consensus in the country (see McClosky and Zaller 1984). Or commentators' positions may be indicators of network biases, including subtle influences of reporters and editors upon the selection of news sources and upon the ways in which stories are filmed and reported. Or, again, commentators and other sources with whom they agree may (correctly or not) be perceived by the public as reflecting a climate of opinion or an emerging national consensus on an issue, which may weigh heavily with citizens as they form their own opinions (see Lippmann 1922; Noelle-Neumann 1973). With our present data, we cannot distinguish among these possibilities. But news commentators either constitute or stand for major influences on public opinion.

Experts

. . . [T]hose we have categorized as "experts" have quite a substantial impact on public opinion. Their credibility may be high because of their actual or portrayed experience and expertise and nonpartisan status. It is not unreasonable for members of the public to give great weight to experts' statements and positions, particularly when complex technical questions affect the merits of policy alternatives.

The existence of a reciprocal process, influence by public opinion upon experts, cannot be ruled out (particularly to the extent that the audience-seeking media decide who is an expert based on the popularity of his or her policy views), but it is probably limited in the short run because experts do not face immediate electoral pressures—that is, public attitudes may ulti-mately influence who are considered experts and what their basic values are, but once established, experts are less likely than presidents or other elected officials to bend quickly with the winds of opinion.

One striking example of the influence of expert opinion as reported in the media concerns the Senate vote on the SALT II arms limitation treaty. Public support for the treaty dropped 5.5% from February to March 1979 and 19% from June to November. During both periods many retired generals and arms experts spoke out or testified against the treaty, citing difficulties of verification and an allegedly unequal balance of forces favoring the Soviets.

Presidents

. . . [N]umerous cases support the inference that popular presidents' actions and statements reported in the media do affect public opinion. These include President Nixon's persistent opposition to accelerating U.S. troop withdrawals from Vietnam during 1969, 1970, and 1971; Reagan's 1981 argument for AWACS airplane sales to Saudi Arabia; Carter's 1977–78 increased attention to Arab countries; Carter's early 1980 movement (during a temporary peak in popularity) toward toughness in the Iranian hostage crisis; Reagan's 1982 bellicose posturing toward the Soviet Union; Ford's 1974–75 defense of military spending; Ford's 1976 and Carter's 1980 advocacies of cuts in domestic spending; and, perhaps, Nixon's 1972–73 support for wage and price controls.

On the other hand, as our regression results showed, unpopular presi-dents do not have much success at opinion leadership. In a number of cases unpopular presidents made serious efforts to advocate policies but failed to persuade the public. This was true of Ford's attempts to increase mili-tary spending in 1976 and his resistance to jobs programs and health and education spending in the same year. Jimmy Carter in early 1979, with his popularity at 43% approval and falling, failed to rally support for SALT II. Carter was also unsuccessful at gaining significant ground on gasoline rationing, the military draft, or the Equal Rights Amendment in 1979 and 1980. Even Ronald Reagan, when near a low point of popularity (44%) in mid-1982, failed to move opinion toward more approval of a school prayer amendment to the Constitution. Because this distinction between popular and unpopular presidents emerged clearly in our previous analysis of newspaper data (Page and Shapiro 1984), we are inclined to believe that it is real (though modest in magnitude) even though the popular president effect does not quite reach statistical significance. . . .

Interest Groups

Our regression analysis indicated that groups and individuals representing various special interests, taken together, tend to have a negative effect on public opinion. Our examination of the cases supports this point but also suggests that certain kinds of groups may have positive effects while others have negative impact.

We found many cases (more than 20) in which public opinion unequivocally moved *away* from positions advocated by groups and individuals representing special interests. In some cases the groups may have belatedly spoken up after public opinion had already started moving against their positions, producing a spurious negative relationship. But in many instances they seem actually to have antagonized the public and created a genuine adverse effect.

Such cases include Vietnam War protesters from 1969 to 1970, protesters against draft registration in 1980, and perhaps the nuclear freeze movement in 1982. U.S. citizens have a long history of opposition to demonstrators and protesters, even peaceful ones, and apparently tend not to accept them as credible or legitimate sources of opinion leadership. . . .

In general, the public apparently tends to be uninfluenced (or negatively influenced) by the positions of groups whose interests are perceived to be selfish or narrow, while it responds more favorably to groups and individuals thought to be concerned with broadly defined public interests. The best examples of the latter in our data are environmental groups and perhaps also general "public interest" groups like Common Cause.

From 1973 to 1974, for example, support for leasing federal land to oil companies declined as TV news reported conservationists challenging the positions of the profit-seeking and presumably less credible oil companies. During the same period, support for a freeze on gasoline, heating, and power prices increased a bit despite opposition by gas station owners and oil companies.

Not only business corporations, but also some mass membership groups representing blacks, women, the poor, Jews, and organized labor seem to have been held in disrepute and to have had null or negative effects on opinion about issues of direct concern to them, including social welfare policies and some Middle East issues. . . .

Conclusion

We believe we have identified the main influences on short-term and medium-term opinion change.

Our analysis does not offer a full account of certain glacial, long-term shifts in public opinion that reflect major social, technological, and demographic changes such as rising educational levels, cohort replacement, racial migration, or alterations in the family or the workplace. The decades-long transformations in public attitudes about civil liberties, civil rights, abortion, and other matters surely rest (at least in an ultimate causal sense) upon such social changes. . . . If news reports play a part in such major opinion shifts, they may do so mainly as transmitters of more fundamental forces.

Within the realm of short- and medium-term effects, however, we have had striking success at finding out what moves public opinion. Our TV news variables, together with opinion at the time of an initial survey, account for well over 90% of the variance in public opinion at the time of a second survey. The news variables alone account for nearly half the variance in opinion change. . . .

The processes of opinion change are not simple. In order to account for changes between two opinion surveys, for example, it is essential to examine media content before the first survey. *Discrepancies* between current news and prior news (or prior opinion) are important. Part of the media impact is temporary so that there is a tendency for opinion in the T1–T2 period to drift back, to move in a direction opposite to the thrust of the media content prior to T1.

Moreover, it is important to distinguish among news *sources* rather than aggregating all media content together. The effects of news from different sources vary widely.

Among the sources we examined, the estimated impact of news commentary is strongest of all, on a per-story basis, though such messages are aired less frequently than those from other sources. The causal status of this finding, however, is uncertain. Commentary may be an indicator of broader influences, such as media bias in the selection and presentation of other news, of consensus among the U.S. media or elites generally, or of a perceived public consensus.

Experts, those perceived as having experience and technical knowledge and nonpartisan credibility, also have very sizable effects. A policy alternative that experts testify is ineffective or unworkable tends to lose public favor; an alternative hailed as efficient or necessary tends to gain favor.

We found that messages communicated through the media from or about popular presidents tend to have positive effects on opinion. Presidents respond to public desires, but they can also lead public opinion (see Page and Shapiro 1984). Active presidential effort can be expected to yield a 5- or 10-percentage point change in opinion over the course of a few months.

News commentators, experts, and popular presidents have in common a high level of credibility, which we believe is crucial to their influence on the public. Rational citizens accept information and analysis only from those they trust. In contrast, news sources with low credibility, such as unpopular presidents or groups perceived to represent narrow interests, generally have no effect, or even a negative impact, on public opinion.

Some of these findings might be thought to be limited to the recent period we studied, in which the public has relied heavily on TV and is better educated and more attentive to politics than U.S. citizens in the past. Our confidence in the generality of the findings, however, is bolstered by their consistency with our previous analysis (using newspaper stories) of opinion change from 1935 onward (see Page and Shapiro 1983b, 1984). This similarity also reinforces the observation that the national news media in the U.S. are very much of a piece. They all tend to report the same kinds of messages concerning public policy, from the same sources. This can be attributed to the norms and incentives—and the organizational and market structure—of the news industry and especially to the pervasiveness of the wire services (see Epstein 1973; Gans 1980; Roshco 1975). In this respect the contents of one medium is a good indicator of the content of many media.

In terms of our concerns about democratic theory, it is interesting to observe that relatively neutral information providers like experts and news commentators apparently have more positive effects (at least direct effects) than do self-serving interest groups. It is also interesting that popular presidents, who presumably tend to embody the values and goals of the public, are more able than unpopular ones to influence opinions about policy. These findings suggest that objective information may play a significant part in opinion formation and change and that certain of the more blatant efforts to manipulate opinion are not successful.

On the other hand, unobtrusive indirect effects by special interests—through influences on experts and commentators, for example—may be more dangerous than would be a direct clash of interests in full public view. Clearly there is much more to be learned before we can be confident about the fundamental sources of influence on public opinion. The same is true of judging the quality of information received by the public.

In order to judge to what extent the public benefits from constructive political leadership and education and to what extent it suffers from deception and manipulation, we need to examine the truth or falsehood, the logic or illogic, of the statements and actions of those who succeed at gaining the public's trust (see Bennett 1983; Edelman 1964; Miliband 1969; Wise 1973; contrast Braestrup 1983; Robinson 1976; Rothman 1979). This applies to the sources whose messages are conveyed through the media and to the media themselves. There is much to learn about whether various sources lie or mislead or tell the truth; about how accurately or inaccurately the media report what the sources say and do; and about the causes of any systematic distortions or biases in the selection and reporting of policy-related news.

Notes

1. Numbers for those naming a network as their primary news source were as follows: Fox, 520; CBS, 258; CNN, 466; ABC, 315; NBC, 420; NPR/PBS, 91. All findings in this section were statistically significant at the $p < 0.05$ level, except where noted.

References

Bennett, W. Lance. 1983. *News: The Politics of Illusion*. New York: Longman.

Braestrup, Peter. 1983. *Big Story*. New Haven, Conn.: Yale University Press.

Chaffee, Steven H. 1975. *Political Communication: Enduring Issues for Research*. Beverly Hills: Sage.

Cook, Fay Lomax, Tom R. Tyler, Edward G. Goetz, Margaret T. Gordon, David Protess, Donna R. Leff, and Harvey L. Molotch. 1983. Media and Agenda Setting: Effects on the Public, Interest Group Leaders, Policy Makers, and Policy. *Public Opinion Quarterly* 47:16–35.

Davis, James A. 1975. Communism, Conformity, Cohorts, and Categories: American Tolerance in 1954 and 1972–73. *American Journal of Sociology* 81:491–513.

Downs, Anthony. 1957. *An Economic Theory of Democracy*. New York: Harper.

Edelman, Murray. 1964. *The Symbolic Uses of Politics*. Urbana: University of Illinois Press.

Epstein, Edward J. 1973. *News from Nowhere*. New York: Random House.

Erbring, Lutz, Edie N. Goldenberg, and Arthur H. Miller. 1980. Front Page News and Real World Cues: A New Look at Agenda-Setting by the Media. *American Journal of Political Science* 24:16–49.

Freeman, Howard E., H. Ashley Weeks, and Walter J. Wertheimer. 1955. News Commentator Effect: A Study in Knowledge and Opinion Change. *Public Opinion Quarterly* 19:209–15.

Funkhauser, G. Ray. 1973. The Issues of the Sixties: An Exploratory Study in the Dynamics of Public Opinion. *Public Opinion Quarterly* 37:63–75.

Gans, Herbert J. 1980. *Deciding What's News*. New York: Vintage.

Graber, Doris A. 1984. *Mass Media and American Politics*. 2d ed. Washington, D.C.: Congressional Quarterly.

Hallin, Daniel C. 1984. The Media, the War in Vietnam, and Political Support: A Critique of the Thesis of an Oppositional Media. *Journal of Politics* 46:2–24.

Hovland, Carl I., and Walter Weiss. 1951–52. The Influence of Source Credibility on Communication Effectiveness. *Public Opinion Quarterly* 16:635–50.

Iyengar, Shanto, Mark D. Peters, and Donald R. Kinder. 1982. Experimental Demonstrations of the "Not-So-Minimal" Consequences of Television News Programs. *American Political Science Review* 76:848–58.

Jaccard, James. 1981. Toward Theories of Persuasion and Belief Change. *Journal of Personality and Social Psychology* 40:260–69.

Katz, Elihu, and Paul F. Lazarsfeld. 1965. *Personal Influence: The Part Played by People in the Flow of Communications.* Glencoe, Ill.: Free Press.

Klapper, Joseph T. 1960. *The Effects of Mass Communication.* Glencoe, Ill.: Free Press.

Kraus, Sidney, and Dennis Davis. 1976. *The Effects of Mass Communication on Political Behavior.* University Park: Pennsylvania State University Press.

Lippmann, Walter. 1922. *Public Opinion.* New York: Macmillan.

McClosky, Herbert, and John Zaller. 1984. *The American Ethos: Public Attitudes toward Capitalism and Democracy.* Cambridge, Mass.: Harvard University Press.

McCombs, Maxwell E., and Donald L. Shaw. 1972. The Agenda-Setting Function of the Mass Media. *Public Opinion Quarterly* 36:176–87.

McGuire, William J. 1986. The Myth of Mass Media Effectiveness: Savagings and Salvagings. In *Public Communication and Behavior,* ed. George Comstock. New York: Academic Press.

MacKuen, Michael B. 1981. Social Communications and Mass Policy Agenda. In *More than News: Media Power in Public Affairs,* ed. Michael B. MacKuen and Steven L. Coombs. Beverly Hills: Sage.

MacKuen, Michael B. 1984. Exposure to Information, Belief Integration, and Individual Responsiveness to Agenda Change. *American Political Science Review* 78:372–91.

Miliband, Ralph. 1969. *The State in Capitalist Society.* London: Quartet.

Noelle-Neumann, Elisabeth. 1973. Return to the Concept of Powerful Mass Media. In *Studies in Broadcasting,* ed. H. Eguchi and K. Sata, 67–112. Tokyo: The Nippon Hoso Kyokai.

Noelle-Neumann, Elisabeth. 1980. Mass Media and Social Change in Developed Societies. In *Mass Communication Review Yearbook.* Vol. 1, ed. G. Cleveland Wilhoit and Harold de Bock. Beverly Hills: Sage.

Noelle-Neumann, Elisabeth. 1984. *The Spiral of Silence.* Chicago: University of Chicago Press.

Page, Benjamin I., and Robert Y. Shapiro. 1982. Changes in Americans' Policy Preferences, 1935–1979. *Public Opinion Quarterly* 46:24–42.

Page, Benjamin I., and Robert Y. Shapiro. 1983a. Effects of Public Opinion on Policy. *American Political Science Review* 77:175–90.

Page, Benjamin I., and Robert Y. Shapiro. 1983b. The Mass Media and Changes in Americans' Policy Preferences: A Preliminary Analysis. Paper presented at the annual meeting of the Midwest Political Science Association, Chicago.

Page, Benjamin I., and Robert Y. Shapiro. 1984. Presidents as Opinion Leaders: Some New Evidence. *Policy Studies Journal* 12:649–61.

Page, Benjamin I., Robert Y. Shapiro, and Glenn R. Dempsey. 1984. Television News and Changes in Americans' Policy Preferences. Paper presented at the annual meeting of the Midwest Political Science Association, Chicago.

Page, Benjamin I., Robert Y. Shapiro, and Glenn R. Dempsey. 1985a. The Mass Media Do Affect Policy Preferences. Paper presented at the annual meeting of the American Association for Public Opinion Research, McAfee, N.J.

Page, Benjamin I., Robert Y. Shapiro, and Glenn R. Dempsey. 1985b. What Moves Public Opinion. Paper presented at the annual meeting of the American Political Science Association, New Orleans.

Robinson, Michael J. 1976. Public Affairs Television and the Growth of Political Malaise: The Case of "The Selling of the Pentagon." *American Political Science Review* 70:409–32.

Roshco, Bernard. 1975. *Newsmaking.* Chicago: University of Chicago Press.

Rothman, Stanley. 1979. The Mass Media in Post-Industrial Society. In *The Third Century: America as a Post-Industrial Society,* ed. Seymour Martin Lipset, 346–88. Stanford: Hoover Institution.

Schattschneider, E. E. 1960. *The Semisovereign People.* New York: Holt.

Wagner, Joseph. 1983. Media Do Make a Difference: The Differential Impact of the Mass Media in the 1976 Presidential Race. *American Journal of Political Science* 27:407–30.

Wise, David. 1973. *The Politics of Lying.* New York: Vintage.

Zaller, John. 1985. *The Diffusion of Political Attitudes.* Princeton University. Photocopy.

8

DISDAINING THE MEDIA: THE AMERICAN PUBLIC'S CHANGING ATTITUDES TOWARD THE NEWS

Paul Gronke and Timothy Cook

Editor's Note

Politics becomes precarious when polls show that citizens are losing trust in the institutions that serve their political needs. Paul Gronke and Timothy Cook charted trends in Americans' confidence in the media from 1973 to 2004 and then analyzed the reasons for the sharp plunge in trust. Chapter 8 highlights their surprising findings; it omits the details of their painstaking research. While overall confidence in media as institutions has indeed dropped precipitously, this overall finding masks many variations in the nature of audiences and situations. Most important, audiences still retain confidence in their personally chosen news outlets. Americans therefore can continue to dodge the troubling question of what happens when people lose confidence in the press. The research also shows that contrary to widely held beliefs, confidence in media does not necessarily move in tandem with confidence in other major institutions in public life.

When this essay was written, Paul Gronke was a professor of political science at Reed College, and Timothy Cook was a professor of journalism at Louisiana State University. Gronke and Cook were collaborating on a study of public trust in institutions, which was designed to expand and deepen the research presented in Cook's seminal book *Governing with the News: The News Media as a Political Institution.* Timothy Cook's untimely death in 2006 ended the collaboration.

In the early 1970s, in the wake of Watergate and a presidential impeachment, one of the key players in that scandal—the news media—rode

Source: Excerpted from Paul Gronke and Timothy Cook, "Disdaining the Media: The American Public's Changing Attitudes toward the News," in *Political Communication,* 24:3 (July 2007): 259–281. Reprinted by permission of Taylor & Francis Group, http://www.informaworld.com.

high in public esteem. Harris and National Opinion Research Center surveys from that time period reveal that "the people running the press" were trusted and admired, not far below (if at all) those most trusted of American institutions, the military and the Supreme Court, and considerably higher than the more overtly political institutions: Congress and the presidency (Lipset & Schneider, 1987, Table 2-1; W. L. Bennett, 1998, Figure 1). Looking back on that decade, Lipset and Schneider (1987, p. 69) noted a trend "of increasing relative esteem" for the press. Not only were the news media favorably perceived, but also survey research in the 1970s and 1980s revealed that the aggregate level of public confidence in the news media varied in ways largely independent of public confidence in other institutions. To Lipset and Schneider (1987, p. 65), this meant that the press, along with organized religion, were "'guiding' institutions, outside the normal political and economic order, and to some extent 'critics' of that order." To the extent that there was any connection, confidence in the press rose when confidence in other branches, especially the executive, fell, in a "modest but noticeable see-saw relationship" (Lipset & Schneider, 1987, p. 55).[1]

Even after restrictions on press access during the United States' invasion of Grenada in 1983 seemed to occasion little overt outrage, public criticism of the news media remained fairly limited (Gergen, 1984; Schneider & Lewis, 1985; Whitney, 1985; Robinson & Kohut, 1988). Citizens were, to be sure, critical of the tendencies they perceived for the news media to be unfair, biased, and preoccupied with bad news. Nonetheless, the public was satisfied with the overall performance of the news outlets with which they were most familiar, rarely provided a majority in favor of government restrictions on the media (ones that reporters strongly opposed), and even viewed the news media as a whole more positively than other institutions. . . .

By contrast, by the late 1990s, in the wake of another presidential scandal and another presidential impeachment, the news media were no longer so favorably viewed. Indeed, of all the institutions examined in the yearly General Social Survey (GSS), public confidence in the press has suffered the steepest decline . . . (see . . . FitzSimon & McGill, 1995 [and Table 8-1]). The ratings of the news media, which were once seen as independent of views toward other political institutions, are now more strongly correlated with them (S. Bennett et al., 1999). According to surveys conducted by the Pew Research Center for the People and the Press (1998c, 1999b), the public is more inclined to say that "the news media gets in the way of society solving its problems," and that news organizations generally "don't care about the people they report on" and "try to cover up their mistakes." Overall, the news media are now seen as exercising too much influence, leading to a sharp erosion in the former reticence about governmental intervention to improve the news (Smith & Lichter, 1997, Exhibit 3–4).

Table 8-1   Confidence in the press (GSS pooled)

Variable	Demographics		Plus political		Plus institutional attachments		Plus general confidence	
	Coeff.	t	Coeff.	t	Coeff.	t	Coeff.	t
Education	**-0.007**	-2.180	**-0.007**	-2.182	**-0.007**	-2.049	**-0.008**	-2.234
Age	**-0.003**	-5.664	**-0.003**	-4.776	**-0.003**	-3.931	**-0.001**	-2.016
Income	**-0.023**	-6.123	**-0.020**	-5.441	**-0.022**	-5.739	**-0.017**	-4.371
Race (Black)	0.020	0.723	**-0.079**	-2.835	**-0.064**	-2.250	0.001	0.035
Gender (female)	-0.030	-1.673	**-0.043**	-2.368	-0.028	-1.551	-0.013	-0.718
Party identification			**-0.047**	-9.423	**-0.046**	-9.256	**-0.052**	-10.252
Political views			**-0.072**	-10.330	**-0.067**	-9.543	**-0.071**	-9.885
Shared partisanship			**-0.018**	-3.826	**-0.018**	-3.899	**-0.032**	-6.818
Strength of partisanship					0.010	1.022	**-0.037**	-3.774
Attend religious services					*-0.018*	-5.069	**-0.033**	-9.127
Job satisfaction					0.013	1.173	-0.025	-1.038
Improved financial state					**0.062**	2.586	**-0.033**	-2.883
Generalized confidence							*0.482*	43.217
Ancillary parameters								
Constant	1.126	16.695	1.091	16.146	1.061	15.110	1.323	18.433
Mu(1)	1.628	117.950	1.647	117.865	1.649	117.794	1.735	118.327
No. of cases	16,535		16,535		16,535		16,535	
-2*[LL(0)–LL(1)]	813		1,123		1,188		2,875	
% correctly predicted	56.10		56.67		56.58		58.60	
Pseudo R^2	.03		.04		.04		.10	

Note: Data were derived from the General Social Survey, 1973–1998. Entries are maximum likelihood ordinal probit estimates. Models were estimated in Stata 6 and Limdep 7.0. Boldface estimates are more than two times their standard error, boldface italic estimates are more than three times.

This sea change in the American public's attitudes toward the news media is a familiar story. Distinguished reporters themselves have recounted it many times. For instance, E. J. Dionne Jr.'s most recent diagnosis of the ills of American politics, *They only Look Dead* (1996), followed on James Fallows's *Breaking the News* (1996) and said flatly "Americans hate the press" and that "we are now in a middle of a new revolt against the journalistic order." Journalists, when they received awards in 1999 for their defense of the First Amendment, said much the same thing in their acceptance speeches. Marvin Kalb (1999, p. 9), for instance, ominously pointed out, "The American press is lucky that the First Amendment was passed more than 200 years ago; there is little reason to believe that it would be passed today, and there is increasing reason to believe that the American people have lost confidence in much of the press to do the right things." John Seigenthaler likewise noted in October 1999 that "public hostility toward the press today is 'more pronounced, more profound' than at any time in the past half-century" ("Public Distrust," 1999, p. 1). . . .

Indeed, the unpopularity of the news media is taken nowadays to be so obvious that it barely deserves discussion. . . .

But to What Effect?

Invariably, we must answer the "so what?" question. Seeing that confidence in the press has slumped, even (if not especially) among its former admirers, may not say very much about real-world implications.

Our results here show that the public's confidence in the news media has eroded considerably—and tellingly, across a variety of groups, including those that previously had been most positive toward them. The Pew Center for the People and the Press (1999a) found, as of February 1999, that the American public was more critical of "news organizations generally," increasingly tending to choose the more negative of a pair of opposite phrases, particularly as compared to the previous times that the public was asked the same questions in the mid-1980s. In short, citizens seem consistent; the results we obtain are not simply the by-product of their response to a particular question.

All of this raises doubts about the public *legitimacy* of news media power. Indeed, when asked directly, citizens tend to say that "the news media have too much influence over what happens in the world today," as in a Harris poll from late 1996 where 58% said "too much," 7% "too little," and 33% "just about the right amount" (Smith & Lichter, 1997, Exhibit 3–4). Relatedly, the same poll showed a narrow majority of respondents responding that the news media abuse freedom of the press (52% vs. 41% endorsing "use this freedom responsibly"), a larger majority indicating that "the news media tend to favor one side" (63% vs. 33% answering that "the news media deal fairly with all sides"), and 74% saying they see either a great deal or fair amount of political bias in news coverage (Smith & Lichter 1997, Exhibits 3–5, 3–7, and 5–7).

. . . [A]s opposed to the beginning of our time period, when the news media were more frequently seen to be performing a positive political social function as a watchdog over government, citizens nowadays have tended to see them as enmeshed with other national institutions. Sixty-three percent in the 1996 Harris poll responded that the "news media are . . . often influenced by powerful people and organizations," whereas only 30% answered that "the news media are pretty independent" (Smith & Lichter, 1997, Exhibit 3–7). Not that the public has entirely abandoned the watchdog function as a worthwhile goal—the 1996 Harris poll found that the two activities that the public was most inclined to find the media put too little emphasis on were "holding public officials accountable for what they do" (45% said too little) and "protecting the public from abuses of power" (43% said too little), and strong majorities endorsed each as "very important" activities for the media (Smith & Lichter, 1997, Exhibits 2–4 and 2–5). In effect, the critique of the news media as a whole seems to be not that they are overly adversarial, but that they are seen to be part of the same disdained and distant structure of political power.

Does this decline in the trust given to the news media, and to journalists, then suggest a crisis for the institutional media? After all, these findings would seem to undermine the conclusion that the news media, as a political and social institution, "are expected to preside over a societal and/or political sector" (Cook, 2005, p. 70) by both elites and the mass public. Yet the public's apparent lack of confidence in the news media as a whole may or may not undermine the institutional place of the news media very much.

We need to distinguish between confidence in the news media as a whole and support for particular news outlets. It may be that while citizens are skittish about trusting the news media, they still find their overall day-to-day performance to be acceptable. Just as citizens usually dislike Congress far more than their own representative in Congress or often disapprove of the health care system in the United States at the same time they approve of their own physician or see discrimination against women occurring frequently in the world at large but rarely in their immediate surroundings (Mutz & Flemming, 1999), they may disapprove of the news media as a whole or of journalists taken as a group yet still be satisfied with the news outlets to which they attend.

. . . The American public regularly expresses favorability levels exceeding 80% in local television news, their local newspaper, and network television news, except for one anomalous drop in favorability expressed toward network news from June 1994–June 1995, and again in December 1997 (the latter surely an impact of the blanket coverage given to the Lewinsky scandal). . . .

Like Congress, the work of journalists is increasingly visible to the public. Moreover, there is often negative news about the sloppy processes, ethical missteps, and mistakes of both members of Congress and journalists. In addition, there is often unrelenting criticism against both from the spin control of the White House. Citizens have ready sources of data about Congress and its members as a whole as well as about "the news media" and "journalists" as a whole. As with Congress, the public appears disinclined to give the news media any slack. A *Newsweek* poll conducted in July 1998, after a series of well-publicized journalistic mishaps and scandals, asked its respondents, "Do you see these recent cases of media inaccuracy as isolated incidents involving a few specific reporters and news organizations, or do they make you less likely to trust the news media's reporting in general?" Thirty percent chose the former, 62% the latter.[2] As perhaps should have been expected, the public is satisfied and positive about the performance of the individual news outlets they use, much more so than they are about the institutional news media or journalists. . . .

Conclusions

We now have the beginnings of a clearer understanding of the American public's attitudes toward the news media. What then have we learned? We would point to several conclusions:

There is strong evidence that the confidence expressed by the public toward the leaders of the press has shifted substantially, both on the average and with a near disappearance of the number of people who report "a great deal" and a huge upswing in the 1990s in the proportions who say "hardly any" confidence. Although the GSS data show a steeper decline, we find similar results over time for the Harris surveys for the same time period as well, giving further reinforcement to the notion that Americans' confidence in the news media did indeed shift to a much more negative assessment from the early 1970s to the late 1990s.

Although we must be tentative, confidence in the press is only partly connected with that accorded to other institutions. In particular, from 1973 to 1998, confidence in the press started out at a higher level than other institutions and ended up at a lower level. These different trajectories again suggest that the press be conceptualized differently than the bulk of other institutions. Moreover, the substantial effect that improved family finances, attending religious services, and shared partisanship have upon confidence in the press, opposite to the effect that these variables have on generalized confidence, suggests that there are different factors at work in each case.

It is true that confidence in the press is strongly predicted by a measure of generalized confidence in other institutions, suggesting that it is very much connected with other institutions as opposed to operating from outside the social and political order, as Lipset and Schneider (1987) suggested for the 1970s and 1980s. However, confidence in the press is not a mere extension of how citizens judge other institutions in general, as income, partisanship, ideology, shared partisanship, strength of partisanship, and religiosity all have substantial independent effects upon confidence in the press over and above the impact of generalized confidence. Put otherwise, lower income, moving from Democrat to Republican, moving from liberal to conservative, identifying with the party in power, and increasing strength of party identification all push toward lower ratings than what we would have predicted on the basis of generalized confidence alone. This reminds us of one of the central riddles that we have to note: Those who express confidence in most political and social institutions are not always those who do the same for the press, especially those with the greatest stake in the current political system.

Consequently, we can do more than simply note how confidence in the press has fallen over time and point out certain years when this occurred (and offer educated speculation about why that might occur). More to the point, confidence in the press has fallen in part because those groups that formerly constituted a core of support for the press (Democrats, liberals, partisans in opposition to the party in power) have shrunk considerably over the last three decades. However, we also point out that as of 1998, many of the essential distinctions between Americans in confidence toward the press had collapsed. In particular, the gaps between Democrats and Republicans and between liberals and conservatives all but disappeared in 1998. The former is not unprecedented and reflects the tendency for Republicans and Democrats seemingly to pay close attention to which party occupies the White House when it comes to having confidence in the press. However, the disappearance of the liberal-conservative distinction in 1998 is new, and it will bear watching to see if this is a one-time-only short-term result (presumably) of the Lewinsky affair or if this indicates a beginning of a new trend. In effect, however, this was a double whammy for journalism, as those segments of the population that were most inclined to be critical of the press both grew in proportion and increased in negativity at the same time.

Finally, although the press as a whole is judged increasingly negatively, such results do not tell the whole story. From the mid-1980s to the late 1990s, the confidence ratings for the press as a whole fell substantially according to the GSS data. However, approval ratings of news organizations (local television news, network television news, and hometown daily newspapers) were almost flat during this same period. Even if we were to conclude (and we do not) that the GSS result suggests that "Americans hate the media," we would note that these results are no indication of a crisis for the public's relationship with American journalism as a whole. Americans do not disdain the news, even while they are increasingly critical of the news media as a whole.

Much of this may reflect a split not only between their preference for the known quantity of the news over the distant and poorly understood institution known as "the press," but also between their approval of the information they receive and their disapproval of the practices and procedures that they see journalists pursuing.

. . . [A]t this juncture, we have a richly detailed—and mixed—picture of Americans' attitudes toward the news media. Such a depiction can and should give pause to both the champions and the detractors of American journalism (and American politics). We would note that the increasing willingness of Americans to report "hardly any" confidence in the leaders of "the press" is important, not merely in removing some degree of political legitimacy from the institutional practices of journalists but in also, we surmise, encouraging an erosion in the onetime support of the privileges journalists claim on behalf of freedom of the press. We are by no means convinced that this is a negative development.[3] Yet on the other hand, we clearly do not see a crisis that would impel disgusted readers and viewers away from the news outlets to which they attend, however haphazardly and sporadically, quite apart from the even greater satisfaction and support with the news media's performance that Pew Research Center (1998d) surveys have recently documented for Washington elites. The collective power of the news media may not then be very well respected or appreciated, but there seems to be little threat to the continuation of that power.

Notes

1. See also Becker, Cobbey, and Sobowale (1978) for similar results in the early 1970s.
2. *Newsweek* poll conducted by Princeton Survey Research Associates, July 9–10, 1998, Question R09, accessed from the POLL archive of the Roper Center for Public Opinion Research, University of Connecticut. See also the Media Studies Center poll discussed by McClain (1998) that noted that relatively few people had heard of the June scandals (the highest was 42% reporting hearing of the CNN/*Time* retraction of the nerve gas report), but large majorities had concluded that journalists often or sometimes invent stories, plagiarize, use unethical or illegal tactics, and make factual errors.
3. One of us (Cook, 1998, 2nd ed., 2005) has argued for a rethinking of standard notions of freedom of the press to encourage—as political doctrine and jurisprudence once did more heavily—the rights of the public to the information it requires to participate in politics alongside the rights of news organizations to disseminate what they see fit.

References

Barry, D. (1999, January 9–10). Leaning journalism. *International Herald Tribune*, p. 20.
Becker, L. B., Cobbey, R. E., & Sobowale, I. A. (1978). Public support for the press. *Journalism Quarterly, 55*, 421–430.

Benett, S. E., Rhine, S. L., Flickinger, R. L., & Bennett, L. (1999). "Video malaise" revisited: Public trust in the media and government. *Harvard International Journal of Press/Politics, 4*(4), 8–23.

Bennett, W. L. (1998). The uncivic culture: Communication, lifestyle, and the rise of lifestyle politics. *PS: Political Science and Politics, 31,* 741–762.

Bennett, W. L., Gressett, L. A., & Haltom, W. (1985). Repairing the news: A case study of the news paradigm. *Journal of Communication, 35*(2), 50–68.

Blendon, R. J., Benson, J. M., Morin, R., Altman, D. E., Brodie, M., Brossard, M., et al. (1997). Changing attitudes in America. In J. S. Nye Jr., P. D. Zelikow, & D. C. King (Eds), *Why people don't trust government* (pp. 205–215). Cambridge, MA: Harvard University Press.

Brehm, J., & Rahn, W. (1997). Individual level evidence for the causes and consequences of social capital. *American Journal of Political Science, 41,* 999–1023.

Cater, D. (1959). *The fourth branch of government.* Boston: Houghton Mifflin.

Cook, T. E. (1998). *Governing with the news* (2nd ed., 2005). Chicago: University of Chicago Press.

Cook, T. E., & Gronke, P. (2005). The skeptical American: Revisiting the meanings of trust in government and confidence in institutions. *Journal of Politics, 67*(3).

Cooper, J. (1999). The puzzle of distrust. In J. Cooper (Ed.), *Congress and the decline of public trust* (pp. 1–26). Boulder, CO: Westview Press.

Craig, S. C. (1993). *The malevolent leaders: Popular discontent in America.* Boulder, CO: Westview Press.

Dalton, R. (2000). Value change and democracy. In S. J. Pharr & R. D. Putnam (Eds.), *Disaffected democracies: What's troubling the trilateral countries?* (pp. 252–269). Princeton, NJ: Princeton University Press.

Dautrich, K., & Hartley, T. (1999). *How the news media hail American voters: Causes, consequences, and remedies.* New York: Columbia University Press.

Dennis, J. (1975). Trends in public support for the American party system. *British Journal of Political Science, 5,* 187–230.

Dionne, E. J., Jr. (1996). *They only look dead: Why progressives will dominate the next political era.* New York: Simon & Schuster.

Döring, H. (1992). Higher education and confidence in institutions: A secondary analysis of the "European Values Survey," 1981–83. *West European Politics, 15,* 126–146.

Erskine, H. (1970–1971). The polls: Opinion of the news media. *Public Opinion Quarterly, 34,* 630–643.

Fallows, J. (1996). *Breaking the news: How the media undermine American democracy.* New York: Pantheon.

FitzSimon, M., & McGill, L. T. (1995). The citizen as media critic. *Media Studies Journal, 9,* 91–101.

Freedom Forum and Newseum News. (1999). Public distrust threatens free press, former editor warns.

Gergen, D. R. (1984). The message to the media. *Public Opinion, 7*(2), 5–8.

Gronke, P., & Cook, T. E. (2001). *Dimensions of institutional trust: How distinct is confidence in the media?* Paper presented at the annual meeting of the Midwest Political Science Association, Chicago, IL.

Gronke, P., & Feaver, P. D. (1999). *The foundations of institutional trust: Reexamining public confidence in the U.S. military from a civil-military perspective.* Paper presented at the annual meeting of the American Political Science Association, Atlanta, GA.

Hayduk, L. A. (1987). *Structural equation modeling with LISREL.* Baltimore: Johns Hopkins University Press.

Hibbing, J., & Theiss-Morse, E. (1995). *Congress as public enemy.* New York: Cambridge University Press.

Kalb, M. (1999). *Freedom of the press? Too radical a proposition for the timid of today.* Speech presented at the Ford Hall Forum, Boston.

King, D. C. (1997). The polarization of American parties and mistrust of government. In S. Nye, Jr., P. D. Zelikow, & D. C. King (Eds.), *Why people don't trust government* (pp. 155–178). Cambridge, MA: Harvard University Press.

Lipset, S. M., & Schneider, W. (1987). *The confidence gap.* Baltimore: Johns Hopkins University Press.

McAllister, I. (1999). The economic performance of governments. In P. Norris (Ed.), *Critical citizens: Global support for democratic governance* (pp. 188–203). New York: Oxford University Press.

McClain, D. L. (1998, October 19). Scandals don't much harm an already bad reputation. *New York Times,* p. C4.

Mutz, D. C., & Flemming, G. N. (1999). How good people make bad collectives: A social-psychological perspective on public attitudes toward Congress. In J. Cooper (Ed.), *Congress and the decline of public trust* (pp. 79–99). Boulder, CO: Westview Press.

Newton, K. (1999). Social and political trust in established democracies. In P. Norris (Ed.), *Critical citizens: Global support for democratic governance* (pp. 169–187). New York: Oxford University Press.

Newton, K., & Norris, P. (2000). Confidence in public institutions: Faith culture, or preformance? In S. J. Pharr & R. D. Putnam (Eds.), *Disaffected democracies: What's troubling the trilateral countries?* (pp. 52–73). Princeton, NJ: Princeton University Press.

Norris, P. (Ed.). (1999a). *Critical citizens: Global support for democratic governance.* New York: Oxford University Press.

Norris, P. (1999b). Institutional explanations for political support. In P. Norris (Ed.), *Critical citizens: Global support for democractic governance* (pp. 217–235). New York: Oxford University Press.

Nye, J. S., Jr., Zelikow, P. D., & King, D. C. (Eds.) (1997). *Why people don't trust government.* Cambridge, MA: Harvard University Press.

Orren, G. (1997). Fall from grace: The public's loss of faith in government. In J. S. Nye, Jr., P. D. Zelikow, & D. C. King (Eds.), *Why people don't trust government* (pp. 77–107). Cambridge, MA: Harvard University Press.

Overby, C. L. (1999). Media: Too much Talk, not enough action. *Freedom Forum and Newseum News, 6,* 3.

Pew Research Center for the People and the Press. (1998a). *Internet news takes of: Event-driven news audiences.* Retrieved from http://www.people-press.org/med98rpt.htm with questionnaire results at http://www.people-press.org/med98que.htm

Pew Research Center for the People and the Press. (1998b). *Pew's poll numbers: Clinton moral authority slips: Phone calls, not polls, may sway Congress: 20 million go online for Starr report.* Retrieved from http://www.people-press.org/starrpt .htm with questionnaire results at http://www.people-press.org/starrque.htm

Pew Research Center for the People and the Press. (1998c). *Popular policies and unpopular press lift Clinton ratings: Scandal reporting faulted for bias and inaccuracy.* Retrieved from http://www.people-press.org/feb98rpt.htm with questionnaire results at http://www.people-press.org/feb98que.htm

Pew Research Center for the People and the Press. (1998d). *Washington leaders wary of public opinion: Public appetite for government misjudged.* Retrieved from http://www.people-press.org/leadrpt.htm with questionnaire results at http:// www.people-press.org/leadque.htm

Pew Research Center for the People and the Press. (1999a). *Public votes for continuity and change in 2000: Big doubts about news media's values.* Retrieved from http://www.people-press.org/feb99rpt.htm with questionnaire results at http:// www.people-press.org/feb99que.htm

Pew Research Center for the People and the Press. (1999b). *Striking the balance: Audience interests, business pressures and journalists' values.* Retrieved from http://www.people-press.org/press99rpt.htm with questionnaire results at http:// www.people-press.org/press99que.htm

Pharr, S. J., & Putnam, R. D. (Eds.). (2000). *Disaffected democracies: What's troubling the trilateral countries?* Princeton, NJ: Princeton University Press.

Robinson, M. J., & Kohut, A. (1988). Believability and the press. *Public Opinion Quarterly, 52,* 174–189.

Sanford, B. W. (1999). *Don't shoot the messenger: How our growing hatred of the media threatens free speech for all of us.* New York: Free Press.

Schneider, W., & Lewis, I. A. (1985). Views on the news. *Public Opinion, 8*(4), 6–11, 58–59.

Smith, T. J., III, & Lichter, S. R. (1997). *What the people want from the press.* Washington, DC: Center for Media and Public Affairs.

Sparrow, B. (1999). *Uncertain guardians: The news media as a political institution.* Baltimore: Johns Hopkins University Press.

Stimson, J. A. (1985). Regression in space and time: A statistical essay. *American Journal of Political Science, 29,* 914–947.

Tuchman, G. (1972). Objectivity as strategic ritual: An examination of newsmen's notions of objectivity. *American Journal of Sociology, 77,* 660–679.

Verba, S., Schlozman, K. L., & Brady, H. E. (1995). *Voice and equality: Civic voluntarism in American politics.* Cambridge, MA: Harvard University Press.

Weatherford, M. S. (1992). Measuring political legitimacy. *American Political Science Review, 86,* 149–166.

Weisberg, H. (1981). A multidimensional conceptualization of party identification. *Political Behavior, 2,* 33–60.

Whitney, D. C. (1985). The media and the people—Americans' experience with the news media: A fifty-year review. Unpublished manuscript, Gannett Center.

9

HOW SOFT NEWS BRINGS POLICY ISSUES TO THE INATTENTIVE PUBLIC

Matthew A. Baum

Editor's Note

Ordinary Americans, as well as pundits and scholars, have voiced alarm in recent decades about the sharp decline in the public's consumption of political news offered by traditional media. They blame the decline primarily on waning interest in politics, and they fear that many citizens are becoming dropouts who largely ignore politics. When that happens, government is forced to rely on unrepresentative samples of public opinions. That unduly enhances the influence of knowledgeable elites. Matthew A. Baum is among the growing group of public opinion scholars who assess the political content of popular soft news programs as possible substitute sources for citizen enlightenment about vital political issues. His pioneering research provides strong evidence that soft news does, indeed, inform citizens about current politics. It helps to level the political playing field by reducing the knowledge gap between hard news loyalists and defectors.

  Baum was an assistant professor in the Department of Political Science at the University of California, Los Angeles, when he wrote this essay. His research focused on American foreign policy, mass media, public opinion, and politics. The selection presented here became part of a book-length study published in 2003 by Princeton University Press under the title *Soft News Goes to War: Public Opinion and American Foreign Policy in the Media Age.*

  People who are not interested in politics often get their news from sources quite different from those of their politically engaged counterparts (Chaffee

---

Source: Matthew A. Baum, "Sex, Lies, and War: How Soft News Brings Foreign Policy to the Inattentive Public," in *American Political Science Review,* 96:1 (March 2002): 91–109. Copyright © 2002 by the American Political Science Association. Reprinted with the permission of Cambridge University Press.

and Kanihan 1997). While alternative news sources for the politically uninvolved have long been available, the last two decades have witnessed a dramatic expansion in the number and diversity of entertainment-oriented, quasi-news media outlets, sometimes referred to collectively as the soft news media.

Political scientists, including public opinion scholars, have mostly ignored the soft news media. And, indeed, most of the time these media eschew discussion of politics and public policy, in favor of more "down-market" topics, such as celebrity gossip, crime dramas, disasters, or other dramatic human-interest stories (Patterson 2000; Kalb 1998). Yet, as I shall demonstrate, on occasion, the soft news media *do* convey substantive information concerning a select few high-profile political issues, prominently among them foreign policy crises. This suggests the proliferation of soft news may have meaningful implications for politics, including foreign policy.

Scholars have long pondered the barriers to information and political participation confronting democratic citizens. The traditional scholarly consensus has held that the mass public is woefully ignorant about politics and foreign affairs (Delli Carpini and Keeter 1996; Converse 1964; Almond 1950), and hence, with rare exceptions, only relatively narrow segments of the public—the so-called "attentive public" or "issue publics"—pay attention to public policy or wield any meaningful influence on policymakers (Graebner 1983; Cohen 1973). By, in effect, broadening access to information about *some* political issues, soft news coverage of politics may challenge this perspective, at least in part. If a substantial portion of the public that would otherwise remain aloof from politics is able to learn about high-profile political issues, such as foreign crises, from the soft news media, this may expand the size of the attentive public, at least in times of crisis. And a great deal of research has shown that intense public scrutiny, when it arises, can influence policymakers, both in Congress and the White House (Baum 2000; Powlick 1995; Bosso 1989).

This possibility raises a number of questions. First, to what extent and in what circumstances do the entertainment-oriented, soft news media convey information about serious political issues? Second, what types of political topics appeal to such media outlets? Third, how might their coverage differ from that found in traditional news sources? Finally, who is likely to consume political news presented in this entertainment-oriented media environment, and why? These are the primary questions motivating the present study.

I argue that for many individuals who are not interested in politics or foreign policy, soft news increasingly serves as an alternative to the traditional news media as a source of information about a select few political issues, including foreign policy crises. This is because the soft news media are in the business of packaging human drama as entertainment. And, like celebrity murder trials and sex scandals—the usual fare of soft news outlets—some political issues, prominently among them foreign crises, are easily framed as compelling human dramas. As a result, the soft news media have increased many politically inattentive individuals' exposure to information about select high-profile political issues, primarily those involving scandal, violence, heroism, or other forms of human drama. Yet public opinion scholars have largely failed to consider how this might influence public views of politics.

This study focuses primarily on foreign policy crises. My argument, however, is general, and so not unique to foreign policy. Indeed, it also applies to a fairly narrow range of domestic political issues. Nonetheless, I focus on foreign crises for three reasons. First, *ceteris paribus,* foreign crises are more likely than most issues to transcend traditional partisan boundaries. Hence, public attention to foreign crises is relatively less likely to be affected by heightened public cynicism regarding partisan politics (Nye, Zelikow, and King 1997; Dionne 1991). Second, beyond celebrity murder trials and sex scandals, few issues are as likely to capture the public's imagination as the prospect of large-scale violence and the potential death of large numbers of Americans at the hands of a clearly identifiable villain. Combined, these two factors make foreign crises an appealing subject matter for the largely apolitical, entertainment-oriented soft news media. Third, Americans know and care less about foreign than domestic affairs (Graber 1984), especially in the post–Cold War era (Moisy 1997; Holsti 1996), and most foreign policy news is typically ignored entirely by the soft news media. Hence, while my argument extends beyond foreign policy, I nonetheless focus on foreign crises as, in effect, a "most difficult" test of the argument.

. . . I argue that by repackaging news about select political issues, including foreign crises, as entertainment, soft news dramatically reduces the cognitive costs of paying attention. As a result, even individuals who are not interested in politics may be willing to pay attention to such information.

Soft News Coverage of Foreign Crises

. . . [A]ny political relevance of soft news depends on the extent to which such programs actually cover political issues, such as foreign crises. And, indeed, *soft news programs have covered every major U.S. foreign military crisis since 1990.* I searched program transcripts, using Lexis-Nexis, and *TV Guide* listings for a variety of soft news programs to determine whether and to what extent they covered the Persian Gulf War, the ongoing series of post–Gulf War crises with Iraq, and four other high-profile U.S. foreign crises of the past decade—Somalia, Haiti, Bosnia, and Kosovo. Where such transcripts were inaccessible (e.g., *Oprah Winfrey*), I contacted several programs directly. For purposes of comparison, I also searched Lexis-Nexis for soft news coverage of several more traditional and less dramatic political issues. . . . Table 9–1 presents the results of these inquiries. These figures—which represent the number of *separate broadcasts* of each program that addressed a given issue—are extremely conservative, due to limited availability of transcripts, sporadic program listings, and unwillingness of some programs to provide the requested information, as well as recent start-dates or cancellation of several of the programs.

To determine whether these raw figures constitute "significant" coverage, I compared soft news coverage of four foreign crises in the 1990s with coverage of those crises on ABC's *World News Tonight*. The results indicated that, taken together, the number of separate broadcasts of the TV talk shows listed in Table 9–1 mentioning the U.S. interventions in Bosnia and Kosovo, combined, was equivalent to 73% of the total number of separate broadcasts of *World News Tonight* which mentioned those conflicts. The corresponding figure for Somalia and Haiti, combined, was over half (52%) as many broadcasts. Indeed, the number of separate broadcasts mentioning Bosnia presented on one tabloid news program, *Extra,* is equivalent to nearly half (46%) of the total number of *World News Tonight* broadcasts mentioning Bosnia. While soft news programs predictably offered significantly less coverage of these crises than the network news—for instance, network newscasts more frequently present multiple stories on a given topic within a single broadcast and tend to offer greater depth of coverage—these figures nonetheless appear far from trivial.

How Soft News Programs Cover Foreign Crises

While, like traditional news outlets, soft news programs do appear to cover foreign crises regularly, they do not necessarily do so in the same manner. Where traditional news outlets typically cover political stories in manners unappealing—either too complex or too arcane—to individuals who are not intrinsically interested in politics, the soft news media self-consciously frame issues in highly accessible terms—which I call "cheap framing"—emphasizing dramatic and sensational human-interest stories, intended primarily to appeal to an entertainment-seeking audience.

Neuman, Just, and Crigler (1992) identify five common frames readily recognized and understood by most individuals. These include "us vs. them," "human impact," "powerlessness," "economic," and "morality." To this list, Powlick and Katz (1998) add an "injustice" frame. Graber (1984) found that several of these frames—"human impact," "morality," and "injustice"— resonated strongly with her interview subjects.[1] Not surprisingly, these are the prevalent themes found in the soft news media. . . .

A review of the content of soft news coverage of several 1990s foreign crises [shows that in] each case, rather than focus on the more arcane aspects of these crises, such as military tactics or geopolitical ramifications, the soft news media tended to focus on highly accessible themes likely to appeal to viewers who were not necessarily watching to learn about military strategy or international diplomacy. For instance, during the Persian Gulf War, while CNN and the major networks filled the airwaves with graphic images of precision bombs and interviews with military experts, the daytime talk shows hosted by Oprah Winfrey, Geraldo Rivera, and Sally Jesse Raphael, as well as *A Current Affair,* focused on the personal hardships faced by spouses of soldiers serving in the Gulf and on the psychological trauma suffered by families of Americans being held prisoner in Iraq as "human shields."

Similarly, in mid-1995, in covering the escalating U.S. military involvement in Bosnia, a review of the nightly news broadcasts of the three major networks indicates that they addressed a broad range of issues—including international diplomacy, military tactics, the role of NATO, "nation building," and ethnic cleansing, to name only a few. In contrast, the soft news media devoted most of their coverage to a single dramatic story: the travails of U.S. fighter pilot Scott O'Grady, who was shot down over enemy territory on June 2, 1995. Captain O'Grady's heroic story of surviving behind enemy lines for 5 days on a diet of insects and grass, before being rescued by NATO forces, represented an ideal made-for-soft-news human drama. To determine the nature and extent of soft news coverage of Bosnia in June 1995, I reviewed Lexis-Nexis transcripts from 12 soft news programs for which the appropriate data were accessible.[2] I found that of 35 total broadcasts on these 12 shows addressing the conflict in Bosnia, 30 (or 86%) featured the O'Grady story. Of course, traditional news programs also covered the story. Yet, in the latter case, this was merely one of *many* storylines. The three major networks, combined, covered the O'Grady story in only 13 of 57 (or 23%) June 1995 national news broadcasts in which Bosnia was addressed. . . .

Incidental Attention

. . . [F]or many Americans, politics, including foreign policy, is of little interest.

Those who consider politics a waste of time are unlikely to pay attention to political information unless the time and effort required to do so (i.e., the expected costs) are extremely small, thereby removing any incentive to ignore it (Salomon 1984). One means of minimizing the costs associated with paying attention to low-benefit political information might be to attach or "piggyback" it to low-cost entertainment-oriented information. This would allow individuals to learn about politics passively (Neuman, Just, and Crigler 1992; Zukin with Snyder 1984), even if they are neither interested in the subject matter nor motivated to learn about it (Zukin with Snyder 1984; Robinson 1974; Wamsley and Pride 1972; Blumler and McQuail 1969; Fitzsimmons and Osburn 1968; Krugman 1965). Political information might thus become a free bonus, or *incidental by-product,* of paying attention to entertainment-oriented information.[3] In effect, piggybacking might, on occasion, render any

Table 9-1   Partial Listings of Soft News Coverage of 1990s U.S. Foreign Crises and Other Political Issues

Program		Number of separate broadcasts addressing issue										
	Gulf War	Somalia	Haiti	Bosnia	Iraq (1992–1999)	Kosovo	1996 primaries	1998 elections	Regulate tobacco	NAFTA	WTO	Lewinsky scandal
Network news magazines												
Dateline NBC	—	4	8	17	52	13	4	4	1	1	0	16
20/20	42	3	4	8	20	10	0	1	0	0	0	4
Primetime Live	36	8	4	11	16	—	3	0	0	1	0	3
48 Hours	2	3	4	3	8	1	2	2	0	0	0	2
60 Minutes	14	4	8	17	51	16	2	1	1	2	2	2
Average	23.5	4.4	5.6	11.2	29.4	29.0	2.2	1.6	0.40	0.80	0.40	5.4
Late-night TV talk shows												
Jay Leno	—	—	39	25	102	14	48	0	0	15	0	45
David Letterman	—	4	20	32	88	21	35	1	0	27	0	37
Conan O'Brien	—	3	22	14	53	4	23	0	0	25	0	30
Politically Incorrect	—	—	—	19	55	15	31	1	5	0	1	34
Average	—	3.5	27.0	22.5	74.5	13.5	34.3	0.50	1.3	16.8	0.25	36.5
Daytime TV talk shows												
Oprah Winfrey	3	6	8	8	4	—	—	—	—	—	—	—

Rosie O'Donnell	—	—	3	4	10	—	1	0	0	0	1
Regis and Kathie Lee	6	5	10	13	7	0	0	0	4	0	6
Geraldo Rivera	6	3	40	13	—	0	0	0	0	0	29
Phil Donahue	—	37	26	59	58	5	5	—	0	0	—
Average	*4.5*	*12.8*	*11.5*	*24*	*18.4*	*8.5*	*1.67*	*0.33*	*0.0*	*1.0*	*12.0*
Network TV soft news											
Extra	—	16	116	62	8	1	1	0	0	0	24
Entertainment Tonight	—	4	16	7	2	0	1	1	0	0	15
Inside Edition	—	4	11	24	3	2	1	0	1	1	28
A Current Affair	4	1	8	7	—	2	—	—	0	0	—
Average	*4.0*	*6.3*	*37.8*	*25*	*4.3*	*1.3*	*1.0*	*0.33*	*0.25*	*0.25*	*22.3*
Cable TV soft news											
E! Network	3	3	26	6	3	2	0	0	0	0	36
Black Entertainment Television	—	23	3	12	6	0	0	0	2	1	8
Comedy Central's *Daily Show*	—	—	3	21	16	—	1	1	3	0	11
MTV News	—	7	11	4	7	19	1	0	2	0	5
Average	*3.0*	*11.0*	*10.8*	*10.8*	*8.0*	*7.0*	*0.50*	*0.25*	*1.75*	*0.25*	*15.0*
Talk radio											
Howard Stern Show	—	—	18	47	32	13	2	1	0	0	28

Note: "—" indicates either that a given program was not on the air at the time of a given event or that transcripts were unavailable. In several cases, these data exclude "Operation Desert Fox," the December 16–19, 1998, bombing campaign against Iraq.

trade-off between being entertained and learning about politics moot by, in effect, transforming a select few of the major political issues of the day *into* the entertainment that people seek.[4]

This does not imply that transforming news into entertainment will affect all viewers similarly. Indeed, survey evidence . . . indicates that most people who consume traditional news do so primarily (albeit not exclusively) to learn about the issues of the day. This suggests that increasing the entertainment value of news is unlikely to affect significantly these individuals' attentiveness to political news. Indeed, such individuals have already determined that political news is worth their time and effort. Watching soft news programs is unlikely to affect this calculus, even if they occasionally cover political issues. Rather, only individuals who would not otherwise be exposed to politics are likely to be affected by encountering political coverage in the soft news media, or by piggybacking.

Yet, even for the latter, politically uninterested individuals, piggybacking is possible only if information about a political issue can be attached to entertainment-oriented information *without* increasing the costs of paying attention. And this requires framing the information in terms accessible to even politically disengaged individuals (i.e., cheap framing).[5] Paying attention to news that employs highly accessible frames requires less cognitive energy than paying attention to traditional news formats, which might provoke greater cognitive conflict (Krugman and Hartley 1970). Such information is cheap. Indeed, absent cheap framing, piggybacking would almost certainly fail. In fact, for many individuals, if information about a political issue can be piggybacked to low-cost and high benefit, entertainment-oriented information, the associated costs of paying attention are virtually eliminated.

This discussion suggests that by engaging in cheap framing and piggybacking, the soft news media may substantially reduce the expected costs of paying attention to those issues that lend themselves to these practices, such as political sex scandals, celebrity murder trials, and foreign policy crises. This, in turn, might induce individuals who do not normally seek information about politics or foreign affairs to attend to *some* information about such issues, even if their intrinsic interest, per se, remains low.

Summary and Hypotheses

Most of the time, the soft news media avoid politics entirely, in favor of more sensational issues, such as crime dramas, scandals, and celebrity gossip. Many entertainment-seeking television viewers may therefore remain largely uninformed about the day-to-day political issues facing the nation. When, however, an issue crosses over, via piggybacking, from network newscasts to the soft news media, a far broader audience will likely confront it. And unlike the relatively mundane or arcane presentation of political information offered by network newscasts, soft news programs employ cheap framing to appeal to entertainment-seeking audiences. Hence, for many individuals, the expected benefit of learning about politics, per se, is quite small. Yet the cognitive costs of paying attention to information about select political issues, including foreign crises, may, on occasion, be smaller still, due in no small measure to the efforts of soft news programmers to exploit such issues' previously untapped entertainment value and resulting suitability for piggybacking. A number of hypotheses follow from the theory. Four of these, which I test in the next section, are as follows.

> H1: People watch soft news programs to be entertained, not to learn about politics or foreign affairs.

> H2: *Ceteris paribus,* people who are uninterested in foreign affairs and consume soft news should be more attentive to foreign crises (and other similarly accessible issues) than their counterparts who are similarly uninterested in foreign affairs but do not consume soft news.

> H3: *Ceteris paribus,* soft news consumption should be *most* strongly positively related to foreign crisis attentiveness among the *least* politically engaged members of society and *least* strongly positively related to attentiveness among the *most* politically engaged members of the public.

> H4: *Ceteris paribus,* other *less* accessible or dramatic, or *more* partisan, political issues are less likely to be covered by the soft news media, and hence, attentiveness to such issues should *not* be significantly related to consumption of soft news.

[Editor's note: Information about the statistical tests has been sharply abbreviated.]

Why People Watch Soft News

. . . Might some individuals tune in to soft news programs with the explicit intent of learning about foreign crises or other political issues? Such individuals may reason that, when a crisis or other major issue arises, the soft news media will offer more interesting coverage than network newscasts or newspapers. If so, the incidental by-product model would be irrelevant. Hypothesis 1, however, predicts that soft news viewers watch such programs for their entertainment value, *not* to learn about politics. To test this hypothesis, I employ a 1996 survey (Pew Center Media Consumption poll, May 1996), which asked respondents the extent to which they prefer news about entertainment, famous people, crime, national politics, or international affairs (among other topics), as well as to what extent they consume a variety of soft news media.

I created an *entertainment news interest index,* based on the first three items mentioned above and a *soft news consumption index* based upon the latter series of questions. If information about foreign crises, or other political issues, is being piggybacked to entertainment programming, primarily as an incidental by-product, then we should observe a strong positive correlation between interest in entertainment-oriented news and consumption of soft news media, but *not* between interest in news about international affairs or national politics and soft news consumption. In fact, this is just what I find. The entertainment news interest index correlates with the soft news consumption index at an impressive 0.40. The corresponding correlations with interest in international affairs and interest in national politics are nearly zero. . . . This strongly suggests that to the extent that individuals are receiving information about foreign crises, or other national political issues, in the soft news media, they are doing so not by design but, rather, as an incidental by-product of seeking entertainment. Any information about foreign crises or national politics appears in these data to be piggybacked to entertainment-oriented news. This result clearly supports Hypothesis 1.

Soft News Consumption and Following Foreign Crises

For the next investigation, my data are drawn from the aforementioned 1996 Pew Center survey of public media consumption habits. In addition to asking respondents which types of television and radio programming, magazines, and newspapers they watch, listen to, and read, the survey also asked if respondents had followed . . . three foreign crisis–related issues: Bosnia, the Israel-Lebanon conflict, and a congressional debate on terrorism. . . .

. . . As one might anticipate, consumption of hard news is strongly positively associated with attentiveness to each foreign crisis ($p < 0.001$), as is political knowledge in the terrorism and Lebanon models. Interest in international affairs is also positively and significantly related to respondents' attentiveness to the three issues ($p < 0.001$). Most importantly for my purposes, however, exposure to the soft news media is positively and significantly associated with attentiveness to each crisis, thereby, in each instance, supporting Hypothesis 2.

To determine whether exposure to soft news exerts differing effects on respondents with varying levels of overall interest in international affairs, I interact the latter variable with the soft news index. The results strongly support Hypothesis 3. The interaction term is significant, or nearly so, and correctly signed, in all three models ($p < 0.01$, $p < 0.056$, and $p < 0.073$). Because logit coefficients are difficult to interpret, I translate the coefficients on the key variables into probabilities, with all controls held constant at their mean values. The results indicate that, for individuals who report following international affairs "very" or "fairly" closely, exposure to soft news matters little for attentiveness to any of the three foreign crisis issues. Yet individuals who follow international affairs less closely (representing over one-third of the respondents) *do* appear to learn about each issue through the soft news media. Consistent with Hypothesis 3, the relationships are strongest for respondents who claim to follow international affairs "not at all" closely. . . .

. . . [T]he soft news effect is substantial. As soft news consumption increases, the corresponding probabilities of following the Israel-Lebanon conflict, antiterrorism debate, and Bosnia intervention "fairly closely" increase by 19 (from 0.09 to 0.28), 34 (from 0.08 to 0.42), and 41 (from 0.10 to 0.51) percentage points, respectively. Each of these results clearly supports Hypothesis 3, suggesting that respondents who are uninterested in international affairs are nonetheless exposed to information about all three crisis issues through the soft news media.[6]

The question remains whether, as predicted by Hypothesis 4, the above interaction disappears if the respondents are asked about an issue covered intensely by the traditional news media but *not* by the soft news media. If the interaction persists, this would suggest that the above relationships may be artifacts of some omitted variable(s), such as, perhaps, greater overall media exposure by soft news consumers. One appropriate political issue for addressing this question is a presidential primary election. Primaries are highly partisan events and, hence, less appealing to a politically cynical populace. They ought therefore to be less amenable than foreign crises to cheap framing and piggybacking. . . . In fact, consistent with Hypothesis 4 . . . the soft news media appear in these relationships to contribute to attentiveness to foreign crises but *not* to the 1996 presidential primaries. . . .

Conclusion

Beginning in the 1980s, news broadcasters, facing unprecedented competitive pressures, came to recognize that real-life human drama could attract a large audience and could be produced at a far lower cost than fictional drama. According to Danny Schechter, a former producer for CNN and ABC's news magazine *20/20*, the Persian Gulf War drove home for news executives the huge ratings potential of military conflicts, which could be realized by transforming war reporting into a made-for-television soap opera:

> It started with the Gulf War—the packaging of news, the graphics, the music, the classification of stories. . . . Everybody benefited by saturation coverage. The more channels, the more a sedated public will respond to this. . . . If you can get an audience hooked, breathlessly awaiting every fresh disclosure with a recognizable cast of characters they can either love or hate, with a dramatic arc and a certain coming down to a deadline, you have a winner in terms of building audience. (Scott 1998)

Through cheap framing, the soft news media have successfully piggy-backed information about foreign crises (and other highly accessible issues, such as the Lewinsky scandal) to entertainment-oriented information. Soft news consumers thereby gain information about such issues as an incidental by-product of seeking entertainment. My statistical investigations demonstrated that individuals *do* learn about these types of issues—but *not* other, less accessible or dramatic issues—from the soft news media, without necessarily tuning in with the intention of doing so.

Substantial scholarly research has shown that public opinion can, at least sometimes, influence policy outcomes, including in foreign policy (Kernell 1997; Powlick 1995; Bartels 1991; Ostrom and Job 1986; Page and Shapiro 1983). And even *minimal* attention to politics through the mass media disproportionately increases partisan stability in voting (Zukin 1977). This suggests that soft news media coverage of foreign policy may have significant practical consequences for American politics. Indeed, while viewers of many of these programs are not among the most politically engaged Americans (Davis and Owen 1998), low-attention individuals do vote in significant numbers. . . . While determining the precise policy effects of this phenomenon is beyond the scope of this project, in a democratic political system, in which leaders are directly accountable to the public, it seems unlikely that heightened awareness of policy decision making by a previously disengaged segment of the population would be entirely without consequence.

Indeed, I have presented some evidence suggesting that the soft news media may not necessarily cover political issues in the same way that traditional news programs do. And research has shown that the *nature* of the political information people consume can influence the substance of the opinions they express (Iyengar and Kinder 1987). This, in turn, raises the possibility that, at least in some instances, and regarding some issues, the opinions of individuals whose primary source of political information is the soft news media might differ materially from those of their more politically attentive counterparts. . . .

My findings further suggest that some of the barriers to information and political participation confronting democratic citizens may be falling. Where America's foreign policy was once the domain of a fairly small "foreign policy elite," the soft news media appear to have, to some extent, "democratized" foreign policy. This represents both a challenge and an opportunity for America's political leaders. It is a challenge because leaders can no longer count on communicating effectively with the American people solely through traditional news outlets (Baum and Kernell 1999; Hess 1998). To reach those segments of the public who eagerly reach for their remotes any time traditional political news appears on the screen, leaders must reformulate their messages in terms that appeal to programs preferred by these politically uninterested individuals.

The rise of the soft news media also offers an opportunity, because, to the extent that they are able to adapt their messages accordingly, soft news outlets allow leaders to communicate with segments of the population that have traditionally tuned out politics and foreign affairs entirely. This may allow future leaders to expand their support coalitions beyond the traditionally attentive segments of the population. Broader support coalitions, in turn, may translate into more effective leadership, particularly in difficult times.

Finally, from the citizens' perspective, one might be tempted to take heart from the apparent leveling-off of attentiveness to foreign policy across differing groups of Americans. After all, a more broadly attentive public might yield more broad-based participation in the political process. Many democratic theorists would likely consider this a desirable outcome. Yet it is unclear whether more information necessarily makes better citizens, particularly if the quality or diversity of that information is suspect. Indeed, one might also be tempted to wonder about the implications of a citizenry learning about the world through the relatively narrow lens of the entertainment-oriented soft news media.

Notes

1. These findings complement a large literature in social psychology on individual media uses and gratification. This literature (e.g., Katz, Blumler, and Gurevitch 1973–1974; Katzman 1972; Katz and Foulkes 1962) argues that individuals use the media to fulfill various social and psychological needs, including diversion, easing social tension and conflict, establishing substitute personal relationships, reinforcing personal identity and values, gaining comfort through familiarity, learning about social problems, and surveillance. In fact, the frames most frequently employed by typical individuals are directly linked to several of the predominant uses of the media identified by psychologists.

2. The programs I reviewed included *Extra, Dateline, Jay Leno, David Letterman, Conan O'Brien, A Current Affair, Live with Regis and Kathy Lee, Entertainment Tonight, Howard Stern, E! News Daily, The E! Gossip Show,* and *The Geraldo Rivera Show.*

3. Passive learning is possible because individuals are more likely to accept information presented in a nonconflictual manner, which does not arouse excitement (Krugman and Hartley 1970). Individuals learn passively by first *choosing* to expose themselves to a particular type of information (e.g., political news), say by watching the network news, but then surrendering control of the *specific* information to which they are exposed (Zukin and Snyder 1984). For instance, individuals unwilling to *read* about a political issue in the newspaper may be willing to *watch* a news story about the issue, even if they are not particularly interested in the subject matter, simply because watching television requires less effort (Eveland and Scheufele 2000). Incidental learning is merely an extreme form of passive learning, whereby the individual actively seeks one variety of

information, say entertainment, and is unwittingly exposed to and accepts information of another sort entirely (e.g., political news).

4. This does not imply that the distinction between traditional and soft news has disappeared or that politically apathetic individuals have come to anticipate heightened benefits from consuming political news. . . . [However,] information attended to by a viewer due to its entertainment value may have the unintended effect of influencing that individual's attitudes toward other things, such as, say, a foreign policy crisis.

5. While there are many potential sources of accessibility, none approach the overwhelming predominance of the mass media in determining which issues command public attention, at least temporarily (Iyengar 1990; Krugman and Hartley 1970). Krugman and Hartley (1970) note that, as an ideal vehicle for passive learning, television has allowed many people to develop opinions on serious issues about which they would previously have replied "don't know" if queried (because they would have avoided learning about such issues).

6. The relationships are strongest for the antiterrorism debate (which is clearly linked by the public to international terrorism). This is most likely due, in large measure, to the national trauma produced by the World Trade Center and Oklahoma City bombings. Millions of Americans perceived themselves as holding a personal stake in the terrorism debate, and so it was a more immediate concern (and thus more accessible) than Bosnia or the Israel-Lebanon conflict.

References

Almond, Gabriel A. 1950. *The American People and Foreign Policy.* New York: Harcourt, Brace.

Bartels, Larry M. 1991. "Constituency Opinion and Congressional Policy Making: The Reagan Defense Buildup." *American Political Science Review* 85 (June): 457–74.

Baum, Matthew A. 2000. *Tabloid Wars: The Mass Media, Public Opinion and the Use of Force Abroad,* Ph.D. dissertation. San Diego: University of California.

Baum, Matthew A., and Sam Kernell. 1999. "Has Cable Ended the Golden Age of Presidential Television?" *American Political Science Review* 93 (March): 99–114.

Blumler, Jay G., and Denis McQuail. 1969. *Television in Politics: Its Uses and Influence.* Chicago: University of Chicago Press.

Bosso, Christopher J. 1989. "Setting the Agenda: Mass Media and the Discovery of Famine in Ethiopia." In *Manipulating Public Opinion: Essays on Public Opinion as a Dependent Variable,* eds. Michael Margolis and Gary A. Mauser. Pacific Grove, CA: Brooks/Cole. Pp. 153–74.

Chaffee, Steven H., and Stacey F. Kanihan. 1997. "Learning About Politics from the Mass Media." *Political Communication* 14 (October–December): 421–30.

Cohen, Bernard C. 1973. *The Public's Impact on Foreign Policy.* Boston: Little, Brown.

Converse, Philip E. 1964. "The Nature of Belief Systems in Mass Publics." In *Ideology and Discontent,* ed. David E. Apter. New York: Free Press. Pp. 206–61.

Davis, Richard, and Diana Owen. 1998. *New Media and American Politics*. New York and Oxford: Oxford University Press.

Delli Carpini, Michael X., and Scott Keeter. 1996. *What Americans Know About Politics and Why It Matters*. New Haven, CT: Yale University Press.

Dionne, E. J. 1991. *Why Americans Hate Politics*. New York: Simon & Schuster.

Eveland, William P., and Dietram A. Scheufele. 2000. "Connecting News Media Use with Gaps in Knowledge and Participation." *Political Communication* 17 (July–September): 215–37.

Fitzsimmons, Stephen J., and Hobart G. Osburn. 1968. "The Impact of Social Issues and Public Affairs Television Documentaries." *Public Opinion Quarterly* 32 (Autumn): 379–97.

Graber, Doris A. 1984. *Processing the News: How People Tame the Information Tide*. New York: Longman.

Graebner, Norman A. 1983. "Public Opinion and Foreign Policy: A Pragmatic View." In *Interaction: Foreign Policy and Public Policy*, eds. E. D. Piper and R. J. Turchik. Washington, DC: American Enterprise Institute. Pp. 11–34.

Hess, Stephen. 1998. "The Once to Future Worlds of Presidents Communicating." *Presidential Studies Quarterly* 28 (Fall): 748.

Holsti, Ole R. 1996. *Public Opinion and American Foreign Policy*. Ann Arbor: University of Michigan Press.

Iyengar, Shanto. 1990. "Shortcuts to Political Knowledge: The Role of Selective Attention and Accessibility." In *Information and Democratic Processes*, eds. John A. Ferejohn and James H. Kuklinski. Urbana and Chicago: University of Illinois Press. Pp. 160–85.

Iyengar, Shanto, and Donald R. Kinder. 1987. *News that Matters*. Chicago: University of Chicago Press.

Kalb, Marvin. 1998. "The Rise of the 'New News': A Case Study of Two Root Causes of the Modern Scandal Coverage." Discussion Paper D-34 (October). Cambridge, MA: Joan Shorenstein Center on the Press, Politics and Public Policy, Harvard University.

Katz, Elihu, and David Foulkes. 1962. "On the Use of the Mass Media as 'Escape': Clarification of a Concept." *Public Opinion Quarterly* 26 (Autumn): 377–88.

Katz, Elihu, Jay G. Blumler, and Michael Gurevitch. 1973–1974. "Uses and Gratifications Research." *Public Opinion Quarterly* 37 (Winter): 509–23.

Katzman, Natan. 1972. "Television Soap Operas: What's Been Going on Anyway?" *Public Opinion Quarterly* 36 (Summer): 200–12.

Kelly, Stanley, Jr., and Thad W. Mirer. 1974. "The Simple Act of Voting." *American Political Science Review* 68 (January): 572–91.

Kernell, Samuel. 1997. *Going Public: New Strategies of Presidential Leadership*, 3rd ed. Washington, DC: CQ Press.

Krugman, Herbert. 1965. "The Impact of Television Advertising: Learning Without Involvement." *Public Opinion Quarterly* 29 (Autumn): 349–56.

Krugman, Herbert E., and Eugene L. Hartley. 1970. "Passive Learning from Television." *Public Opinion Quarterly* 34 (Summer): 184–90.

Moisy, Claude. 1997. "Myths of the Global Information Village." *Foreign Policy* 107 (Summer): 78–87.

Neuman, W. Russell, Marion R. Just, and Ann R. Crigler. 1992. *Common Knowledge: News and the Construction of Political Meaning.* Chicago: University of Chicago Press.

Nye, Joseph S., Philip D. Zelikow, and David C. King, eds. 1997. *Why People Don't Trust Government.* Cambridge, MA: Harvard University Press.

Ostrom, Charles W., Jr., and Brian L. Job. 1986. "The President and the Political Use of Force." *American Political Science Review* 80 (June): 541–66.

Page, Benjamin I., and Robert Y. Shapiro. 1983. "Effects of Public Opinion on Policy." *American Political Science Review* 77 (March): 175–90.

Patterson, Thomas E. 2000. "Doing Well and Doing Good." Faculty Research Working Paper Series, RWP01–001 (December). Cambridge, MA: John F. Kennedy School of Government, Harvard University.

Powlick, Philip J. 1995. "The Sources of Public Opinion for American Foreign Policy Officials." *International Studies Quarterly* 39 (December): 427–52.

Powlick, Philip J., and Andrew Z. Katz. 1998. "Testing a Model of Public Opinion-Foreign Policy Linkage: Public Opinion in Two Carter Foreign Policy Decisions." Presented at the 1998 Meeting of the Midwest Political Science Association, Chicago.

Robinson, Michael. 1974. "The Impact of the Televised Watergate Hearings." *Journal of Communication* 24 (Spring): 17–30.

Salomon, Gavriel. 1984. "Television Is 'Easy' and Print Is 'Tough': The Differential Investment of Mental Effort in Learning as a Function of Perceptions and Attributions." *Journal of Educational Psychology* 76 (December): 647–58.

Scott, Janny. 1998. "The President Under Fire: The Media; A Media Race Enters Waters Still Uncharted." *The New York Times* 1 February, Late Edition-Final, Sect. 1: 1.

Wamsley, Gary, and Richard A. Pride. 1972. "Television Network News: Rethinking the Iceberg Problem." *Western Political Quarterly* 25 (Summer): 434–50.

Zukin, Cliff. 1977. "A Reconsideration of the Effects of Information on Partisan Stability." *Public Opinion Quarterly* 41 (Summer): 244–54.

Zukin, Cliff, and Robin Snyder. 1984. "Passive Learning: When the Media Environment Is the Message." *Public Opinion Quarterly* 48 (Autumn): 629–38.

10

NEWS COVERAGE EFFECTS ON PUBLIC OPINION ABOUT CRIME

Frank D. Gilliam Jr. and Shanto Iyengar

Editor's Note

Ample news stories about crime have made fear of criminals a pervasive and powerful force at all levels of political life. This fear motivates citizens to avoid neighborhoods where crime reputedly thrives and leads them to shun contacts with demographic groups deemed to be prone to criminal acts. Crime and justice system issues, including the appropriateness of penalties, are hotly debated staples in many election campaigns. Yet despite the prominence of such issues, the factual situations surrounding crimes are routinely ignored. Instead, policies and behaviors are governed by the stereotypical images of crime that pervade the community. To a large extent, these images are spread through the news media. What have the media wrought, and what are the consequences? Frank D. Gilliam Jr. and Shanto Iyengar provide answers based on cleverly designed experimental research.

Gilliam was a professor and the associate vice chancellor at the University of California, Los Angeles, and founder of its Center for Communications and Community when this research was published. He specialized in racial and ethnic politics, the mass media, and electoral behavior. Iyengar was the Chandler Professor of Communication and a professor of political science at Stanford University and the director of its Political Communication Laboratory. He had authored numerous pathbreaking books about the effects of television on American politics and was well known for pioneering experimental research.

Source: Excerpts from "Super-Predators or Victims of Societal Neglect? Framing Effects in Juvenile Crime Coverage" by Franklin D. Gilliam, Jr., and Shanto Iyengar from *Framing American Politics,* edited by Karen Callaghan and Frauke Schnell. © 2005. Reprinted by permission of the University of Pittsburgh Press.

Throughout the early and mid-1990s pundits warned of an impending youth-crime epidemic (DiIulio 1995). To many observers (e.g., Bennett, DiIulio, and Walters 1996), the increasing frequency of juvenile violent crime signified that America was now home to a new breed of so-called super-predators—amoral, radically impulsive, and brutally cold-blooded preadults who murder, assault, rape, burglarize, deal deadly drugs, engage in gang warfare, and generally wreak communal havoc (Bennett, DiIulio, and Walters 1996, 27; Berkman 1995). As proof, analysts noted that teenage homicides and violent-crime arrests doubled between the mid-1980s and the mid-1990s, the number of gun homicides tripled, and juvenile gang murders quadrupled (Bennett, DiLulio, and Walters 1996). Indeed, talk of violent, remorseless teen "super-predators" quickly became part of the public discourse. As criminologist James Fox observed, "Unless we act today, we're going to have a bloodbath when these kids grow up" (quoted in Garrett 1995).

. . . Public alarm over juvenile crime through the mid-1990s was heightened by extensive media coverage. Of course, young people (especially minority youth) who engage in criminal violence are especially newsworthy (see Males 1996; Dorfman et al. 1995); senseless acts of violence by "glassy-eyed, remorseless" teenagers in gang attire (Berry and Manning-Miller 1996) satisfy the media's programming needs. As general trends in American public opinion suggest, the growing reach of local news contributed to increased support for punitive remedies aimed at youth offenders (Dorfman et al. 1995; Gilliam 1998). For instance, the public called for more aggressive law enforcement, and in response policy makers across the country proposed and adopted more severe sanctions on adolescent crime, such as incarceration in adult facilities, trying juveniles as adults, the death penalty, and "three strikes" legislation (Alderman 1994; Jacobius 1996; Tang 1994; Walinsky 1995). Thus the rate of juvenile crime and the increased visibility of juvenile crime to the public through the news media—frequently featuring non-white teenagers engaged in the most violent of acts—were thought to have contributed to the high levels of public concern for crime.

In summary, the reality of violent crime in the mid-1990s was that an individual's age and ethnicity could realistically be considered "threatening" attributes. Our objective in this chapter is to examine the extent to which the public's attitudes toward crime reflect these cues. More specifically, we test the proposition that people become more fearful of crime and more committed advocates of punitive measures for dealing with violent crime when the news media frame the issue in ways that highlight the juvenile and non-white attributes of perpetrators.

The Research Design

We treat the two relevant characteristics of individual perpetrators (race and youth) as orthogonal factors in a fully crossed experimental design. A recently broadcast news story dealing with increased police patrols in the city of Long Beach provided the experimental stimulus. The story described armed police patrols of high-crime areas and the eventual arrest of two males. We manipulated the age of the suspects indirectly by depicting the police activity either as a general effort to reduce crime or, alternatively, as an attempt to curb gang-related crime. Thus, we altered the anchor's introductory lead-in so that the police operation was described as either a "crime sweep" (the words appeared on the television screen during the anchor's introduction) or a "gang sweep" (this label was substituted for "crime sweep" during the lead-in, and later the reporter referred to the suspects as "gang members"). With the exception of these two variations, the gang and non-gang versions of the news report were equivalent.

The race/ethnicity manipulation was more direct. Because the original report included police photographs of the two suspects, we were able to insert different "mug shots" corresponding to different ethnic groups. Depending on the experimental condition, the photos of the two suspects featured African Americans, whites, Hispanics, or Asians. Except for the substitution of the photographs, the news reports were identical in content and appearance.

Experimental participants watched a fifteen-minute videotaped local newscast (including commercials) described as having been selected at random from news programs broadcast during the past week. The objective of the study was said to be "selective perception" of news reports. Depending upon the condition to which they were assigned (at random), participants watched one of the following versions of the news story on the Long Beach police patrols.

1. The "crime-sweep" report that included the close-up photo of the two suspects
2. The "crime-sweep" report, but with all references to particular suspects eliminated
3. The "gang-sweep" report that included the close-up photo of the two suspects
4. The "gang-sweep" report, but devoid of any reference to individual suspects

Control participants watched the same newscast, but without any story on crime. In place of the crime report, they watched a story on a partial solar eclipse.

The design allows us to investigate a variety of questions. First, we can compare viewers' responses to news reports featuring non-white perpetrators (operationally defined as the conditions featuring African Americans and Hispanics) with their responses to coverage in which the suspects were white or Asian or to coverage in which there was no information about specific perpetrators. Second, we can estimate the effects of youth-related crime on public attitudes by comparing reactions to the "gang-sweep" and "crime-sweep" conditions. Third, we can isolate the interactive effects, if any, between the youth and ethnicity factors. Perhaps viewers feel especially threatened when the crime involves juvenile gangs and the gang members are non-white.

In addition to the additive and interactive effects of perpetrator ethnicity and age, we can also assess the relative influence of visual cues (photographs of faces) and semantic cues (the "crime-sweep" versus "gang-sweep" labels) in news coverage of crime. Simple comparison of the difference in viewer responses between the "gang-sweep" and "crime-sweep" conditions that excluded pictures of the suspects with the baseline condition in which there was no reference to crime at all provides an estimate of the effects of crime coverage that lacks visual information about individual perpetrators. A parallel comparison of the gang- and non-gang-related conditions in which photographs of the perpetrator appear reveals the degree to which "pictures speak louder than words."

The report on crime was inserted into the middle position of the newscast, following the first commercial break. Except for the news story on crime, the newscasts were identical. None of the other stories appearing in the newscast concerned crime or matters of race.

The experimental "sample" consisted of residents of West Los Angeles who were recruited through flyers and announcements in newsletters offering fifteen dollars for participation in "media research." The age of the participants ranged from eighteen to sixty-four. Fifty-one percent were white, 30 percent were black, 4 percent were Asian, and 7 percent were Latinos. Fifty-two percent were women. The participants were relatively well educated (40 percent had graduated from college) and, in keeping with the local area, more Democratic than Republican (47 versus 22 percent) in their partisan loyalty.

The experiment was administered during the fall of 1995 at a major shopping mall in West Los Angeles in a two-room suite that was furnished casually with couches, lounge chairs, potted plants, and so on. Participants could browse through magazines and newspapers, snack on cookies and coffee, or (in many cases) chat with fellow participants who were friends or colleagues.

On their arrival, participants were given their instructions and then completed a short pretest questionnaire concerning their social background, party identification and political ideology, level of interest in political affairs, and media habits. They then watched the videotape of the newscast. At the end of the videotape, participants completed a lengthy questionnaire that included questions about their evaluations of various news programs and prominent journalists; their opinions concerning various issues in the news; their recall of particular news stories; their beliefs about the attributes of particular racial/ethnic groups; and, of course, crime. After completing the questionnaire, subjects were debriefed in full (including a full explanation of the experimental procedures) and paid.

Testing the Super-Predator Hypothesis

Our primary interest lies in examining the effects of news coverage on public opinion toward crime. Two facets of opinion are especially relevant to the "super-predator" hypothesis—fear of violent crime and support for punitive criminal justice policies. . . .

. . . The underlying premise of the hypothesis is that minority offenders are especially threatening to the public. Therefore, we expect that people will become more fearful and punitive when they are exposed to news stories that feature "super-predators." Table 10–1 presents the results of parallel analysis-of-variance tests for the impact of the age (gang sweep versus crime sweep) and ethnicity (non-white versus white/Asian) manipulations on the indices of fear and punitiveness. The top half of the table reveals a robust main effect of the youth-crime manipulation on fear of crime ($p < .05$). As expected, exposure to news coverage of gang-related crime boosted fear by a factor of 10 percent (in relation to news coverage of ordinary crime). Despite their heightened fear, viewers were *not* more likely to mention punitive accounts of crime when they encountered the "gang-sweep" frame. To the contrary, the gang frame made participants significantly ($p < .02$) less punitive in their approach to crime. Thus, these results provide only partial confirmation of the super-predator hypothesis; people are especially threatened by youthful offenders, but youth crime does not prompt them to prescribe harsh treatment of offenders.

The effects of the race/ethnicity manipulation are presented in the second half of Table 10–1. Both measures show the expected pattern—higher levels of fear and punitiveness when the suspects were non-white—but both patterns are weak. If we subject the data to a more pointed test of the hypothesis by comparing the conditions with non-white suspects with those featuring whites or Asians, the results are more telling. The lower level of punitiveness when the suspect is either Asian or white is significant at the .05 level. In the case of fear, the difference is less dramatic ($p < .15$). As compared with their counterparts who encountered Asian or white suspects in news coverage of crime, participants who saw Hispanic or African American suspects were significantly more punitive and somewhat more fearful. These results thus validate the racial component of the super-predator hypothesis.

Table 10-1   Fear of Crime and Punitiveness by Types of Crime and Race of Suspect

	Type of crime coverage		
	Gang crime	No crime coverage	Ordinary crime
Fear of crime	.58 (132)	.45 (65)	.48 (155)
		F-value: 3.91, p < .05	
Punitiveness	.80 (132)	1.06 (65)	1.18 (155)
		F-value: 3.96, p < .02	

	Race of suspects		
	Asian/white	No crime coverage	Non-white
Fear of crime	.50 (99)	.45 (65)	.57 (95)
		F-value: 2.21, ns	
Punitiveness	.88 (99)	1.06 (65)	1.16 (95)
		F-value: 1.36, ns	

How is it that people are more fearful of crime but at the same time are less willing to favor punitive measures when presented with youthful offenders? Perhaps the study participants, following the model of criminal law, reasoned that preadults should not be held individually accountable for their actions. Moreover, gangs are collectivities, making it difficult to pinpoint responsibility. The distinctiveness of the gang label is also suggested by the finding that the significant differences in punitiveness elicited by the race/ethnicity manipulation were conditioned by the distinction between gang crime and ordinary crime. That is, we detected evidence of an interaction between reference to gang crime and the suspects' race. When the news is not framed in gang-related terms, non-white offenders elicit more punitive responses than white or Asian offenders. When the report refers to gangs, on the other hand, the ethnicity cue becomes less informative and participants make no distinction between the white/Asian and black/Hispanic suspects. In effect, the gang frame makes participants noticeably less punitive in their attitudes irrespective of the suspects' race.

Verbal versus Visual Cues

The analysis to this point has ignored qualitative differences in the depiction of crime. Specifically, the differences reported in Table 10–2 were calculated across the conditions that featured both verbal and visual cues (the "gang-sweep" or "crime-sweep" label followed by photos of the two suspects) and conditions that provided only the verbal cue. The effects of the "verbal only" and "verbal plus visual" conditions are presented in Table 10–2.

Table 10-2   Verbal versus Visual Framing of Crime

| | Type of crime coverage | | | | |
| | Gang crime | | No crime coverage | Ordinary crime | |
	Pictures	No pictures		No pictures	Pictures
Fear of crime	.58 (88)	.59 (44)	.45 (65)	.48 (155)	.50 (106)
			F-value: 2.25, p < .06		
Punitiveness	.77 (88)	.84 (44)	1.06 (65)	1.10 (49)	1.22 (106)
			F-value: 2.08, p < .08		

These results do little to support the maxim that pictures are more persuasive than words. In general, the addition of the photographs of the suspects did not strengthen the manipulation. In the case of gang-related crime, the presence of the visual cues, if anything, tended to reduce viewers' fear and punitiveness. On the other side of the manipulation (ordinary crime), the pattern was reversed; participants tended to be more fearful and punitive when the news story included photographs of the suspects. While none of these differences is statistically significant, the pattern suggests that the conceptual distinction between gang-related crime and garden-variety crime takes precedence over the presence or absence of visual cues concerning individual suspects. When viewers are forewarned that the crime in question is gang related, exposure to the pictures of two "gang members" serves to make them slightly less punitive. On the other hand, when viewers are not led to anticipate gang involvement in crime, exposure to the identical pictures elicits slightly higher levels of punitiveness. . . .

Fear of crime was equally affected by exposure to juvenile crime and non-white offenders. Among participants who watched the news report on gang-related crime, fear of crime increased by 9 percent; for participants who encountered Hispanic or African American suspects the increase was 8 percent. The interaction of the youth and race factors proved insignificant. That is, the effects of the suspects' race proved uniform in the gang-crime and ordinary-crime versions of the news report.

Turning to the control variables, women and blacks were especially fearful of crime. These individual differences are in keeping with the literature on victimization and fear of crime. In addition to race and gender, people who watch local news on a regular basis are more likely to fear crime, suggesting that the distinctive agenda of local newscasts has been passed on to the audience.

. . . [W]hites, Republicans, and conservatives were in the vanguard of the punitive approach to crime. People who tune in to local news regularly were not only more likely to fear crime; they were also significantly more punitive in their outlook.

In all, our results provide mixed support for the super-predator hypothesis. We found that exposure to news reports featuring juvenile and non-white offenders triggered more responses reflecting concern about crime (as compared with groups who were exposed to crime stories featuring other categories of perpetrators), but there was no outpouring of support for punitive criminal justice policies. Our subjects actually expressed less punitive attitudes when they were exposed to juvenile offenders, no matter what the perpetrators' ethnicity. Apparently, people believed, or at least hoped, that youthful offenders could be reformed with appropriate intervention.

. . . [W]eakness in design and measurement, combined with a significantly changed context, accounts for the incomplete rendering of the super-predator hypothesis. With this in mind, we conducted a second study designed to overcome the liabilities. . . . We paid special attention to securing a more typically episodic news treatment, limiting the analysis to white and black youth, revising dependent measures to reflect views specific to youth crime, and incorporating the role of the violent-crime victim into the youth-crime news narrative. . . . [W]e constructed [a] 3 × 3 design in which we manipulated the crime role and the presence of racial cues in crime news. Subjects were randomly assigned to one of nine conditions (i.e., white perpetrator, no perpetrator, black perpetrator × white victim, no victim, black victim). Depending upon the condition to which they were assigned, subjects watched a news story on crime that included a close-up photo of the suspect and/or victim. . . . [T]he photo depicted either a youthful African American or a white male. The report on crime was inserted into the middle position of the newscast, following the first commercial break. Except for the news story on crime, the newscasts were identical in all other respects. None of the remaining stories on the tape concerned crime or matters of race. . . .

. . . Initial analysis indicated that the critical influence on crime attitudes concerned the pairing of white victim with black perpetrator. There was no statistically significant difference as a function of other configurations of race of perpetrator, race of victim, and crime role. Thus, we conducted parallel analyses for the main effects of exposure to the white victim or black perpetrator (controlling for several common individual differences including education, income, age, gender, marital status, ideology, and party identification) on subjects' crime attitudes.

Table 10–3 presents the results of the second study. The top third of the table provides moderate support for our expectations. For example, exposure to the white-victim condition was associated with a significant increase in fear of random street violence and teen crime and violence. Similarly, exposure to the black-perpetrator condition increased fear of random street violence but did not have an appreciable impact on fear of adolescent crime or punitive crime solutions.

Table 10-3 Impact of TV News by Crime Role and Race of Subject

	Threat of teen crime	Punitive solutions	Fear of random street violence
All subjects (N = 300)			
White victim	2.36*	2.22**	1.90
Non-white victim	2.23	2.09	1.87
Black perpetrator	2.32*	2.15	1.89
Non-black perpetrator	2.25	2.12	1.88
White subjects (N = 132)			
White victim	2.43**	2.27*	1.96
Non-white victim	2.13	2.11	1.82
Black perpetrator	2.39*	2.29**	1.81
Non-black perpetrator	2.17	2.11	1.90
Black subjects (N = 85)			
White victim	2.41	2.26	1.79
Non-white victim	2.41	2.14	1.84
Black perpetrator	2.45	2.20	1.90
Non-black perpetrator	2.40	2.17	1.80

$*p < .10$ $**p < .05$

These results are produced, in large part, by the significant difference between white and African American study participants. Thus the second third of the table examines the impact of the dominant frame on whites' crime attitudes. The results of this analysis provide more solid support for the super-predator perspective in four of the six relevant comparisons. In other words, exposure to either a white victim or a black perpetrator was related to heightened fear of youth crime and support for punitive juvenile justice policies. On the other hand, there were no measurable effects on more general fear of crime attitudes. Finally, the last third of the table repeats the analysis for black subjects. The main finding is that the manipulations do not influence African Americans' crime attitudes (see also Gilliam and Iyengar 2000). Presumably this is a result of the fact that African Americans are more likely to have a deeper pool of experiences upon which to base judgments. In other words, they do not rely as heavily on the news media for information about their community.

Discussion

Our results describe a cascade of effects that reveal subtle variations in the applicability of the super-predator hypothesis. Contrary to expectations, our study participants were reluctant to punish juvenile criminals in the context of gang involvement, regardless of the race of the perpetrator. The gang manipulation in our study effectively reduced the proportion of viewers who offered consistently punitive attributions of responsibility. . . . Once the behavior of individuals is placed in the context of gang activity, the public's outlook seems to shift from the failings of individuals to the shortcomings of the broader society. Thematic frames thus lead to societal attributions of responsibility (Iyengar 1991).

. . . Nonetheless, there is still strong support for the super-predator hypothesis as the dominant youth-crime frame available to the American public. Our second study strengthened the mild findings in the first experiment. For example, among white study participants, exposure to the black perpetrator significantly increased the number of people fearful of teen crime and supportive of more punitive juvenile justice policies like placing youth in adult detention facilities. This is all the more interesting given that the black/white juvenile murder-arrest rate is at the lowest it has been in two decades (Snyder 2002).

The addition of the crime role—perpetrator or victim—as an element of the news frame yielded interesting insights. For example, exposure to white teen victims in and of itself raised fear levels and support for punitive crime policies among white participants. In other words, people gain no added leverage by knowing the identity or race of the alleged perpetrator. Simply knowing that the victim was white increased the proportion of harsh crime attitudes.

All told, our evidence suggests the following generalizations. First, both semantic and visual cues condition public attitudes on crime. The word *gang* appears to associate crime with violence and youthful perpetrators. Accordingly, people exposed to the cue become both more fearful of crime and less enthusiastic about punitive remedies. It is worth noting that the effects of the gang cue on support for punitive remedies were "color-blind"—study participants were more lenient with youthful offenders, no matter what their ethnicity. At the same time, our evidence also demonstrated considerable traces of race-based reasoning about crime. Exposure to non-white perpetrators or white victims was sufficient to move the audience in a more punitive direction. In this respect ordinary citizens seem more consistently race oriented than the judicial process. Criminal sentencing, as is well documented, is most extreme when the case involves both a white victim and a non-white perpetrator (Sidanius and Pratto 1999). The court of public opinion, however, is insensitive to perpetrator-victim permutations; the mere presence of a non-white perpetrator or white victim is sufficient to elicit an extreme "sentence."

References

Alderman, J. 1994. Leading the public: The media's focus on crime shaped sentiment. Public Perspective 5:26–27.

Bennett, W. Lance, J. J. DiIulio Jr., and J. P. Walters. 1996. Body count: Moral poverty . . . and how to win America's war against crime and drugs. New York: Simon and Schuster.

Berkman, H. 1995. A gunshot in Boston sends tremors nationwide. National Law Journal 18 (October 9, 1995).

Berry, V., and C. Manning-Miller. 1996. Mediated messages and African-American culture. Thousand Oaks, CA: Sage Publications.

DiIulio, J. J., Jr. 1995. The coming of the super-predators. Weekly Standard (November 27):23.

Dorfman, L., K. Woodruff, V. Chavez, and L. Wallack. 1995. Youth and violence on local television news. Unpublished report, Berkeley Media Studies Group.

Garrett, L. 1995. Murder by teens has soared. New York Newsday (February 17).

Gilliam, Frank, Jr. 1998. Reframing childcare: The impact of local television news. Washington, DC: Charles S. Benton Foundation.

Gilliam, Frank, Jr., and Shanto Iyengar. 2000. Prime suspects: The impact of local television news on attitudes about crime and race. American Journal of Political Science 44:560–73.

Iyengar, Shanto. 1991. Is anyone responsible? How television frames political issues. Chicago: University of Chicago Press.

Jacobius, A. 1996. Going gangbusters: Prosecutors fight gangs with injunctions banning conduct such as using beepers and applying graffiti. American Bar Association Journal 82:24–26.

Males, M. 1996. The scapegoat generation: America's war on adolescents. Monroe, ME: Common Courage Press.

Sidanius, Jim, and Felicia Pratto. 1999. Social dominance: An intergroup theory of social hierarchy and oppression. Cambridge: Cambridge University Press.

Snyder, H. 2002. Juvenile arrests 2000. Washington, DC: Office of Juvenile Justice and Delinquency Prevention.

Tang, B. 1994. INS/VGTF and the NYPD. Police Chief 61:33–36.

Walinsky, A. 1995. The crisis of public order. Atlantic (July):39–54.

11

WANTED, DEAD OR ALIVE: MEDIA FRAMES, FRAME ADOPTION, AND SUPPORT FOR THE WAR IN AFGHANISTAN

Jill A. Edy and Patrick C. Meirick

Editor's Note

When news stories present newsworthy events from a variety of perspectives, which perspective, if any, dominates public opinion? What are the consequences for peoples' views about these events as well as their preferences for particular policies and for public policy outcomes? Chapter 11 presents findings from one of the rare studies that answers these questions based on contemporaneous polls taken in the field immediately after a major crisis. The crisis, in this case, was the September 11, 2001, attack on the United States. The authors' findings reveal that the effects of media framing are far more complex when measurements are taken in natural environments than when they are taken in laboratories that create experimental studies. In real-life settings, audience members combine elements of news media frames in various ways and develop their policy preferences to match their own perspectives. The media frames are important ingredients in this process but compete with other influences that enhance or diminish their impact.

Jill A. Edy and Patrick C. Meirick were serving as associate professors in the Department of Communication at the University of Oklahoma when they wrote this essay. Both had already made major contributions to public opinion studies.

In the weeks that followed the September 11 attacks in the United States, Americans turned to the news media to help them understand what was happening and what it meant. From moment to moment, they got different

Source: Excerpted from Jill A. Edy and Patrick C. Meirick, "Wanted, Dead or Alive: Media Frames, Frame Adoption, and Support for the War in Afghanistan," in *Journal of Communication,* 57:1 (March 2007): 119–141. Reprinted by permission of John Wiley and Sons.

answers, for like most terrorist acts, the September 11 attacks were more than criminal but not exactly martial. Addressing the nation on September 20, President Bush said, "On September 11th, [the] enemies of freedom committed an act of war against our country" (Bush, 2001, para. 12). But he also justified his focus on the Taliban leadership of Afghanistan by saying, "By aiding and abetting murder, the Taliban regime is committing murder" (Bush, 2001, para. 20). The FBI, the Justice Department, and various law enforcement agencies investigated the incident and attempted to beef up domestic security. They also worked to determine the origin of envelopes laced with anthrax that were being mailed to various government and media offices. Meanwhile, the Departments of State and Defense and the U.S. military responded to the attack's international dimensions as they might to an act of war. On October 7, with widespread American public support, the U.S. military launched air strikes against Afghanistan.

Available theories of media/government relationships (e.g., Bennett, 1990) suggest that both the criminal and the militaristic aspects of September 11 were represented in the news media because each of these frames had important official sponsors. Second-level, or aspect, agenda setting would predict that whichever theme appears most frequently in the news media is also the most likely to be internalized by citizens. Yet, available research on framing offers few predictions about how audiences might have responded to such a media environment. To date, framing studies have considered either the construction of frames in naturally occurring media texts or the effects of experimenter-created frames on subjects. There is little nonexperimental work in the vein of what Scheufele (2000) calls frame setting, the process by which media frames affect audience frames—a process analogous in level, if not in mechanism, to that of agenda setting. Moreover, early studies of framing (e.g., Iyengar, 1987) explored the impacts of a single frame on audience opinion, whereas more recent studies (e.g., Druckman, 2004) have examined the impacts of carefully balanced opposing frames. September 11 coverage, in contrast, involved competing frames that were not necessarily oppositional. Thus, although the literature on framing effects has grown apace, it remains difficult to connect the theoretical findings to actual political discourse. In this paper, we attempt to bridge those gaps by examining how competing frames that are present in the media are adopted by audiences and how those frames, once adopted, influence public support for a policy. We first conduct a content analysis to document the extent to which the news media used a crime frame versus a war frame in their September 11 coverage in the weeks after the event. We then use survey data to explore how audiences adopted components of these competing frames. Finally, we examine the consequences of the frames adopted for public support of military action in Afghanistan. Our research design allows for the possibility that audiences adopt portions of media frames rather than adopting frames in their entirety, and thus that audiences combine framing elements in unexpected ways that impact their support for policies. The results offer a richer picture of how framing works in natural settings. . . .

Method

Content Analysis

In moving our study of framing from the laboratory to the real world, we lose the ability to reconstruct precisely what media content our audience has seen. Early agenda-setting studies resolved a similar challenge by documenting the content of local media in the areas where the studies were conducted. Our problem is somewhat more complex because our survey respondents lived all over Tennessee (a largely rural state in the southeastern United States). This makes elite print media like the *New York Times* or the *Washington Post* unlikely information sources for our audience. Indeed, our respondents probably shared almost no print media in common, for there are four larger cities in Tennessee (Memphis, Nashville, Knoxville, and Chattanooga) and many small municipalities, each with its own newspaper. Add to this the likelihood that people selectively exposed themselves to news sources, and the complexities of recreating citizens' media environment multiplies.

Rather than trying to reconstruct each survey respondent's specific media environment, we examined the one resource likely to be common to all of them: national broadcast network news.[1] Transcripts of nightly national news content from CBS, ABC, and NBC that mentioned the word "September" were coded from October 15 through November 2, 2001. By mid-October, the attacks in New York and Washington were consistently being referred to by the date they occurred, and we have several reasons to believe that this search term caught most of the relevant news. . . .

Content was coded at the level of the paragraph as fitting a war frame, a crime frame, a mixed crime and war frame, or as neither. Over 1,600 paragraphs appearing in 152 stories were coded. Intercoder reliability for the overall distribution of frames, based on double coding a systematic random sample of 10% of the stories, was .87 using Brennan and Prediger's kappa. . . .

Respondents

Our respondents were 328 Tennessee residents who were part of a split-ballot, random-digit-dial telephone survey of 614 Tennesseans conducted from October 22 until November 2, 2001. The poll's response rate was 34.57%. . . .

About 58% of respondents were women and 83% were White, with 9.4% identifying as African American and another 7.1% belonging to other racial groups. The mean age was 42 years and the median family income category was \$35,001–\$40,000. About a third had completed at least a 4-year college degree. Politically, the sample was a bit right of center, with 37% identifying themselves as Republicans and 29% as Democrats.

Survey Measures

. . . The survey measured how respondents framed September 11 on two basic dimensions of frames (Entman, 1993): problem definition and desired remedy. Each was measured as a dichotomous variable. To identify problem definition, respondents were asked if the people who died on September 11 were murder victims (crime) or war casualties (war). To identify their desired remedy, respondents were asked what they wanted to happen to the perpetrators of the September 11 attacks: to be killed on the battlefield (war) or to be tried in court (crime). . . .

Three questions were asked regarding support for military action in Afghanistan under certain circumstances. The first question simply asked for the respondents' attitudes about military action in Afghanistan. The second asked how they would feel about a ground invasion of Afghanistan, and the third asked for attitudes toward a ground invasion with civilian casualties. Responses were given on a 4-point scale from strongly oppose to strongly approve. The three items were averaged to form a scale ($a = .68$) that is our main measure of support for military action. We also use responses to the three items in a repeated-measures analysis; although levels of support for the war are extraordinarily high in the simplest formulation, support drops off sharply as potential negative outcomes are added to the questions.

Results

Content Analysis of Media Frames

National broadcast television news reports reveal that two distinct frames were applied to the events of September 11 during late October of 2001. As the war in Afghanistan got under way, with the first air strikes occurring on October 7, reporters interpreted its significance in terms of the attacks of September 11. At the same time, they reported the ongoing criminal investigations into both the September 11 attacks and the envelopes of anthrax spores that had subsequently been sent to congressional offices, television network news organizations, and others. Table 11–1 reveals that the war frame appears more frequently than the crime frame by a ratio of about two to one. All three networks used both frames. ABC was the most balanced (11.9% war and 10.2% crime), whereas CBS (18.05% and 8.42%) and NBC (17.13% and 10.28%) more closely approximated the overall average. Each network also included a substantial number of paragraphs that contained both war and crime elements—nearly 12% of the total. . . .

Table 11–1   Distribution of Frames by Network

Source	War Frame	Crime Frame	Mixed	Neither	Total
All networks	15.9 (257)	9.5 (153)	12.1 (195)	62.5 (1,007)	100 (1,612)
ABC	11.9 (57)	10.2 (49)	8.8 (42)	69.2 (332)	100 (480)
NBC	17.1 (80)	10.3 (48)	16.1 (75)	56.5 (264)	100 (467)
CBS	18.1 (120)	8.4 (56)	11.7 (78)	61.8 (411)	100 (665)

Note: Each cell shows percentage of paragraphs in transcripts within each media outlet containing each type of frame, followed by the raw number in parentheses.

Frame Adoption

. . . [A] chi-square goodness-of-fit test was run comparing the observed frequencies of frame adoption (pure war, pure crime, and mixed) in the sample to the frequencies of such pure and mixed frames in the media. The result was significant ($\chi^2 = 86.00$, $df = 2$, $p < .001$), which indicates that the public's frame adoption looked nothing like the pattern that would be expected based on the frequency of these frames on the network news. Pure war was the most frequent media frame but the least frequent audience frame, whereas pure crime was the most frequent audience frame, consistent with a resonance explanation.

. . . [We] had asked how common it would be for people to adopt mixed frames. The rather surprising answer: Almost half (49%) adopted frame components that represented a mix of crime and war frames. Table 11–2 shows the frequencies with which our respondents adopted problem definitions and preferred remedies of war and crime frames. Initially, we had thought that problem definitions would be fairly consistent with preferred remedies so that a scale of war-frame endorsement could be created. As it

Table 11–2   Typology of Frame Component Endorsement

Desired Remedy	Problem Definition		Total, % (N)
	Crime: 9/11 Dead Are Murder Victims, % (N)	War: 9/11 Dead Are War Casualties, % (N)	
Crime: Try perpetrators in court	Pure crime, 35.3 (103)	War crime, 16.1 (47)	51.4 (150)
War: Kill perpetrators in battle	Vengeance, 32.9 (96)	Pure war, 15.8 (46)	48.6 (142)
Total	68.2 (199)	31.8 (93)	100 (292)

Note: $\chi^2 = .038$, $p = .846$.

turned out, however, respondents' problem definitions were not at all related to their preferred remedies (χ^2 = .038, p = .846, r = .01).

This result suggested not a scale but rather a typology based on answers to our two framing questions. Some 35% of the respondents said they thought of the September 11 dead as murder victims and wanted to see the perpetrators tried (pure crime), whereas 16% said they thought of the September 11 dead as war casualties and wanted to see the perpetrators killed in battle (pure war). Of those subscribing to mixed frames, 33% said they saw the September 11 dead as murder victims and wanted to see the perpetrators killed in battle (vengeance) and 16% said they saw the September 11 dead as war casualties and wanted to see the perpetrators tried (war crime).

Framing Effects

. . . An analysis of variance (ANOVA) finds that there are significant differences in support for military action in Afghanistan among the four categories of this typology, $F(3, 287)$ = 10.89, p < .001. Those who employed a vengeance frame were the most supportive of the war in Afghanistan overall (M = 3.29, SD = .55), followed closely by those who embraced a pure war frame (M = 3.24, SD = .66). Those who applied a pure crime frame (M = 2.99, SD = .52) were less supportive of the war, and those adopting a war-crime frame (M = 2.76, SD = .68) were less supportive yet. . . . [A]ll means were significantly different at p < .05 except for the vengeance and pure war frames. . . .

Discussion

We had hypothesized that consistent adoption of a war frame would be associated with support for military action in Afghanistan, but we soon found that adopting one component (e.g., problem definition) of a war frame was independent of adopting another such component (e.g., desired remedy). Taken as a whole, our analysis suggests the complexity of the framing phenomenon. Respondents seem not to have simply adopted the frames presented in the media. Confronted with competing frames, they appear to have cobbled them together to build stories of their own. We thus find it difficult to talk about war frames and crime frames per se, but we can talk about the consequences of the different frame components and the ways in which they were assembled. . . .

. . . Druckman (2004) argues that presented with opposing frames, people express genuine opinions—that is, opinions that appear to be unaffected by their exposure to frames. In his study, respondents exposed to opposing frames revert to the opinions they expressed in the experimental pretest. Our data are not precisely comparable to his, but they suggest that something more complex may be going on. First, respondents' social location appears to affect which framing elements they adopt. Respondents who belong to groups that are more likely to be sent to fight a war, for example, are less likely to want to see the perpetrators of the September 11 attacks killed in battle. Second, both respondents' social location and the frames they adopt exert independent effects upon their support for the war in Afghanistan. In other words, the frames do not appear to "cancel each other out," leaving genuine opinion. Rather, the sense that respondents make of public issues seems to be influenced by their social location (which may make their preferences appear genuine), but their sense of the situation has a unique impact on support for the policy over and above that explained by social location. All of this suggests that experimental framing studies to date may not have captured the complexity of what it is people are actually doing when they process political information.

Our findings also expand our understanding of the relationship between frames and the moral valence assigned to public issues (e.g., Chong, 1996; Entman, 1993; Nelson, 2004; Nelson & Oxley, 1999). Experiments on framing effects have manipulated the moral valence assigned to public events, and Entman's work argues that the frame-construction process assigns a moral valence to public events. Other work has suggested the likelihood of adopting a media frame is influenced by subjects' existing beliefs and values (Domke et al., 1998; Price et al., 1997). Our findings reveal the possibility that something else may be going on: Respondents may use their own moral compasses to evaluate and combine frame elements instead of deriving moral valences from the frames. We had expected that a crime-consistent problem definition—perceiving those who died on September 11 as murder victims—would be associated with lesser support for military action in Afghanistan. Instead, those who saw the dead as murder victims were more supportive. This may reflect public moral outrage over the attacks. Outrage is frequently a factor in mobilizing people (Gamson, 1992), and condemnation of the enemy and its actions is often part of the public justification for military action. "Murder victim" is a concept more fraught with moral outrage than "war casualty," for it connotes that the dead cannot be blamed and that the attack was clearly intentional, unlawful and immoral. Defining those who died as war casualties, on the other hand, connotes that the attack took place in the context of a recognized bilateral conflict in which killing is not always morally wrong.

Indeed, each combination of problem definition and desired remedy suggests a different moral judgment about September 11. A "pure crime" perspective conceptualizes the events of September 11 as an attack on individuals by individuals, a moral judgment that suggests a need to redress private wrongs but that is also likely to find the expansion of punishment beyond those directly responsible morally unacceptable. In contrast, the "vengeance frame" makes the group responsible for attacks on individuals. Because the group is guilty, inflicting harm on group members who may have played no direct role in the attacks is morally acceptable. Indeed, there may be an "eye-for-an-eye" logic behind the relative willingness of those subscribing to this frame to inflict civilian casualties in Afghanistan. A "pure war" frame describes an attack on a group by a group, creating an "us-versus-them" evaluation that justifies military action on grounds of self-defense. However, the moral valence of such a posture is subtly different from that of pure crime or vengeance in that it invokes the idea of self-defense rather than seeking redress on behalf of others. A "war-crime frame" invokes its own unique moral judgment. Like the war frame, it defines its user as a member of a wronged group; however, it identifies not a general "enemy" but specific "criminals" responsible for the wrong.

This assessment of the moral valence of the frames finds some support in an examination of the point at which those in each category of the typology cease to support the war. Those who wanted to see the perpetrators of September 11 killed in battle (the adopters of the pure war and vengeance frames) are the most supportive of the war, and they remain supportive of the war even in the face of civilian casualties. In contrast, those who want to see the offenders tried by a court (those adopting the pure crime and war-crime frames) typically oppose the war in Afghanistan if it means civilian casualties. This connection between desired remedy and support for the policy makes sense. Those who wished to see the perpetrators tried could logically support the war, but shooting innocent bystanders (civilians) in the process of capturing the "bad guys" may have seemed like going too far. Those who saw this purely as war may have been more accepting because such outcomes are often perceived as regrettable but necessary in war, whereas those who saw this as vengeance may have been willing to exact retribution for the wrong done to innocent Americans.

Exploring respondents' understanding of September 11 in light of the multidimensional frames present in the news reveals that their support for the war in Afghanistan was much more complex than it first appears. On the surface, public support for the war in Afghanistan looks overwhelming. Moreover, such support was not "soft": Large majorities of Americans remained committed to the war in Afghanistan in the face of ground invasion, and even in the event of civilian casualties, support hovered around 50%. Yet, the diversity of frame adoption revealed in this study suggests that different Americans supported the war for different reasons. These findings are remarkably different from those of most experimental framing studies, which typically represent framing in public discourse as a struggle between divergent groups over how a public issue should be understood and suggest that framing effects are a zero-sum game. Evidence from this study reveals that framing also can be a coalition-building phenomenon. Frames can be distinct from yet harmonious with other frames, and people can support the same policy for different reasons. Beneath the overwhelming support were several distinct understandings of what September 11 meant and how the war in Afghanistan related to that meaning. . . .

Notes

1. We focused on network news for several reasons. First, it is unclear what content to select for coding on 24-hour cable news networks, whereas the nightly news on the networks makes for an obvious coding target. Second, although cable news saw a huge ratings increase after September 11, the combined audiences of the top three cable news networks (CNN, FOX News, and MSNBC) still averaged less than 2% of American adults at their September peak (Althaus, 2002). The Center for Media and Public Affairs (n.d.) continues to conduct studies of the network nightly news, excluding cable news because "[t]hough the cable news programs attract a lot of media attention, the highest-rated show on cable attracts one-tenth of the audience that Tom Brokaw, Peter Jennings, and Dan Rather do." Third, one study has found that FOX News and CNN framed the immediate aftermath of the September 11 attacks much the same way that the networks did and used criminal frames with almost identical frequency (Li, Lindsay, & Mogensen, 2002).

References

Althaus, S. (2002). American news consumption during times of national crisis. *PS: Political Science & Politics, 35*, 517–521.

American Association for Public Opinion Research. (2006). *Standard definitions: Final dispositions of case codes and outcome rates for surveys* (4th ed.). Lenexa, KS: Author.

Baumgartner, F. R., & Jones, B. (1993). *Agendas and instabilities in American politics.* Chicago: University of Chicago Press.

Bennett, W. L. (1990). Toward a theory of press-state relations. *Journal of Communication, 40*, 103–125.

Bush, G. W. (2001, September 20). Address to a joint session of Congress and the American people. Retrieved August 25, 2005, from http://www.whitehouse.gov/news/releases/2001/09/20010920-8.html

Center for Media and Public Affairs. (n.d.). Network news studies. Retrieved May 24, 2006, from http://www.cmpa.com/networkNewsStudies/index.htm

Chong, D. (1996). Creating common frames of reference on political issues. In D. C. Mutz, P. M. Sniderman, & R. A. Brody (Eds.), *Political persuasion and attitude change* (pp. 195–224). Ann Arbor, MI: University of Michigan Press.

Domke, D., Shah, D. V., & Wackman, D. B. (1998). Media priming effects: Accessibility, association, and activation. *International Journal of Public Opinion Research, 10*, 51–74.

Druckman, J. N. (2004). Political preference formation: Competition, deliberation, and the (ir)relevance of framing effects. *American Political Science Review,* 98, 671–686.

Entman, R. M. (1991). Framing coverage of international news: Contrasts in narratives of the KAL and Iran Air incidents. *Journal of Communication,* 41(4), 6–27.

Entman, R. M. (1993). Framing: Toward clarification of a fractured paradigm. *Journal of Communication,* 43, 51–58.

Entman, R. M. (2003). Cascading activation: Contesting the White House's frame after 9/11. *Political Communication,* 20, 415–432.

Gamson, W. A. (1992). *Talking politics.* Cambridge, U.K.: Cambridge University Press.

Gamson, W. A., & Modigliani, A. (1989). Media discourse and public opinion on nuclear power: A constructionist approach. *American Journal of Sociology,* 95, 1–37.

Goffman, E. (1974). *Frame analysis.* Philadelphia: University of Pennsylvania Press.

Graber, D. A. (1990). Seeing is remembering: How visuals contribute to learning from television news. *Journal of Communication,* 40(3), 134–155.

Hall, S. (1982). The rediscovery of ideology: The return of the repressed in media studies. In M. Gurevitch, T. Bennett, J. Curran, & J. Woollacott (Eds.), *Culture, society and the media* (pp. 56–90). London: Methuen.

Iyengar, S. (1987). Television news and citizens' explanations of national affairs. *American Political Science Review,* 81, 815–831.

Iyengar, S. (1991). *Is anyone responsible? How television frames political issues.* Chicago: University of Chicago Press.

Iyengar, S., & Kinder, D. (1987). *News that matters: Television and American opinion.* Chicago: University of Chicago Press.

Kahneman, D., & Tversky, A. (1984). Choice, values and frames. *American Psychologist,* 39, 341–350.

Keeter, S., Miller, C., Kohut, A., Groves, R. M., & Presser, S. (2000). Consequences of reducing nonresponse in a national telephone survey. *Public Opinion Quarterly,* 64, 125–148.

Li, X., Lindsay, L. F., & Mogensen, K. (2002, August). Media in a crisis situation involving national interest: A content analysis of the TV networks coverage of the 9/11 incident during the first eight hours. Paper presented at the 2002 convention of the Association for Education in Journalism and Mass Communication, Miami, FL.

McCombs, M. (1997). New frontiers in agenda-setting: Agendas of attributes and frames. *Mass Comm Review,* 24(1,2), 32–52.

McCombs, M., Llamas, J. P., Lopez-Escobar, E., & Rey, F. (1997). Candidate images in Spanish elections: Second-level agenda-setting effects. *Journalism & Mass Communication Quarterly,* 74, 703–717.

Morley, D. (1980). *The "Nationwide" audience: Structure and decoding.* London: British Film Institute.

NBC Nightly News. (2001, October 31). [Television broadcast]. New York: National Broadcasting Company.

Nelson, T. E. (2004). Policy goals, public rhetoric, and political attitudes. *Journal of Politics, 66,* 581–605.

Nelson, T. E., & Oxley, Z. M. (1999). Issue framing effects on belief importance and opinion. *Journal of Politics,* 61, 1040–1068.

Price, V., & Tewksbury, D. (1997). News values and public opinion: A theoretical account of media priming and framing. In G. Barnett & F. J. Boster (Eds.), *Progress in the communication sciences* (pp. 173–212). Greenwich, CT: Ablex.

Price, V., Tewksbury, D., & Powers, E. (1997). Switching trains of thought: The impact of news frames on readers' cognitive responses. *Communication Research,* 24, 481–506.

Scheufele, D. A. (2000). Agenda-setting, priming, and framing revisited: Another look at cognitive effects of political communication. *Mass Communication and Society,* 3, 297–316.

Shah, D. V., Watts, M. D., Domke, D., & Fan, D. P. (2002). News framing and cueing of issue regimes: Explaining Clinton's public approval in spite of scandal. *Public Opinion Quarterly,* 66, 339–370.

Sniderman, P. M., & Theriault, S. M. (2004). The structure of political argument and the logic of issue framing. In W. E. Saris & P. M. Sniderman (Eds.), *Studies in public opinion: Attitudes, nonattitudes, measurement error, and change* (pp. 133–165). Princeton, NJ: Princeton University Press.

Stone, D. A. (1989). Causal stories and the formation of policy agendas. *Political Science Quarterly,* 104, 281–300.

Tversky, A., & Kahneman, D. (1981). The framing of decisions and the psychology of choice. *Science,* 211, 453–458.

White, H. (1987). *The content of the form: Narrative discourse and historical representation.* Baltimore, MD: The Johns Hopkins University Press.

Valentino, N. A. (1999). Crime news and the priming of racial attitudes during evaluations of the president. *Public Opinion Quarterly,* 63, 293–320.

Zaller, J. (1992). *The nature and origins of mass opinion.* New York: Cambridge University Press.

12

AUDIENCE FRAGMENTATION AND POLITICAL INEQUALITY IN THE POST-BROADCAST MEDIA ENVIRONMENT

Markus Prior

Editor's Note

Markus Prior argues that the proliferation of news sources is segmenting the nation into news buffs and entertainment buffs. The news buffs, who feast on the rich flow of news, shape the opinion currents that drive politics. The entertainment buffs are choosing to isolate themselves from politics, indulging in light amusement instead. The inequalities in political interest and participation that distinguish news buffs from entertainment buffs impair the quality of American democracy. A government based on impoverished opinion sources becomes less representative and less effective because the pool of informed citizens is smaller, turnout at elections is reduced, and political polarization is enhanced.

Markus Prior expressed the views quoted in Chapter 12 in Post-broadcast Democracy, a book based on his doctoral dissertation. The book was published when he was an assistant professor of politics and public affairs at the Woodrow Wilson School of Public Affairs at Princeton University. The dissertation won the American Political Science Association's 2005 E.E. Schattschneider Award for the year's best dissertation about American government.

... Media Environments and Political Behavior

Before television, news was more difficult. Understanding the news required a relatively high level of ability, so learning about politics was more strongly determined by formal education and cognitive skills. Broadcast

Source: Excerpted from Markus Prior, *Post-Broadcast Democracy: How Media Choice Increases Inequality in Political Involvement and Polarizes Elections,* New York: Cambridge University Press, 2007, Chapter 8. Copyright (c) 2007 by Markus Prior. Reprinted with the permission of Cambridge University Press.

television provided less educated citizens with more basic information, which increased their political knowledge and their likelihood of going to the polls (at least relative to the more educated). Starting in the 1970s, cable television slowly offered television viewers more programming choices. Some viewers—the entertainment fans—began to abandon the nightly newscasts in favor of more entertaining programs. In the low-choice environment, they encountered politics at least occasionally because they liked watching television—even television news—more than most other leisure activities. Neuman (1996, 19) characterized this pattern as "politics by default." Cable television and the Internet have transformed "politics by default" into politics by choice. By their own choice, entertainment fans learn less about politics than they used to and vote less often.

"Politics by default" made the 1960s and 1970s a period of unusually widespread news consumption. More people watched television news in this period than at any other time. Only television, by virtue of being both easy to follow and hard to resist, drew the less educated into the news audience. That news reaches fewer people today is thus not an irregularity, but rather a return to the days before television. The anomaly that stands out is that so many Americans decided to watch the news in the 1960s and 1970s, even though nobody forced them, and they were happy to abandon the news as soon as alternatives became available.

The transition from the low-choice environment to the high-choice world of cable and Internet reversed trends generated by the advent of broadcast television. For example, broadcast television lowered inequality in political involvement before cable and the Internet increased it again. But the changes underlying the two transitions involved different subpopulations. The advent of broadcast television modified the relationship between ability and political involvement, but it did little to change the effect of motivation. Cable television and the Internet, in contrast, confer greater importance to individual motivations in seeking political information out of the mass of other content. At the same time, they leave the role of ability more or less constant. In other words, broadcast television helped the less educated learn more about politics, whether or not they were particularly motivated to follow the news. The current high-choice environment concentrates political knowledge among those who like the news largely independent of their levels of education or cognitive skills. (Education continues to affect political learning in the high-choice media environment, but media content preferences are increasingly important predictors and only weakly related to education.)

Widespread news consumption was not the only consequence of the unusual broadcast television environment. . . . [T]he 1960s and 1970s stand out because of their relative equality in political involvement, a direct result of the broad reach of broadcast news. Elections, too, were unusual in the 1960s and 1970s. The impact of party identification on vote decisions dropped to its modern low point (Bartels 2000). Electoral volatility was higher than either today or in the middle of the twentieth century (Bartels 1998). Politicians took atypically moderate positions, both in Congress and during their election campaigns (Ansolabehere, Snyder, and Stewart 2000; Poole and Rosenthal 1997). I have argued that the relative absence of polarization in this period reflects the properties of the low-choice media environment. Because the political views of less educated citizens who were led to the polls by broadcast television were less firmly grounded in partisanship, they were more susceptible to nonpartisan voting cues such as incumbency. Although this did not have a systematic effect in presidential elections, where partisan cues dominate, it did affect congressional elections. The symbiosis between local television stations and members of Congress allowed incumbents to dominate the airwaves and send favorable cues. As a result, incumbents increased their vote shares as television spread across the country.

Beginning in the 1970s, greater media choice widened the turnout gap between news and entertainment fans. Advances in cable technology and the emergence of the Internet continue to feed this gap today. As a result of the fact that those who do not tune out are more partisan, greater turnout inequality produces more polarized elections. Entertainment fans are less partisan than those who continue to follow politics and vote in the high-choice media environment. The stronger partisan preferences of remaining voters reduce the volatility of election outcomes. Elections become more strongly determined by partisanship even though partisanship in the public as a whole has changed to a much lesser degree.

Many Americans live in a high-choice media environment already. More than 80 percent of them have access to cable or satellite television. More than half access the Internet from their homes. With the transition from low choice to high choice so far advanced, have the bulk of the political changes happened already? In some ways, the biggest change that cable television brought about was the removal of the quasi-monopoly for news in the early evening. Once the first dozen cable channels removed this monopoly, the structural reasons for inflated news audiences had largely disappeared. Yet even though cable television removed the biggest bottleneck in the quest for around-the-clock entertainment, Internet access accelerated the effect, according to my analysis. Access to two new media appears to roughly double the impact of preferences compared to either one of them.

Analog cable systems and dial-up Internet connections—currently the modal ways of new media access—are only the first technological steps toward greater choice. The convergence of media is likely to increasingly blur the difference between cable and the Internet. Digital transmission will without a doubt multiply the number of choices and the efficiency of choosing.

In the absence of preference changes, future technological advances such as video-on-demand and widespread broadband access are likely to exacerbate inequality. Media content preferences will only become more important for our understanding of American politics. . . .

. . . Extraordinary circumstances can temporarily disturb these trends. With greater media choice, entertainment fans leave the news audience. But under extraordinary circumstances, many of them return. In the aftermath of the terrorist attacks on September 11, 2001, Americans watched news and visited news Web sites in record numbers (Althaus 2002; Prior 2002). . . . [T]he media environment and people's motivations both contributed to these unusual spurts of political involvement. Interest in the news surrounding the attacks was obviously very high. But the media environment, too, was temporarily changed as the broadcast networks provided uninterrupted news coverage for four days and many cable channels, including MTV, TNT, and ESPN, carried news feeds instead of their usual entertainment and sports programming. The military interventions in Iraq in 1991 and 2003 also increased news interest considerably, though not nearly as much as 9/11 (Althaus 2002; Baum 2003b; Gantz and Greenberg 1993). The impact of content preferences is bound to be muted in these moments of crisis. . . .

The list of interesting questions for future research does not end there. In addition to the strength of content preferences, the opportunity to act upon them should condition the effects on political involvement. In the Opportunity-Motivation-Ability framework (Delli Carpini and Keeter 1996; Luskin 1987) that laid the foundation for the Conditional Learning Model, the media environment is not the only element of learning opportunity. Even a strong news fan in a high-choice media environment may not pick up a great deal of information if other things keep her busy. Employment status, child-rearing obligations, and many other demands on time should affect the relationship between preferences, news exposure, and political involvement. Moreover, media content preferences are clearly not the only motivational determinant of content selection. With respect to the choice between news and entertainment, the most obvious other contender seems to be a sense of civic duty. Some people may not like news as much as entertainment, but they still follow it because they consider it their duty as citizens to be informed about the major political issues of the day. We might expect a greater impact of civic duty, too, in the high-choice media environment where entertainment lures whenever news is an option. Convenience, social interactions, and incomplete information about viewing choices can all dilute the relationship between content preferences and viewing decisions. One purpose of media marketing, after all, is to get people to follow programming they would not otherwise select. Yet despite these distorting influences, even the simple distinction between a taste for news and a taste for entertainment has proved to drive content selection and its political consequences to a remarkable degree.

Another possible objection to the power of media choice concerns not the demand for different programming, but its supply. Actual choice between different types of media content, not simply the number of channels or media, is the key variable behind many of the effects described in this book. Access to a medium, the measure I use in the empirical analysis, is nothing more than a convenient simplification. Some have argued that actual choice between different content has not increased much at all as a result of technological advances. Barber (1998–9, 578–9), for example, contends that "despite the fact that outlets for their product have multiplied, there has been little real substantive diversification. . . . The actual content available is pretty much identical with what was available on the networks ten years ago. . . . Media giants make nonsense of the theoretical diversification of the technology."

Although Barber overstates his case and although cable television would still make it easier to select one's preferred content, even if media content had not changed at all, he offers a useful warning against technological determinism and urges continued attention to the impact of media consolidation. The prediction that "a thousand niches will bloom" (Rich 2002) in the high-choice media environment needs an empirical assessment. Even leaving aside the issue of media ownership concentration, the choice between different news formats is clearly not limitless. News is costly, so demand needs to surpass a profitability threshold for news formats to be available (unless news production is subsidized by the government). Television news is available around the clock (although not always live even on most twenty-four-hour news channels), but some issues are covered more than others. Quality of news and the resources devoted to specific issues vary. If the potential audience for an issue is too small, the fixed costs of covering the issue can outweigh the benefits that news providers can expect, so the issue may receive little or no coverage. In principle, similar constraints apply for online news (Hamilton 2004, 190–4). Geographical boundaries and proximity to the media outlet are largely irrelevant for online news, however. Internet users can easily access news from other regions of the country or from foreign media outlets. Although economic constraints are present for online news, "the low fixed costs of website operation and potential for aggregating like-minded individuals from many different areas or countries implies great variety in news provision on the Internet" (Hamilton 2004, 192). . . .

Media Environments and the Interpretation of Political Trends

. . . The decline of network news audiences over the last two and a half decades has been interpreted as a sign of waning political interest and a disappearing sense of civic duty. Yet this interpretation ignores the circumstances under which high news ratings emerged. Taking into account these circumstances yields a very different conclusion. News consumption can change even while people's media content preferences (and their civic duty and their political interest and their trust in the media) remain constant. In this case, cable television and later the Internet modified the relationship between content preferences and news exposure. The decline in news audiences was not caused by reduced political interest. . . . Interest in politics was simply never as high as audience shares for evening news suggested. A combined three-quarter market share for the three network newscasts takes on a different meaning if one considers that people had hardly any viewing alternatives.

The same caution is warranted when interpreting the recent partisan polarization of elections. Many analysts believe that America has become a deeply polarized nation. This study provides a corrective to this view. Comparing survey data from the 1970s to today's polls, analysts often jump to the conclusion that the public has become vastly more partisan. This sets off a hunt to explain how individuals were converted from ambivalent moderates to rabid partisans. I have provided a less radical explanation for the polarization of elections in recent decades. Greater media choice has made partisans more likely to vote and moderates more likely to abstain. Politics by choice is inherently more polarized than politics by default. This is not to deny that conversion may have played some role. But a far simpler change, higher turnout of partisan news-seekers and lower turnout of less partisan entertainment fans, contributes to polarization. This change polarizes elections but leaves the country as moderate and indifferent as it used to be. . . .

The negative impact of television on political involvement even among people who were primarily attracted by television entertainment was initially limited because the amount and availability of entertainment was limited too. Television may have offered them more vivid and convenient diversion than either movie theatres or radio, but political engagement among entertainment fans took a greater hit after cable television opened the floodgates for entertainment. Again, however, increasing knowledge and turnout rates among news fans compensated at least partly for this decline. . . .

The Voluntary Origins of Political Inequality

. . . Having the opportunity to view hundreds of television channels makes for more satisfying viewing than being limited to just three or four. And being able to choose from among hundreds of television channels and thousands of Web sites is even better. Despite the occasional difficulty in finding the desired content online or doubt about the added value of another dozen new cable channels, few inhabitants of the high-choice media environment would like to turn back the clock.

Yet although this wide variety means greater viewing, reading, and listening pleasures, the implications of greater choice for the health of democracy are more ambiguous. Rising inequality in political involvement and increasing partisan polarization of elections make it more difficult for a democratic system to achieve equal representation of citizens' interests. Unlike most other forms of inequality, however, this one arises due to voluntary consumption decisions. Entertainment fans abandon politics not because it has become harder for them to be involved—many people would argue the contrary—but because they decide to devote their time to media that promise greater gratification than the news. The mounting inequality between news fans and entertainment fans is due to preference differences, not differences in abilities or resources. In this regard, the contrast to the pre-television media environment is stark. Print media and even radio excluded those with low cognitive abilities and little education; entertainment fans in the current high-choice environment exclude themselves. This trend creates a question for modern democracies: When media users get what they want all the time, does anyone get hurt?

The voluntary basis of rising inequality in political involvement clashes with the conventional wisdom on the implications of the "digital divide." Many casual observers emphasize the great promise new technologies hold for democracy. They deplore current socioeconomic inequalities in access to new media but predict increasing political knowledge and participation for current have-nots after these inequalities have been overcome. The notion of Conditional Political Learning leads to the decidedly less optimistic conclusion that any gap based on socioeconomic status will be eclipsed by a preference-based gap once access to new media becomes cheaper and more widely available. . . .

. . . Mere access to the Internet is only one of many aspects of the divide. Differences in hardware, software, and connection speed all introduce additional inequality. Using the Internet in a library or at school is not the same as using it in one's own home. Demographic differences in access to the Internet persist today. Unlike broadcast television and radio, the Internet is a service that is available only for a regular fee (at least in today's business model), not a product that, once purchased, provides free access to media content. It is not a foregone conclusion that almost every American will eventually have easy and efficient access to the wealth of political information online. . . .

It is not immediately clear if the rising inequality in political involvement hurts social welfare. I have so far eschewed assessing my empirical findings in light of some normative standard. In some sense, assessing political involvement among entertainment fans does not need a normative standard: Their political knowledge and turnout rates are dropping. And they surely did not drop from such highs that their involvement in the high-choice environment represents a welcome decline to more healthy levels. Yet, it is not convincing to argue reflexively that only maximum political involvement creates the conditions under which democracy can function. Both the Downsian perspective of political ignorance as rational and Schudson's (1998; 2000) recent reconsideration of what makes a "good citizen" force us to specify more carefully how well and how equally informed we need an electorate to be.

In Schudson's view, the ideal of an informed citizen who carefully studies political issues and candidate platforms before casting a vote needs adjustment. It was, first of all, always an ideal against which most citizens looked ill-informed and ineffective. But, argues Schudson, it also ignores an arena for citizenship that has expanded dramatically in the last fifty years. Beginning with the civil rights movement, litigation became a way to instigate social change that gave citizens both the opportunity and the obligation to claim their rights: "The new model of citizenship added the courtroom to the voting booth as a locus of civic participation" (1998, 250). Together with increasing regulatory powers of the federal government, the "rights revolution" extended the reach of politics into many areas of private life. This new dimension has added considerable complexity to the role of the citizen, making citizenship "a year-around and daylong activity" (1998, 311). Although Schudson does not deny the benefits of an informed citizenry, it is neither realistic nor necessary, in his view, to expect citizens to be well informed about every aspect of their increasingly complex role in society. Instead, he proposes a modified model of citizenship, the "monitorial citizen." Rather than being widely knowledgeable about politics, citizens merely need to "be informed enough and alert enough to identify danger to their personal good and danger to the public good" (Schudson 2000, 22). In order to fulfill this "monitoring obligation," citizens "engage in environmental surveillance rather than information-gathering" (1998, 310–11).

How do the news junkies, Switchers, and entertainment fans that we have encountered in this book measure up against Schudson's model of citizenship? Even by his relaxed standards, the citizenry in the high-choice media environment seems handicapped by the growing inequality of political involvement. The drop in news exposure and knowledge among entertainment fans reduces the monitoring capabilities among the electorate. According to Schudson (1998, 310), "monitorial citizens scan (rather than read) the informational environment in a way so that they may be alerted on a very wide variety of issues for a very wide variety of ends." Although available data do not allow a precise assessment, this does not sound like the entertainment fans we have encountered in this book. Many of them probably do considerably less than "scan . . . the informational environment." It is doubtful that entertainment fans can be effective monitors. To the extent that the success of Schudson's model depends on monitoring by all or most citizens, my empirical analysis indicates a growing problem for democracy.

An optimist might grant that entertainment fans would not make good monitors but point out that the high-choice media environment provides news junkies with unprecedented resources to perform as monitorial citizens. If it is not necessary for all citizens to engage in monitoring because some citizens can in fact fill in as monitors for others, the expansion of media choice could actually make it easier to spot the dangers. Can news junkies be super-monitorial citizens? News junkies certainly look like excellent monitors. They consume a lot of information—and a lot more than before the choice explosion. Collectively at least, they may be quite close to the ideal of an informed citizenry. They also take advantage of new media technologies to share and debate the results of the monitoring. (Perhaps we should think of bloggers as the quintessential monitorial citizens of our day.) Most importantly, news junkies do not mind the monitoring obligation. They enjoy following the news. According to an optimistic interpretation, the less equitable knowledge distribution benefits democracy (in the absence of a change in the mean) because those who become more knowledgeable guide policy in a more "enlightened" direction.

Empirical evidence dampens the optimism. Because politicians pay more attention to voters than nonvoters (e.g., Griffin and Newman 2005; Rosenstone and Hansen 1993), the views of politically less-motivated citizens may not be reflected in political outcomes as much as before. Polls may not adequately represent the views of the electorate because respondents who lack information give responses that do not reflect their preferences or do not provide substantive responses at all (Althaus 2003).

The optimistic interpretation rises and falls with the validity of one key assumption: The happily monitoring news junkies will keep the interests of the happily news-avoiding entertainment fans in mind. For that to happen, either the super-monitorial news junkies of the high-choice media environment would have to approximate a random sample of the population, in which case their political views would correspond roughly to the views of entertainment fans. Or, if news junkies resemble an elitist sample of activists, they would have to consider the collective interest of the citizenry, rather than their own self interest, while performing their monitoring tasks.

Demographically, news fans and entertainment fans are remarkably similar. Although my analysis produced a few significant demographic differences, they were substantively very small. The only partial exception was a sizable age difference between news and entertainment fans. . . . Yet despite demographic similarities, it is far from obvious that news fans can effectively and fairly represent the interests of their friends, colleagues, and relatives who prefer to avoid the news. In one respect, news fans differ substantially from entertainment fans: They are far more partisan. At the very least, this encourages candidates to take more extreme political positions, especially in primaries (Aldrich 1995; Fiorina 1999). News junkies are unlikely to advocate the moderate policy positions that entertainment fans seem to favor. . . .

Audience Fragmentation

Recent years have seen a lively discussion of the societal and political implications of new media technologies. First and foremost, people have more choice. Increasingly, they also have the opportunity to customize their media use and to filter out content in advance. Some scholars have sounded the alarm bells over these developments, warning of dire consequences of customization, fragmentation, and segmentation. In *Breaking Up America,* Turow (1997, 2, 7) sees the emergence of "electronic equivalents of gated communities" and "lifestyle segregation." Sunstein (2001) predicts the demise of "shared experiences" and increasing group polarization as media users select only content with which they agree in the first place. Others emphasize the benefits of choice and customization (e.g., Negroponte 1995). In this debate, some seemingly mundane conceptual details have not received enough consideration.

Audience fragmentation, the starting point for this debate, is empirically well established. As the number of television channels increases, the audience for any one channel declines and more channels gain at least some viewers. Audience fragmentation increases the diversity of media exposure in the aggregate. This much is uncontroversial. But audience fragmentation tells us nothing about the diversity of individuals' media use. Individuals may take advantage of greater media choice either by watching a mix of many newly available channels or by "bingeing on their favorites" (Webster 2005, 369). Webster (1986; 2005) uses the concept of "audience polarization" to capture the concentration of viewing of a particular channel. If a few viewers account for most of the channel's viewing, its audience is polarized. If viewing is distributed across a large number of people who individually make up only a small share of the channel's viewing, audience polarization is low. From the viewer's perspective, audience polarization is high when people watch a lot of a particular program format or genre and not much else. . . .

. . . Audience fragmentation in particular need not doom civic life. Certain kinds of fragmentation seem completely harmless. Imagine three individuals in the fall of 2005, John, Larry, and Claire, who all used to watch *Friends.* Now John watches *Desperate Housewives,* Larry watches *South Park,* and Claire watches *Lost.* The proliferation of choices allows people who used to watch the same entertainment programming to now watch different entertainment programming. It is hard to see how this change threatens our society (except perhaps in that John, Larry, and Claire cannot talk about the same show at work—which might itself be an incentive to coordinate on one show and limit fragmentation).

Likewise, if John, Larry, and Claire all used to watch the *CBS Evening News with Dan Rather,* but now John watches the *NBC Nightly News,* Larry watches *The Situation Room,* and Claire tunes in to *Special Report with Brit Hume,* the political implications of fragmentation are limited. Although they now watch different news programs, the three of them still learn roughly the same things about politics. To the extent that exposure to political information motivates political participation, none of the three would seem to be less likely to participate than in the past.

In one respect, this fragmentation of news audiences does seem to make democracy more vulnerable. If some former Rather viewers switch to very conservative outlets, while others turn to a news source with a decidedly liberal slant, their political views may polarize. Such a trend has raised concerns because it might limit the diversity of arguments that viewers encounter and expose them to biased information. . . .

Even if some media exposure is indeed selective with regard to partisan slant, ideological audience specialization poses a lesser problem than audience specialization along the fault lines of news and entertainment. The latter not only exacerbates inequalities in political involvement, it also contributes to partisan polarization in a very different way. Ideological audience specialization raises the specter of partisan polarization because exposure to ideologically biased political content may persuade moderates or reinforce partisans. . . . [T]here are fewer moderate voters today not because they have been converted by increasingly partisan media, but because they have been lost to entertainment. They are still alive and moderate, but politically less relevant because of their tendency to abstain. . . .

References

Aldrich, John. 1995. *Why Parties?* Chicago: University of Chicago Press.

Althaus, Scott L. 2002. American News Consumption During Times of National Crisis. *PS: Political Science and Politics* 35 (3):517–21.

———. 2003. *Collective Preferences in Democratic Politics.* Cambridge: Cambridge University Press.

Ansolabehere, Stephen. 2001. Candidate Positioning in U.S. House Elections. *American Journal of Political Science* 45 (1):136–59.

Ansolabehere, Stephen, James M. Snyder, Jr., and Charles Stewart III. 2000. "Old Voters, New Voters, and the Personal Vote: Using Redistricting to Measure the Incumbency Advantage." *American Journal of Political Science* 44 (1): 27–34.

Barber, Benjamin R. 1998–9. Three Scenarios for the Future of Technology and Strong Democracy. *Political Science Quarterly* 113 (4):573–89.

Bartels, Larry M. 1998. Electoral Continuity and Change, 1868–1996. *Electoral Studies* 17 (31):301–26.

———. 2000. Partisanship and Voting Behavior, 1952–1996. *American Journal of Political Science* 44 (1):35–50.

Baum, Matthew A. 2003b. *Soft News Goes to War.* Princeton, New Jersey: Princeton University Press.

Delli Carpini, Michael X., and Scott Keeter. 1996. *What Americans Know About Politics and Why It Matters.* New Haven, Connecticut: Yale University Press.

Fiorina, Morris P. 1999. *Whatever Happened to the Median Voter?* Paper presented at the MIT Conference on Parties and Congress, Cambridge, Massachusetts, October 2.

Gantz, Walter, and Bradley S. Greenberg. 1993. Patterns of Diffusion and Information-Seeking. In *Desert Storm and the Mass Media,* edited by Bradley S. Greenberg and Walter Gantz (pp. 166–81). Cresskill, New Jersey: Hampton Press.

Griffin, John D., and Brian Newman. 2005. Are Voters Better Represented? *Journal of Politics* 67 (4):1206–27.

Hamilton, James T. 2004. *All the News That's Fit to Sell: How the Market Transforms Information into News.* Princeton, New Jersey: Princeton University Press.

Luskin, Robert C. 1987. Measuring Political Sophistication. *American Journal of Political Science* 31 (4): 856–99.

Negroponte, Nicholas. 1995. *Being Digital.* New York: Knopf.

Neuman, W. Russell. 1996. Political Communication Infrastructure. *The Annals of the American Academy of Political and Social Science* 546:9–21.

Poole, Keith T., and Howard Rosenthal. 1997. *Congress: A Political-Economic History of Roll Call Voting.* New York: Oxford University Press.

Prior, Markus. 2002. Political Knowledge after September 11. *PS: Political Science and Politics* 35 (3):523–9.

Rich, Frank. 2002. The Weight of an Anchor. *New York Times Magazine,* May 35.

Rosenstone, Steven J., and John Mark Hansen. 1993. *Mobilization, Participation, and Democracy in America.* New York: MacMillan.

Schudson, Michael. 1998. *The Good Citizen: A History of American Civic Life.* New York: Martin Kessler Books.

———. 2000. Good Citizens and Bad History: Today's Political Ideas in Historical Perspective. *Communication Review* 4 (1):1–20.

Sunstein, Cass R. 2001. *Republic.Com.* Princeton, New Jersey: Princeton University Press.

Turow, Joseph. 1997. *Breaking up America: Advertisers and the New Media World.* Chicago: University of Chicago Press.

Webster, James G. 1986. Audience Behavior in the New Media Environment. *Journal of Communication* 36 (3):77–91.

———. 2005. Beneath the Veneer of Fragmentation: Television Audience Polarization in a Multichannel World. *Journal of Communication* 55 (2):366–82.

Young, Dannagal G., and Russ Tisinger. 2006. Dispelling Late-Night Myths: News Consumption among Late-Night Comedy Viewers and the Predictors of Exposure to Various Late-Night Shows. *Harvard International Journal of Press/Politics* 11 (3):113–34.

Part III

INFLUENCING ELECTION OUTCOMES

Doris Graber

When it comes to running for office or campaigning for or against a particular policy, practicing politicians are always seriously concerned about media effects. Along with their campaign organizations, they spend much time, effort, and money to influence the outcome with the help of favorable media attention. If their candidates or causes lose, they frequently blame the tone of media coverage or the lack of adequate media coverage for the defeat. Given the importance of elections in democratic societies, scholars and campaign professionals who actually conduct the campaigns have devoted inordinate amounts of time to studying and analyzing the campaigning process. Research is becoming increasingly sophisticated because new tools are available and because the supply of campaign messages has been mushrooming.

The readings in part III scrutinize several important aspects of news media coverage of election campaigns. Selections depict the kinds of images that emerge from news stories, advertisements, and the Internet. Authors speculate about the political consequences of this coverage and raise questions about the ability and effectiveness of the press in informing the public about the real issues at stake in each election.

Part III begins with an analysis of election coverage that focuses on an extremely important facet—the content presented through audiovisuals. Given the omnipresence of audiovisual messages in nearly all kinds of modern media, the dearth of systematic audiovisual content analysis is truly surprising. Lack of reliable, practical, and low-cost analysis methods has been the major barrier. Maria Elizabeth Grabe and Erik Page Bucy head the small group of scholars who have breached it. They scrutinized sounds and visuals from presidential elections ranging from 1992 through 2004.

Their analysis shows that audiovisual content on television and the Internet supplies citizens with a rich array of readily usable cues for making sensible voting decisions. When tests of civic knowledge include questions about audiovisual information in addition to queries about verbal information, citizens' knowledge scores surge from the common ranking of "abysmal" to a hope-generating "adequate."

Political advertisements by candidates, their supporters, and their opponents are among the most important and controversial sources of election information. They are important because they introduce voters to salient parts of the candidate's biography; they are controversial because the prose reflects a one-sided, uncritical account produced by the candidate's hired campaign aides. Political scientist Darrell M. West discusses the persuasive power of well-crafted advertisements that manage to tap expertly into viewers' predispositions. He provides evidence that confirms that commercials alter the public's knowledge and appraisals of candidates. Impending defeats can turn into victories and vice versa depending on the quality of political commercials.

The theme of the essay that follows is that election news flows in American presidential campaigns are inadequate and obstruct, rather than enhance, informed voting by average citizens. Thomas E. Patterson argues that major changes in candidate nomination methods and election procedures have emasculated political parties. The news media have stepped into the void, but their structures and goals are ill suited to providing the guidance that voters need to make sound political judgments. Consequently, the quality of American presidential election campaigns has sunk to dangerously low levels.

Patterson's pessimism is counterbalanced by Rachel Gibson's optimism. She talks about the "revitalization of politics" thanks to the birth of the "new media." Gibson explores the multiple channels that Barack Obama used in 2008 to win the U.S. presidency in an extraordinarily vibrant, information-rich campaign. New media made it possible to reach many more voters than ever before with messages tailored to their interests and needs. They allowed Americans of all ages and stations of life to respond personally to these messages and to craft and disseminate their own messages to selected audiences. Gibson predicts that these developments herald a revolution in citizen participation in government. The Internet is making a reality of Lincoln's promise at Gettysburg that "government by the people," will not perish, because citizens' views do indeed shape public policies and election outcomes.

To check whether Gibson's perceptions represent typical academic ivory-tower views, unsullied by the realities that actual participants face in actual battles over media coverage, the next chapter features the reports of campaign strategists who participated in the 2008 presidential contest. Nicolle Wallace served as an advisor to Republican candidate John McCain; Anita Dunn advised Democratic candidate Barack Obama. Their reports show that both are seriously concerned about the quality of press coverage.

A particularly ugly aspect of these concerns is highlighted by the final selection. Much political advertising strikes a sharply negative chord. So do many of the news stories in the printed press and in television, radio, and Internet broadcasts. There is a veritable flood of nasty accusations and predictions of doom should opposition candidates and parties come to power. Larry J. Sabato's essay explains why negative stories dominate presidential campaigns and why the consequences are unfortunate. The viciousness of current campaign journalism, which instantly reaches millions of Americans, harms electoral politics. It discourages worthy new entrants, fatally wounds the political careers of many well-qualified contenders, and leaves deep personal and political scars on scores more.

13

NEWS AND THE VISUAL FRAMING OF ELECTIONS

Maria Elizabeth Grabe and Erik Page Bucy

Editor's Note

Electing well-qualified public officials is arguably citizens' most important obligation in democracies. News stories are their main sources of information. Grabe and Bucy charge that most scholarly analyses of the merits of televised election news are inadequate, even misleading, because they ignore the content of visual messages. Their research on audiovisuals broadcast on television news during presidential elections in 1992, 1996, 2000, and 2004 focuses on sound bites and image bites, their soundless counterparts that actually are more prevalent.

The meticulously researched findings show that visuals provide citizens with a rich array of readily usable cues for making sensible voting decisions, based on television and Internet news, including news found on social networking sites. The news stories' visual cues differ from those provided by the verbal news flows that dominate print media and that have been the basis for rating, and bemoaning, citizens' lack of political competence. When visual learning is included, citizens' knowledge scores surge.

Both authors were associate professors at Indiana University, Bloomington, when their book was published. Their main affiliation was with the Department of Telecommunications, with secondary affiliations to the political science department. Maria Elizabeth Grabe also held an appointment as a research associate in the political science department of the University of Pretoria, South Africa; Erik Page Bucy held an adjunct associate professorship in Indiana's School of Informatics.

. . . Despite the visual nature of television, research analyzing the content of presidential-candidate appearances on the news has focused almost exclusively on the verbal side of the message, documenting the amount of time candidates are simultaneously seen and heard (Hallin 1992, Lichter 2001), the length and tone of their statements (Lowry & Shidler 1995, Lowry & Shidler 1998, Robinson & Sheehan 1983), and the interpretive frames journalists use to package sound bites in televised reports (Levy 1981, Steele & Barnhurst 1997). Yet such preoccupation with the shrinking sound bite, which treats the accompanying visuals as accidental elements of televised political speech, not only overlooks television's single most distinguishing feature—its ability to generate a real-time stream of images rich in referential meaning—but also fails to consider the influence that images have on viewers (Meyrowitz 1985, Newhagen 2002). As the information-processing literature has shown, these effects are considerable when compared to the verbal component of the news. Moreover, fixation on sound bite length assumes that the longer the sound bite, the better the quality of news coverage (Russomanno & Everett 1995, Stephens 1998).

Our investigation calls these assumptions into question and makes a decisive turn toward the visual dimension of media politics. Despite the academic emphasis on policy debate and issue discussion in election campaigns, expressive displays emitted by candidates do not lose their relevance to audiences— or to journalists and other critics—when broadcast on the nightly news. Indeed, owing to the close-up nature of television, they arguably take on added importance, as Hillary Clinton's emotional moment during the 2008 New Hampshire primary aptly illustrated (see Givhan 2008, Kantor 2008). Given the rise of a more interpretive style of broadcast journalism since the 1980s, with reporters and correspondents inserting more of their own opinion and commentary into political coverage and candidates being verbally confined to an ever dwindling amount of air time (Barnhurst & Steele 1997, Hallin 1992), news visuals have assumed an increasingly central yet largely unrecognized role in informing viewers (Lehtonen 1988).

With regard to the volume of coverage, the question that has to be asked is whether image bites now occupy more candidate airtime than sound bites—and what the implications of this development might be for democratic politics. . . .

. . . Even in the era of online news and cell phone news feeds, network newscasts still draw the largest audiences for news (Lichter 2001, Project for Excellence in Journalism 2004). The continued prominence of network news and dependence of political campaigns on audiovisual media promotes unprecedented viewer scrutiny of candidates. Widescreen and high-definition television monitors also bring candidates into closer view than ever. Indeed, "never before have leaders been in such frequent, widespread, and close-up visual contact with followers" (Bucy & Bradley 2004, p. 61). Despite this, however, scholarly analyses of sound bites generally ignore the experimental research relating to television visuals and focus instead on the length of candidate statements aired on the evening news. . . .

Sound Bite News

. . . Although efforts have been made to offer presidential candidates more time on the network evening news, as when CBS unilaterally decided in 1992 to maintain a 30-second sound bite minimum (which the network quickly revised downward to 20 seconds and subsequently abandoned; Ross 1992), the average length of sound bites continues to decline. In 1988, the mean sound bite length was 9.8 seconds; by the 2000 election the mean length had contracted another 20%, down to 7.8 seconds (Lichter 2001). During this time period, with the exception of the unusual 1992 general election campaign, which featured three ostensibly major candidates—the two major party nominees plus Independent Ross Perot—the total number of campaign stories and minutes of news time devoted to general election news decreased while the frequency and proportion of journalists' speaking time increased (Lichter 2001, Steele & Barnhurst, 1997, Grabe et al. 1999). . . .

. . . Only analyzing sound bite and campaign story *length,* however, ignores the *content* of candidate statements and overlooks the possibility that even the briefest of comments or utterances may have sizable political impact (Russomanno & Everett 1995, Stephens 1998, Clayman 1995, Scheuer 1999). Take, for example, George H. W. Bush's 1988 convention pledge: "Read my lips: no new taxes," reprised by the Democrats to detrimental effect during the 1992 campaign. The Clinton campaign exploited Bush's fateful guarantee, which consultant James Carville described as "the most famous broken promise in the history of American politics" (quoted in Hegedus & Pennebaker 1993), in both advertising and televised debates. In the third and final debate, Clinton cast the pledge as a cynical ploy that reflected on Bush's character. "The mistake that was made was making the 'read my lips' promise in the first place just to get elected, knowing what the size of the deficit was. You just can't promise something like that just to get elected if you know that circumstances may overtake you" (quoted in Hegedus and Pennebaker 1993). Similarly, the Republicans in 2004 used a short but contradictory statement by John Kerry to critique his lack of resolve. When pressed by a heckler about why he had voted against an appropriations bill to support the war in Iraq, Kerry said, "I actually did vote for the $87 billion [bill] before I voted against it" (quoted in Thomas 2004, p. 70). Technically, he was referring to different *versions* of the bill, but this critical point was lost in translation. Kerry was subsequently branded as a "flip-flopper," an image powerfully reinforced in George W. Bush's campaign advertising, and one that he never managed to shake.

Under certain circumstances, then, even short sound bites can have political consequences, particularly when recycled in advertising and other campaign attacks. Yet blanket criticism of the *shrinking* sound bite reflects the untested assumption that brief candidate statements invariably misinform voters, contribute to a distorted view of the campaign, and negatively impact the speaker's candidacy while longer actualities enhance news quality, increase voter learning, and improve a candidate's prospects for election. The sheer *length* of a sound bite does not necessarily correlate with increased substance: politicians are famous for filling rooms (and broadcasts) with hot air. . . .

To move beyond concerns about length, sound bite *content* should also be considered. Previous research has analyzed candidate statements for their informational context or origin (Lowry & Shidler 1995, Lowry & Shidler 1998) but sound bite substance has not been explicitly examined in news analysis. Therefore, we investigate the substantive content or meaning of these "snappy snippets of taped comment or news." . . . [W]e identified seven options of sound bite content, including: speaking time devoted to policy positions, reactions to the news, attacks on opponents, defending one's role in a controversy, predicting victory, calls to rally the troops, and an "other" category for cases that did not fit. The duration of sound bite substance was recorded in seconds, with each sound bite assigned to a single content option.

Findings for Sound Bite Content

The largest portion of sound bite time, 40.79%, was spent on attacks against opponents, whereas only 3.52% of bite time was allocated to defenses against attacks (see Table 13–1). Thus, the biggest chunk of bite content was taken up by attack and defense rhetoric. Another sizable portion of bite time, 29.88%, contained candidate statements on issues, either explaining policy positions or responding to news events of national and international interest. Declarations of victory and appeals for voter support—calls to "rally the

Table 13–1   Content of Sound Bites

Sound Bite Content	Percentage of Total Bite Time (1992–2004 combined)
Attacks on opponents	40.79
Defensive rhetoric	3.52
Issue discussion of policies or news events	29.88
Calls to rally supporters	11.09
Other	14.72

troops"—took up 11.09% of bite time. Another 14.72% of bite time was taken up by topics that did not fit into the above options. . . .

The mean durations for these content categories remained reasonably stable over time. Only one category, defenses against attacks, fluctuated significantly across elections. . . .

Image Bite News

Sound bites play an important, if not controversial, role in election coverage, but the biggest untold story of televised coverage of presidential campaigns is the prevalence of candidate *image bites*. Although scholars have called for greater attention to "video bites" (Lowry & Shidler 1995, Lowry & Shidler 1998) and systematic investigation of news visuals generally (Graber 1996, Graber 2001), the visual aspect of news remains understudied. Research on ambient or background sound in television news (e.g., cheering, jeering, music, natural sound) is perhaps even more overlooked than visuals, despite its potentially powerful communicative outcomes. This is due in part to a normative, social-scientific bias against audiovisual media and a tendency to dismiss television as a superficial or entertainment medium that lacks the seriousness of print. As Graber (2001, p. 93) has observed, "The belief that audiovisuals are poor carriers of important political information has become so ingrained in conventional wisdom that it has throttled research."

Yet the myth that television is an intellectual lightweight is convincingly countered by empirical findings that show television news to be positively associated with political knowledge (Drew & Weaver 2006, Putnam 2000) and experimental literature that has demonstrated how emotional displays of political leaders are capable of influencing viewer attitudes even when embedded in the background of a TV newscast during which the leader's voice is not heard (Bucy 2000, Masters & Sullivan 1993). Investigation of image bites seems duly warranted on several accounts. First, nonverbal emotional displays can serve as a potent vehicle for expression by candidates, whether intended or not. Second, viewers readily distinguish between different types of televised displays, which are frequently shown at close-up range—and increasingly in high definition. And third, the emotional and evaluative reactions that viewers experience upon exposure to visual portrayals of candidates can translate into lasting feelings, attitudes, and political behaviors (Bucy 2003, Lanzetta et al. 1985).

Lacking the pithy verbal content of sound bites, image bites are nevertheless informationally and politically potent. Indeed, in the course of a few ill-advised seconds during a speech to supporters on the night of the 2004 Iowa caucuses, Howard Dean issued a shrill call to rally the troops and demonstrated the power of an image bite to undermine a candidate's electoral viability. In news commentaries after the episode, Dean was characterized as having "blown up his presidential aspirations . . . with what appeared to be a painful, primal scream" (Kamen 2004, p. A25). . . . Both sound and image bites derive their notoriety and persuasive force at the extremes, particularly from gaffes and iconic moments. At their most memorable, they are characterized on the one hand by the signature expressions of perceived greatness and, on the other, by the irreparable slips and embarrassing acts that destroy candidacies. . . .

In American politics, televised nonverbal displays "have proved both disastrous and beneficial for those seeking or holding public office" (Shields & MacDowell 1987, p. 78). As for their salutary consequences, iconic image bites are the stuff of which lasting impressions are made. These are the signature expressions and desirable candidate behaviors that inspire and reassure while capturing the larger meaning of a political performance. In recent elections two episodes stand out, both from acceptance speeches at Democratic National Conventions. In 2004, John Kerry invoked his war-hero past (but not his anti-Vietnam activism) by bounding to the podium, saluting convention-goers, and proclaiming, "I'm John Kerry and I'm reporting for duty." The line—borrowed from an old Wesley Clark speech—"brought down the house" (Thomas 2004, p. 81). The image of Kerry saluting delegates reinforced the convention message of "a strong America," and his performance, in the words of one convention delegate, offered "a true reflection of his patriotism and his life" (quoted in Nagourney 2004, p. Al). Four years earlier, Al Gore's extended embrace of his wife as he made his way to the podium for his 2000 acceptance speech made headlines and seemed to give Gore a better than expected postconvention bounce. The "20-point kiss," as it came to be known (Klein 2006) also put candidate Gore in an improved political position. . . .

. . . During a political debate, major speech, or other high-profile televised event, a few seconds of the wrong nonverbal cues could lead to a fall in the polls, accompanied by eroded faith in leadership ability (Meyrowitz 1985, Edelman 1964). As a consequence, the communicative behavior and visual presentation of public figures has become increasingly central to evaluations of political effectiveness. . . .

Over each of the four elections analyzed, image bites made up a substantially larger percentage of total campaign coverage than sound bites. . . .

Overall, there was a significant difference between the amount of time that candidates appeared in sound and image bites per story. . . . Candidates were featured more prominently in image bites than sound bites. Although the average duration of all sound and image bites within stories did not vary significantly over time, a consistent increase in image bite lengths could be observed (see Fig. 13–1). Sound bite durations per story show a less consistent pattern, increasing from 1992 to 2000, then decreasing notably in 2004. . . .

Figure 13–1   Average total duration of candidate sound and image bites over time

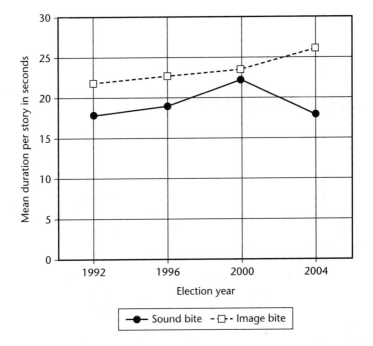

Discussion

Images are the *lingua franca* of politics, yet they remain among the least scrutinized and least understood aspects of political news. Image bites do not reveal the logic of candidate arguments or the details of policy positions. However, for a critical component of the electorate, which is only semi attentive to civic affairs (Neuman 1986), political decisions may be based more on affective attachments and nonverbal signals expressed by leading politicians on television than careful consideration of issue positions (Bucy 2000). Indeed, in a political environment increasingly dependent upon electronic media, an awkward, unappealing, or inappropriate communication style is becoming difficult to counteract with policy proposals—and may become the focus of public discussion. . . . This sort of nonverbal information is precisely what television excels at presenting. Appreciating the information value of candidate displays, and therefore of the potential influence of image bites, opens a window on understanding television news that did not appear to exist when the audio track alone was treated as important. . . .

Clayman (1995, p. 119) describes the reproduction of candidate quotations and sound bites as a "profoundly consequential matter" for democracy. "As the news media have become increasingly central to the conduct of public affairs, political battles are now waged largely through the brief verbal excerpts that make their way into the daily news." If sound bites are largely issue oriented, as our analysis has found, then their contribution to policy debates—and to highlighting differences between candidates during elections—may be more substantial than commonly assumed. This is particularly relevant to partisan politics. The very nature of broadcast media, with their fast-paced editing and increasing audiovisual speed, resists long, complex messages. Broadcast news, as with television generally, acts as a "simplifying lens," in the words of Scheuer (1999) favoring clear-cut issues over diffuse or complicated policy discussions (see also Patterson 1980).

On account of this structural or nonideological bias, Scheuer maintains, television's sound bite sensibility ultimately favors political ideas and positions on the Right, which tend to be clear-cut, self-regarding, and easier to articulate than positions on the Left, which tend to involve contextual explanations of remote causes or effects and advocate the welfare of others. Television, he asserts, filters out "complex ideas in favor of blunt emotional messages that appeal to the self and to narrower moral-political impulses" (Scheuer 1999, p. 10). Conservative promises to cut taxes and safeguard individual rights, for instance, are an easier sell than liberal ideas about the need to increase social welfare spending and use taxpayer money to develop alternative energy sources. As a result, news coverage and other television fare function as a brake on liberal ideas while acting as an accelerator of conservative messages and values. To Scheuer (p. 10), the medium's "increasing dominance of our political culture has been a central factor in the resurgence of American conservatism" and eclipse of liberalism in recent decades. . . .

Perhaps most striking in this analysis were the findings for candidate image bites, which constituted a greater percentage of total campaign coverage than sound bites. This result was expected, given television's status as a visual medium. Consistent with this pattern, candidates were featured more often in image bites ($M = 22.99$ seconds per news story) than they were in sound bites ($M = 18.59$ seconds). Even as sound bites continue to shrink, the amount of time candidates are appearing visually in newscasts is actually *increasing* in duration, rising gradually each election year. This suggests that viewers of the evening news are receiving more direct visual cues about candidates than verbal information. Because pictures are perceived as firsthand knowledge about political actors and events, including presidential candidates and campaign-related developments, news visuals are undoubtedly delivering more information to viewers than previously acknowledged. With greater appreciation for visual processing, nonverbal communication, and voter learning from television news, research can begin to redress this oversight by investigating the effects of image bites on political evaluations and outcomes (see, for example, Benjamin and Shapiro 2009).

Given that presidential candidates were seen in image bites more than twice as much as journalists over all election years (M = 22.99 seconds per story compared to M = 9.13 seconds), the journalistic domination of broadcast news is not as one-sided or complete as commonly argued. If using a verbal yardstick to measure candidate appearances on the evening news, the airtime available to candidates has indeed declined. However, if using the *shown but not heard* visual standard, the amount of time allocated to candidates relative to journalists is quite favorable. Granted, candidates are speaking less, but this does not mean that viewers are receiving no useful political knowledge. Visuals carry a plenitude of social information, and the nonverbal communication they convey forms the basis of political impressions and assessments. . . .

. . . The Informational Consequences of Television News

Before jumping on the denunciatory bandwagon, critics of media and politics would do well to heed some of the more consequential findings from the emerging interdisciplinary science of image processing and reconsider television news from a visual perspective. Converging results from political psychology, neuroscience, public opinion research, and even economics are difficult to dismiss—and worth a closer look. New and ongoing studies are showing how (1) viewers of television news are as politically informed and motivated as readers of newspapers and other print media revered by the word culture; (2) visual forms of political knowledge equalize gender, race, and educational differences—and may more effectively predict voter turnout than traditional measures of verbal knowledge; and (3) thin-slice exemplars of political stimuli, namely, candidate photographs and 10-second image bites, provide viewers with enough social information to make reliable inferences about candidate competence and electoral suitability. Except perhaps for concerns about the quality of political discourse, these findings effectively neutralize criticism that television does not perform a useful civic duty. . . .

. . . [V]isuals convey information on multiple levels. Facial displays and other aspects of expressive behavior form the basis of inferences about more enduring candidate qualities, especially character and electoral viability, influencing support among voters. As our analyses have shown, it is not just the type of display but the timing of different modes of nonverbal behavior (agonic versus hedonic) that makes a difference in building or weakening voter support. Aggression, for example, is not conducive to rallying support when a candidate is behind in the polls or after a poor debate performance. Al Gore's intensifying agonic behavior during the final three weeks of the

2000 election shows how exhibiting too much anger/threat in the context of dwindling public support can have an injurious result. George W. Bush, on the other hand, demonstrated how emphasizing positive displays of happiness/reassurance toward Election Day can sustain a candidate in a tight race.

Moreover, how camera angles and other packaging features are employed in newscasts can greatly transform the content and embedded meaning of campaign news stories. Our analysis revealed positive correlations between tracking poll data and beneficial packaging features for Bob Dole in 1996 and George W. Bush in 2000, and negative correlations for detrimental packaging of Bill Clinton and George H. W. Bush in 1992, Al Gore in 2000, and John Kerry in 2004. If persistently applied, visual packaging can affect candidate support by either enhancing or undermining perceptions of leadership and momentum. We also found evidence showing how visual framing can dampen candidate appeal, as it did for the polling numbers of George H. W. Bush, Al Gore, and John Kerry. . . .

. . . [I]nferences made from visual depictions of candidates occur rapidly, if not automatically, influencing subsequent information processing about candidates even if not consciously contemplated (Todorov et al. 2005, p. 1623). Visual portrayals, in this sense, may prime later judgments about political viability and shape the criteria by which candidates are evaluated, including their policy positions. Hence, visual information complements verbal knowledge—and vice versa. . . .

In addition to priming subsequent evaluations, visuals serve as a foundation for decision making in their own right. Visual information from thin-slice exposures of political candidates seems to function effectively as a forecasting tool, predicting electoral outcomes on par with more conventional measures such as retrospective evaluations of the incumbent or economic conditions (Benjamin & Shapiro 2009). Visual knowledge as indexed by candidate photographs is both demographically equalizing and associated with political competence, predicting voter turnout in congressional and presidential elections. Even on measures of verbal knowledge, network news viewing has been consistently associated with political learning and works in conjunction with other hard news use[d] to generate interest in the campaign. None of these effects would occur if news visuals truly made no appeal to reason and merely served as visual decoration for verbal narratives.

When considering visuals as information, a distinction needs to be made between factual knowledge and social information of the kind that news visuals provide. Table 13–2 compares factual and social information types in relation to four key contextual dimensions: the media that are associated with them, biological predispositions to attend to them, cognitive competence to process them, and social constructions of their informational

Table 13–2 Comparison of Factual and Social Information Types

	Information Types	
	Factual	Social
Media	Word-based	Visually based
	Dependent on literacy	Independent of literacy requirements
	Biased toward print media	Biased toward television, visual media
	Present in audio track of television news	Present in video track of television news
Biology	Developed late in hominoid evolution	Developed early in hominoid evolution
	No specialized brain centers for reading	Specialized brain centers for visual processing
	Emerges within cognitive band of processing (500 msec and above)	Emerges within biological band of processing (50 msec and above)
Cognition	Difficult to recall	Easy to recall
	Requires extensive rehearsal for memory	Requires minimal rehearsal for memory
	Most useful with a political schema	Not dependent on a political schema
	Permits slow inferences of politically relevant traits	Enables quick inferences of politically relevant traits
	Overriden by compelling visuals	Assigned priority over spoken words
Culture	Viewed as a marker of intellect	Viewed as a marker of "idiocy"
	Culturally constructed as rational	Culturally constructed as emotional
	Associated with elites, sophistication	Associated with nonelites, lack of sophistication
	Socially stratifying, exclusionary	Socially equalizing, inclusionary

status in society. Clearly, these information types are not as cleanly separated as we have listed here for comparative purposes. Yet, the comparison illustrates how elites have managed to construct the information offered in print media as the acme of civic knowledge—despite the biological and cognitive predisposition of humans to absorb social information from visual-based media.

The point-by-point comparisons between factual and social information leave little room to doubt the arbitrariness of crowning print media, and their dissemination of facts, as democratizing. Indeed, if democratic theory and practice truly valued the participation of *the people,* especially citizens from lower levels of the social strata, the recognition that visuals impart valuable political knowledge would be better integrated into public debate and the research agendas of scholars. . . .

Rationality as it is usually discussed implies the deployment of factual knowledge into an elaborated political schema, or semantic memory network, upon which citizens are assumed to base reasoned decisions. This is a limited view of voter competence. As work on visual knowledge documents, memory associations derived from news visuals provide an equally potent foundation for decision making—for a vast proportion of the electorate. Indeed, visuals are highly efficient conduits of information that highlight inconsistencies and facilitate connections between candidates, their political stances, and voter evaluations. Moreover, visuals handily outperform the written and spoken word in tests of both long- and short-term memory.

We have asked, and perhaps gotten, all that we can from newspapers and other print media. Perhaps the time is right to reconsider the value of television to informing voters. Indeed, television news appears to have a more positive relationship with democracy than previously acknowledged. Since news visuals convey substantive social information and influence candidate support, they should be regarded as indices of political knowledge that work in conjunction with verbal messages to cultivate civic competence. The visually informed voter uses a varying combination of factual and social information from media and other sources to assess political developments and arrive at intelligent decisions. Visually informed voters may not possess extensive procedural knowledge of institutional processes or an encyclopedic memory for the names of important public figures but they may be remarkably adept at recognizing the faces of those figures and knowing what policies the person behind the name stands for.

With the growing availability of and access to full-motion images in the online environment, the arbitrary devaluation of visuals may begin to reverse course. The separation between factual and social forms of information might also be bridged by a new generation of citizens whose use of social networking, file-sharing, and online news sites to share, consume, and produce media content can be seen as part of a multichannel process of media participation in civic and political life (see Bucy and Gregson 2001). There is reason for cautious optimism in this regard, as 40% of citizens between 18 and 29 routinely turn to online sources, including social networking sites, not only to share files but also to learn about politics and engage in debate (Pew Research Center 2008).

Just as control of knowledge had to be wrested from the medieval monasteries to open new intellectual vistas and allow the slow democratization of society, so an emerging medium might compel a reconsideration of print culture standards for defining knowledge. Likewise, just as Latin was replaced by common dialects such as English and German to advance liberty and human emancipation, so a converged medium might help change and eventually overturn the rationalist paradigm's insistence that verbal language is paramount to or the sole standard of an informed and participating citizenry. Despite its declining market share and, some would say, likely extinction, network news has played a fundamental but underappreciated role in realizing these transformations with inordinate speed.

References

Barnhurst, Kevin G., and Catherine A. Steele. 1997. Image-bite news: The visual coverage of elections on U.S. television, 1968–1992. *Press/Politics* 2(1):40–58.

Benjamin, Daniel J., and Jesse M. Shapiro. 2009. Thin-slice forecasts of gubernatorial elections. *Review of Economics and Statistics* 91(3):523–536.

Bucy, Erik P. 2000. Emotional and evaluative consequences of inappropriate leader displays. *Communication Research* 27(2):194–226.

Bucy, Erik P. 2003. Emotion, presidential communication, and traumatic news: Processing the World Trade Center attacks. *Harvard International Journal of Press/Politics* 8(4):76–96.

Bucy, Erik P., and Kimberly S. Gregson. 2001. Media participation: A legitimizing mechanism of mass democracy. *New Media and Society* 3(3):359–382.

Bucy, Erik P., and Samuel D. Bradley. 2004. Presidential expressions and viewer emotion: Counterempathic responses to televised leader displays. *Social Science Information/Information sur les Sciences Sociales* 43(1):59–94.

Clayman, Steven E. 1995. Defining moments, presidential debates, and the dynamics of quotability. *Journal of Communication* 45(3):118–146.

Drew, Dan D., and David H. Weaver. 2006. Voter learning in the 2004 presidential election: Did the media matter? *Journalism and Mass Communication Quarterly* 83(1):25–42.

Edelman, Murray. 1964. *The symbolic uses of politics.* Urbana: University of Illinois Press.

Givhan, Robin. 2008, January 8. A chink in the steely façade of Hillary Clinton. *Washington Post*, p. C1.

Grabe, Maria Elizabeth, Shuhua Zhou, and Brooke Barnett. 1999. Sourcing and reporting in news magazine programs: *60 Minutes* versus *Hard Copy*. *Journalism and Mass Communication Quarterly* 76(2):293–311.

Graber, Doris A. 2001. *Processing politics: Learning from television in the Internet age.* Chicago: University of Chicago Press.

Graber, Doris A. 1996. Say it with pictures. *Annals of the American Academy of Political and Social Science* 546:85–96.

Hallin, Daniel C. 1992. Sound bite news: Television coverage of elections, 1968–1988. *Journal of Communication* 42(2):5–24.

Hegedus, Chris, and D. Alan Pennebaker. 1993. *The war room.* Santa Monica, CA: Trimark Home Video.

Kamen, Al. 2004, January 21. A meltdown in history. *Washington Post*, p. A25.

Kantor, Jodi. 2008, January 9. A show of emotion that reverberated beyond the campaign. *New York Times,* p. A14.

Klein, Joe. 2006. *Politics lost: How American democracy was trivialized by people who think you're stupid.* New York: Doubleday.

Lanzetta, John T., Dennis G. Sullivan, Roger D. Masters, and Gregory J. McHugo. 1985. Emotional and cognitive responses to televised images of political leaders.

In *Mass media and political thought: An information-processing approach,* ed. Sidney Kraus and Richard M. Perloff, pp. 85–116. Beverly Hills, CA: Sage.

Lehtonen, Jaako. 1988. The information society and the new competence. *American Behavioral Scientist* 32(2):104–111.

Levy, Mark R. 1981. Disdaining the news. *Journal of Communication* 31(3):24–31.

Lichter, S. Robert. 2001. A plague on both parties: Substance and fairness in TV election news. *Harvard International Journal of Press/Politics* 6(3):8–30.

Lowry, Dennis T., and Jon A. Shidler. 1995. The biters and the bitten: An analysis of network TV news bias in campaign '92. *Journalism and Mass Communication Quarterly* 69(2):341–361.

Lowry, Dennis T., and Jon A. Shidler. 1998. The sound bites, the biters, and the bitten: A two-campaign test of the anti-incumbent bias hypothesis in network TV news. *Journalism and Mass Communication Quarterly* 75(4):719–729.

Masters, Roger D., and Denis G. Sullivan. 1993. Nonverbal behavior and leadership: Emotion and cognition in political information processing. In *Explorations in political psychology,* ed. Shanto Iyengar and William J. McGuire, pp. 150–182. Durham, NC: Duke University Press.

Meyrowitz, Joshua. 1985. *No sense of place: The impact of electronic media on social behavior.* New York: Oxford University Press.

Nagourney, Adam. 2004, July 30. Kerry accepts nomination, telling party that he'll restore "trust and credibility." *New York Times,* p. Al.

Neuman, W. Russell. 1986. *The paradox of mass politics: Knowledge and opinion in the American electorate.* Cambridge, MA: Harvard University Press.

Newhagen, John E. 2002. The role of meaning construction in the process of persuasion for viewers of television images. In *The persuasion handbook: Developments in theory and practice,* ed. James. P. Dillard and Michael W. Pau, pp. 729–748. Thousand Oaks, CA: Sage.

Patterson, Thomas E. 1980. *The mass media election: How Americans choose their election.* New York: Praeger.

Pew Research Center. 2008. The Internet gains in politics. Retrieved June 2, 2008, from http://www.pewinternet.org/PPF/r/234/source/rss/reportdisplay.asp. Accessed June 2, 2008.

Project for Excellence in Journalism. 2004. *The state of the news media 2004.* http://www.stateofthenewsmedia.org/. Accessed January 15, 2006.

Putnam, Robert D. 2000. *Bowling alone: The collapse and revival of American community.* New York: Simon and Schuster.

Robinson, Michael J., and Margaret A. Sheehan. 1983. *Over the wire and on TV: CBS and UPI in campaign '80.* New York: Russell Sage Foundation.

Ross, E. 1992, September 25. Networks adjust election coverage. *Christian Science Monitor,* p. 12.

Russomanno, Joseph A., and Stephen E. Everett. 1995. Candidate sound bites: Too much concern over length? *Journal of Broadcasting and Electronic Media* 39(3):408–415.

Scheuer, Jeffrey. 1999. *The sound bite society: Television and the American mind.* New York: Four Walls Eight Windows.

Shields, Stephanie A., and Kathleen A. MacDowell. 1987. "Appropriate" emotion in politics: Judgments of a televised debate. *Journal of Communication* 37(4):78–89.

Steele, Catherine A., and Kevin G. Barnhurst. 1996. The journalism of opinion: Network news coverage of U.S. presidential campaigns, 1968–1988. *Critical Studies in Mass Communication* 13(3):187–209.

Stephens, Mitchell. 1998. *The rise of the image, the fall of the word.* New York: Oxford University Press.

Thomas, Evan. 2004, November 15. Trench warfare. *Newsweek,* pp. 62–81.

Todorov, Alexander, Anesu N. Mandisodza, Amir Goren, and Crystal C. Hall. 2005. Inferences of competence from faces predict election outcomes. *Science,* 308(10):1623–1626.

14

LEARNING ABOUT THE CANDIDATES

Darrell M. West

Editor's Note

"Air Wars" is the name Darrell M. West uses for television advertising in presidential and senatorial election campaigns. The name is very fitting because commercials are the chief strategic tools that candidates employ in their battles to win the nominations and the final elections. Through spot advertisements and longer commercials, each candidate tries to persuade voters that he or she is the most likeable, most qualified, and most electable choice and that opposing candidates are inferior on most scores.

The evidence clearly shows that advertisements set the tone of the campaign and are a major source of information for voters and a key factor in their votes. That is why high-level candidates spend a huge share of their campaign budgets on designing, producing, and airing commercials rather than relying on the free publicity provided by news stories. That is also why there is more truth than ever before to the old adage, "money is the mother's milk of politics."

West was the vice president and director of governance studies at the Brookings Institution in Washington, D.C., when this essay was published. He had previously been a Distinguished Professor of Political Science and Public Policy at Brown University and the director of its Taubman Center for Public Policy. West has been a prolific author, writing books and articles about mass media and elections with a focus on advertising and the corrupting influence of campaign financing. He has also been a frequent political commentator for several major national newspapers and television news outlets.

Source: Darrell M. West, *Air Wars: Television Advertising in Election Campaigns, 1952–2008*, 5th ed., Washington, D.C.: CQ Press, 2010, Chapter 5. Reprinted by permission of CQ Press, a division of SAGE Publications.

Early efforts to study the impact of ads emphasized learning about substantive matters: Do the media provide information that increases voters' knowledge of where candidates stand on the issues? To the pleasant surprise of scholars, research from the 1970s revealed that voters who watched ads got more information than did those exposed only to television news.[1] Experimental work also supported claims about the educational virtues of commercials.[2] Ads did not help candidates create new political images based on personality; rather, political commercials allowed viewers to learn about the issues.

Notwithstanding the undeniable trend of these studies, researchers have persisted in their efforts to examine the effects of advertising. Great changes have taken place in the structure of political campaigns since earlier research was completed. New electoral arenas have arisen that do not have the stabilizing features of past settings. Furthermore, recent campaign experiences run contrary to interpretations that emphasize the educational virtues of commercials. Television is thought to have played a crucial, and not very positive, role in a number of races, a state of affairs that has renewed concern about the power of ads to alter citizens' beliefs.[3]

Indeed, recent studies have found that voters do not often cast ballots based on the issues. Citizens form many impressions during the course of election campaigns, from views about candidates' issue positions and personal characteristics to feelings about the electoral prospects of specific candidates, and those views are decisive. As ads have become more gripping emotionally, *affective models* that describe feelings are crucial to evaluations of candidates' fortunes.[4]

Favorability is an example of an affective dimension important to voter choice. Citizens often support the candidates they like and oppose those they dislike. If they dislike all, they vote for the ones they dislike the least. Anything that raises a candidate's favorability also increases the likelihood of selection.[5] Candidates devote much attention to making themselves appear more likable. Values that are widely shared, such as patriotism and pride in national accomplishments, help candidates increase their favorability ratings among voters. Conversely, hard-hitting ads are used to pinpoint the opposition's flaws.

The opening up of the electoral process has brought new factors such as electability and familiarity to the forefront. *Electability* refers to citizens' perceptions of a candidate's prospects for winning the election in November. Impressions of electability can increase voters' support of a candidate because citizens do not want to waste their votes. *Familiarity* is important as a threshold requirement. Candidates must become known to do well at election time. The development of a campaign structure that encourages less widely known candidates to run makes citizens' assessments of a candidate's prospects a potentially important area of inquiry.

Advertising and the Electoral Context

Past work on television advertising has focused on a particular kind of electoral setting—presidential general elections. For example, Thomas Patterson and Robert McClure's findings were based on the campaign that ended in Richard Nixon's landslide victory over George McGovern. The ads' apparent lack of effect on voters' assessments of the candidates is not surprising in light of the lopsided race and the fact that by the time of the initial survey in September public perceptions of the two candidates had largely been determined. In that situation, it was appropriate for Patterson and McClure to conclude that people "know too much" to be influenced by ads.[6]

However, as Patterson and McClure pointed out, other electoral settings display greater opportunities for advertising to have measurable effects. Nominating campaigns and Senate races show extensive shifts in voters' assessments of the candidates. Presidential nominations often have unfamiliar contenders vying for the votes of citizens who hold few prior beliefs about the candidates. In these settings, television commercials can play a major role in providing crucial information about the candidates.

Advertising is particularly important when news media time is scarce. In 1980, Ken Bode, then a reporter for NBC, recounted a letter written to him by Republican senator Bob Dole of Kansas following his unsuccessful nominating campaign: "Dear Ken, I would appreciate knowing how much coverage my campaign received by NBC from the date of my announcement to my final withdrawal. I've been told my total coverage by NBC amounted to fourteen seconds."[7]

Senate races also have become heavily media oriented. Candidates spend a lot of money on television advertising, and Senate contests have taken on the roller-coaster qualities of nominating affairs. Many Senate elections feature volatile races involving unknown challengers. Because some observers have speculated about the effects of advertising, it is important to study advertising in nominating and Senate campaigns to determine whether its impact varies with the electoral setting. . . .

The Impact of the Campaign

When looking at how ads and the campaign affected voter perceptions of the candidates, it is clear there were important effects. Those who saw Nixon ads in 1972 were more likely to see him as wishing to uphold commitments made to other nations. The same phenomenon emerged in the 1988 nominating process. During that year, exposure to ads influenced people's perceptions of the issue positions of Dukakis (on the military), Gore (on unfair competition from Japan), and George Bush (on deficit reduction). The 1992 race helped viewers understand Buchanan's and Clinton's stances on the economy and

Paul Tsongas's on competition from Japan. Each candidate ran ads that made these subjects central to his campaign.[8] During the general election, Clinton worked hard to stake out claims to particular issues to prevent Republicans from trespassing on traditionally Democratic ground, as Bush had done in 1988 when he campaigned on promises to become the environmental and education president. But Clinton's strategy also created problems for himself. One of the criticisms directed against him in spring focus groups was that he was difficult to pin down: "If you asked his favorite color he'd say 'Plaid,'" stated one focus group participant.[9]

Ads had an impact on viewers' assessments of candidates' images, likability, and electability that was at least as strong as the effect on viewers' assessments of issue positions. In terms of perceptions of likability, commercials had a significant impact in many elections. For Gore and Bush in 2000, ad exposure was related to favorability ratings; the same was true for Buchanan and Perot in 1992 and for Senate candidates in 1974 and 1990. In terms of electability, the strongest ad impact came with Dukakis in the 1988 nominating process, but effects were present for Nixon in 1972, Carter in 1976, Buchanan and Clinton in 1992, and Clinton in 1996. Conversely, people who saw Bush's ads in 1992 had a negative sense of the president's electability.

Some campaigners were able to mold public perceptions of personal traits. Those who watched Carter ads saw him as an able leader, and those who saw Gore ads in 1988 felt he was likely to care about people. Those who watched Clinton ads in the spring of 1992 believed that he was a caring individual. The ads helped create a positive view of his character, which countered the negative coverage received after Gennifer Flowers came forward to claim he had an affair with her.[10]

In the 2000 presidential general election, I looked at the connection between a viewer thinking Gore and Bush, respectively, were electable and that person seeing news and ads for the candidates. Those individuals who saw Gore's ads were more likely to report that he was electable. The same was true for Bush to an even greater extent. In 1996, those who said they saw Clinton's ads were much more likely to cite him as electable, whereas those who saw Dole's ads were significantly more likely to say he was not electable. Seeing Perot's ads or the TV news had no impact on his electability.

The weak results for Perot's ads in 1996 contrast clearly with the situation in 1992. That year, Perot's ads were the most memorable and provided a dramatic boost for the Texan in the closing weeks of the campaign. In contrast, people in 1996 who said they saw Perot's ads were not more likely to recognize him, like him, or feel that he was electable.[11] Part of the problem related to his ad-buy strategy. Unlike in 1992, when he aired $60 million in ads during the last month of the election and dramatically outspent both Clinton and Bush, he did not choose to do this in 1996.

There also were interesting relationships between viewers seeing TV news and candidates' ads and how those viewers saw candidates' personal qualities and political views. In 2000, those who saw Gore's commercials were more likely to see him as providing fiscal discipline and less likely to believe that Bush would do so. However, those who reported seeing national television news concluded the opposite: that Bush would be fiscally responsible and caring and that Gore would not likely be either.[12]

In 2004, ads were linked to changing perceptions of the candidates. Voter impressions shifted during the course of the campaign. Using national surveys undertaken by CBS News/*New York Times*, it is apparent that Kerry was far less known (57 percent recognition level in March 2004) than Bush (82 percent recognition), but became about as well known as the president by the end of October. Throughout most of the campaign, Bush held a higher favorability rating than did Kerry.

From the beginning of the general election in spring 2004, Bush attacked Kerry as a wishy-washy politician who told voters what they wanted to hear. This perception stuck with voters as the polling data revealed that Bush consistently had a huge advantage over Kerry in people's views that he says what he believes. For example, in mid-October, 59 percent portrayed Bush as saying what he believed, compared to 37 percent who felt that way about Kerry.

Bush also neutralized a traditional Democratic strength, that of being seen as caring and compassionate and understanding the needs of ordinary people. Ever since Herbert Hoover's inaction in the face of the Great Depression in the 1930s, voters have seen Democrats as caring more about ordinary folks than Republicans. However, on this key dimension, Bush was able to narrow the perception gap. Whereas in mid-October 51 percent thought Kerry understood the needs of everyday people, 44 percent felt that way about Bush. For a president whose tax cut policies had benefited wealthy Americans and who had passed billions in tax breaks for corporations, this represented a major victory. In addition, Bush tarred Kerry with the code word "liberal," similar to what his father had done to Dukakis in 1988. At the beginning of the general election, 39 percent of registered voters saw Kerry as a liberal; by mid-October, this number had risen to 56 percent.

In short, Bush used attack ads to portray Kerry unfavorably. He characterized the Massachusetts Democrat as a doctrinaire liberal who was also wishy-washy and unprincipled. These two critiques are noteworthy because in some respects, they are inconsistent: It is difficult to be simultaneously wishy-washy and a doctrinaire liberal. However, by repeating these messages over and over, Bush was able to reinforce these perceptions about Kerry.

In 2008, Obama and McCain started out with similar recognition and favorability levels. . . . [Seventy] percent of registered voters in a January 2008 national survey recognized McCain, whereas 71 percent recognized Obama. McCain had a 57 percent favorability rating, compared to Obama's 55 percent. By the end of the general election, however, Obama held a ten-point favorability advantage over McCain. The decline of foreign policy issues such as the Iraq War and international terrorism and the rise of domestic economic issues clearly played to Obama's advantage. Public opinion surveys demonstrated that voters perceived Democrats as having a stronger capacity to handle economic issues than Republicans. Since the terrain was favorable to Democrats, the public opinion climate helped create sympathetic feelings toward the Democratic nominee.

Obama's ads played on voter anxiety about the economy by reminding people that Republicans had been in charge for eight years and that the economy had deteriorated during that time. The United States had gone from a $1 trillion budget surplus to a deficit of the same size. The combination of a weak economy and strong communications effort helped people see Obama as a caring and compassionate individual who would understand their needs. This neutralized McCain's experience advantage and offset the GOP nominee's virtue of being seen as a stronger commander in chief.

Ads and the Vote

Recent campaigns offer interesting opportunities to investigate how ads affect the vote.[13] . . .

In 2004, voters started the general election showing an eight-percentage-point lead for President Bush (by a 46 to 38 percent margin). The president's advantage reflected several strengths. At that point, Kerry was not very well known. The president was also aided by voter perceptions that he was a strong leader serving in troubled times. But by the end of July, right after the Democratic convention, Kerry moved to his first lead in the race. According to the CBS News/*New York Times* national surveys, Kerry was supported by 48 percent of voters, compared to 43 percent supporting Bush. Kerry's rise reflected a well-received convention acceptance speech and the positive press coverage that accompanied this presentation.

However, August proved to be a very difficult month for Kerry. His campaign was not able to go on the air with commercials because he had exhausted his nomination funds and did not want to use his scarce general election dollars. At the same time, outside groups such as the Swift Boat Veterans for Truth were attacking Kerry's Vietnam record and alleging he was not trustworthy. Under these circumstances, he was not able to sustain his advantage. By September, Bush had regained the lead (50 to 41 percent).

Throughout the remainder of the fall, though, the two candidates were locked in a tight race. Kerry's support rose slightly during the three presidential debates; his strong performance boosted voter backing of his candidacy. But Bush maintained his own support by attacking Kerry's liberal record and inconsistent stances on terrorism. One ad entitled "Wolves" started airing October 22. It showed a pack of wolves running through woods, while a female announcer spoke of the dangers confronting the world and how "Kerry and liberals in Congress" had voted to cut spending on intelligence-gathering in the 1990s. The commercial claimed that weakness invited danger and encouraged those who wanted to harm America. By the end of the campaign, Bush's post-debate slump had disappeared: On a 51 to 48 percent popular vote, Bush beat Kerry and won reelection.

In April 2008, Obama started with a 51 to 40 percent lead over McCain. As shown in Table 14–1, he was able to maintain this lead until early September, when McCain for the first time edged to a two-point lead. Russia had invaded Georgia in August, and McCain had taken a very tough foreign policy stance, calling for cutting ties to Russia and enlarging NATO to include Eastern European countries, a position strongly opposed by Russia.

However, this lead did not hold up for long. In mid-September, major financial institutions melted down, which put economic news back on the front page. In short order, the national government was forced to put public monies into major banks, and Congress enacted a landmark $700 billion financial rescue program. Between September 12 to 16, Obama surged back to a five-point lead, and soon his margin was up to double-digits. In the last survey, Obama led McCain by 51 to 40 percent, identical to the margin he had held in April.

Table 14–1   Voter Preferences during the 2008 Campaign

	April 3	May 3	July 7–12	July 31–Aug. 5	Aug. 29–31	Sept. 5–7	Sept. 12–16	Sept. 27–30	Oct. 10–13	Oct. 19–22	Oct. 25–29
McCain	40%	40%	39%	39%	40%	46%	43%	40%	39%	39%	40%
Obama	51	51	45	45	48	44	48	49	53	52	51
Unsure	9	9	16	16	12	10	9	11	8	9	9

Source: CBS News/*New York Times* national surveys.

Note: Entries indicate the percentage of voter support for each candidate.

Conclusion

To summarize, ads are one of the major ways in which citizens learn about the candidates. From advertisements, voters develop perceptions about personal qualities, values, electability, and issue positions. Not only are these perceptions important for the candidates, they affect the vote. Citizens often support those candidates they like, with whom they share values and who they feel are electable.

Ads do not operate autonomously. People bring prior beliefs such as party attachments, ideological stances, and life experiences relating to their age, gender, education, and race. For this reason, candidates undertake detailed research on voter opinions. Campaign commercials must dovetail with a person's background and political orientation for an ad to be effective. If a spot does not resonate with people, it will not inform viewers in the manner desired by candidates.

Notes

1. Thomas Patterson and Robert McClure, *The Unseeing Eye* (New York: Putnam's, 1976).
2. Ronald Mulder, "The Effects of Televised Political Ads in the 1975 Chicago Mayoral Election," *Journalism Quarterly* 56 (1979): 25–36; Charles Atkin, Lawrence Bowen, Oguz Nayman, and Kenneth Sheinkopf, "Quality versus Quantity in Televised Political Ads," *Public Opinion Quarterly* 37 (1973): 209–224.
3. Kathleen Jamieson, *Packaging the Presidency,* 2nd ed. (New York: Oxford University Press, 1992); Edwin Diamond and Stephen Bates, *The Spot* (Cambridge: MIT Press, 1984); L. Patrick Devlin, "Contrasts in Presidential Campaign Commercials of 1988," *American Behavioral Scientist* 32 (1989): 389–414.
4. Larry Bartels, *Presidential Primaries and the Dynamics of Public Choice* (Princeton: Princeton University Press, 1988); Edie Goldenberg and Michael Traugott, *Campaigning for Congress* (Washington, D.C.: CQ Press, 1984), 85–91.
5. See Stanley Kelley Jr. and Thad Mirer, "The Simple Act of Voting," *American Political Science Review* 68 (1974): 572–591.
6. Quoted in Patterson and McClure, *The Unseeing Eye,* 130.
7. On hearing this story at a post-election campaign seminar, John Anderson quipped that Dole's fourteen seconds consisted of a news report about his car breaking down in New Hampshire. Both stories are taken from Jonathan Moore, ed., *Campaign for President: 1980 in Retrospect* (Cambridge, Mass.: Ballinger, 1981), 129–130.
8. Interview with Elizabeth Kolbert, July 20, 1992.
9. "How He Won," *Newsweek,* November/December 1992 (special issue), 40.
10. Marion Just, Ann Crigler, Dean Alger, Timothy Cook, Montague Kern, and Darrell M. West, *Cross Talk* (Chicago: University of Chicago Press, 1996).
11. For question wording, see Darrell M. West, *Air Wars,* 2nd ed. (Washington, D.C.: CQ Press, 1997), chap. 6, note 21.
12. Ibid., note 21.
13. Marion Just, Ann Crigler, Dean Alger, Timothy Cook, Montague Kern, and Darrell M. West, *Cross Talk* (Chicago: University of Chicago Press, 1996.)

15

THE MISCAST INSTITUTION

Thomas E. Patterson

Editor's Note

There is much "out of order" in presidential election campaigns. The mass media are miscast into filling the political role that political parties ought to play. The norms of journalism and the commercial goals of the press are at odds with the political values that should guide election campaigns in democracies. The candidates are miscast into serving a public relations function designed to snare, rather than enlighten, voters. This forces these candidates to make and keep politically disastrous promises. The voters are equally miscast. They cannot fill the void of political savvy left by ill-functioning parties. Their voting choices, therefore, lack sound political grounding. The news media are neither inclined nor equipped to supply them with the type of information they need to vote intelligently.

This study, drawn from his book *Out of Order,* was written while Thomas E. Patterson was a professor of political science at the Maxwell School of Citizenship and Public Affairs at Syracuse University. The book received the American Political Science Association's Graber Award as the best book of the decade in political communication. The American Association for Public Opinion Research named an earlier Patterson book, *The Unseeing Eye: The Myth of Television Power in National Politics,* published in 1976 with Robert McClure, one of the fifty most influential books about public opinion in the past half century. Patterson has also published two acclaimed American government texts.

The United States is the only democracy that organizes its national election campaign around the news media. Even if the media did not want the responsibility for organizing the campaign, it is theirs by virtue of an election system built upon entrepreneurial candidacies, floating voters, freewheeling interest groups, and weak political parties.

It is an unworkable arrangement: the press is not equipped to give order and direction to a presidential campaign. And when we expect it to do so, we set ourselves up for yet another turbulent election.

The campaign is chaotic largely because the press is not a political institution and has no capacity for organizing the election in a coherent manner. . . .

The news is a highly refracted version of reality. . . . The press's restless search for the riveting story works against its intention to provide the voters with a reliable picture of the campaign. It is a formidable job to present society's problems in ways that voters can understand and act upon. The news media cannot do the job consistently well. Walter Lippmann put it plainly when he said that a press-based politics "is not workable. And when you consider the nature of news, it is not even thinkable."[1] . . .

* * *

The press's role in presidential elections is in large part the result of a void that was created when America's political parties surrendered their control over the nominating process. Through 1968, nominations were determined by the parties' elected and organizational leaders. Primary elections were held in several states, but they were not decisive. A candidate could demonstrate through the primaries that he had a chance of winning the fall election, as John Kennedy, the nation's first Catholic president, did with his primary victories in Protestant West Virginia and Wisconsin in 1960.

Nevertheless, real power rested with the party leadership rather than the primary electorate. . . . The nominating system changed fundamentally after the bitter presidential campaign of 1968. . . .

. . . [I]n the Democratic party [it] changed from a mixed system of one-third primary states and two-thirds convention states, controlled by party elites, to a reformed system in which nearly three-fourths of the delegates to the national convention were chosen by the voters in primary elections. Many Democratic state legislatures passed primary-election laws, thereby binding Republicans to the change as well.[2] Serious contenders for nomination would now have to appeal directly to the voters. . . .

Jimmy Carter's efforts in the year preceding his 1976 presidential nomination exemplified the new reality. Instead of making the traditional rounds among party leaders, Carter traveled about the country meeting with journalists. When the New York Times's R. W. Apple wrote a front-page story about Carter's bright prospects one Sunday in October 1975, his outlook indeed brightened. Other journalists followed with their Carter stories and helped to propel the long-shot Georgian to his party's nomination. Carter would not have won under the old rules.

Of course, the news media's influence in presidential selection had not been inconsequential in earlier times, and in a few instances it had even been crucial. Wendell Willkie was an obscure businessman until the publisher Henry Luce decided that he would make a good president. Luce used his magazines *Time, Life,* and *Fortune* to give Willkie the prominence necessary to win the Republican nomination in 1940. . . .

Nevertheless, the media's role today in helping to establish the election agenda is different from what it was in the past. Once upon a time, the press occasionally played an important part in the nomination of presidential candidates. Now its function is always a key one. The news media do not entirely determine who will win the nomination, but no candidate can succeed without the press. The road to nomination now runs through the newsrooms.

Reform Democrats did not take the character of the news media into account when they changed the presidential election process in the early 1970s. Their goal was admirable enough. The system required a change that would give the voters' preferences more weight in the nominating process. But the reformers disregarded the desirability of also creating a process that was deliberative and would allow for the reflective choice of a nominee. In their determination to abolish the old system, they gave almost no thought to the dynamics of the new one. . . .

The modern campaign requires the press to play a constructive role. When the parties established a nominating process that is essentially a free-for-all between self-generated candidacies, the task of bringing the candidates and voters together in a common effort was superimposed on a media system that was built for other purposes. The press was no longer asked only to keep an eye out for wrongdoing and to provide a conduit for candidates to convey their messages to the voters. It was also expected to guide the voters' decisions. It was obliged to inspect the candidates' platforms, judge their fitness for the nation's highest office, and determine their electability—functions the parties had performed in the past. In addition, the press had to carry out these tasks in a way that would enable the voters to exercise *their* discretion effectively in the choice of nominees.

The columnist Russell Baker hinted at these new responsibilities when he described the press as the "Great Mentioner." The nominating campaign of a candidate who is largely ignored by the media is almost certainly futile, while the campaign of one who receives close attention gets an important boost. In this sense, the press performs the party's traditional role of screening potential nominees for the presidency—deciding which ones are worthy of serious consideration by the electorate and which ones can be dismissed as also-rans. The press also helps to establish the significance of the primaries and caucuses, deciding which ones are critical and how well the candidates must perform in them to be taken seriously.

The press's responsibilities, however, go far beyond news decisions that allocate coverage among the contending contests and candidates. The de facto premise of today's nominating system is that the media will direct the voters toward a clear understanding of what is at stake in choosing one candidate rather than another. Whereas the general election acquires stability from the competition between the parties, the nominating stage is relatively undefined. It features self-starting candidates, all of whom clamor for public attention, each claiming to be the proper representative of his party's legacy and future. It is this confusing situation that the press is expected to clarify.[3]

A press-based system seems as if it ought to work. The public gets a nearly firsthand look at the candidates. The alternatives are out in the open for all to see. What could be better?

The belief that the press can substitute for political institutions is widespread. Many journalists, perhaps most of them, assume they can do it effectively.[4] Scholars who study the media also accept the idea that the press can organize elections. Every four years, they suggest that the campaign could be made coherent if the media would only report it differently.[5]

However, the press merely appears to have the capacity to organize the voters' alternatives in a coherent way. The news creates a pseudocommunity: citizens feel that they are part of a functioning whole until they try to act upon their news-created awareness. . . . The press can raise the public's consciousness, but the news itself cannot organize public opinion in any meaningful way. . . .

The proper organization of electoral opinion requires an institution with certain characteristics. It must be capable of seeing the larger picture—of looking at the world as a whole and not in small pieces. It must have incentives that cause it to identify and organize those interests that are making demands for policy representation. And it must be accountable for its choices, so that the public can reward it when satisfied and force amendments when dissatisfied.[6] The press has none of these characteristics. The media has its special strengths, but they do not include these strengths.

The press is a very different kind of organization from the political party, whose role it acquired. A party is driven by the steady force of its traditions and constituent interests. . . . The press, in contrast, is "a restless beacon."[7] Its concern is the new, the unusual, and the sensational. Its agenda shifts abruptly when a new development breaks.[8] The party has the incentive—the possibility of acquiring political power—to give order and voice to society's values. Its raison d'être is to articulate interests and to forge them into a winning coalition. The press has no such incentive and no such purpose. Its objective is the discovery and development of good stories.[9] . . .

The press is also not politically accountable. The political party is made accountable by a formal mechanism—elections. The vote gives officeholders a reason to act in the majority's interest, and it offers citizens an opportunity to boot from office anyone they feel has failed them. Thousands of elected officials have lost their jobs this way. The public has no comparable hold on the press. Journalists are neither chosen by the people nor removable by them. Irate citizens may stop watching a news program or buying a newspaper that angers them, but no major daily newspaper or television station has ever gone out of business as a result.

Other democracies have recognized the inappropriateness of press-based elections. Although national voting in all Western democracies is media-centered in the sense that candidates depend primarily on mass communication to reach the voters, no other democracy has a system in which the press fills the role traditionally played by the political party.[10] Journalists in other democracies actively participate in the campaign process, but their efforts take place within an electoral structure built around political institutions. In the United States, however, national elections are referendums in which the candidates stand alone before the electorate and have no choice but to filter their appeals through the lens of the news media.

. . . [T]he presidential election system has become unpredictable. The nominating phase is especially volatile; with relatively small changes in luck, timing, or circumstance, several nominating races might have turned out differently. There is no purpose behind an electoral system in which the vote is impulsive and the outcome can hinge on random circumstance or minor issues. Stability and consistency are the characteristics of a properly functioning institution. Disorder is a sure sign of a defective system. Although pundits have explained the unpredictability of recent elections in terms of events and personalities peculiar to each campaign, the answer lies deeper—in the electoral system itself. It places responsibilities on its principals—the voters, the candidates, and the journalists—that they cannot meet or that magnify their shortcomings.

* * *

The voters' problem is one of overload. The presidential election system places extraordinary demands on voters, particularly during the nominating phase. These races often attract a large field of contenders, most of whom are newcomers to national politics. The voters are expected to grasp quickly what the candidates represent, but the task is daunting. . . . Nor can it be assumed that the campaign itself will inform the electorate. At the time of nomination, half or more of the party's rank-and-file voters had no clear idea of where Carter (1976), Mondale (1984), Bush and Dukakis (1988), and Clinton (1992) stood on various issues.[11] . . . The Republicans' nomination of Ronald Reagan in 1980 is particularly revealing of the public's lack of information. . . . When asked to place Reagan on an ideological scale, 43 percent said they did not know where to place him, 10 percent said he was a liberal, and 6 percent identified him as a moderate.[12]

Nominating campaigns are imposing affairs. They are waged between entrepreneurial candidates whose support is derived from groups and elites joined together solely for that one election. Primary elections are not in the least bit like general elections, which offer a choice between a "Republican" and a "Democrat." If these labels mean less today than in the past, they still represent a voting guideline for many Americans. But a primary election presents to voters little more than a list of names.[13] There is no established label associated with these names, no stable core of supporters, and typically the appeals that dominate one election are unlike those emphasized in others. . . . Voters are not stupid, but they have been saddled with an impossible task. The news media consistently overestimate the voters' knowledge of the candidates and the speed with which they acquire it. . . .

Voters would not necessarily be able to make the optimal choice even if they had perfect information. A poll of New Hampshire voters in 1976 reportedly showed that when each Democratic candidate was paired off successively with each of the others, Jimmy Carter came out near the bottom. . . . Yet he won the primary. New Hampshire's voters divided their support somewhat evenly among the other Democratic contenders, enabling the less favored choice, Carter, to finish first with 28 percent of the vote. The possibility that someone other than the consensual alternative will emerge victorious exists in every multicandidate primary.

There was a time when America's policymakers understood that the voters should not be assigned this type of election decision, even if they were able to make it. Citizens are not Aristotles who fill their time studying politics. People have full lives to lead: children to raise, jobs to perform, skills to acquire, leisure activities to pursue. People have little time for attending to politics in their daily lives, and their appetite for political information is weak. . . . How, then, can we expect primary-election voters to inform themselves about a half-dozen little-known contenders and line them up on the basis of policy and other factors in order to make an informed choice?

Of course, voters *will* choose. Each state has a primary or a caucus, and enough voters participate to make it look as though a reasoned choice has been made. In reality, the voters act on the basis of little information and without the means to select the optimal candidate in a crowded race.

The modern system of picking presidents also places burdens on the candidates that they should not be required to carry. Some of the demands are grotesque. A U.S. presidential campaign requires nearly a two-year stint in the bowels of television studios, motel rooms, and fast-food restaurants. . . .

The system can make it difficult for a person who holds high office to run for nomination. In 1980, Howard Baker's duties as Senate minority leader kept him from campaigning effectively, and he was easily defeated. . . . The strongest candidate for nomination is often someone, like Carter in 1976 and Reagan in 1980, who is out of office. . . .

Advocates of the present system argue that the grueling campaign is an appropriate test of a candidate's ability to withstand the rigors of the presidency. This proposition is a dubious one. It is easy to imagine someone who would make a superb president but who hates a year-long campaign effort or would wilt under its demands. . . .

The current system makes it impossible for the public to choose its president from the full range of legitimate contenders. The demands of a present-day nominating campaign require candidates to decide far in advance of the presidential election day whether they will make the run. If they wait too long to get into the race, they will find their funding and organization to be hopelessly inadequate. Moreover, a candidate who wins the nomination but then loses the general election is likely to acquire a loser's image which may hinder any subsequent run for the presidency. As a consequence, any potential candidate is forced into a strategic decision long before the campaign formally begins. . . .

For those who run, the electoral system is a barrier to true leadership. Candidates are self-starters who organize their own campaigns. . . . As entrepreneurs, they look for support from wherever they can plausibly get it. In the past, the parties buffered the relationship between candidates and groups. Today, it is very difficult for candidates to ignore the demands of interest groups or to confine them to their proper place. Indeed, the modern candidate has every reason for tirelessly courting interest groups—nominating campaigns *are* factional politics. . . .

Contrary to the press's chronic complaint, the central problem of the modern campaign is not that presidential candidates make promises they do not intend to keep; instead, it is that candidates make scores of promises they ought not to make but must try to keep.[14] Politicians with a reputation for breaking promises do not get very far. They attract votes by making commitments and fulfilling them. But it is the nature of the modern campaign to encourage them to overpromise. In this sense, the campaign brings them *too* close to the public they serve. . . .

Politics, like the marketplace, cannot function without ambition. The challenge, as the political scientist James Ceaser notes, is "to discover some way to create a degree of harmony between behavior that satisfies personal ambition and behavior that promotes the public good."[15] All of the nation's great presidents—Washington, Jefferson, Jackson, Lincoln, Franklin D. Roosevelt—were men of towering ambition, but their drive was directed toward constructive leadership.

The electoral reforms of the early 1970s have served to channel ambition in the wrong direction. Today's nominating system is a wide-open process that forces candidates into petty forms of politics. Without partisan differences to separate them, candidates for nomination must find other ways to distinguish themselves from competitors. They often rely on personality appeals of the ingratiating kind. . . .

An electoral system should strengthen the character of the office that it is designed to fill. The modern system of electing presidents undermines the presidential office.[16] The writers of the Constitution believed that unrestrained politicking encouraged demagoguery and special-interest politics,[17] and would degenerate eventually into majority tyranny. If we know now that the Framers were wrong in their belief in the inevitability of a tyrannical majority, we also know that they were right in their belief that an overemphasis on campaigning results in excessive appeals to self-interest and momentary passions.

More than in the candidates or the voters, the problem of the modern presidential campaign lies in the role assigned to the press. Its traditional role is that of a watchdog. In the campaign, this has meant that journalists have assumed responsibility for protecting the public against deceitful, corrupt, or incompetent candidates. The press still plays this watchdog role, and necessarily so. This vital function, however, is different from the role that was thrust on the press when the nominating system was opened wide in the early 1970s.

The new role conflicts with the old one. The critical stance of the watchdog is not to be confused with the constructive task of the coalition-builder. The new role requires the press to act in constructive ways to bring candidates and voters together.

The press has never fully come to grips with the contradictions between its newly acquired and traditional roles. New responsibilities have been imposed on top of older orientations. . . . If the media are capable of organizing presidential choice in a meaningful way, it would be despite the fact that the media were not designed for this purpose. . . . The public schools, for example, have been asked to compensate for the breakup of the traditional American family. The prospects for success are as hopeless as the task is thankless. The same is true of the press in its efforts to fill the role once played by the political party. . . . [T]he press is not a substitute for political institutions. A press-based electoral system is not a suitable basis for that most pivotal of all decisions, the choice of a president.

Notes

1. Walter Lippmann, *Public Opinion* (1922; reprint, New York: Free Press, 1965), p. 229.
2. William Crotty and John S. Jackson III, *Presidential Primaries and Nominations* (Washington, D.C.: American Enterprise Institute, 1977), pp. 44–49.
3. Michael J. Robinson, "Television and American Politics: 1956–1976," in *Reader in Public Opinion and Communication,* 3rd ed., ed. Morris Janowitz and Paul Hirsch (New York: Free Press, 1981), p. 109.
4. See "The Press and the Presidential Campaign, 1988" (Seminar proceedings of the American Press Institute, Reston, Va., December 6, 1988).
5. Ibid.
6. See Everett Carll Ladd, *American Political Parties* (New York: Norton, 1970), p. 2.
7. Lippmann, *Public Opinion,* p. 229.
8. Richard Davis, *The Press and American Politics* (New York: Longman, 1992), pp. 21–27.
9. James David Barber, "Characters in the Campaign: The Literary Problem," in *Race for the Presidency,* ed. James David Barber (Englewood Cliffs, N.J.: Prentice-Hall, 1978), pp. 114–17.
10. Holli Semetko, Jay G. Blumler, Michael Gurevitch, and David H. Weaver, with Steve Barkin and G. Cleveland Wilhoit, *The Formation of Campaign Agendas* (Hillsdale, N.J.: Lawrence Erlbaum, 1991), pp. 3, 4.
11. See, for example, Thomas E. Patterson, *The Mass Media Election* (New York: Praeger, 1980), p. 167, and Paul Taylor, *See How They Run* (New York: Knopf, 1990), pp. 202–03.
12. Scott Keeter and Cliff Zukin, *Uninformed Choice: The Failure of the New Presidential Nominating System* (New York: Praeger, 1983), pp. 110, 136.
13. Austin Ranney, *Channels of Power* (New York: Basic Books, 1983), p. 93.
14. Theodore Lowi, *The Personal President: Power Invested, Promise Unfulfilled* (Ithaca, N.Y.: Cornell University Press, 1985), p. 11.
15. James W. Ceaser, *Presidential Selection: Theory and Development* (Princeton, N.J.: Princeton University Press, 1979), p. 11.
16. Ibid., p. 310.
17. Ibid., pp. 82–83.

16

NEW MEDIA AND THE REVITALISATION OF POLITICS

Rachel Gibson

Editor's Note

Patterson's negative views about news media campaign coverage, set forth in chapter 15, are counterbalanced by the far more positive views of Internet scholars who envision a new age of popular participation in government, especially in election campaigns. Political scientist Rachel Gibson, a British scholar, talks about "citizen campaigns" and uses Barack Obama's 2008 presidential campaign as an example. She considers it a model for major changes in campaigns and the information flows that they generate and that nourish them. Average citizens have resumed their role as active participants and have become powerful forces that shape election outcomes.

Rachel Gibson was a professor of political science at the Institute for Social Change at the University of Manchester when this essay was completed. Scholars at the institute are drawn from multiple disciplines and focus their studies on the causes and consequences of social change. Gibson had previously held an appointment as a professor of new media studies at the University of Leicester. Research fellowships had taken her to other European countries and to Australia. She was a principal investigator on the Australian Election Study and the Australian Survey of Social Attitudes. She has been a leading scholar in Internet research of political messages.

Introduction

 . . . [T]here has been a significant decline in the levels of support and popular trust enjoyed by our representative institutions and elected officials in recent decades (Norris 1999; Pharr and Putnam 2000), particularly in respect to parties' civic strength and levels of voter attachment (Dalton and Wattenberg 2001).

Source: Excerpted from Rachel Gibson, "New Media and the Revitalisation of Politics," in *Representation,* 45:3 (September 2009): 289–99. Reprinted by permission of Taylor & Francis Group, http://www.informaworld.com.

My purpose here, then, is to ask whether the new information and communication technologies (ICTs), particularly the newer user-driven applications synonymous with the 'Web 2.0' era, offer the possibility for a rejuvenation of formal politics, *sui generis* of the debate over the scale and particular sources of the problem. In a nutshell, do the new technologies of blogs, social networking and video-sharing sites present politicians with new and meaningful ways to stimulate popular interest and participation in established politics and the representative process? To address this question we take evidence from one of the most acclaimed e-campaigns to date, that of the Democratic nominee Barack Obama's in his bid for the US Presidency in 2008. Without wishing to steal too much thunder from our conclusions, it can be revealed at this point that the answer arrived at is a tentative yes: democratic benefits do appear to be associated with the use of Web 2.0 tools, although one must remember that even in e-politics, context is king. . . . [T]ranslated into offline mobilisation . . . these efforts helped to sustain him in the race, if to not win the election itself. The adoption and adaptation of these strategies, therefore, would understandably be of interest to politicians and parties around the world. Here we seek to identify what lay at the heart of Obama's successful use of the new media in 2008 and how they might be of utility for British parties in 2010.

The Problem: Media Culpa?

Before turning to examine the idea of e-democracy as a 'rescue remedy' for contemporary politics, let me first summarise the key points of the critique of . . . the role of the media in fostering the growing anti-politics culture. While the main source of the growing disenchantment and even hatred of politics and politicians is located within the political class itself and its zeal for outsourcing key governing tasks in recent years—a practice that has giv[en] rise to 'a form of decision-making without full democratic accountability'— the media and particularly television are also to bear significant responsibility for the current levels of discontent. Echoing the criticisms of a number of American authors from Patterson (1993) to Putnam (2000), the electronic media are regarded as complicit in fostering the general disaffection and cynicism toward all things political. Through its 'dumbing down' of news content, fusing of commentary and reporting and concentration on the competitive, scandalous and personality-led aspects of politics rather than the substantive issues at stake, the media are seen to have both trivialised and tarnished the practice of politics in the public mind. This hollowing-out of serious debate has been accompanied by the adoption of more adversarial interview tactics by journalists in interviewing politicians. Such methods, while they might bolster the integrity and independence of the fourth estate, only serve to deepen the culture of contempt towards politicians in the long run, it is argued, as the 'default' message transmitted to the public is that politicians are withholding the truth from you, the listener/viewer.

While this notion of a media-driven malaise has been countered by a number of scholars who see its influence as more limited and even positive or benign (Brians and Wattenberg 1996; Norris 1999; Patterson and McClure 1976), the idea that the established media have not always served as a force for the democratic good is one that has taken firm root within academic and popular discourse over recent decades. Indeed the perceived association between mass media and democratic decline goes some way towards explaining the highly enthusiastic reception that the new media, in the shape of the Internet, received in the early 1990s. As use of the digital communication technologies began to spread across the demos, cyber-optimists such as Howard Rheingold, Nicholas Negroponte and Amitai Etzioni were quick to identify their capacity for devolving power to citizens and strengthening civic ties and networks (Negroponte 1995; Etzioni and Etzioni 1997). Despite facing criticism from cyber-pessimists who predicted instead the fragmentation and enervation of the citizen body as new ICTs spread across society, and also from more empirically-driven cyber-sceptics who argued against any significant changes taking place in either direction, promoters of e-democracy appear to have had their hopes revived with the arrival of the Web 2.0 era. These new user-driven modes of Internet interaction are seen as promoting the voice of the mass over established elites (Surowiecki 2005; Grannick 2006; Leadbeater 2007). Blogging and social networking tools are seen to hold great promise for reviving democratic practice in particular. In the news reporting context, blogs are seen to provide a low-cost means of publishing news and alternative perspectives, giving greater prominence to citizen journalists vis-à-vis established media pundits (Deuze 2003). Aggregative feed services give the masses an ability to select and edit their news content, removing or at least reducing the agenda-setting power of a few unelected gatekeepers sitting atop centralised media conglomerates based in capital cities. In the civic realm, social networking sites offer organisations the opportunity to mobilise quickly at the national and international level around a single issue and then disperse (Pickerill 2004; Pickerill et al. 2008; Rheingold 2003). In short, compared with previous forms of media, the Internet is seen to offer a new opportunity to spread 'power to the people' and thus present the possibility for a serious challenge, if not an antidote, to current anti-politics woes.

The Solution: New Media Campaigning Obama-style?

The question to be addressed here is the extent to which such expectations of the new media are indeed justified. Can these new forms of web-enabled activism really offer a way to engage and re-engage voters behaviourally in politics, and attitudinally inject a new sense of optimism and trust into politicians and our system of representative government? Clearly addressing the question through an audit and assessment of the array of e-democracy initiatives that parties, parliaments and governments in the UK and elsewhere have undertaken is beyond the scope of this article. What is possible, however, is a more focused account of one arena of formal political activity—that of the election campaign—where it does appear from recent events in the US that the new media are being used to activate voters, and where some genuine revitalising potential for democracy appears to exist. We turn here to examine these events more closely, paying particular attention to the tools used by the Obama campaign team and the type of participatory involvement they stimulated. Finally we ask whether they can work outside of the American context?

The growth of 'bottom-up' campaigns

The roots, if not the birth, of citizen-campaigning can be traced to the arrival of Howard Dean on the political landscape of the US in 2004. Despite ultimately failing to gain his party's nomination, his rise from unknown governor of a small north-eastern state to front-runner status in the Democratic primaries in late 2003 marked for many a 'coming of age' of the Internet as a political medium. Although his uncompromising anti-war message struck a strong chord with party activists, his ability to raise funds and volunteers was strongly linked to his strategic use of the Internet. It was his leverage of 'mousepads' as well as 'shoe leather,' as one former campaign worker put it, that succeeded in putting Dean ahead (Teachout and Streeter 2007). Central to the campaign's success was its 'Dean for America' blog and email lists, which according to its national director Joe Trippi were critical in personalising relationships with supporters and developing a sense of joint-ownership of the Dean candidacy, foreshadowing the 'Yes we can!' philosophy of Barack Obama. Indeed Trippi, in his account of his experiences during that campaign, talks extensively about the way in which the technology was explicitly used to break down the 'us and them' mentality that had dominated previous presidential campaigning 'war rooms' and establish a new grass- or netroots supporter-led model (Trippi 2004).

Although Trippi and Dean may have been the first effective users of new ICTs to build a citizen-campaign network, the Obama team operating in the new Web 2.0 era arguably took it to new and dizzying heights. Trippi himself captured the escalation in operations very succinctly when he observed that if the Dean campaign was the Wright brothers of 'bottom-up' campaigns, as he terms it, then that of the Illinois senator has been Apollo 11 (Trippi 2008). The widening of the campaign organisational base to encompass a host of ordinary citizens through the new forms of social media proved to be one of the hallmarks of the campaign. At the heart of the operation and central to the promoting the grassroots online efforts was the 'MyBO' space built into the official website. Here a range of self-organising tools were made available to users that allowed them to sign up as mini-campaign managers. They could establish a fundraising page, start a campaign blog, set up a political group and recruit members or simply email a prepared message out to their online social networks to advertise Obama's policy positions. At a later stage in the campaign, Democrat voter databases were even opened up to registered supporters to download coordinates for local area canvassing. The campaign also deployed and made use of externally developed software to organise its fieldwork such as Central Desktop, to recruit thousands of precinct campaign volunteers in advance of the 'super Tuesday' primaries. In the last stages of the campaign attention shifted to mobile phones with the 'Call Friends' application being rolled out for download to I-phones. The software effectively converted the phone into a personal campaign tool, with address books becoming databanks for the targeted messaging of friends and family to urge them to vote for Obama. As the campaign blog pointed out, this would generate thousands of additional personal contacts in key swing states, some of which might then go on to generate votes.

Outside these campaign-sponsored initiatives, citizen and candidates' use of third-party-provided platforms expanded dramatically in the 2008 election cycle. YouTube in particular proved to be a highly popular tool for the distribution of official and also non-official political advertising to a worldwide audience. The 37-minute 'More Perfect Union' speech given by Obama in March 2008, designed to address the growing tensions over the racially charged statements of his former pastor, Revd Jeremiah Wright, became the most popular clip on the US video channel soon after it was posted and was viewed almost five million times prior to the election (Vargas 2008a). Efforts beyond Obama's formal video production unit also proved highly popular, with one anonymously posted anti–Hillary Clinton clip, portraying her as a 'Big Brother' figure as well as the more light-hearted 'Obama girl' also gaining several million hits. YouTube was also notable in providing an alternative forum for candidate debates and promoting 'ordinary' voters' questions during the 2008 primary season, although it did utilise the power of the mainstream media to promote itself to a wider audience, working with CNN and an editorial team of established journalists.

Other examples of new media opportunities that allowed individuals to assume a more directing or organising role in the campaign occurred via initiatives such as 'Voter-Voter,' a US-based site that took the YouTube model one step further by allowing individuals to upload their home-made campaign ads, select a target audience and then pay for their material to be shown on local television. 'ActBlue,' while functioning as a political action committee and channel for donations to Democratic candidates, also strongly promoted 'DIY' tools for users to engage in fundraising and campaign organising in their own right. Use was also made of less politically oriented sites such as Eventful.com and Meetup.com, which focused on bridging the online-offline gap by channelling e-votes or chat into real-world events. The former was harnessed early on by John Edwards, a Democratic primary contender, to ask his supporters where he should show up on the campaign trail. The results ended up taking him to Columbus, Kentucky, a surprising destination given its population numbered only 229. However, the momentum in its favour appeared to increase as the initiative was seen as an opportunity to promote 'small town' America over the bigger cities that typically dominate the campaign trail.

Democratic renewal?

The key question to emerge from these developments, for our purposes, is how far they show the new media to be capable of challenging and even countering the growing disconnect between citizens and the state. . . . [D]o the new user-centred digital technologies provide a means of stemming the 'anti-politics' tide? The answer provided in this article, as noted in the introduction, is a qualified affirmative. One might be tempted to dismiss the new techniques, viewed individually, as a series of interesting albeit experimental and even quirky additions to the seasoned activist's toolbox. Viewed collectively, however, they share, it is argued, a facility for promoting the role of ordinary voters in the production, management and even message development of a political campaign. From the simple act of circulating campaign-relevant information within one's online social circle and posting on a blog to more strategic interventions such as the production of web ads and/or independent fundraising sites, these techniques are seen as combining to allow more citizens to become more directly involved in the course of the election. In order to help define or distil out the commonality or underlying logic behind these political uses of Web 2.0 technologies in the election, the term 'citizen-campaigning' is developed to apply to the new web-enabled participatory practices that were observed. Of course it is accepted that not all of the activities captured under this label were necessarily new, since many involved the re-expression of existing types of involvement such as political discussion, contacting, volunteering and donating. However, what is seen to be a significant change was the collective and proactive manner in which the practices were promoted and engaged in. So rather than individuals simply being called on to make a 'one-off' transaction with the party in terms of sending money or pledging their vote to a door-to-door/telephone canvasser, they were offered the means to spread the word themselves, producing a new more self-directing, spontaneous and socially embedded (rather than institutionally driven) layer of political action during the campaign.

Identification and definition of the new form of citizen empowerment being fuelled by the new wave of web technologies is, however, just one step towards addressing the question under consideration here. It is the wider implications of these developments for the thesis of democratic decline that forms our central focus. In brief, we argue that the main effects of citizen-campaigning in terms of a regeneration/revitalisation of the wider polity are threefold. First, in organisational terms one immediate effect is the shifting or at least rebalancing of the locus of control from the central headquarters or the campaign 'war room' out to the new volunteer army of field operatives. In place of the 'one size fits all' hierarchical model that dominated presidential campaigns in the 1990s, we find a plethora of smaller, locally developed and personalised networks of persuasion. . . . Herein lies the second, less immediate but perhaps even more powerful, renewal potential of citizen-campaigning. For seasoned operatives such as Joe Trippi, such a downward push in campaign operation constitutes nothing less than a political revolution, a 'quantum leap' towards a new kind of grassroots politics in which citizens become active and involved once again in their parties' and candidates' future. Beyond the e-campaign practitioners and devotees, however, it is evident that such activities do fit well within the scholarly framework referred to earlier which pinpoints the growth in 'elite-challenging' modes of political behaviour and new participatory norms within Western democracies. Indeed, what is perhaps most exciting for e-democracy advocates . . . to observe is not only that we are seeing these more self-directing modes of activity emerging in the online context but that they are occurring within the sphere of conventional politics as well, rather than the more typical arenas of unconventional or protest politics. Citizen-campaigning, it seems, might just serve as a means for siphoning off some of the new radicalism and participatory energy held by the 'new values' generation, and channelling it into the representative sphere.

A third and even longer-term way that citizen-campaigning might engineer some type of democratic renewal lies in the wider domain of attitudes and norms. These new forms of web-enabled participation, if engaged in extensively and consistently enough, should help in promoting a closer sense of connection between voters and candidates and even parties. In using these tools to become more proactive and involved with a political campaign, individuals enter into more of a 'partnering' relationship with those they elect, which may lead to the development [of] a greater sense of ownership and stake in the outcome. Further, the more socially embedded and personalised nature of contacting that this type of engagement spawns may then ripple out to a wider grassroots base, increasing the perceptions of candidates' authenticity and trustworthiness, and in turn levels of participatory involvement.

Any empirical assessment of these claims is inevitably a complex and prolonged task. Certainly it is evident from the US experience that not all citizens are taking advantage of the opportunities for co-production and co-organisation that the new web tools afford. Thus any investigation of the democratising impact of citizen-campaigning would need to pay particular attention to exactly who is active in the new networks, how representative they are of wider society and how sustainable they are over time. In lieu of such nuanced data it is possible at this point to marshal a couple of sources of evidence that may help us address at least some general questions about the scale of the uptake and enthusiasm for citizen-campaigning among the public more widely. Our first port of call in this regard is the report from the Pew Internet and American Life Project on the 2008 election which reports levels of involvement among the US population in the e-campaign. Its findings are actually rather heartening in terms of the scope of people's political engagement with Web 2.0 tools and particularly those more socially oriented applications, with one in ten of Americans claiming to have used Facebook or MySpace for political activity during 2008 (including befriending a politician or starting/joining a political group). This was particularly pronounced among those under 30 years of age. Similar numbers were reported as forwarding or posting some kind of political commentary or writing during the election and five per cent of all adults said that they posted their own commentary to a news group or blog. Fifteen per cent of email users reported sending an election-related message to friends and family during the campaign and, perhaps more significantly given our notion of 'ripple out' effects, just over one third of email users reported receiving campaign-relevant email. Not surprisingly, when the political affiliation of those politically engaging via Web 2.0 tools was investigated, there was clear evidence that it was Obama's supporters who were most active (Smith and Rainie 2008). Unfortunately the levels of political experience of those involved with these more active forms of e-campaigning is not reported, which means claiming any greater mobilising effects is not possible at this stage.

Beyond survey data, however, an alternative metric for judging the democratising claims for citizen-campaigning can be seen in the scale and structure of fundraising efforts during the 2008 race, which broke all records in terms of the amounts donated. While John McCain was among the first generation of candidates to reveal the fundraising power of the Internet in 2000, and Howard Dean sharpened the use of these tactics, raising a total of $27 million online during the 2004 primaries (Talbot 2009), the 2008 race saw the full realisation of the Internet's potential to fill the campaign coffers. One early starter in the chase for online donations was Republican Ron Paul, who raised an astonishing $6 million in one day in December 2007 (Stirland 2007). Barack Obama, however, proved to be the wunderkind of Internet fund-raising, reportedly raising over $600 million in total, with a substantial portion of this coming from online sources (Luo 2008). While the amount itself is noteworthy, more compelling in regard to levels of democratic engagement is the donor structure underlying that record-breaking haul. According to *Washington Post* reporters, most of the donations made online were around $80 and were made by up to 3 million individuals (Vargas 2008b). The emergence of such a broad and shallow pool of small 'investors' in the campaign contrasted sharply with the deeper networks of high-dollar donors that had characterised US presidential elections in the past (Vargas 2008a). Comments by Simon Rosenberg, a former member of Bill Clinton's first presidential campaign, neatly reflected the change presented by the Obama approach, as he noted that 'compared to our 1992 campaign, this is like a multinational corporation versus a non-profit' (Rayner 2008). Such observations also provide some validity to the argument that the online political engagement inspired by the Obama campaign widened active participation among the electorate compared with previous elections. In the longer term, should this pattern be maintained and strengthened, then it may go some way towards combating public cynicism about money buying undue influence over politicians for the wealthy few.

Citizen Campaigning in the UK?

Early into their account Hay *et al.* note that a democratising of all our collective institutions for decision-making is vital if citizens are not merely going to be empowered into a few narrow fields. Revitalising politics will mean challenging arenas that have effectively become depoliticised—arenas in which unelected managers, professionals and experts now dominate. It is the argument of this paper that the new forms of web-enabled citizen-campaigning offer one means of making this challenge and affecting this change within the electoral context. How far it can operate in the party-dominated environment of UK politics, however, is a question that requires further and deeper scrutiny.

The US, with its weaker party control of candidates and campaigns and lack of an established membership body, clearly provides a ripe context for this more devolved approach to electioneering. Building a team of volunteers from scratch is time-consuming and expensive. The increased resources and reduced costs that citizen-campaigning offers to political hopefuls, therefore, provides a powerful incentive for its adoption. In addition, use of federalism in the United States means that there are more frequent elections and thus more opportunities for innovation and experimentation than in Britain, which experiences a national election once every five years. Finally, the more liberal campaign finance rules of the US can also be seen as a spur to citizen-campaigning. The change of rules in 2002, permitting individuals to donate a maximum of $2,300 to candidates in particular has spawned the growth of so-called 'bundling,' whereby donors gather sums from many different individuals in an organisation or community that they then hand on to the campaign. The networked web environment provides a highly efficient means for the non-expert to engage in this type of bulk fund-raising.

Such constraints notwithstanding, there are a number of bases for expecting the new types of campaign-related citizen activism to emerge in the UK in the next general election. Practically, parties have already starting making use of new social media tools to set up new national supporter networks, with a number of leading and lesser known politicians now enjoying profiles on Facebook and MySpace. One of the most prominent practitioners, Liberal Democrat Steve Webb, was reported to have said that he would be using Facebook to consult voters on their views about the Liberal Democrat manifesto (Carlin 2007). In addition, dedicated online discussion forums for policy consultation with members and the wider public have been trialled, such as Labour's 'Let's Talk' and the Liberal Democrats' 'Have Your Say.' Politicians and parties have also moved into the online video market, with the Conservative leader David Cameron setting up his own personal channel, 'Webcameron,' shortly followed by Labour Vision and official party sites established on the popular video-sharing site YouTube. At the local level, the parties have been encouraged to use online technologies to help increase the involvement of members in decisions, while easing the demands and requirements for membership (Hain 2004; Miliband 2005; Katwala and Brooks 2005; Creasey and Alexander 2006; Cruddas and Harris 2007). Perhaps more significantly, there has also been growth in the less official uses of the technology by party members and affiliated networks. Conservative bloggers such as Iain Dale and Tom Montgomery have attracted a wide audience and become mouthpieces for Tory grassroots opinion. Many individual party members now make use of social networking tools such as Facebook and MySpace to network with other sympathisers and promote their party (Francoli and Ward 2008).

Whether this 'peace-time' commitment to wiring up the grassroots is continued and developed in the election period to mobilise and integrate ordinary citizens into the campaign organisational infrastructure remains to be seen. The benefits of citizen campaigning in terms of efficiency gains are clear, particularly for the minor parties that have fewer resources to draw on. In addition the potential boost in mass participation and ability to forge closer relationships with voters via citizen-campaigning is no doubt a highly appealing prospect for the major parties facing membership declines and criticism for seeming out of touch and unresponsive. However, such benefits need to be weighed up against possible longer-term downsides. While democracy is about ensuring a wide range of voices are heard in the public arena, it is also about decision-making and arriving at consensus. Citizen-campaigning, while it may provide a new outlet and stimulus for popular engagement, also presents a challenge to those seeking to convey a coherent and consistent message, with multiple campaigns possibly running on a party's or candidates' behalf. How those numerous and possibly conflicting viewpoints are reconciled into policy alternatives as the campaign proceeds, and especially if it succeeds, may prove crucial to sustaining the newly mobilised constituency of support. Once elected to office by the mousepads of citizen-campaigners, how does the politician satisfy the potentially diverse coalition of newly energised supporters that can lay claim to his/her victory? To what extent is it realistic to expect the partnership to continue and what mechanisms would be required to transfer powers of co-direction and co-production to the governing arena? While such a rewiring of the system may ultimately prove technologically feasible, given current developments in e-government, such a scenario is some years away. Is there, therefore, a potential for citizen-campaigning to heighten popular disillusionment with politics as it energises and expands the pool of stakeholders and constituencies of interest, only to deflate hopes and expectations by confronting them with government as usual? How far citizen-campaigning can serve to counteract declines in public trust in our key democratic bodies and their performance in the longer term is clearly a topic for future research.

References

Brians, C., and M. Wattenberg. 1996. Campaign issue knowledge and salience: Comparing commercials, TV news, and newspapers. *American Journal of Political Science* 40:172–193.

Carlin, B. 2007. Lib Dems enlist Facebook for manifesto views. Telegraph.co.uk, available online at http://www.telegraph.co.uk/news/uknews/1563426/Lib-Dems-enlist-Facebook-for-manifesto-views.html (accessed 24 May 2009).

Creasy, S., and D. Alexander. 2006. *Serving a Cause, Serving a Community: The Role of Political Parties in Today's Britain*. London: Demos.

Cruddas, J., and J. Harris. 2007. *Fit for Purpose: A Programme for Labour Party Renewal*. London: Compass.

Dalton, R. J. 2006. *Citizen Politics: Public Opinion and Political Parties in Advanced Western Democracies*, 4th edn. Washington, DC: CQ Press.

Dalton, R. J. 2008. *The Good Citizen: How a Younger Generation Is Reshaping American Politics*. Washington, DC: CQ Press.

Dalton, R., and M. Wattenberg, eds. 2001. *Parties without Partisans: Political Change in Advanced Industrial Democracies*. Oxford: Oxford University Press.

Deuze, M. 2003. The web and its journalisms: Considering the consequences of different types of news media online. *New Media and Society* 5(2): 203–230.

Etzioni, A., and O. Etzioni. 1997. Editorial: Communities: Virtual vs. real. *Science* 277 (5324): 295.

Francoli, M., and S. J. Ward. 2008. 21st century soapboxes? MPs and their blogs. *Information Polity* 13(1–2): 21–39.

Grannick, J. 2006. Saving democracy with Web 2.0. *Wired,* available online at http://www.wired.com/software/webservices/commentary/circuitcourt/2006/10/72001 (accessed 7 March 2009).

Hain, P. 2004. *The Future Party.* London: Catalyst.

Hindman, M. 2005. The real lessons of Howard Dean: Reflections on the first digital campaign. *Perspectives on Politics* 3(1): 121–8.

Katwala, S., and R. Brooks. 2005. Come together. *Fabian Review,* autumn: 10–14.

Keen, A. 2007. *Cult of the Amateur.* London: Nicholas Brealey.

Leadbeater, C. 2007. *We Think: The Power of Mass Creativity.* London: Profile.

Luo, M. 2008. Obama recasts the fund-raising landscape. *New York Times Online,* 20 October, available online at http://www.nytimes.eom/2008/10/20/us/politics/20donate.html?_r=1&hp=&pagewanted=print&oref=slogin (accessed 27 October 2008).

Miliband, E. 2005. Digging up the grassroots. *Fabian Review,* autumn: 15–18.

Negroponte, N. 1995. *Being Digital.* New York: Vintage Books.

Norris, P., ed. 1999. *Critical Citizens: Global Support for Democratic Government.* Oxford: Oxford University Press.

Patterson, T. E. 1993. *Out of Order.* New York: Alfred A. Knopf.

Patterson, T., and R. D. McClure. 1976. *The Unseeing Eye: The Myth of Television Power in National Politics.* New York: Putnam.

Pharr, S. J., and R. D. Putnam, eds. 2000. *Disaffected Democracies: What's Troubling the Trilateral Countries?* Princeton, NJ: Princeton University Press.

Pickerill, J. 2004. *Cyberprotest: Environmental Activism Online.* Manchester: University of Manchester Press.

Pickerill, J., K. Gillian, and F. Webster. 2008. *Anti-war Activism: New Media and Protest in the Information Age.* Basingstoke: Palgrave Macmillan.

Putnam, R. D. 2000. *Bowling Alone: The Collapse and Revival of American Community.* London: Simon and Schuster.

Rayner, G. 2008. How the Internet helped propel Barack Obama to the White House. *The Daily Telegraph,* 5 November, available at http://www.telegraph.co.uk/news/worldnews/northamerica/usa/barackobama/3387174/How-the-Internet-helped-propel-Barack-Obama-to-the-White-House.html (accessed July 2009).

Rheingold, H. 2003. *Smart Mobs: The Next Social Revolution.* Cambridge, MA: Basic Books.

Smith, A., and L. Rainie. 2008. *The Internet and the 2008 Election.* Pew Internet and American Life Project Report, issued 15 June 2008, available online at http://www.pewinternet.org/~/media//Files/Reports/2008/PIP_2008_election.pdf.pdf (accessed 24 May 2009).

Stirland, S. L. 2007. Ron Paul supporters make history with $6 million online haul. *Wired Blog Network,* 17 December, available online at http://blog.wired.com/27bstroke6/2007/12/ron-paul-suppor.html (accessed 22 May 2009).

Stirland, S. L. 2008. Propelled by Internet, Barack Obama wins presidency. *Wired Blog Network*, 4 November, available online at http://blog.wired.com/27bstroke6/2008/11/propelled-by-in.html (accessed 20 February 2009).

Surowiecki, J. 2005. *The Wisdom of Crowds*. New York: Anchor Books.

Talbot, D. 2009. The geeks behind Obama's web strategy. *Boston Globe*, 8 January, available online at http://www.boston.com/news/politics/2008/articles/2009/01/08/the_geeks_behind_obamas_web_strategy (accessed 6 March 2009).

Teachout, Z., and T. Streeter. 2007. *Mousepads, Shoe Leather, and Hope*. Boulder, CO: Paradigm Publishers.

Trippi, J. 2004. *The Revolution Will Not Be Televised*. New York: Regan Books.

Trippi, J. 2008. Author's note—2nd edition of *The Revolution Will Not Be Televised*, available online at http://joetrippi.com/blog/?cat=2&paged=2 (accessed 18 October 2008).

Vargas, J. A. 2008a. Politics is no longer local. It's viral. *Washington Post*, 15 March, available online at http:/www.washingtonpost.com/wpdyn/content/article/2008/12/26/AR2008122601131.html (accessed 15 March 2009).

Vargas, J. A. 2008b. Obama raised half a billion online. *The Clickocracy*, available online at http://voices.washingtonpost.com/44/2008/11/20/Obama_raised_half_a_billion_on.html (accessed 20 February 2009).

17

ELECTING THE PRESIDENT 2008: THE INSIDERS' VIEW

Nicolle Wallace and Anita Dunn

Editor's Note

Shortly after the 2008 presidential election, top strategists and consultants for the Democratic and Republican campaigns met for a retrospective analysis. Chapter 17 is based on a portion of their taped conversations. It assesses media coverage of the 2008 campaign from the insider's perspective of two seasoned professionals who worked with the candidates during the final campaign stages. Nicolle Wallace served as an advisor to Republican candidate John McCain; Anita Dunn advised Democratic candidate Barack Obama. Both advisors expressed serious concerns about the quality of press coverage.

Wallace's experiences included service in the 2004 Bush campaign, service as the director of communications for the White House, and service in the news media realm as a political analyst at CBS news. Dunn had been a career political strategist and communications advisor for nearly thirty years when she became part of Obama's campaign staff. She had previously worked with Democratic Party leaders including Senator Tom Daschle and Representative Nancy Pelosi. Kathleen Hall Jamieson, a professor of communication at the Annenberg School for Communication of the University of Pennsylvania, edited the transcripts of the discussions at the meetings.

The Campaign and the Press

Nicolle Wallace [McCain advisor]

The notion that John McCain changed vis-à-vis the media should be corrected. The media had that backward. John McCain was sad that the media had changed so drastically from 2000. He missed the media from

2000. The media in 2000 were a press corps that got on a bus and spent a day talking about an issue. They would usually have to say to him, "Senator McCain, we'd love to keep talking to you, but we've got to file." They'd take the benefit of all that conversation and file.

The media of 2008 would get on a bus leg in the middle of a conversation, type out a blog about how his sock was down or didn't match his shoe. He was sad that their industry had put these pressures on them, that they could no longer have discussions about issues that took place over the course of the day, as you rolled around on the bus for eight hours.

I think he also missed the media of 2000 because in 2000 they had access to him on the bus but they also included images or sounds or other things that they saw on a campaign trail. By 2008, the only thing that made air were questions about Viagra—the gotcha moment. I think he remained quite distraught for what had happened to journalism.

It did change a lot between 2000 and 2008. Howard Kurtz (of CNN and the *Washington Post*) came out with us and said, "You know, all these guys back here, some of them were 12 [years old] in 2000. So, they don't even know what they're talking about. And they say they miss the John McCain of 2000." He asked, "What does Senator McCain think?" I said, "He just chuckles and says he misses the press corps of the year 2000 and of the 2000 campaign." I think the media can't help itself when they're part of a story. The coverage of the relationship between John McCain and the media was always about the media.

We paid a big price for his commitment to accessibility. John McCain can't and won't be handled. It's not as if campaign staff would say, "No media." He'd laugh at you and say, "Get out of Elisabeth Bumiller's [*New York Times* reporter] seat." It's not as if anyone said to him, "Enough." He finally saw an inability to communicate a message over the course of the summer which, once the Democratic primary ended, really mattered. Since we didn't have resources, we relied on those news cycles. It's why the "show me" ads, as we called them, were part of our strategy. We didn't have curtain number two, three or four. We really relied on our media. We just couldn't spare any more news cycles to insipid conversations about Viagra. So, we made a decision to change our interactions. We moved them out of the back of the bus. We started using that for speech writing and working. It became a traveling office instead of a rolling press conference. We really tried to change our approach to [the] message.

Another thought, I don't know how many of you have ever come home with a new puppy. How many people have ever come home with a puppy? Raised a puppy? I had a very smart, willful, stubborn puppy. I'd say, "Why is she jumping?" She'd bark right at my face. The trainer said, "She has impulse control problems. You need to train her to resist the impulse." And I said,

"How do I do that?" We had a whole bag of hot dogs that we'd carry around. You literally train an animal out of the impulse to express every urge.

The media has an impulse control problem. It cannot help itself. It cannot help itself from jumping on the seediest or the most unseemly or the most unsubstantiated rumor. Then all the reporters who have plenty of impulse control, who are working real stories or looking at issues feel all these puppies breathing down their neck, because they're chasing the hot dogs.

What we ended up with in the big cauldron of political coverage was really a lot [of] crap. Some did a good job. But the changes in journalism made it harder for someone like Dan Balz or Adam Nagourney or Elisabeth Bumiller to spend the day working her contacts, making calls, talking with campaigns and writing a story. Because every 30 minutes, she's on her Blackberry and someone's filed about how, at the last event—someone threw a naked Palin Barbie. And someone has to file that. There was so much junk in that system. It leaves a lot of questions for journalists and journalism to examine. When something bad happens at a government agency, sometimes the best way to investigate it is a self-audit. It's probably a moment in political coverage for political journalism inside some of the best journalism schools to look inside and ask what they want to be. Because to turn the really good political journalists into people who have to compete with . . . the bloggers all day is a different deal. It's a different beat. Steve and I used to say, we ran the last campaign of the last century of campaigns in media acts. It will be viewed as quaint that we rolled around on a bus with a pool.

I was at the White House for six years. And one of the things we started grappling with was what's a journalist? People who wrote online articles for websites hosted by companies say, we're in-house journalists. What is a journalist? And what's their obligation vis-à-vis political coverage?

I know that NBC internally grappled with the presence of Keith Olbermann on its brand. We had a lot of meetings at the highest levels of NBC. I think Brian Williams is a very, very committed journalist. But Keith Olbermann said some of the ugliest, nastiest things, things that I wouldn't repeat in mixed company about Cindy McCain, about the Palin kids. I mean, forget about the politicians. They sign up for it. But when you've got both candidates ruling spouses and kids off bounds, and you've got Keith Olbermann saying really nasty things, it makes the relationship with the news side of the network hard. All we ever said was, "It's a difficult thing for us. It's difficult for us to sit here or to pull back the curtain and share with you when on the way to the bathroom, we could run into Keith Olbermann."

I know NBC grapples with it. They have made business decisions that are what they are. I joined the campaign in April of '08, and I said, "You better hope and pray that we lose, because we are on such a bad path that—[I] don't know what would happen if Senator McCain had won and had to continue to deal with MSNBC and NBC."

I think by the end, it was in a more positive place, largely through the efforts of Tom Brokaw, Brian Williams, and people like Chuck Todd, people who took very seriously our concerns about the MSNBC, NBC family. . . .

When you're in communications, you're drinking out of the fire hose. You've got all the news created by your own campaign to deal with, the ads, the ads that come from the other side. You've got the changing and evolving relationship with the political press. And then you're always on the front line of whatever is coming your way from, in our case, a very organized, very strategic, very methodical opponent.

It was certainly not a campaign without challenges and I worked for a candidate who really gets the media and really valued the relationships that he had. What I came away with is that there are still places in journalism where source reporting, where those relationships really matter.

I believe that it's worth examining whether in this election newspapers, your local dailies and to a slightly lesser extent, the national papers and network television coverage and local television coverage, reemerged as arbiters of the information that got through to the most number of voters. There were certainly things that were spread on the Internet. But they were largely seen by groups of voters that were very much interested and in favor of one candidate or the other. I think news outlets and television networks can now become something different and just as useful, and perhaps even more valuable. And that is organizers and prioritizers of information.

Anita Dunn [Obama advisor]

I joined the Obama campaign in January of 2008 and I was a friend of the Obama campaign throughout 2007. I had not worked on the 2004 presidential campaign. When I came on a regular basis in January of 2008, right after New Hampshire, one of the first things that everyone said to me was, "You will be astonished when you go out on the bus the first time, and you see how young everybody is." Astonished wasn't even the word. I thought, "Geez, I thought everybody on the campaign was so young." The time I walked into the campaign, I'd never felt older in my life. You can only imagine what the Obama campaign was like.

I think what Nicolle has just said is extraordinarily important, which is that the nature of campaign coverage in 2008 was totally reactive. It was non-stop. There was no context and no analysis. I was shocked for at least two days, until we figured out exactly how we wanted to play it.

We were in the primaries up against one of the more famous political machines of the last century, the Clintons, the legendary war room people. They had an aggressive press operation. What was interesting to me was the ability that our campaign developed with the help of Jon [Carson] and—and Joe Rospers and the people in New Media, to communicate around the filter. You need to feed cable and the Internet with content. We would occasionally say [cynically], "They need new bright, shiny things to go play with," which would be that [web] advertising we forced [the ad team] to produce. We tried to resist that and keep our campaign integrity for a while but at the end of the day, there was a national narrative that cable and the Internet were telling. There was a campaign they were talking about that was actually not the real campaign. That was, to me, one of the most interesting things I've ever seen.

Those of us who are old grew up in an era in which you were taught that your earned media, your press, should support what your paid media were doing. In this world, what you were doing in the press was supposed to reinforce what you were doing in the paid media. Your speeches, your surrogates, and everybody were supposed to be saying the same thing.

What you've increasingly got in 2008, at least from our campaign, was what I call the total disconnect. You had this bizarre national narrative, this weird 24-hour national campaign that was being played out on cable and on blogs and on Internet sites. . . .

The new news cycle began at 10:00 at night when the [Washington] Post or the [New York] Times would actually post their pieces that would be in the paper the next morning. By the time folks like my neighbors who read the paper [read it], we'd be eight news cycles past them. We already would've produced advertising to respond to what was in the paper or we would've made the decision not to respond.

We decided very quickly that we were going to force the media to actually cover the campaign on our terms. We had a reputation, to some extent deserved, for a level of discipline, [for] not leaking. We didn't always have it in the primary but by the general, we'd gotten it down fairly well. Part of that was the decision we made that we would force the coverage to our campaign events, to the things the campaign did and we would not talk about anything else. For instance, we never gave a process interview to the New York Times, to either of their very good reporters who cover politics.

I don't think we ever gave the candidate an interview with Adam Nagourney after October 2007. Certainly not on my watch, as we like to say. We tried to force them to cover what was happening as opposed to the back story about what was happening. That was a source of great conflict between us and our press corps. They complained continually about our lack of accessibility but, at the end of the day, forcing them to cover what we wanted them to cover was incredibly important to us.

One of the things that we did was communicate, by and large, most of our news to our supporters. We did that mostly because we really cared about our supporters. When the Clinton people joined the campaign, after the primary was over, one of the most surprising things for them was how much time we spent in meetings talking about how we were going to talk to our supporters about something. In the VP roll-out, the Obama campaign people's starting assumption was that we were going to tell our supporters before we told the press. Clinton people were surprised by the idea that we weren't going to give the story to the AP first after cutting a deal with [AP political reporter] Ron Fournier.

We handled our money announcement in the same way. It was how we did our Invesco [acceptance speech at the Democratic Convention] announcement. David Plouffe would do "hostage-looking" videos [videos akin to those showing hostages pleading for release]. Parenthetically, I'm always surprised when I see that we ended up spending 36.4 million in Florida because in August we did a video to our supporters telling them we were going to spend 39 million there. I'm stunned at how close we came.

When we made the announcement that we were leaving the public financing system, we told our supporters [first].

By September, interviews with national print reporters were nonexistent because there was very little reason at the end of the day to do them. We did national electronic because that's how people get their information. Print does not drive news. Internet drives cable; cable drives networks. If you want a story in the *Post* or the *Times* to drive news, you have to consciously make it a news driver. You produce an ad. You do a conference call. . . .

We actually decided that in light of the scarce time of Barack Obama, our press priorities were battleground states. Everything in our campaign was driven by battleground states.

The third thing, . . . when we saw slack times in the primary, we didn't have a problem because there was always another primary, some news-making event, for reporters to cover. During the general, we didn't have that. We had three debates in that big stretch of time. So we needed to create events. That was a big driving force behind our 30-minute program. [We did these things] almost as a way to kill the clock because if we were filling that space, you [in the McCain campaign] weren't. A huge part of what we were trying to do in the general election was to keep you from filling that space. The McCain [campaign] tortured us all summer and we were not happy about that whatsoever.

The place where I think the press [produced] its worst coverage of the general election was in the total absence of any kind of scrutiny of the issue on which we spent the most money in the general election, health care. I worked from Chicago. When I started going to battleground states for debate prep, the first state we went to was Florida. That was the first time I'd actually been in a battleground television market, was able to see the amount of advertising we were doing. All we saw in Illinois was national cable. [After watching TV in Florida] I thought, "Oh, my gosh. You see on paper how many advertising dollars are going into markets but it's different being in Tampa and seeing how much money was being spent behind [the issue of] health care."

When we were in Asheville, North Carolina, preparing for the second debate, the number of times I saw the "ball of string and the left-right arrows" health care ad, which anybody who was in a battleground state saw at least 2,000 times, was pretty stunning. The fact is, there was a real health care debate. We brought it up in the debates. John McCain brought it up in the debates. There was a huge difference of opinion. Because, I'm assuming, of financial constraints, you guys didn't advertise on it, you couldn't answer. . . .

. . . I thought [the campaigns' emphasis on health care and the national news] was a very good example of how what was going on in the battleground states with voters was almost totally disconnected from the national narrative. [The focus there was on] Bill Ayers and the Sarah Palin interviews. [Meanwhile] there was a whole campaign going on that people [were seeing in our ads] in battleground states, [or hearing when they] were being contacted by Jon Carson's folks. . . .

We actually went back to the model where we communicated about the content we were airing advertising about. Amazing how that actually worked. Local media would cover the issues. That still works out there. You go to Toledo, Ohio, and make a speech about health care, and the Toledo paper and the Toledo TV stations say, "Barack Obama was here today talking about health care" as opposed to, "Barack Obama, who is still reeling from the accusation that his crowd was too big yesterday, came to make a pathetic excuse about why he's not a celebrity." . . .

Nicolle Wallace

I was on the road full time. John McCain did one to three hours of battleground media every day. We didn't do it for the kind of spiritual, meaningful reasons that the Obama campaign did it. Compared to the other campaign, we had no money. We did it because we felt it was important to go around the filter and communicate directly with our voters. So, we did two to three hours of battleground media, I'd say every day from the middle of August until Election Day. That would usually include at least one, sometimes two, satellite tours into target states. Wherever he went, Senator McCain would sit down with three or four network affiliate reporters in a market and the print reporters. So, it was usually five reporters in a local market, plus a sat[ellite] tour, and if we were hitting two states, he'd do that twice. . . .

In my first job at the White House in 2001, I ran the Office of Media Affairs, which is the regional press office for all the reporters that don't go to the briefing room every day. Whatever the President did that day, we'd send their way, and the stories were tracked. I am dying to see how that washes out in this White House.

In this campaign, people in the battleground states had a conversation for 15 months about how crappy the economy was. [By contrast] the national media only talked about it for the last six weeks. In Michigan, we were getting questions about their unemployment rate, the state of their economy, and the auto industry for a year. I don't remember the network mix turning to almost purely economy until the last five, six weeks.

Anita Dunn

They didn't. We got economic questions during the primary because our primary process went so much longer. But the questions [from the national media focused on] why we weren't connecting better on the economy, as opposed to [concentrating on] the extraordinary amount of policy that we put out. I think we put out more policy [positions] than any campaign ever has. And [we] continually tweaked the policy.

Every morning in the general election, we'd send somebody from our campaign out and the questions would [not only] be ludicrous [but also] would have nothing to do with what we were seeing in any polling.

We would sit down in our Sunday planning meetings and map out the idiotic press ads that we were going to need for the week. One of the things that we discovered was that our regular ads, the ads we were running for voters, weren't covered because [the press didn't consider them] interesting enough. They just worked.

Nicolle Wallace

Too substantive. It is an Alice in Wonderland scenario. I've done this for 12 years. I wouldn't have done this for as long as I have if I didn't really like a lot of people in the media. There are plenty of people in the media who if given a truth serum, would not say things too discordant with what we've said.

Anita Dunn

It was like the Wild West out there. . . . I think that part of the reputation we got for being such control freaks was because we simply were trying to control the things we could control. By the general election, we'd figured out how we could game the system to do what we wanted to do and at the same time, keep everybody busy, giving them content to keep 'em busy while you actually went out . . . and won the campaigns.

18

OPEN SEASON: HOW THE NEWS MEDIA COVER PRESIDENTIAL CAMPAIGNS IN THE AGE OF ATTACK JOURNALISM

Larry J. Sabato

Editor's Note

Modern presidential campaign coverage is often mean-spirited and ugly. It destroys candidates' political careers by magnifying their human foibles and physical infirmities. Larry J. Sabato shows how attack journalism inflicted deep political wounds on Democratic presidential candidate Michael Dukakis and Republican vice presidential candidate Dan Quayle during the 1988 presidential campaign. The consequences of such treatment, Sabato concludes, are candidates who are increasingly secretive because they fear reporters and reporters who cover less substantive news because they are obsessed with detecting scandals. Deprived of information needed to make sound choices, the public becomes ever more distrustful and filled with disgust for politicians as well as the press.

Sabato was the Robert Kent Gooch Professor of Government and Foreign Affairs at the University of Virginia when this essay was written. He is the founder and director of the University of Virginia's Center for Politics and a former Rhodes Scholar and Danforth Fellow. His best-known book, *Feeding Frenzy: Attack Journalism & American Politics,* published in 1991, made the phrase *feeding frenzy* part of America's political lexicon. Sabato has been a prolific, highly respected writer and commentator on political campaigns.

Source: Under the Watchful Eye: Managing Presidential Campaigns in the Television Era, ed. Mathew D. McCubbins, Washington, D.C.: Congressional Quarterly Press, 1992. Reprinted by permission of CQ Press, a division of SAGE Publications.

. . . The issue of character has always been present in American politics—not for his policy positions was George Washington made our first president—but rarely, if ever, has character been such a pivotal concern in presidential elections, both primary and general, as it has since 1976. . . .

Whatever the precise historical origins of the character trend in reporting, it is undergirded by certain assumptions—some valid, others dubious. First and most important of all, *the press correctly perceives that it has mainly replaced the political parties as the "screening committee" that winnows the field of candidates and filters out the weaker or more unlucky contenders.* Second, many reporters, again correctly, recognize the mistakes made under the rules of lapdog journalism and see the need to tell people about candidate foibles that affect public performance. Third, the press assumes that it is giving the public what it wants and expects, more or less. Television is the primary factor here, having served not only as handmaiden and perhaps mother to the age of personality politics but also conditioning its audience to think about the private lives of "the rich and famous."

Less convincing, however, are a number of other assumptions about elections and the character issue made by the press. Some journalists insist upon their obligation to reveal everything of significance discovered about a candidate's private habits; to do otherwise, they say, is antidemocratic and elitist. Such arguments ignore the press's professional obligation to exercise reasonable judgment about what is fit to be printed or aired as well as what is most important for a busy and inattentive public to absorb. Other reporters claim that character matters so much because policy matters so little, that the issues change frequently and the pollsters and consultants determine the candidates' policy stands anyway.

Perhaps most troubling is the almost universally accepted belief that private conduct affects the course of public action. Unquestionably, private behavior can have public consequences. However, it is far from certain that private vice inevitably leads to corrupt, immoral leadership or that private virtue produces public good. Indeed, the argument can be made that many lives run on two separate tracks (one public, one private) that should be judged independently. In any event, a focus on character becomes not an attempt to construct the mosaic of qualities that make up an individual but rather a strained effort to find a sometimes manufactured pattern of errors or shortcomings that will automatically disqualify a candidate. . . .

Not surprisingly, politicians react rather badly to the treatment they receive from the modern press. Convinced that the media have but one conspiratorial goal—to hurt or destroy them—the pols respond by restricting journalists' access, except under highly controlled situations. Kept at arm's length and out of the candidate's way, reporters have the sense of being enclosed behind trick mirrors: they can see and hear the candidate, but not vice versa.

Their natural, human frustrations grow throughout the grueling months on the road, augmented by many other elements, including a campaign's secrecy, deceptions, and selective leaks to rival newsmen, as well as the well-developed egos of candidates and their staffs. Despite being denied access, the press is expected to provide visibility for the candidate, to retail his or her bromides. Broadcast journalists especially seem trapped by their need for good video and punchy soundbites and with regret find themselves falling into the snares set by the campaign consultants—airing verbatim the manufactured message and photoclip of the day. The press's enforced isolation and the programmed nature of its assignments produce boredom as well as disgruntlement, yet the professionalism of the better journalists will not permit them to let their personal discontent show in the reports they file.

These conditions inevitably cause reporters to strike back at the first opportunity. Whether it is emphasizing a candidate gaffe, airing an unconfirmed rumor, or publicizing a revelation about the candidate's personal life, the press uses a frenzy to fight the stage managers, generate some excitement, and seize control of the campaign agenda. Media emotions have been so bottled and compressed that even the smallest deviation from the campaign's prepared script is trumpeted as a major development. . . .

Does press frustration, among other factors, ever result in uneven treatment of presidential candidates, a tilt to one side or the other, further helping to foster attack journalism? In other words, are the news media biased? One of the enduring questions of journalism, its answer is simple and unavoidable: of course they are. Journalists are fallible human beings who inevitably have values, preferences, and attitudes galore—some conscious and others subconscious—all reflected at one time or another in the subjects or slants selected for coverage. To revise and extend the famous comment of Iran-Contra defendant Oliver North's attorney Brendan Sullivan, reporters are not potted plants. . . .

. . . [P]ress bias of all kinds—partisan, agenda setting, and nonideological—has influenced the development of junkyard-dog journalism in covering presidents and presidential candidates. But ideological bias is not the be-all and end-all that critics on both the right and left often insist it is. Press tilt has a marginal effect, no more, no less.

Two Cases of Attack Journalism in the 1988 Presidential Election: Dukakis and Quayle

Michael Dukakis's 1988 mental-health controversy is one of the most despicable episodes in recent American politics. The corrosive rumor that the Democratic presidential nominee had undergone psychiatric treatment for severe depression began to circulate in earnest at the July 1988 national party convention. The agents of the rumormongering were "LaRouchies," adherents of the extremist cult headed by Lyndon LaRouche, who claims, among other loony absurdities, that Queen Elizabeth II is part of the international drug cartel.[1]

Shortly after the Democratic convention, the Bush campaign—with its candidate trailing substantially in the polls—began a covert operation to build on the foundation laid by the LaRouchies. As first reported by columnists Rowland Evans and Robert Novak,[2] Bush manager Lee Atwater's lieutenants asked outside Republican operatives and political consultants to call their reporter contacts about the matter. These experienced strategists knew exactly the right approach in order not to leave fingerprints, explains Steve Roberts of *U.S. News & World Report:*

> They asked us, "Gee, have you heard anything about Dukakis's treatment? Is it true?" They're spreading the rumor, but it sounds innocent enough: they're just suggesting that you look into it, and maybe giving you a valuable tip as well.[3]

Many newspapers, including the *Baltimore Sun* and the *Washington Post,* at first refused to run any mention of the Dukakis rumor since it could not be substantiated.[4] But on August 3 an incident occurred that made it impossible, in their view, not to cover the rumor. During a White House press conference a correspondent for *Executive Intelligence Review,* a LaRouche organization magazine, asked Reagan if he thought Dukakis should make his medical records public. A jovial Reagan replied, "Look, I'm not going to pick on an invalid." Reagan half apologized a few hours later ("I was just trying to be funny and it didn't work"), but his weak attempt at humor propelled into the headlines a rumor that had been only simmering on the edge of public consciousness.

Whether spontaneous or planned, there is little doubt that "Reagan and the Bush people weren't a bit sorry once it happened," as CNN's Frank Sesno asserts.[5] The Bush camp immediately tried to capitalize on and prolong the controversy by releasing a report from the White House doctor describing their nominee's health in glowing terms.[6] But this was a sideshow compared with the rumor itself. The mental-health controversy yanked the Dukakis effort off track and forced the candidate and then his doctor to hold their own press conference on the subject, attracting still more public attention to a completely phony allegation. False though it was, the charge nonetheless disturbed many Americans, raising serious doubts about a candidate who was still relatively unknown to many of them. "It burst our bubble at a critical time and cost us half our fourteen-point [poll] lead," claims the Dukakis staff's senior adviser, Kirk O'Donnell. "It was one of the election's turning points; the whole affair seemed to affect Dukakis profoundly, and he never again had the same buoyant, enthusiastic approach to the campaign."[7]

As is usually the case, the candidate unnecessarily complicated his own situation. Until events forced his hand, Dukakis stubbornly refused to release his medical records or an adequate summary of them despite advance warning that the mental-health issue might be raised. But the press can by no means be exonerated. While focusing on the relatively innocent casualty, most journalists gave light treatment to the perpetrators. In retrospect, several news people said they regretted not devoting more attention to the LaRouche role in spreading the rumor, given his followers' well-deserved reputation as "dirty tricksters."[8]

Overall, one of the most important lessons of the Dukakis mental-health episode is that caution must be exercised in reporting on presidential campaign rumors. "The media are really liable for criticism when we get stampeded by competitive instincts into publishing or airing stories that shouldn't be on the record," says National Public Radio's Nina Totenberg. "We were stampeded on the Dukakis story, and we should never have let it happen."[9]

The perils of vice-presidential candidate Dan Quayle became perhaps the most riveting and certainly the most excessive feature of 1988's general election. For nearly three weeks, coverage of the presidential campaign became mainly coverage of Quayle. Most major newspapers assigned an extraordinary number of reporters to the story (up to two dozen), and the national networks devoted from two-thirds to more than four-fifths of their total evening-news campaign minutes to Quayle. Combined with the juicy material being investigated, this bumper crop of journalists and stories produced, in the words of a top Bush/Quayle campaign official, "the most blatant example of political vivisection that I've ever seen on any individual at any time; it really surpassed a feeding frenzy and became almost a religious experience for many reporters." Balance in coverage, always in short supply, was almost absent. First one controversy and then another about Quayle's early life mesmerized the press, while little effort was made to examine the most relevant parts of his record, such as his congressional career.

It was the big-ticket items about Quayle—his National Guard service, the alleged love affair with Paula Parkinson, and his academic record—that attracted the most attention. At the convention, wild rumors flew, notably the false allegation that Quayle's family had paid fifty thousand dollars to gain him admission to the Guard. It was unquestionably legitimate for the press to raise the National Guard issue, although once the picture became clear— Quayle's family did pull strings, but not to an unconscionable degree—some journalists appeared unwilling to let it go. Far less legitimate was the press's resurrection of a counterfeit, dead-and-buried episode involving lobbyist Paula Parkinson. As soon as Quayle was selected for the vice-presidential nomination, television and print journalists began mentioning the 1980 sex-for-influence "scandal," despite the fact that Quayle had long ago been cleared of any wrongdoing and involvement with Parkinson. "When Quayle's name came up as a vice-presidential possibility, before his selection, the word passed among reporters that Bush couldn't choose Quayle because of his 'Paula problem,'" admitted one television newsman. "It was the loosest kind of sloppy association . . . as if nobody bothered to go back and refresh their memory about the facts of the case."

Some of the rumors about Quayle engulfing the press corps stretched even farther back into his past than did the womanizing gossip. Quayle's academic record was particularly fertile ground for rumormongers. By his own admission, the vice-presidential nominee had been a mediocre student, and the evidence produced during the campaign suggests that mediocre was a charitable description. At the time, however, a rumor swept through Quayle's alma mater, DePauw University, that he had been caught plagiarizing during his senior year. This rumor, which cited a specific teacher and class, was widely accepted as true and became part of the Quayle legend on campus.

Within a day of Quayle's selection as the vice-presidential nominee, the rumor had reached the New Orleans GOP convention hall. Hours after the convention was adjourned, the *Wall Street Journal* published a lengthy article on Quayle's problems, noting unsubstantiated "rumors" of a "cheating incident."[10] This story helped to push the plagiarism rumor high up on the list of must-do Quayle rumors, and soon the press hunt was on—for every DePauw academic who had ever taught Quayle, for fellow students to whom he might have confided his sin, even for a supposedly mysterious extant paper or bluebook in which Quayle's cheating was indelibly recorded for posterity.

As it happens, the plagiarism allegation against Quayle appears to have a logical explanation, and it was apparently first uncovered by the painstaking research of two *Wall Street Journal* reporters, Jill Abramson and James B. Stewart (the latter a graduate of DePauw, which fortuitously gave him a leg up on the competition). Abramson and Stewart managed to locate almost every DePauw student who had been a member of Quayle's fraternity, Delta Kappa Epsilon, during his undergraduate years. Approximately ten did remember a plagiarism incident from 1969 (Quayle's year of graduation), and the guilty student was in fact a golf-playing senior who was a political science major and a member of the fraternity—but not Quayle. The similarities were striking and the mix-up understandable after the passage of nearly twenty years. What was remarkable, however, was the fact that an undistinguished student such as Quayle would be so vividly remembered by the faculty. Abramson and Stewart also uncovered the reason for this, and even two decades after the fact their finding makes a political science professor blanch. Quayle was one of only two 1969 seniors to fail the political science comprehensive exam, a requirement for graduation. (He passed it on the second try.) Abramson's conclusion was reasonable: "Jim Stewart and I believed that people had confused Quayle's failure on the comprehensive exam with his . . . fraternity brother's plagiarism, especially since both events . . . occurred at the same time."[11] Unfortunately for Quayle, however (and also for the public), this explanation did not reach print, even though it might have provided a fair antidote to the earlier rumor-promoting article. Instead, the assumption that Quayle must have cheated his way through college solidified and led to other academically oriented rumors and questions, among them how a student with such a poor undergraduate record could gain admission to law school.

An observer reviewing the academic stories about Quayle is primarily struck by two elements. First, despite the windstorm of rumor that repeatedly swept over the press corps, there was much fine, solid reporting, with appropriate restraint shown about publishing rumors, except for the original *Journal* article mentioning plagiarism and some pieces about Quayle's law-school admission. Of equal note, however, was the overwhelming emphasis on his undergraduate performance. As any longtime teacher knows, students frequently commit youthful errors and indiscretions that do not necessarily indicate their potential or future development. Thus, once again, the question of balance is raised. How much emphasis should have been placed on, and precious resources devoted to, Quayle's life in his early twenties compared with his relatively ignored senatorial career in his thirties?

Consequences

Having examined some of the truths about feeding frenzies, we now turn to their consequences. Attack journalism has major repercussions on the institution that spawns it—the press—including how it operates, what the public thinks of it, and whether it helps or hurts the development of productive public discourse. The candidates and their campaigns are also obviously directly affected by the ways and means of frenzy coverage, in terms of which politicians win and lose and the manner of their running. The voters' view of politics—optimistic or pessimistic, idealistic or cynical—is partly a by-product of what they learn about the subject from the news media. Above all, the dozens of feeding frenzies in recent times have had substantial and cumulative effects on the American political system, not only determining the kinds of issues discussed in campaigns but also influencing the types of people attracted to the electoral arena.

One of the great ironies of contemporary journalism is that the effort to report more about candidates has resulted in the news media often learning less than ever before. Wise politicians today regard their every statement as being on the record, even if not used immediately—perhaps turning up the next time the news person writes a profile. Thus the pols are much more guarded around journalists than they used to be, much more careful to apply polish and project the proper image at all times. The dissolution of trust between the two groups has meant that "journalists are kept at an arm's length by fearful politicians, and to some degree the public's knowledge suffers because reporters have a less well-rounded view of these guys," says Jerry terHorst, Gerald Ford's first press secretary and former *Detroit News* reporter.[12] The results are easily seen in the way in which presidential elections are conducted. Ever since Richard Nixon's 1968 presidential campaign, the press's access to most candidates has been tightly controlled, with journalists kept at a distance on and off the trail.[13] And as 1988 demonstrated, the less accessible candidate (Bush) was better able to communicate his message than the more accessible one (Dukakis); the kinder and gentler rewards of victory went to the nominee who was better able to keep the pesky media at bay. . . .

Consequences for the Presidential Candidates

The two cases of attack journalism examined above provide a reliable indication of a frenzy's consequences for a politician. The rumors of Dukakis's mental impairment certainly took his campaign off its stride and probably played at least some role in his defeat. And the attack on Quayle may have permanently damaged his chance of ever being elected to the presidency. Despite somewhat more positive coverage of Quayle during the 1992 campaign, his press secretary, David Beckwith, sees little likelihood that his boss can overcome the frenzy-generated image burdens any time soon: "For the indefinite future there will be lingering questions about Quayle based on what people saw or thought they saw in the [1988] campaign, and it's going to be with him for a number of years."[14] Quayle can be certain that remnants of his past frenzy will resurface and develop in his next campaign. . . .

Consequences for Voters

To voters, what seems most galling about attack journalism in presidential election campaigns is not the indignities and unfairness inflicted on candidates, however bothersome they may be. Rather, people often appear to be irate that candidates are eliminated before the electorate speaks, that irreversible political verdicts are rendered by journalists instead of by the rightful jury of citizens at the polls. The press sometimes seems akin to the Queen of Hearts in *Alice's Adventures in Wonderland,* who declares, "Sentences first—verdicts afterwards."

The denial of electoral choice is an obvious consequence of some frenzies, yet the news media's greatest impact on voters is not in the winnowing of candidates but in the encouragement of cynicism. There is no doubt that the media, particularly television, have the power to influence people's attitudes. With the decline of political parties, news publications and broadcasts have become the dominant means by which citizens learn about public officials; and while news slants cannot change most individuals' basic views and orientation, they can dramatically affect *what* people think about and *how* they approach a given subject.[15] . . .

Consequences for the Political System

The enhanced—some would say inordinate—influence of the contemporary press is pushing the American political system in certain unmistakable directions. On the positive side are the increased openness and accountability visible in government and campaigns during the last two decades. This is balanced by two disturbing consequences of modern press coverage: the trivialization of political discourse and the dissuasion of promising presidential candidacies.

As to the former, the news media have had plenty of company in impoverishing the debate, most notably from politicians and their television consultants. Nonetheless, journalists cannot escape some of the responsibility. First, the press itself has aided and abetted the lowering of the evidentiary standards held necessary to make a charge stick. In addition to the publication of rumor and the insinuation of guilt by means of innuendo, news outlets are willing to target indiscriminately not just real ethical problems, but possible problems and the perception of possible problems. Second, the media often give equal treatment to venial and mortal sins, rushing to make every garden-variety scandal another Watergate. Such behavior not only engenders cynicism, but also cheapens and dulls the collective national sense of moral outrage that ought to be husbanded for the real thing. Third, the press often devotes far more resources to the insignificant gaffe than to issues of profound national and global impact. On many occasions, peccadilloes have supplanted serious debate over policy on the front pages.

The second troubling consequence of media coverage has to do with the recruitment of presidential candidates.[16] Simply put, the price of power has been raised dramatically, too high for some outstanding potential officeholders.[17] An individual contemplating a run for office must now accept the possibility of almost unlimited intrusion into his or her financial and personal life. Every investment made, every affair conducted, every private sin committed from college years on may one day wind up on television or in a headline. For a reasonably sane and moderately sensitive person, this is a daunting realization, with potentially hurtful results not just for the candidate but for his or her immediate family and friends. American society today may well be losing the services of many exceptionally talented individuals who could make outstanding contributions to the commonweal, but who understandably will not subject themselves and their loved ones to abusive, intrusive press coverage. . . .

Fortunately, we have not yet reached the point where only the brazen enter public service, but surely the emotional costs of running for office are rising. Intensified press scrutiny of private lives and the publication of unsubstantiated rumors have become a major part of this problem. After every election cycle, reflective journalists express regret for recent excesses and promise to do better, but sadly the abuses continue. No sooner had the 1992 presidential campaign begun in earnest than Democratic front-runner Bill Clinton was sidetracked for a time by unproven allegations from an Arkansas woman, Gennifer Flowers, about an extramarital affair. The charges were initially published in a supermarket tabloid, the *Star,* and while some news outlets at first downplayed the story because of the questionable source, others ballyhooed it so extravagantly that Clinton was forced to respond, thus legitimizing full coverage by virtually all news organizations.

This classic case of lowest-common-denominator journalism guaranteed the continued preeminence of the character issue for yet another presidential campaign cycle, and in many ways the situation frustrated reporters and voters alike. Both groups can fairly be faulted for this trivialization of campaign coverage: reporters for printing and airing unproven rumors, and voters for watching and subscribing to the news outlets that were the worst offenders. But journalists and their audiences also have it within their power by means of professional judgment and consumer choice to change old habits and bad practice.[18] Hope springs eternal . . . and in the meantime, attack journalism flourishes.

Notes

1. Dennis King, *Lyndon LaRouche and the New American Fascism* (Garden City, N.Y.: Doubleday, 1989). See especially 121–122.
2. Rowland Evans and Robert Novak, "Behind Those Dukakis Rumors," *Washington Post,* August 8, 1988, A13. Reporters from six major news organizations (all three networks, the *Washington Post, U.S. News & World Report,* and the *Los Angeles Times*) told us they had been contacted by Bush operatives about the rumor, and they knew of colleagues at other outlets who had also been called. See also Thomas B. Rosenstiel and Paul Houston, "Rumor Mill: The Media Try to Cope," *Los Angeles Times,* August 5, 1988, 1, 18.
3. Roberts interview.
4. See Edward Walsh, "Dukakis Acts to Kill Rumor," *Washington Post,* August 4, 1988, A1, 6.
5. Frank Sesno, interview with author, Charlottesville, Va., September 27, 1989.
6. Gerald M. Boyd, "Doctor Describes Bush as 'Active and Healthy,'" *New York Times,* August 6, 1988.
7. Kirk O'Donnell, telephone interview with author, June 29, 1990.
8. Dennis King, in *Lyndon LaRouche,* 122, commented upon "the usual [media] reluctance to cover anything relating to LaRouche."

9. Nina Totenberg, telephone interview with author, October 4, 1989.

10. Jill Abramson and James B. Stewart, "Quayle Initially Failed a Major Exam at DePauw, Former School Official Says," *Wall Street Journal,* August 23, 1988, 54.

11. Jill Abramson, interview with author, Washington, D.C., August 4, 1989.

12. Jerald terHorst, interview with author, Washington, D.C., August 4, 1990.

13. See Joseph McGinniss, *The Selling of the President 1968* (New York: Trident, 1969).

14. David Beckwith, telephone interview with author, December 27, 1989. For example, David Broder and Bob Woodward wrote an influential and generally positive series assessing Quayle's career that ran in the *Washington Post* January 12, 1992. The series helped to take some of the disparaging edge off Quayle's image.

15. Shanto Iyengar and Donald R. Kinder, *News That Matters: Television and American Opinion* (Chicago: University of Chicago Press, 1988); Thomas E. Patterson, *The Mass Media Election* (New York: Praeger, 1980); Charles Press and Kenneth VerBurg, *American Politicians and Journalists* (Glenview, Ill.: Scott, Foresman, 1988), 62–66; Shanto Iyengar, Mark D. Peters, and Donald Kinder, "Experimental Demonstrations of the 'Not So Minimal' Consequences of Television News Programs," *American Political Science Review* 76 (December 1982): 848–858; and Roy L. Behr and Shanto Iyengar, "Television News and Real-World Cues and Changes in the Public Agenda," *Public Opinion Quarterly* 49 (Spring 1985): 38–57.

16. On this general subject, see also Laurence I. Barrett, "Rethinking the Fair Games Rules," *Time* 130 (November 30, 1987): 76, 78; Richard Cohen, "The Vice of Virtue," *Washington Post,* March 10, 1989, A23; Charles Krauthammer, "Political Potshots," *Washington Post,* March 1, 1989; Norman Ornstein, "The Post's Campaign to Wreck Congress," May 29, 1989, A25; and "Ethicsgate," *Wall Street Journal* editorial, July 15, 1983, 26.

17. Increasing intrusiveness and scrutiny are also factors in the lessened attractiveness of nonelective governmental service. See Lloyd M. Cutler, "Balancing the Ethics Code," *Washington Post,* March 13, 1989, A15; Ann Devroy, "Current Climate of Caution: Expanded FBI Checks Slow Confirmations," *Washington Post,* March 13, 1989, A1, 4–5.

18. Some remedies from the perspectives of both journalists and news consumers are proposed in Larry J. Sabato, *Feeding Frenzy: Attack Journalism and American Politics* (New York: The Free Press, 1991), Chapter 8.

Part IV

CONTROLLING MEDIA POWER: POLITICAL ACTORS VERSUS THE PRESS

Doris Graber

Political actors try to control how journalists portray them and their causes. Who will win this perennial struggle is always uncertain because journalists have their own views about people and issues. These views shape their choices when they are bombarded with multiple, often conflicting, versions of stories.

Part IV begins with analyses of the many approaches that presidents use to control how media depict their activities. The opening essays also show that the media often become the chief battleground where presidents and congresses fight, win, or lose major political battles. The spotlight next turns to congressional efforts to use media coverage as a policy tool. Legislators want the mainstream news media to frame stories in ways that support each legislator's political objectives. Whether they succeed or fail largely depends on the symmetry between the news outlet's preferred perspectives and the legislator's goals.

A case study follows in the next chapter. It demonstrates that ordinary citizens, bereft of the glamour associated with high-level public office, still can almost certainly capture media attention, albeit at high cost. The concluding essays then confirm that the Internet is making it much easier than ever for ordinary citizens' messages to reach large audiences even when traditional media deny them access.

The essay by Stephen J. Farnsworth and S. Robert Lichter that opens part IV discusses defensive tactics that presidents can use when hounded by journalists in hot pursuit of salacious stories. President Clinton, accused in a flood of media stories of lying under oath, multiple adulterous liaisons, and shady real estate deals, managed to beat back his accusers by generating stories that maligned their motivations and denied the gravity of his alleged offenses. The news media felt compelled to cover his rebuttals because they came from the nation's president. Clinton's stories convinced the public that he deserved forgiveness and support as a victim of vicious politically motivated assaults. Congress then failed to oust him from office because it was loath to impeach an embattled president who had retained public support. With the grudging aid of the media, Clinton's well-publicized counterattack had succeeded.

President Theodore Roosevelt called the presidency a "bully pulpit" because he deemed it an ideal platform for persuasive advocacy of his political agenda. The word "bully" meant "wonderful." Most presidents agree and therefore go public to overcome opposing views. Chapter 20 reports how President Bush used the going-public strategy to win passage of the controversial Patriot Act in 2001. The president's skillfully timed messages, their well-chosen themes, and subsequent favorable news coverage about the legislation were instrumental in passing the act. They created an environment that intimidated Bush's opponents and pressured legislators to quickly approve the act without voicing their objections.

The chapter by Patrick J. Sellers, which follows, also deals with efforts to move political battles from the protective, inside-the-government environment into the glare of media publicity. Sellers investigated how minority parties—Republicans in this instance—managed to air their objections to Democratic policies in the news media in hopes of turning the tide of public opinion and weakening support for their opposition. Their success was partial. They received favorable coverage from Republican-oriented media but not from their Democratic-leaning counterparts.

In the next essay, Doug McAdam tells how the leaders of the American civil rights movement in the 1960s managed to structure their demonstrations so that they would attract extensive favorable media coverage. The secret lay in provoking vicious and visible repressive actions against the movement, making it a pitiable victim and its enemies despicable assailants. The strategy worked well, and the ultimate outcome was a spate of civil rights legislation designed to protect citizens of color from racial discrimination.

The concluding essays in part IV deal with various aspects of new media. Chapter 23, on the "Al Jazeera effect," discusses the shift of power away from the Western mainstream media to voices in other parts of the globe. In this case, the shift is to another news medium. Al Jazeera is an international news network based in the Middle East that reports news from multiple non-Western perspectives. Much of it differs sharply from Western views. The Internet permits people across the globe to access Al Jazeera's offerings. The network has adopted a global orientation, highlighting news from all parts of the world, including many regions that Western media have largely neglected.

The final chapter, by Richard Davis, provides reassuring evidence that the media world is accommodating yet another technology-driven revolution. In the past, it was able to adapt to the printing press, the telephone, and television. Now it is adapting to the Internet with its millions of blogs. As always, accommodation requires declining elites to yield some power to the newcomers, to incorporate the new technologies into older methods of operation, and to work with new types of entrepreneurs. Davis shows that bloggers and professional journalists are perfecting new symbiotic relationships.

19

THE STRUGGLE OVER SHAPING THE NEWS

Stephen J. Farnsworth and S. Robert Lichter

Editor's Note

What journalists cover and how they cover it can determine winners and losers in the political game. The struggle over shaping the news becomes fierce when major political actors—tarred with scandals and under lethal attack from their opponents—and the feuding parties vie for media support. The odds favor the attackers because the media, ever hungry for audience-catching tales, are likely to give full coverage to lurid details about misbehavior in high places. There is no better example of such a battle than the saga of President Clinton's political survival, and even resurrection, after flood tides of scandal coverage that culminated in an impeachment trial. Stephen J. Farnsworth and S. Robert Lichter reveal the kinds of tactics that embattled chief executives have used successfully in the past to counter damaging stories and inflict heavy wounds on their opponents.

When this essay was written, Farnsworth was an associate professor of political science at the University of Mary Washington. His writings about television coverage of the presidency benefit from his experiences as a journalist. Lichter was a professor of communication at George Mason University and the president of the Center for Media and Public Affairs, a media research organization in Washington, D.C. His many books chronicle highlights in the interactions between the American press and the national government.

Source: Stephen J. Farnsworth and S. Robert Lichter, "Can't We Talk About Something Else? Covering Presidential Scandals," in *The Mediated Presidency: Television News and Presidential Governance,* Lanham, Md.: Rowman and Littlefield, 2005, chapter 5. Copyright (c) 2005 by Rowman and Littlefield Publishers, Lanham, Md. Reprinted by permission of Rowman and Littlefield Publishers.

While it is clear that scandal coverage has become more pervasive and more negative, scholars disagree about how today's press coverage of personal matters affects public evaluations of presidents once they are in office (Langman 2002). Clinton's public approval numbers, for example, demonstrate the complexity of the link between scandal coverage and public approval ratings. In December 1997, the month before the [Monica Lewinsky sex] scandal broke, the public's rating of Clinton's performance as president stood at a relatively strong 61 percent approval. By January 1999, the month he was acquitted by the Senate, Clinton's approval rating stood even higher—at 69 percent (Cohen 2002).

It turned out that many people distinguished between Clinton's public and private roles in their evaluations. When asked about his character, or what they thought of him as a person, most expressed disapproval. But they kept these feelings separate from their judgments of his job performance. Scholars who have examined public opinion during this time say that Clinton was able to survive the scandal for two main reasons: (1) the economy's strong performance during 1998, and (2) his success in portraying himself as an ideological moderate—and his opponents as extremists—in the years since the Republican electoral victories of 1994 (cf. Cohen 2002; Newman 2002; Wayne 2000; Zaller 1998). On the first point, it may be risky to banish a president who has been in office during economic good times. On the second, public perceptions of Clinton and his opponents helped the president to portray himself as the victim of fanatical opponents bent on using the scandal to exact revenge. . . .

[The Lewinsky Scandal]

. . . [P]ast allegations [of sexual misconduct] had conditioned the media—and the public—to imagine the worst about the politician opponents had nicknamed "Slick Willie." As a result of the disclosures and the developments throughout the year, the Clinton-Lewinsky saga was by far the leading story of 1998. In all, the network evening news shows devoted one-seventh of their airtime that year to this single story (1,636 broadcast reports in all). The Clinton scandals received more attention than the standoff with Iraq, the bombing of U.S. embassies in Africa, the fighting in the Serbian province of Kosovo, the Israeli-Palestinian conflict, nuclear weapons tests in Pakistan and India, and major financial crises in Asia and in Russia *combined*.

The Clinton-Lewinsky scandal coverage also swamped coverage of the 1998 midterm elections. During the fall campaign season (Labor Day, September 7, through Election Day, November 2) there were six times as many stories on the scandal as on the elections. The Texas governor's race, won by future president George W. Bush, was the subject of only three network news reports.

The subsequent impeachment of the president and its aftermath generated over four hundred more stories in 1999, most of them in the first three months of the year, when the media wrapped up the coverage of the scandal after the Senate's failure to convict the president on charges brought by the House. . . .

The White House fought off the allegations through public denials and efforts to "spin" the story as being a personal vendetta against the president. Foremost among the president's defenders was First Lady Hillary Clinton, who spoke on *The Today Show* on NBC on January 27, 1998, to defend her husband and attack his accusers.

> This is the great story here, for anybody willing to find it and write about it and explain it, is this vast right-wing conspiracy that has been conspiring against my husband since the day he announced for president. . . . Having seen so many of these accusations come and go, having seen people profit, you know, like Jerry Falwell, with videos, accusing my husband of committing murder, of drug running, seeing some of the things that are written and said about him, my attitude is, you know, we've been there before and we have seen this before. (Hillary Clinton, quoted in Blaney and Benoit 2001:109)

. . . The 1992 presidential election was won in part by inducing journalists to train their fire on Clinton's adversaries, short-circuiting further critical coverage of Clinton himself (Ceaser and Busch 1993). A similar pattern occurred in the first weeks of the Clinton-Lewinsky scandal. During the first ten days after the story broke, the president was featured in nearly all (93 percent) of the scandal stories. That figure dropped to 70 percent in the following three weeks, even as the percentage focusing on Monica Lewinsky increased from 47 to 59 percent and the share featuring independent counsel Kenneth Starr also rose from 30 to 41 percent. The growing focus on Lewinsky and Starr in media coverage is a measure of the effectiveness of the Clinton team's approach—increasing the media emphasis on the accusers.

. . . Throughout this period, the only consistent on-air support for Clinton came from the White House and the president's lawyers. Even this group, though, found it necessary to reference the president's admission of improper personal conduct in order to argue that he had done nothing to warrant impeachment, such as lying under oath or encouraging others to do so. As a result, even many sound bites from the Clinton team were negative. In fact, a slight majority (52 percent) of the sound bites from the president himself were positive, as he repeatedly admitted to an inappropriate relationship with Monica Lewinsky. "Indeed, I did have a relationship with Ms. Lewinsky that was not appropriate," Clinton said in a CBS *Evening News* report on September 9. In our age of sophisticated presidential spin, a president has rarely evaluated himself as negatively in his public comments as Clinton did during the second half of 1998.

But the strategy of using offense as the best defense continued to bear fruit. . . . Although the tone of the coverage of Clinton was about two-to-one negative during two periods of peak coverage examined here (the first month of the scandal and the two-month period in the summer of 1998, *Media Monitor,* September–October 1998), coverage of Kenneth Starr, Monica Lewinsky, and other scandal figures were about six-to-one negative. . . .

"Wagging the Dog?"

Presidents facing trouble in Washington—whether from scandal, legislative setbacks, or other unpleasantness—often turn to the international arena. Whether or not they do so to distract the media and the public, presidential performances on the world stage often overshadow other issues, particularly long-running scandals. Even during the Clinton-Lewinsky scandal, an international trip served to drive down the volume of scandal coverage. The three networks broadcast fifty-eight stories on the president's trip to China and his policies toward the Asian superpower from June 24 through July 4, 1998, compared to only nineteen stories on the Clinton-Lewinsky scandal. Coverage of the president likewise was more positive, as four out of five sources quoted on the newscasts evaluated his China policies favorably. Many of the positive assessments came from inside the administration and from the president's Chinese hosts, and the White House reveled in its ability to set the news agenda once again.

The Dynamics of Impeachment Coverage

Two weeks after the 1998 midterm elections, the lame-duck U.S. House Judiciary Committee began holding hearings on whether to impeach President Clinton. During the three weeks of coverage (November 19 through December 12, 1998), the networks aired 108 stories that focused on the hearings. True to form, evaluations of Clinton were mainly (62 percent) negative, while on-air assessments of independent counsel Ken Starr were even more negative (69 percent), and congressional Republicans fared worst of all (77 percent negative).

Context can be decisive for a president's fortunes, as coverage of this scandal illustrates. If Republicans had succeeded in their efforts to frame the Clinton-Lewinsky scandal as a criminal matter of perjury—that is, the felony of lying under oath—they might have been able to drive the president from office. Instead, the media frame was largely that the president's alleged lies were of a more personal nature, the foibles of a philandering husband trying to avoid embarrassing himself and his family. That alternative perspective, presented aggressively by Clinton's defenders through 1998, was adopted by many citizens, making it difficult for the House Republicans to turn public opinion against the president (Bennett 2005; Blaney and Benoit 2001; Klein 2002; Owen 2000; Sabato et al. 2000).

Administration efforts to portray the scandal as a mudslinging contest also worked to the president's advantage. Independent counsel Starr could not defend himself effectively while his investigation was continuing. Holding press conferences to rebut attacks by Hillary Clinton and others would only damage his credibility further. In addition, Starr's GOP allies on Capitol Hill could not win the battle for the airwaves against the White House. The media frames of this story were largely along the lines sketched by the executive branch, as is so often the case. The president may not be able to convince reporters to cover something else, but he retains considerable ability to shape the way the story is discussed, even when the topic is a sex scandal.

Whitewater

The impeachment saga was far from the only major scandal of the Clinton presidency. Near the end of Clinton's first year in office, . . . all three networks reported that former Clinton attorney Vincent Foster's files on the Whitewater Development Corporation had not reached federal investigators for more than five months after his suicide. These reports set off a new round of media inquiries into the ethical practices of the First Family and their associates, a range of questions known collectively as Whitewater.

From those first reports on December 20, 1993, through the first three months of 1994, the network evening news shows aired 193 Whitewater stories with over six hours of airtime. Clinton loyalists frequently attached negative motives to those questioning the First Family. Among the most frequent explanations: partisan politics (including opposition to health care reform, and anti–Hillary Clinton and antiwomen sentiment), self-interest (including jealousy, spite, and financial motivations), and a culture of "negativism" that has made political life and the press more mean-spirited. On ABC on January 7, 1994, David Gergen, a communications staffer for Presidents Clinton, Reagan, Ford, and Nixon, blamed "the cannibalism which is loose in our society in which public figures, such as the Clintons . . . get hammered even though they are trying to do the right thing." Only one source in seven (14 percent) suggested the Clintons' accusers were motivated by genuine concern over possible wrongdoing. . . .

The Clinton media strategies during the Whitewater controversy often involved a combination of offense and defense, as would be employed during the Clinton-Lewinsky scandal several years later. Partisan political sources favorable to the Clintons were aggressive in making the Clintons' case in the media. Supportive comments from administration sources outnumbered negative remarks from congressional Republicans by a margin of nearly three to one. Nevertheless, coverage during this period frequently portrayed the president as politically wounded by the Whitewater affair. . . .

* * *

Conclusion

Twenty years of presidential scandals show how presidents remain the central focus of political news, even—perhaps especially—when things go wrong. But that intense media focus on the executive branch provides a key executive branch power: a president's ability to frame a story more successfully than his competitors and opponents. In scandal after scandal, whether Clinton-Lewinsky or Whitewater, the Abu Ghraib torture photos or the Iran-contra affair, presidents have been able to minimize immediate damage to themselves by working to frame the story in a way less hostile to the White House. The plan for responding to a presidential scandal is simple, and it starts with a direct, consistent message that is echoed by all administration officials (Auletta 2004). . . .

But successful politicians are rarely content to stay on defense. Responding to scandals, especially, requires going on offense as well. Administrations respond to an emerging scandal by attacking their opponents, such as by presenting them as ideological fanatics blinded by their hatred of the president. If the scandal is of a sexual nature, no one can launch a more effective retaliatory strike than the First Lady. Depending on the issue, administration defenders may be able to counterattack by questioning the patriotism of opponents. Reporters love conflict, so countercharges are an effective way to stop playing defense and start playing offense. Sometimes the insults can even muddy the waters, obscuring relevant but—from the point of view of the White House—unhelpful evidence.

For the really big crises, triage is an important part of a president's media defense. During the Clinton-Lewinsky affair, Bill Clinton and his defenders frequently admitted to flaws in the president's character, thereby making the president and his team seem more reasonable to reporters and to viewers of television newscasts. While that approach did not draw investigative blood-hounds like Kenneth Starr and Republican members of the House Judiciary Committee off the scent, the public remained convinced throughout the year-long spectacle that the president should not be removed from office. Though the intensely partisan House impeached the president on a near party-line vote, the less ideologically oriented Senate found it impossible to remove from office a figure receiving such high public approval ratings. The White House also employed triage in the wake of the Iran-contra and Whitewater disclosures. Key administration officials and presidential friends took the fall to protect Clinton and Reagan, a particularly effective strategy for relatively popular presidents.

Making things seem more complicated as a scandal progresses can also strengthen a president's position by depriving opponents of the opportunity to make a clear and simple case. The more justifications a president offers for doing something, the harder it will be for opponents to counter the arguments, particularly given the relatively small amount of television news time provided to voices from outside the executive branch. By moving from "weapons of mass destruction" to "weapons of mass destruction programs" to "weapons of mass destruction activities" to the mass graves found in Iraq, the Bush administration offered a number of after-the-fact justifications for why the United States fought in Iraq. If the question on the lips of reporters is, Does Saddam Hussein deserve to remain in power? then the answer about that brutal tyrant is obvious. The more complicated alternative question offered by the war's opponents—Is Saddam Hussein a greater threat to the United States than, say, al Qaeda or North Korea or Iran?—is a question not likely to be answered effectively on time-pressured television newscasts, which may mean the question will not even be asked by a media-savvy politician.

Lying may seem to be an appealing presidential response to an unfolding scandal, but it is clearly a high-risk strategy. There is the substantial chance that one will be caught in the deceit—all the memos; recalled conversations; and, in the case of Bill Clinton, even DNA samples can undermine the claim that one is telling the whole truth. If that happens, videotape of the damning statements—like Nixon's famous "I am not a crook" response to Watergate and Clinton's finger-wagging denial of a sexual relationship with Monica Lewinsky—are shown over and over again. Although Bill Clinton's presidency survived the scandal, his became a greatly weakened administration, just like the post-Iran-contra Reagan presidency.

Every administration has its dissidents, and their inside views can be very damaging, as a variety of insider books about recent presidents illustrate (Clarke 2004; Reich 1998; Stephanopoulos 1999; Suskind 2004; Woodward 1994). . . . While reporters may hesitate to say plainly that a candidate is lying, today's intensely partisan politics provides a variety of people willing to make such a charge. . . .

The Abu Ghraib scandal is [an] example of how the lack of visual images can influence news media coverage. The mass media were particularly slow to pick up on that story (the most famous incidents happened in November 2003), but reporters made up for lost time with saturation coverage after the pictures were published in April 2004. Once pictures become public, they stay public. Six years after the Clinton-Lewinsky scandal broke—when Bill

Clinton started making the rounds of television news programs to peddle his autobiography—news reports illustrating the president's new book returned to the now vintage footage of President Clinton embracing a beret-clad former intern in a White House rope line.

. . . [T]here are limits to how effectively a president can change the subject in midscandal. Indeed, when Clinton sought to engage in foreign policy during scandal periods, some news accounts questioned whether he was doing so to distract the electorate and the press. Bush's efforts in mid-2004 to talk more about a proposed manned space mission to Mars and less about Iraq likewise largely fell flat. . . .

We may be entering an age in which the online news media function as an immense echo chamber, allowing whispered stories to remain alive until mainstream media turn their attention to them. Stories may live longer than ever before, and unsubstantiated allegations may get more attention than ever before as media outlets "race to the bottom" in accuracy in order to be first in this highly competitive industry (cf. Okrent 2004).

References

Auletta, Ken. 2004. "Fortress Bush: How the White House Keeps the Press Under Control." *New Yorker,* February 19.

Bennett, W. Lance. 2005. *News: The Politics of Illusion.* 6th ed. New York: Pearson/ Longman.

Blaney, Joseph R., and William L. Benoit. 2001. *The Clinton Scandals and the Politics of Image Restoration.* Westport, CT: Praeger.

Ceaser, James, and Andrew Busch. 1993. *Upside Down and Inside Out: The 1992 Elections and American Politics.* Lanham, MD: Rowman & Littlefield.

Clarke, Richard A. 2004. *Against All Enemies: Inside America's War on Terror.* New York: Free Press.

Cohen, Jeffrey E. 2002. "The Polls: Policy-Specific Presidential Approval, Part II." *Presidential Studies Quarterly* 32(4): 779–88.

Klein, Joe. 2002. *The Natural: The Misunderstood Presidency of Bill Clinton.* New York: Doubleday.

Langman, Lauren. 2002. "Suppose They Gave a Culture War and No One Came." *American Behavioral Scientist* 46(4): 501–34.

Newman, Brian. 2002. "Bill Clinton's Approval Ratings: The More Things Change the More They Stay the Same." *Political Research Quarterly* 55(4): 781–804.

Okrent, Daniel. 2004. "Weapons of Mass Destruction? Or Mass Distraction?" *New York Times,* May 30.

Owen, Diana. 2000. "Popular Politics and the Clinton/Lewinsky Affair: The Implications of Leadership." *Political Psychology* 21(1): 161–77.

Reich, Robert, 1998. *Locked in the Cabinet.* New York: Vintage.

Sabato, Larry, Mark Stencel, and S. Robert Lichter. 2000. *Peepshow: Media and Politics in an Age of Scandal.* Lanham, MD: Rowman & Littlefield.

Stephanopoulos, George. 1999. *All Too Human: A Political Education*. Boston: Little, Brown.

Suskind, Ron. 2004. *The Price of Loyalty: George W. Bush, the White House, and the Education of Paul O'Neill*. New York: Simon & Schuster.

Wayne, Stephen J. 2000. "Presidential Personality and the Clinton Legacy." In *The Clinton Scandals and the Future of American Government*, ed. Mark J. Rozell and Clyde Wilcox. Washington, DC: Georgetown University Press.

Woodward, Bob. 1994. *The Agenda: Inside the Clinton White House*. New York: Simon & Schuster.

Zaller, John R. 1998. "Monica Lewinsky's Contribution to Political Science." *PS: Political Science & Politics* 31(2): 554–57.

20

GOING PUBLIC AS POLITICAL STRATEGY: THE BUSH ADMINISTRATION, AN ECHOING PRESS, AND PASSAGE OF THE PATRIOT ACT

David Domke, Erica S. Graham, Kevin Coe, Sue Lockett John, and Ted Coopman

Editor's Note

The U.S. Constitution specifies that Congress makes the laws for the nation and the president merely executes them. In reality, presidents usually lay out plans of their legislative priorities and then work hard to create information environments that will pressure Congress to make the necessary laws. When the proposed legislation is controversial because it pits hallowed values against each other, gaining Congressional approval is difficult. Opposition in Congress can derail the president's plans. Passage of the 2001 Patriot Act illustrates how presidents carefully frame and manage messages from the executive branch. Their strategies are designed to entice the news media to echo the president's line of reasoning and to slight coverage of controversial aspects of proposed laws. If the strategy succeeds and the executive branch of the government and the media seem largely in accord, dissenters in Congress are likely to lie low. The research presented in chapter 20 examined messages by the executive branch, congressional dialogs, and news media coverage, along with the overall political climate, to explain how President Bush prevailed over Patriot Act opponents without major overt battles.

When this essay was written, David Domke was a professor and Sue Lockett John and Ted Coopman were doctoral students in the Department of

Source: Excerpted from David Domke, Erica S. Graham, Kevin Coe, Sue Lockett John, and Ted Coopman, "Going Public as Political Strategy: The Bush Administration, an Echoing Press, and Passage of the Patriot Act," in Political Communication, 23:3 (September 2006): 291-312. Reprinted by permission of Taylor & Francis Group, http://www.informaworld.com.

Communication at the University of Washington. Kevin Coe was a doctoral candidate in the Department of Speech Communication at the University of Illinois. Erica S. Graham worked in film development for Everyman Pictures in Los Angeles, California.

Within days of the terrorist attacks of September 11, 2001, U.S. Attorney General John Ashcroft revealed plans for legislation aimed at giving government authorities far-reaching oversight powers to prevent and protect against terrorist activities. Among other provisions, this legislation proposed to give federal agents the ability to detain noncitizens, increase wiretaps, initiate e-mail and Internet surveillance, and intensify the monitoring of student visas. Several organizations and individuals expressed concerns that it followed in a line of previous governmental abuses of civil liberties in the name of U.S. national security (see Brill, 2003; Quenqua, 2001), but President George W. Bush and Ashcroft often spoke publicly on behalf of the law, arguing that it was essential to combat terrorism. The outcome is known, of course. Within weeks of its introduction into Congress, a modestly revised version, ultimately given the acronym USA PATRIOT Act, was adopted with overwhelming support in the Senate (98–1) and by a large majority in the House of Representatives (357–66). The legislation has been a source of controversy since, and by June 2005 nearly 400 local governmental bodies had adopted resolutions opposing parts of the law (Epstein, 2005; Goering, 2005).

This research examined the passage of the Patriot Act by focusing on what Manheim (1991, 1994) has termed "strategic political communications," in which leaders craft their public language with the goal of creating, controlling, distributing, and using mediated messages as a political resource. Prior to September 11, anti-terrorism legislation was a lesser priority for the Bush administration, even though the threat of an attack was widely known in governmental circles (see U.S. Commission on National Security/21st Century, 2001). Following the attacks the administration sought to make a powerful statement to citizens, who were looking for White House leadership and extended sizable support to the president as Bush's ratings surged to nearly 90% public approval (Pew Center, 2001). In such a crisis context, Kernell (1997) has argued, an administration that acts adroitly in its public communications has an opportunity to gain a "near-monopoly control over information" (p. 183), which can go far to foster support for, and adoption of, government policies. With this perspective we analyzed the passage of the Patriot Act, arguing that (a) the administration acted strategically to dominate public discourse and (b) the mainstream press followed the administration's lead, thereby substantially facilitating the president's control of the legislative agenda.

Strategic Communication and the Bush Administration

Research suggests that political elites excel at controlling political and media information environments, particularly in times of national crisis (e.g., Baker & Oneal, 2001; Coe et al., 2004; Domke, 2004; Entman, 1991; Herman, 1993; Riker, 1986; Zaller, 1992, 1994b). In such contexts, *going public* can be a powerful strategy for a presidential administration seeking to influence Congress or other political leaders. In this approach, the president seeks to build public support for policies by speaking directly to citizens and generating positive news content through exchanges with the press; in turn, such public support can pressure Congress to follow the administration's agenda (see Canes-Wrone, 2001; Gelman & King, 1993; Kernell, 1997). Going public is especially likely to be effective in times of national crisis, because favorable surges in public opinion are common and news media treatment of the administration tends to resemble the positive, or at least sympathetic, "honeymoon period" that often follows elections (Brody, 1991; Graber, 1997; Hughes, 1995; Kernell, 1997). Although some suggest that a strategy of going public is not easily identifiable or always successful (Corrigan, 2000; Powell, 1999), evidence suggests the Bush administration used this technique in its post–September 11 launching of the "war on terrorism" and in its 2002 push for congressional and United Nations resolutions on Iraq (see Billeaudeaux et al., 2003; John et al., 2004). At minimum, public support and the likelihood of news media deference made this approach attractive for the administration in its pursuit of the Patriot Act.

The political success of a presidential administration in going public may be dependent on several elements. First, the *timing* of the administration's public communications is crucial. The optimal time to deliver a message is when a political leader can have the greatest control over relevant discourses and has the attention of important audiences (see Hoger & Swem, 2000). In the immediate aftermath of the terrorist attacks, the administration had the nation's attention: An estimated 82 million Americans watched the president's address before Congress on September 20—likely the largest in U.S. history for a political event (see Huff, 2001). With this bully pulpit, the administration was poised to leverage public support to pressure Congress toward passage of the administration-proposed Patriot Act, which was slated to enter Congress through the Judiciary Committees in each chamber. The House committee was known for its partisanship, and in autumn 2001 it was dominated by staunch conservatives and liberals (Brill, 2003). Committee consensus on the anti-terrorism legislation would send the full Congress important signals regarding expected support. It would be strategically adept, therefore, for the administration to focus its communications on the time period when the legislation was being crafted and considered in committee prior to broader debate. With this in mind, we expected that the preponderance of the president and attorney general's public communications about the anti-terrorism legislation occurred before full congressional consideration of the bill began October 11, 2001.

Second, presentation of a *consistent perspective* among administration leaders is an important strategic consideration, because "any appearance of disunity among the president's ranks will be seized by the media as an opportunity for a story" (Maltese, 1994, p. 1; see also Entman, 2003), thereby distracting from the administration's goals. George W. Bush and his administration long have been known for their discipline in staying "on message"— that is, consistently focusing on a few selected points. Under the tutelage of long-time Bush strategist Karl Rove, this approach became an administration hallmark after September 11 (see Broder, 2003; Domke, 2004; Horsey, 2003; Lemann, 2003; Suskind, 2003). As a result, it was rare for a key administration member to publicly offer an opinion counter to or divergent from the president's, a communication strategy of great import when citizens, other politicians, and journalists were looking to the president and administration for guidance. Our expectation, therefore, was that President Bush and Attorney General John Ashcroft (the latter being the architect and primary "point person" for this law) presented a unified message about the anti-terrorism legislation and the perceived need for its congressional passage—thereby producing a set of consistent administration communications about the Patriot Act.

These underlying communication strategies positioned the administration to capitalize on post–September 11 public support by pushing for a strong policy response. In particular, we suggest that the administration emphasized the need for anti-terrorism legislation to be enacted quickly and with considerable political support by Congress. . . . [R]equests for political solidarity became a potent strategy for a White House seeking to advance its legislative agenda in the aftermath of the terrorist attacks. In this crisis context, administration rhetoric about political unity inevitably suggested that other political actors—particularly those in Congress, of course—should stand with the president *in pursuing the administration's goals*. Notably, these White House communication emphases implied that disagreements would be hazardous and unpatriotic. The combination of these content emphases with strategic message timing and unity likely went some distance in offsetting the sensitive civil liberties matters at stake with the Patriot Act. Indeed, it would not be the first time in war contexts that political leaders advocated and justified the suspension of civil liberties by emphasizing national security and evoking feelings of nationalism (see Ayer & Forsythe, 1979; Katz, 1965; Mishler, 1965; Swisher, 1940). . . .

Presidential Discourse and News Coverage in Crisis Contexts

. . . Press coverage about the Patriot Act was expected to follow the administration's discourse—and not potential alternative perspectives—for a number of reasons. First, mainstream journalists rely heavily upon government officials to "index" the range of viewpoints in news coverage (Althaus, Edy, Entman, & Phalen, 1996; Bennett, 1990; Entman & Rojecki, 1993), especially in crisis and national security contexts (Hallin, Manoff, & Weddle, 1993; Billeaudeaux et al., 2003). As Graber (1997) noted, when "life and property are endangered, when sudden death and terror reign: the media largely abandon their adversarial role and become teammates of officialdom in attempts to restore public order, safety, and tranquility" (p. 252). Second, research suggests that news media particularly focus on the president and administration officials early in crises, providing these actors with the platform to define the circumstances and ultimately limit the range of perspectives (e.g., Hutcheson et al., 2004; Zaller & Chiu, 1996). Third, the anti-terrorism legislation originated with the attorney general, a relatively uncommon occurrence; as a result, administration communications about the law became a marker for news media to follow. Finally, Zaller's (1994a) claim that during crises "national unity [is] good politics" (p. 267)—as in publicly popular politics—can be adapted to suggest that national unity is "good news"—as in *publicly popular news*. Fox News Channel, which was accused by some of highly nationalistic coverage post–September 11 (e.g., Rutenberg, 2001), experienced significant ratings increases during this period, consistently surpassing rival CNN. Similarly, many news organizations incorporated the colors of red, white, and blue into their promotions and identifying logos.

These factors increased the likelihood that news content about the Patriot Act would parallel the timing of the administration's communications, while also rarely challenging the administration's themes and perspectives. Such an outcome might be termed *echoing* news coverage, to highlight that news gathered via "objective" means is rarely neutral in a political sense (see Domke, 2004). To be clear, the expectation is not that mainstream U.S. news coverage contained only the administration's voices or perspectives, which would imply that the independent, commercial news media were merely government mouthpieces. News media do sometimes staunchly criticize administration ideas, of course, particularly when other political leaders speak out against the administration. Such dissent, however, was relatively uncommon in the aftermath of September 11. As a result, our expectation was that news coverage about the Patriot Act remained substantially within the parameters of discourse put forward by the Bush administration, exactly the outcome sought by a strategy of going public. In turn, a wide range of scholarship has suggested that news content—both news coverage and editorials—often serves as sources of "opinion leadership" for citizens and members of Congress (e.g., Dalton, Beck, & Huckfeldt, 1998; Huckin, 2002; Powlick, 1995; Schaefer, 1997; Vermeer, 2002). In short, a combination of strategic Bush administration communications and echoing news discourse after September 11 would have done much to pressure other political actors, especially Congress, to respond to administration requests as if they were unchallengeable demands.

Method

This study proceeded in three stages. First, the public communications of President Bush and Attorney General Ashcroft regarding the administration's anti-terrorism legislation were analyzed between the dates of September 11 and October 25, 2001, when Congress passed the Patriot Act. Second, we determined whether administration communications—particularly the timing, themes, and perspectives—predominated in newspaper content, television news, and newspaper editorials during the same dates. Finally, congressional discourse about the legislation was analyzed for potential insight into the role of administration communications and/or news coverage in legislative debate and activity. . . . [See the original text for research procedure details]. . . .

Results . . .

Timing of Communications

Our first expectations were that Bush and Ashcroft were more likely to speak publicly about the anti-terrorism legislation prior to debate in Congress, a crucial period of committee decision making, and that news coverage followed this pattern. With this in mind, administration communications and news coverage were grouped chronologically: when the legislation was being formulated in committees (September 11 to October 10) or from beginning of full congressional discussion through voting (October 11 to October 25). The data supported our expectations. Of their public communications in which they discussed the legislation or components of it, 83% of Bush's and 77% of Ashcroft's occurred during the period of bill formation. Similarly, 80% of newspaper stories, 83% of editorials, and 81% of television news stories appeared before full congressional debate on the bill. These results, then, indicate that administration leaders targeted their messages to the period when they were better able to control public discourse and potentially influence congressional committees, and that news coverage on the legislation closely paralleled the timing of the administration's communications.

Themes and Valence

Our second set of expectations posited that Bush and Ashcroft were unified in their communications; that is, they consistently made similar points about the perceived merits of the anti-terrorism legislation and the necessity of congressional approval. Six themes were present in the administration's discussion of the Patriot Act: success in the "war on terrorism," U.S. security, civil liberties protections, time urgency, unity, and calls for congressional action. Analyses examined how often Bush and Ashcroft in their public communications emphasized these themes and the valence of their discourse (whether they exhibited any disagreement in their perspectives). . . . [F]or four of the six themes Bush and Ashcroft were highly consistent in their public communications about the Patriot Act; indeed, the themes often appeared in two thirds or more of the texts. The only substantial differences between the president and attorney general were in emphases upon time urgency and civil liberties protections, which were much more present in Ashcroft's communications. Two additional points . . . are noteworthy. First, at no time was there valence disagreement between Bush and Ashcroft; they were unequivocally consistent in their claims that the legislation would bring about success in the "war on terrorism" and would improve U.S. security, that civil liberties would be protected, that political unity was important, that time was of the essence, and that Congress needed to act. Second, the president and attorney general did address other matters in their communications. For example, Bush discussed terrorism broadly, the roles of the FBI and CIA, and the world community's support for the United States, while Ashcroft focused on shortcomings of extant anti-terrorism legislation and specific changes he desired. It is our impression that these differing points of emphasis, all part of the administration's broader discourse about terrorism, only served to buttress the administration's push for the Patriot Act.

Of interest next was how these themes were treated in U.S. news coverage of the anti-terrorism legislation. Specifically, we examined the presence and valence of the themes across three forms of news coverage: newspaper articles, television stories, and newspaper editorials.

. . . [N]ews coverage gave significant voice to four of the six themes: U.S. security, civil liberties protections, time urgency, and calls for Congress to act. Each of these was present in between roughly 40% and 80% of news coverage, a presence that fit our expectations that news media would emphasize the same perspectives as administration officials but not to exactly the same degree. Data also indicate that the news coverage about the themes substantially supported the administration's perspectives. The level of *valence congruence* with the administration—that is, when claims in news coverage emphasized only support, without or with reservations—ranged between

83% and 91% for five of the themes, and was at nearly half (45%) for
the civil liberties theme. In addition, across the types of news coverage, the
level of valence congruence for all themes was consistently favorable toward
the administration, ranging from 67% to 77%. As a reminder, any criticism
of the administration's position in a news item warranted a code of critical
valence. In sum, news coverage of the Patriot Act gave significant voice to
many of the same themes as the administration and predominantly contained
perspectives congruent with the administration's.

It appears, then, that civil liberties was the only domain of news about
the Patriot Act in which the administration was substantively contested. This
finding prompted us to closely scrutinize this discourse, beginning with the
administration. One salient point is that the president's comments about civil
liberties occurred in prepared remarks: to FBI and CIA employees, after a
meeting with his national security team, and in a brief statement about congressional action. Bush faced questioning by the press in roughly 40% of his
Patriot Act–related public communications; in *none* of these, however, were
civil liberties discussed. In contrast, seven of the eight times that Ashcroft
publicly discussed civil liberties and the Patriot Act were in news briefings
or in testimony before Congress. These patterns indicate that the attorney
general but not the president encountered debate about the legislation's
treatment of civil liberties. A second point is that the administration without
exception declared that civil liberties would be fully upheld. For example,
Bush said: "I want you to know that every one of the proposals we've made
on Capitol Hill, carried by the Attorney General, has been carefully reviewed.
They are measured requests; they are responsible requests; they are constitutional requests. Ours is a land that values the constitutional rights of every
citizen, and we will honor those rights, of course" (Bush, 2001b). Ashcroft,
meanwhile, commonly used phrasing similar to his September 24 statement
before the House Judiciary Committee that the administration was "conducting this effort with a total commitment to protect the rights and privacy
of all Americans and the constitutional protectors we hold dear" (Ashcroft,
2001). In short, the administration presented its anti-terrorism legislation as
uncompromising on civil liberties.

News content on this matter was more robust—but not among government officials. Roughly half to three fourths of Patriot Act coverage discussed civil liberties, and of this almost half contained some criticisms,
including 43% of news stories, 67% of editorials, and 70% of TV news
stories. Such critical coverage was present, in relative proportion to the total
civil liberties content in each media outlet, across a wide range of analyzed
news organizations. These critiques focused on three potential implications:
for the general thrust of the Constitution, citizens' privacy, and treatment of
minorities and immigrants, emphasized by 82%, 72%, and 44% of critics,

respectively. Notably, though, these concerns were raised almost entirely by non-governmental organizations and individuals, who constituted 83% of all news sources critical of the administration or legislation. For example, according to a *Houston Chronicle* story on September 17, "Some civil libertarians have cautioned against an overreaction to the terrorist attacks. 'We will urge our leaders to continue to uphold the principles of liberty the nation holds dear as they pursue those responsible for this devastating attack on American soil,' Anthony Romero, executive director of the American Civil Liberties Union, said." Among critical news sources, only 16% were members of Congress (of which all but one were Democrats), and none were affiliated with the Bush administration.

Further, close scrutiny revealed that news content with civil liberties criticisms of the legislation also often included claims that supported the administration. Fully 83% of Patriot Act–related news coverage that contained civil liberties concerns also included administration-supportive claims, with the most common emphases being security (in 78% of such content), calls for congressional action (in 44% of such content), and time urgency (in 42% of such content). For example, a *New York Times* article on October 12 identified several civil liberties concerns and quoted Democratic Senator Russell Feingold of Wisconsin, who said that new legislation was necessary but that "we must also make sure those new tools do not become instruments of oppression." These concerns were countered, however, by quotes from Democratic Senator and majority leader Tom Daschle of South Dakota (who the *Times* said delivered a "chilly lecture on the need for immediate action" and "urged that [Feingold's] amendments be shelved"), Democratic Senator and Judiciary Committee Chair Patrick Leahy of Vermont, and Ashcroft—who emphasized time urgency, national security, and a need for congressional action, respectively. Finally, this coverage contained no discussion of providing greater protections for citizens' freedoms and liberties, and only 6% of content discussed potential alternative forms of the legislation. Thus, even in the one domain of Patriot Act news coverage in which the administration was substantively challenged, perspectives supportive of the administration were heavily represented and the possibility of alternative approaches was not.

Congressional Debate

Finally, congressional discussion and activities were analyzed for evidence regarding their relation to administration communications and/or news coverage. We began with the judiciary committees, which were entry points for the anti-terrorism legislation.

The House committee returned a 36–0 vote in favor of the legislation in its report, issued October 11, 2001. . . .

. . . Our analysis identified whether the rationale [Democratic] senators expressed for voting for the legislation paralleled themes in administration communications and news coverage (the theme "calls for Congress to act" was excluded from this analysis) or included claims that the legislation had been satisfactorily modified. In three days of congressional discussion 22 Democrats spoke in the Senate, and 9 voiced no disagreement with the legislation. . . . Among Democrats who expressed disagreement, all cited security as one of the reasons for supporting the bill—an unsurprising but notable finding given this theme's prevalence in news coverage as a response to civil liberties criticisms. Time urgency and a perception of satisfactory modifications to the legislation each were cited by 7 senators, unity was cited by 6, and success in the "war on terrorism" was expressed by 5. . . .

Discussion

Several findings warrant discussion. First, the administration maximized its position as the unchallenged voice of U.S. politics in the weeks after September 11 by timing the large majority of its public communications about the anti-terrorism legislation to occur prior to consideration of the legislation by the full Congress. Polls during the period suggest that the administration's public communications disseminated broadly and with considerable impact on the public. In the days immediately following the attacks, 55% of randomly sampled U.S. adults said that "in order to curb terrorism in this country," it would be "necessary for the average person to give up some civil liberties." One week later, that number had increased to 63%. And in a September 27–28 poll, 72% of adult Americans said the Bush administration was "about right" in its proposed degree of restrictions on civil liberties in response to terrorism, while another 17% said administration goals were going "not far enough" (for all polls, see Roper Center, 2001; see also Huddy, Khatib, & Capelos, 2002). In this milieu, the historically partisan Judiciary Committee in the House of Representatives returned a 36–0 vote favoring the anti-terrorism legislation, and the Senate bypassed its Judiciary Committee due to administration wishes for speed on the bill. The evidence, then, suggests that the administration's strategy of going public produced, or at least helped to secure, its desired outcomes. To be clear, other factors, including support for the legislation or concerns about retrospective voting, likely also contributed to Congress's actions on the Patriot Act. Nonetheless, it is apparent that the administration's public communications were strategically delivered to marshal public support for the legislation and to pressure Congress to act—and quickly.

Second, the message consistency demonstrated in these data by President George W. Bush and Attorney General John Ashcroft did not coincidentally happen—it was carefully orchestrated and not easily achieved. Entman (2003) noted, for example, that "strategically maladroit administrations, such as the Carter and Clinton White Houses, often found news frames spinning out of their control" (p. 422). This was not the case for the Bush administration in its push for the Patriot Act. To the contrary, the administration presented a unified front that gave other political actors and media outlets little to discuss beyond the key themes that Bush and Ashcroft presented (see also Billeaudeaux et al., 2003; Domke, 2004; Hutcheson et al., 2004). In times of political normalcy, journalists might respond to a unified administration by turning to other topics, particularly when there is little public challenge from other elites. Nothing new from the administration would be viewed as no news, period. In a time of crisis, however, journalists see a continuing emphasis upon administration voices to be an appropriate, patriotic function of the press. As a result, news media become far more likely to echo administration messages—an outcome particularly favorable for a White House that is unified in its public voice. Indeed, we suggest that both strategic timing and unity of message among leaders are necessary foundations for success for a presidential administration attempting to go public in the pursuit of particular goals or policies.

It is the case that two themes, civil liberties protections and time urgency, were emphasized significantly more by Ashcroft than by Bush. . . . Regardless, Bush and Ashcroft's differing emphases on these themes helped to make apparent the more-commonplace consistency in public communications across administration leaders. Further, there was absolute consistency in the valence of perspectives emphasized by the president and attorney general. Not once in their public communications did Bush and Ashcroft disagree about what they proposed or how this legislation would make a difference in a campaign against terrorism.

Examination of news coverage also revealed notable patterns, beginning with the significant emphasis given to several administration themes in news coverage about the Patriot Act. Unity and success in the "war on terrorism" were the only administration emphases not to receive substantial attention in the press, perhaps due to reasons that can be explained by journalistic norms and routines. In particular, the administration's claims of time urgency and calls for congressional action neatly fit journalists' interest in political conflict and strategy (see Cappella & Jamieson, 1997; Patterson, 1993), whereas an emphasis upon unity implicitly challenged this same news norm. Furthermore, news is a time-based industry that thrives on the "now." To say—as Ashcroft repeatedly did—that U.S. lives and national security were at stake unless an administration policy was enacted straightaway was to offer the press prime fodder for news copy: historical significance and immediacy. In contrast, the notion of eventual success may have been viewed by journalists as too abstract in a time of tragic realities. At the same time, while not all administration themes were widely amplified in the press, whenever the themes were present in news content the perspectives of the administration were supported in significant measure. Put simply, the press followed the parameters of discourse on this legislation provided by President Bush and Attorney General Ashcroft with only one exception—the extent of protections for civil liberties.

On this matter, news coverage was about evenly split between pro-administration perspectives suggesting the legislation would adequately protect citizens' civil liberties and the views of others who disagreed. It may be that Bush and Ashcroft's lesser emphasis on this theme, relative to their other talking points, provided an opening for a wider range of societal actors to have their voices heard and disseminated. Zaller and Chiu (1996) have shown that in crisis contexts administration leaders are granted first opportunity by mainstream journalists to define the situation; it seems plausible during such periods, then, that not only additional voices but also contrary ones gain a presence in news coverage in direct relation to the volume of administration public communications. To be clear, though, contrary voices were never predominant in Patriot Act coverage: Even critical civil liberties news content often contained administration-supportive claims, particularly themes of security and an action imperative. In a crisis moment such as September 11, these latter emphases likely have greater resonance among the public—due to their connection to fear and temporal events—than future-oriented concerns about civil liberties. Thus, "objective" news coverage of the Patriot Act that sought to balance civil liberties concerns with legislation-supportive claims about security, time urgency, and a need for congressional action inevitably tilted the political field to the administration's benefit. This outcome was further cemented by the presence of leading congressional Democrats speaking in support of the administration in news coverage, while administration critics in news coverage tended primarily to be people outside of government circles.

Further, it is striking that the differing types of media content analyzed—newspaper articles, newspaper editorials, and television news—showed a high degree of similarity in their echoing of the administration's themes and perspectives. It appears that the administration crafted a message that resonated not only with beat reporters but also with editorial boards, a notable result given the latter's greater freedom to criticize an administration's practices. Because "most Americans are exposed to combinations of all the media" (Graber, 1997, p. 189), the echoing of an administration's themes across various forms of media might be viewed—similar to the timing and consistency of leaders' messages—as crucial to the success of a strategy of going public. Locating the same (or closely similar) message across media channels allows an administration to reach differing yet overlapping audiences, as well as to simply reinforce its message. Indeed, there was a dramatic decrease in administration communications *and* each form of news coverage about the Patriot Act once the anti-terrorism legislation was introduced for formal discussion in Congress. The sharp drop in coverage, we suggest, was due not only to the administration's diminished communications about the legislation but also to the development of other news events. . . .

. . . [P]ublicly stated rationale among senators for their voting decisions and occasional congressional comments about the press are suggestive that the themes and perspectives emphasized by the administration, and echoed substantially in news content, contributed to congressional decision making and debate. . . . Our research, then, is consistent with a growing body of scholarship (e.g., Entman, 2003; Coe et al., 2004; Domke, 2004) suggestive that the administration's strategic communications and accompanying news coverage did much to convert the public support after the terrorist attacks into tangible political capital, including administration-desired legislation. . . .

. . . When the White House and congressional leadership line up together, as they did soon after the terrorist attacks and then in the congressional debates examined here, news coverage will be heavily one-sided. In this way, news coverage almost certainly both reflects the decisions of some political actors to rally behind the presidency and contributes to the silencing of potential dissident voices, among the highest political leaders as well as the general public. The result is that the news media functionally play a game of elitist "follow the leader" that suggests others should do the same.

References

Althaus, S. L., Edy, J. A., Entman, R. M., & Phalen, P. (1996). Revising the indexing hypothesis: Officials, media, and the Libya crisis. *Political Communication, 13*, 407–421.

Ashcroft, J. (2001, September 24). Prepared remarks before House Committee on the Judiciary. Retrieved January 26, 2003, from http://www.usdoj.gov/03press/03_2.html

Ayer, W. P., & Forsythe, D. P. (1979). Human rights, national security, and the U.S. Senate: Who votes for what, and why. *International Studies Quarterly, 23*, 303–320.

Baker, W. D., & Oneal, J. R. (2001). Patriotism or opinion leadership? The nature and origins of the "rally 'round the flag" effect. *Journal of Conflict Resolution, 45*, 661–687.

Beasley, V. (2001). The rhetoric of ideological consensus in the United States: American principles and American prose in presidential inaugurals. *Communication Monographs, 68*, 169–183.

Bennett, W. L. (1990). Toward a theory of press-state relations in the United States. *Journal of Communication, 36*, 103–125.

Billeaudeaux, A., Domke, D., Hutcheson, J., & Garland, P. (2003). Newspaper editorials follow the lead of Bush administration. *Newspaper Research Journal, 24*, 166–184.

Billhartz, C. (2001, September 22). Maher's comments lead to show's suspension. *St. Louis Post-Dispatch*, p. A15.

Brill, S. (2003, March 10). After: How America confronted the Sept. 12 era. *Newsweek*, pp. 66–73.

Broder, J. M. (2003, March 23). A nation at war: The commander. *New York Times*, p. B4.

Brody, R. A. (1991). *Assessing the president: The media, elite opinion, and public support*. Stanford, CA: Stanford University Press.

Bush, G. W. (2001a, September 20). Address before a joint session of the Congress on the United States response to the terrorist attacks of September 11. Retrieved January 26, 2003, from http://www.access.gpo.gov/nara/nara003.html

Bush, G. W. (2001b, September 25). Remarks to Federal Bureau of Investigation employees. Retrieved January 26, 2003, from http://www.access.gpo.gov/nara/nara003.html

Canes-Wrone, B. (2001). The president's legislative influence from public appeals. *American Journal of Political Science*, 45, 313–329.

Cappella, J., & Jamieson, K. H. (1997). *Spiral of cynicism: The press and the public good*. New York: Oxford University Press.

Carter, B., & Barringer, F. (2001, September 28). Speech and expression; in patriotic time, dissent is muted. *New York Times*, p. A1.

Coe, K., Domke, D., Graham, E. S., John, S. L., & Pickard, V. W. (2004). No shades of gray: The binary discourse of George W. Bush and an echoing press. *Journal of Communication*, 54, 234–252.

Cooper, T. (2001, September 22). 2 TV stations yank "Politically Incorrect." *Omaha World-Herald*, p. B8.

Corrigan, M. (2000). The transformation of going public: President Clinton, the First Lady, and health care reform. *Political Communication*, 17, 149–168.

Dalton, R. J., Beck, P. A., & Huckfeldt, R. (1998). Partisan cues and the media: Information flows in the 1992 presidential election. *American Political Science Review*, 92, 111–126.

Domke, D. (2004). *God willing? Political fundamentalism in the White House, the "war on terror" and the echoing press*. London: Pluto Press.

Entman, R. M. (1991). Framing U.S. coverage of international news: Contrasts in narratives of the KAL and Iran Air incidents. *Journal of Communication*, 41, 6–27.

Entman, R. M. (2003). Cascading activation: Contesting the White House's frame after 9/11. *Political Communication*, 20, 415–432.

Entman, R. M., & Rojecki, A. (1993). Freezing out the public: Elite and media framing of the U.S. anti-nuclear movement. *Political Communication*, 10, 155–173.

Epstein, E. (2005, June 16). House defies Bush, votes to repeal part of Patriot Act. *San Francisco Chronicle*, p. A1.

Fleischer, A. (2001, September 26). White House press briefing by Ari Fleischer. Retrieved July 21, 2003, from http://www.whitehouse.gov/news/releases/2001/09/20010926-5.html

Gelman, A., & King, G. (1993). Why are American presidential election campaign polls so variable when votes are so predictable? *British Journal of Political Science*, 23, 409–451.

Goering, S. (2005, June 16). Roll back the infringement on civil liberties; renewing the Patriot Act. *Baltimore Sun*, p. A21.

Graber, D. A. (1997). *Mass media and American politics* (5th ed.). Washington, DC: CQ Press.

Hallin, D. C., Manoff, R. K., & Weddle, J. K. (1993). Sourcing patterns of national security reporters. *Journalism Quarterly, 70,* 753–766.

Herman, E. S. (1993). The media's role in U.S. foreign policy. *Journal of International Affairs, 47,* 23–45.

Hoger, E. A., & Swem, L. L. (2000). Public relations and the law in crisis mode: Texaco's initial reaction to incriminating tapes. *Public Relations Review, 26,* 425–445.

Horsey, D. (2003, February 16). Serving up the GOP agenda. *Seattle Post-Intelligencer,* p. G1.

Huckin, T. N. (2002). Textual silence and the discourse of homelessness. *Discourse & Society, 13,* 347–372.

Huddy, L., Khatib, N., & Capelos, T. (2002). The polls-trends: Reactions to the terrorist attacks of September 11, 2001. *Public Opinion Quarterly, 66,* 418–450.

Huff, R. (2001, September 22). Estimated 82M saw speech. *Daily News* (New York). Retrieved February 22, 2005, from http://web.lexis-nexis.com

Hughes, W. J. (1995). The "not-so-genial" conspiracy: The *New York Times* and six presidential "honeymoons." *Journalism and Mass Communication Quarterly, 72,* 841–850.

Hutcheson, J., Domke, D., Billeaudeaux, A., & Garland, P. (2004). U.S. national identity, political elites, and a patriotic press following September 11. *Political Communication, 21,* 27–50.

John, S. L., Domke, D., Coe, K., & Graham, E. S. (2004). *From September 11 to Saddam: George W. Bush, strategic communications, and the "war on terrorism."* Paper presented at the annual conference of the International Communication Association, New Orleans, LA.

Katz, D. (1965). Nationalism and conflict resolution. In H. Kelman (Ed.), *International behavior: A social psychological analysis* (pp. 130–187). New York: Holt, Rinehart & Winston.

Kernell, S. (1997). *Going public: New strategies of presidential leadership* (3rd ed.). Washington, DC: CQ Press.

Lemann, N. (2003, May 12). The controller. *New Yorker,* pp. 68–83.

Maltese, J. A. (1994). *Spin control: The White House Office of Communication and the management of presidential news* (2nd ed.). Chapel Hill: University of North Carolina Press.

Manheim, J. B. (1991). *All of the people, all of the time: Strategic communication and American politics.* Armonk, NY: M. E. Sharpe.

Manheim, J. B. (1994). Strategic public diplomacy. In W. L. Bennett & D. L. Paletz (Eds.), *Taken by storm: The media, public opinion, and U.S. foreign policy in the Gulf War* (pp. 131–148). Chicago: University of Chicago Press.

McDaniel, M. (2001, September 19). "Politically Incorrect" comes under fire for comments about terrorists. *Houston Chronicle*, p. A10.

Mishler, C. (1965). Personal contact in international exchanges. In H. Kelman (Ed.), *International behavior: A social psychological analysis* (pp. 550–561). New York: Holt, Rinehart & Winston.

Patterson, T. E. (1993). *Out of order.* New York: Knopf.

Pew Research Center. (2001, November 28). Terror coverage boosts news media's image. Retrieved January 12, 2006 from http://people-press.org/reports/display .php3?ReportID=143

Powell, R. J. (1999). "Going public" revisited: Presidential speechmaking and the bargaining setting in Congress. *Congress & the Presidency, 26,* 153–171.

Powlick, P. J. (1995). The sources of public opinion for American foreign policy officials. *International Studies Quarterly, 39,* 427–451.

Quenqua, D. (2001, September 24). Left and right join to protect rights. *PR Week (US),* p. 2.

Riker, W. (1986). *The art of political manipulation.* New Haven, CT: Yale University Press.

Roper Center, University of Connecticut. (2001). Public opinion polls on terrorism, database accession numbers 0387650, 0388036, and 0388087.

Rutenberg, J. (2001, December 3). Fox portrays a war of good and evil, and many applaud. *New York Times.* Retrieved December 3, 2001, from http://www.nyt .com

Schaefer, T. M. (1997). Persuading the persuaders: Presidential speeches and editorial opinion. *Political Communication, 14,* 97–111.

Scott, W. A. (1955). Reliability of content analysis: The case of nominal scale coding. *Public Opinion Quarterly, 19,* 321–325.

Suskind, R. (2003, January). Why are these men laughing? *Esquire,* pp. 96–105.

Swisher, C. B. (1940). Civil liberties in war time. *Political Science Quarterly, 55,* 321–347.

United States Commission on National Security/21st Century. (2001, February 15). Road map for national security: Imperative for change. Retrieved July 7, 2003, from http://www.nssg.gov/ PhaseIIIFR.pdf

Vermeer, J. P. (2002). *The view from the states: National politics in local newspaper editorials.* Lanham, MD: Rowman & Littlefield.

Zaller, J. (1992). *The nature and origins of mass opinion.* Cambridge, England: Cambridge University Press.

Zaller, J. (1994a). Elite leadership of mass opinion: New evidence from the Gulf War. In W. L. Bennett & D. L. Paletz (Eds.), *Taken by storm: The media, public opinion and U.S. foreign policy in the Gulf War* (pp. 186–209). Chicago: University of Chicago Press.

Zaller, J. (1994b). Strategic politicians, public opinion, and the Gulf crisis. In W. L. Bennett & D. L. Paletz (Eds.), *Taken by storm: The media, public opinion and U.S. foreign policy in the Gulf War* (pp. 250–274). Chicago: University of Chicago Press.

Zaller, J., & Chiu, D. (1996). Government's little helper: U.S. press coverage of foreign policy crises, 1945–1991. *Political Communication, 13,* 385–405.

21

MANIPULATING THE MESSAGE IN THE U.S. CONGRESS

Patrick J. Sellers

Editor's Note

Members of Congress, just like the president, compete for a spot in the news limelight. They hope and expect that stories about legislative issues will help them win legislative battles. Favorable media coverage is especially crucial for legislators and parties that are in the minority. In the case reported in chapter 21, Democrats and Republicans battled about including extraneous amendments in a bill that funded disaster relief. The minority Democrats opposed the amendments favored by the majority Republicans.

Patrick Sellers analyzed and compared legislators' efforts to gain media attention for their preferred version of the bill. He also examined the actual coverage of the issues in the Democratic-leaning *Washington Post* and the Republican-leaning *Washington Times*. He found that each paper was quite responsive to appeals that resonated with its own leanings. The *Post* heeded the Democrats' appeals and largely ignored the Republicans; the *Times* heeded Republicans and ignored Democrats. In the end, despite their minority status, the Democrats prevailed over the Republicans, and a "clean" bill was passed. That outcome would have been highly unlikely if they had been unable to entice the news media to cover the situation in ways that favored the Democrats' cause.

Patrick J. Sellers was a professor of political science at Indiana University when this research was first published. A 2010 book-length study, *Cycles of Spin: Strategic Communication in the U.S. Congress,* has broadened the scope of the discussion.

At midnight on the evening of June 10, 1997, the Capitol office of Senate Minority Leader Tom Daschle was filled with senators, staff, and reporters.

Source: Excerpted from Patrick J. Sellers, "Manipulating the Message in the U.S. Congress," in *The Harvard International Journal of Press/Politics,* 5:1 (2000): 22–31. Copyright © 2000 by the President and the Fellows of Harvard College and the Massachusetts Institute of Technology. Reprinted by Permission of SAGE Publications, Inc.

Although the Senate was not in session, the Democratic caucus was in the midst of an all-night vigil to call for passage of disaster-relief funding for states struck by severe winter weather. With twenty-six senators participating through the night, the caucus promoted this message nationally with Internet chat rooms, television interviews, and appearances on late-night radio talk shows.

This event is only one example of the increasing efforts by congressional politicians to shape the issue agenda outside Congress. This article presents a case study of these efforts, focusing on the congressional debate over the supplemental appropriations bill in May and June 1997. Control of the issue agenda inside the institution is a central part of congressional politics (Riker 1997). The majority party exerts extensive control over this agenda, and the minority party often works to subvert that control. However, the battle over the congressional agenda extends beyond the internal operations of Congress to issues covered in the news media. Shaping this broader issue agenda can help politicians pursue their policy and electoral goals (Cook 1989). If legislators draw media attention to an issue, they may more successfully move related legislation through Congress. In addition, media attention may publicize legislators' claims and accomplishments to constituents. In this article, I argue that coordinated support for a single media message will increase the likelihood that the message receives news coverage, which in turn boosts the legislators' goals. . . .

Background

Since the 1950s, members of Congress have increasingly operated as individual entrepreneurs, independent of political parties (Ehrenhalt 1983; Kernell 1997). Legislators promote bills and win reelection by themselves, often with little assistance from their party (Kernell 1997; Sinclair 1997). A central part of the legislators' entrepreneurship is increased access to the media (Ansolabehere et al. 1993). Legislators have many strategies for winning favorable media coverage—from carefully planned events with constituents to staff-produced press releases highlighting recent accomplishments (Sellers 1998). These efforts have produced more frequent and direct contact between politicians and voters (Smith 1993).

However, during the last decade, these increasingly entrepreneurial legislators have faced growing problems in realizing their policy and electoral goals. First, inside the legislative arena individual members of Congress each have pursued their individual policy agendas, agendas most relevant to each member's constituents. It has therefore grown more difficult to build and coordinate legislative coalitions to address difficult long-term issues. By solving relatively narrow and short-term problems of their states and districts, legislators find it easier to avoid addressing broader national concerns when trying to win reelection (Ansolabehere et al. 1993). Second, while incumbent reelection rates remain high (Jacobson 1997), legislators face increasing competition in their efforts to win voters' attention. This competition forces each member to work harder to communicate his or her message directly to constituents. Legislators may turn to new technologies, such as the Internet and satellite television, which makes it easier to communicate with constituents. However, television, radio, and print outlets are also using the same technologies to expand their news offerings. As a result, the legislators' messages form only a small part of a growing and potentially overwhelming body of information that the public receives (Ansolabehere et al. 1993). At the same time, public cynicism about Congress has reached new heights, with many voters uninterested in learning about any politician. Reporters may react negatively to individual legislators' attempts to win media attention (Hess 1986).

In response to these problems, members of Congress have increasingly coordinated legislative efforts, often within their party. In particular, legislators in a party may unify their communication efforts around a single message (Herrnson and Patterson 1995; Sinclair 1997). If a large number of legislators join in promoting the same message to the national media in Washington, that message is more likely to receive national news coverage. That coverage may, in turn, further passage of legislation desired by members. Both the resulting legislative accomplishments and the national promotion of the party's message may boost the legislators' electoral fortunes.

Congressional parties and their members can therefore benefit from publicizing their messages on issues before Congress. These media efforts have the effect of expanding a legislative conflict beyond the confines of Congress, involving constituents and interest groups outside the institution. Significantly, the two parties in Congress may not always have an equal incentive to expand a conflict beyond Congress (Schattschneider 1960). Because the majority party controls the levers of the legislative process, it may prefer to keep a conflict inside Congress, where the party exerts greater control. Conversely, the minority party lacks such levers and may ultimately lose a legislative fight that remains inside Congress. The minority therefore has a stronger incentive to expand the conflict beyond Congress. Aggressive promotion of the party's message offers one way to incorporate outside individuals into the conflict, which may increase the minority's chances of legislative success.

In these dynamics of message promotion and conflict expansion, the underlying assumption is that many voices are more effective than one in pushing through the cacophony of information that voters receive. This assumption is reasonable. Reporters are more likely to cover a message if the legislators supporting the message have greater influence over policy outcomes. A large number of legislators form a voting bloc with great influence over policy outcomes, so an issue promoted by many legislators will receive more attention from reporters.

Previous studies of congressional news coverage have not examined the link between message support and coverage. They focused instead on the mentions of individual members or committees in national news sources (Cook 1989; Deering and Smith 1997; Hess 1986; Weaver and Wilhoit 1974). This article examines the link in detail. In a case study of the congressional debate over the supplemental appropriations bill, I analyze how variation in the coordination of message efforts translated into varying media coverage of the two parties' messages. I expect that greater coordination in support of a message is more likely to result in more extensive news coverage of that message.

The Supplemental Appropriations Bill

In early May 1997, the supplemental appropriations bill had almost finished working its way through the legislative process. The bill provided funding for communities struggling with flooding and other severe winter weather. The popularity of the bill encouraged members to attach other legislative proposals in hope of winning quick approval for them. The Republican congressional leadership attached two controversial provisions to the supplemental.

. . . Democrats pushed for passage of a "clean" disaster-relief bill. They attempted to steer debate over the supplemental bill to the hardships caused by the harsh winter weather and the disaster victims' need for federal assistance. The Republicans tried to focus the debate on a different set of issues. . . .

In May, both sides expressed confidence in their strategies. By attaching the two controversial provisions to the supplemental bill, the Republicans appeared confident that their control over the legislative process (as majority party) would allow them to control debate over the bill and win its passage. However, this strategy may have underestimated the ability of the Democrats to expand the conflict beyond the confines of the Senate and focus the media's and the public's attention on the Democratic message. In the actual debate over the supplemental bill, each side did engage the issues promoted by the opposing side, attacking their opponents' claims and arguments on these issues. However, both parties attempted to focus the public debate on issues favoring their interests. . . . In this fight over the supplemental bill, the Democrats won a clear victory. On June 12, the House and Senate passed the bill with neither Republican provision attached (Taylor 1997).

Competing Messages and Media Coverage

I analyzed the parties' campaigns to structure public debate about the supplemental appropriations bill by comparing two types of measures: (1) legislators' support for their party's message and (2) the subsequent coverage of each party's message in the news media. To calculate legislators' support, I used a set of press releases collected from congressional press galleries. The set includes all releases submitted by representatives and senators to four galleries from May 12 to June 14, 1997.[1] Because my analysis of media coverage used two national newspapers based in Washington, D.C., the releases are a valid indicator of legislators' efforts to influence media coverage in these two outlets.

Using the releases for each day, I counted the number of legislators from each party who publicly supported their party's message on the supplemental bill. The mean for congressional Democrats was 2.62 during this period, whereas their counterparts from the GOP averaged 2.03 per day. These low averages are not surprising. The thirty-four-day period includes the Memorial Day congressional recess, when many legislators were not in Washington to promote their party's message to the national media. In addition, the press releases are only one way that legislators attempt to influence national press coverage. The leaderships of both Senate caucuses often organize "floor events," in which groups of a party's legislators obtain an hour or more of floor time and engage in a public discussion promoting the party's message. In addition, legislators hold press conferences in the Capitol, promoting their party's message to the national media. The analysis for this paper, however, relies only on the releases, which makes it harder to find a significant link between legislators' activities and the media coverage.

To assess the national news coverage of the supplemental bill during the thirty-four-day period, I used Lexis-Nexis to download articles from the *Washington Post* and the *Washington Times*. My search was as comprehensive as possible, capturing all articles mentioning "Congress," "president," "Democrat," or "Republican." The search mistakenly captured articles on the Congressional Open (a Maryland golf tournament) and the president of Bolivia, but the next step of coding largely eliminated such undesirable articles. For each paper's articles for each day, I used a word-count computer program to count the number of mentions of important words or phrases in each party's message on the supplemental bill.[2] Significantly, I compiled the words and phrases from the legislators' press releases and not from the articles themselves.

During the thirty-four-day period, both papers gave more coverage to the Democrats' message than to the Republicans'. In the *Post,* the daily average of mentions of the Democrats' themes was 20.71, whereas the GOP mean was 11.94. In the *Times*, the averages were 15.03 and 8.65. The Democratic advantage may partially stem from the actual news events underlying the Democrats' message (continued spring flooding and community rebuilding efforts). The Republicans' issues . . . lacked this type of immediate news event. The actual events surrounding disaster relief supported the Democrats' message and increased the likelihood that the message would be successful— that is, that it would pressure the Republicans to produce a "clean" supplemental appropriations bill.

Linking Message Support and Coverage

The final stage of this analysis compares the legislators' message efforts to the subsequent news coverage. I expect that if more legislators support a party's message, that message will receive more coverage. . . .

. . . In the *Times'* coverage, Republican legislators' support for their party's message is significantly and positively related to subsequent coverage of that message. . . . In contrast, Democrats' support for their party's message appears unrelated to the *Times'* coverage of that message. These patterns are reversed in the *Post*'s coverage. Here, Republicans' support for their party's message does not appear to be linked to the *Post*'s coverage of that message. However, the Democrats' support is positively and significantly related to coverage of their message. . . . In sum, Republicans' support for their message appears to win coverage of that message in the *Times*. Democrats appear to win coverage of their message in the *Post*.

Overall, two aspects of this analysis are most notable. First, the Democrats' victory may be tied to their expansion of the conflict beyond Congress. The Republicans controlled the legislative process inside Congress, which may have led them to believe that they could control public debate over the supplemental bill. However, the Democrats were able to expand the debate beyond Congress by emphasizing the need for immediate disaster relief, which was difficult to dispute. The popularity of this issue may have encouraged many Democratic legislators to support it publicly. When the conflict began to receive coverage in the national media, the Republicans were forced to turn to the more controversial issues (census sampling and the automatic continuing resolution) underlying their legislative proposal. With such divisive issues making up their party's message, legislators from the GOP may have been less willing to promote that message publicly.

Second, in the battle over the supplemental bill, the *Times* appeared more responsive to Republican appeals, whereas the *Post* responded more to the Democrats' message. . . . The papers provided different coverage of the debate over the supplemental bill, and the differences are consistent with the *Times'* reputation as favoring conservative causes and that of the *Post* as granting more favorable coverage to liberal causes.

These differences in coverage and reputation may be linked to decisions by the newspapers' owners and editors to provide different interpretations of news events. The city of Washington contains a sizeable audience for political news, but this audience ranges in ideology from liberal to conservative. As a result, each newspaper may target its coverage to win a different portion of the market. The differences between the *Times'* coverage and the *Post's* coverage may be unlikely to occur in other cities, however. . . .

More generally, the ideas and analytical techniques in this article may help explain other conflicts throughout the world. . . . [C]ompeting sides in a conflict often attempt to build public support for their cause through the news media (McAdam et al. 1996). Leaders of each side work to coordinate the activities of their supporters in order to increase the effectiveness of the appeal for media coverage. Studying legislators' communication efforts in Congress can improve our understanding of how these broader conflicts are manipulated, won, and lost.

Notes

1. They include the House and Senate Radio-Television and Press galleries.
2. For the Democrats' message, I searched for the following words or phrases: *disaster relief, flood relief, clean, vigil, floods, tornadoes, mudslides, natural calamities,* and *no strings attached.* The searches for the Republicans' message included the following: *automatic continuing resolution, shutdown, no shutdown, sampling, census, undercount,* and *non-emergency funds.*

References

Aldrich, John, and David Rohde. 1995. "Theories of the Party in the Legislature and the Transition to Republican Rule in the House." Presented at the annual meeting of the American Political Science Association, Chicago, Aug. 31–Sept. 3.

Ansolabehere, Stephen, Roy Behr, and Shanto Iyengar. 1993. *The Media Game: American Politics in the Television Age.* New York: Macmillan.

Cook, Timothy. 1989. *Making Laws and Making News: Media Strategies in the U.S. House of Representatives.* Washington, D.C.: Brookings Institution.

Deering, Chris, and Steven Smith. 1997. *Committees in Congress.* 3rd Edition. Washington, D.C.: CQ Press.

Ehrenhalt, Alan. 1983. "In the Senate of the '80s, Team Spirit Has Given Way to the Rule of Individuals." *Congressional Quarterly Weekly Report* 41 (Sept. 4): 2182.

Herrnson, Paul, and Kelly Patterson. 1995. "Toward a More Programmatic Democratic Party? Agenda-Setting and Coalition-Building in the House of Representatives." *Polity* 27(4): 607–28.

Hess, Stephen. 1986. *The Ultimate Insiders: U.S. Senators in the National Media.* Washington, D.C.: Brookings Institution.

Jacobson, Gary. 1997. *The Politics of Congressional Elections.* 4th Edition. New York: Longman.

Kernell, Samuel. 1997. *Going Public: New Strategies of Presidential Leadership*. 3rd Edition. Washington, D.C.: Congressional Quarterly Press.

King, Gary. 1989a. *Unifying Political Methodology: The Likelihood Theory of Statistical Inference*. Cambridge: Cambridge University Press.

King, Gary. 1989b. "Variance Specification in Event Count Models: From Restrictive Assumptions to a Generalized Estimator." *American Journal of Political Science* 33 (Aug. 3): 762–84.

Krehbiel, Keith. 1998. *Pivotal Politics: A Theory of U.S. Lawmaking*. Chicago: University of Chicago Press.

McAdam, Doug, John McCarthy, and Mayer Zald. 1996. *Comparative Perspectives on Social Movements*. Cambridge: Cambridge University Press.

Riker, William. 1997. *The Strategy of Rhetoric: Campaigning for the American Constitution*. New Haven: Yale University Press.

Schattschneider, E. E. 1960. *The Semisovereign People: A Realist's View of Democracy in America*. Hinsdale, IL: Dryden Press.

Sellers, Patrick. 1998. "Strategy and Background in Congressional Campaigns." *American Political Science Review* 40(1): 159–72.

Sinclair, Barbara. 1997. *Unorthodox Lawmaking: New Legislative Processes in the U.S. Congress*. Washington, D.C.: Congressional Quarterly Press.

Smith, Steven. 1993. *The American Congress*. Boston: Houghton Mifflin.

Taylor, Andrew. 1997. "Clinton Signs 'Clean' Disaster Aid after Flailing GOP Yields to Veto." *Congressional Quarterly Weekly Report* 55(24) (June 14): 1362.

Weaver, David, and Cleveland Wilhoit. 1974. "News Magazine Visibility of Senators." *Journalism Quarterly* 51(1): 67–72.

22

STRATEGIES OF THE AMERICAN CIVIL RIGHTS MOVEMENT

Doug McAdam

Editor's Note

Democratic governments lose public support when they appear to act in undemocratic ways. Social movements have learned to exploit these image concerns by engaging in disruptive forms of protest in locations where they are hated. They hope to provoke repressive police actions and thereby gain news media attention. News media framing of such incidents is likely to feature a David and Goliath scenario that depicts the protesters as abused victims and the authorities as abusing villains. People who see and hear these graphic stories are apt to side with the victims. Doug McAdam illustrates how the strategy works by tracking the activities of the American civil rights movement during the leadership years of Martin Luther King Jr.

McAdam was a professor of sociology at Stanford University when he wrote this essay. He was the coauthor and coeditor of several books about social movements and American politics. His research has been instrumental in identifying the important roles that news media can play in the success or failure of social movements.

Political movements face at least six strategic hurdles that typically must be surmounted if they are to become a force for social change. Specifically, movement groups must be able to

1. attract new recruits;
2. sustain the morale and commitment of current adherents;
3. generate media coverage, preferably, but not necessarily, of a favorable sort;

Source: Doug McAdam, "The Case of the American Civil Rights Movement," in *Research on Democracy and Society,* Vol. 3, ed. Frederick D. Weil, Oxford, U.K.: Elsevier, 1997, 155–176. Republished with permission from Emerald Group Publishing Limited.

4. mobilize the support of various "bystander publics";
5. constrain the social control options of its opponents; and
6. ultimately shape public policy and state action.

. . . [T]he last four of these goals have been the subject of very little empirical research by movement scholars. In what follows, then, I want to make them the principal focus of attention. Together they constitute the broader "environmental challenge" confronting the movement. . . .

In this chapter, I seek to show how the American civil rights movement was able, through the strategic framing efforts of Martin Luther King Jr. and his Southern Christian Leadership Conference (SCLC), largely to accomplish these four goals. . . .

To fully appreciate the daunting challenge that confronted the civil rights movement, one has to understand the depths of black powerlessness on the eve of the struggle. In 1950, fully two-thirds of all blacks continued to live in the southern United States. Yet, through a combination of legal subterfuge and extralegal intimidation, blacks were effectively barred from political participation in the region. . . .

If change were to come, it would have to be imposed from without. This, of course, meant intervention by the federal government. However, with a moderate Republican, Dwight Eisenhower, in the White House and southern Democrats exercising disproportionate power in Congress, the movement faced a kind of strategic stalemate at the national level as well. To break the stalemate, the movement would have to find a way of pressuring a reluctant federal government to intervene more forcefully in the South. This, in turn, meant attracting favorable media attention as a way of mobilizing popular support for the movement.

Attracting Media Coverage

If one were to conduct an ethnographic study of virtually any social movement organization, be it local or national, one would be very likely to uncover a pervasive concern with media coverage among one's subjects. The fact is, most movements spend considerable time and energy in seeking to attract and shape media coverage of their activities. . . .

The simple fact is that most movements lack the conventional political resources possessed by their opponents and thus must seek to offset this power disparity by appeals to other parties. The media come to be seen—logically, in my view—as the key vehicle for such influence attempts. The civil rights movement represents a prime example of this dynamic in action, and no group in the movement mastered this dynamic and exploited its possibilities better than the SCLC and its leader, Martin Luther King Jr.

The media's fascination with King was evident from the very beginning of the Montgomery, Alabama, bus boycott. Launched in December 1955, the boycott inaugurated the modern civil rights movement and catapulted King into public prominence. From then until his death in April 1968, King never strayed far from the front page and the nightly news. What accounts for King's media staying power, and why were he and the SCLC, alone among movement groups, so successful in attracting favorable media attention? In seeking to answer these questions, I will emphasize the role of three factors.

1. *Disruptive actions are newsworthy.* First, the SCLC and King mastered the art of staging newsworthy disruptions of public order. The first requirement of media coverage is that the event be judged newsworthy. Their experiences in Montgomery convinced King and his lieutenants of the close connection between public disruption and media coverage. All of King's subsequent campaigns were efforts to stage the same kind of highly publicized disruptions of public order that had occurred in Montgomery. Sometimes King failed, as in Albany, Georgia, in 1961–1962, when Police Chief Laurie Pritchett responded to King's tactics with mass arrests but without the violence and disruptions of public order so critical to sustained media attention. At other times in other places—most notably in Birmingham, Alabama, in 1963 and Selma, Alabama, in 1965—local authorities took the bait and responded with the kind of savagery that all but guarantees media attention.

Still, his mastery of the politics of disruption explains only how King and the SCLC were able to attract the media but not the overwhelmingly sympathetic tone of that coverage. Given the openly provocative nature of the King/SCLC strategy, the generally favorable coverage accorded King's actions demands explanation. The key to the puzzle would seem to rest with King's consummate ability to frame his actions in highly resonant and sympathetic ways. The final two factors focus on King's framing efforts, first in conventional ideational terms and then in terms of the signifying function of his tactics.

2. *Ideational framing.* As noted previously, all work on framing betrays an exclusive concern with ideas and their formal expression by movement actors. These conscious ideational pronouncements—speeches, writings, and so on—are an important component of a movement's overall framing effort; and, in accounting for King's success in attracting sympathetic media coverage, much of the credit must go to the substantive content of his thought. Quite simply, no black leader had ever sounded like King before. In his unique blending of familiar Christian themes, conventional democratic theory, and the philosophy of nonviolence, King brought an unusually compelling yet accessible frame to the struggle. First and foremost, there was a deep "resonance" (Snow et al. 1986) to King's thought. Specifically, in employing Christian themes and conventional democratic theory, King succeeded in

grounding the movement in two of the ideational bedrocks of American culture. Second, the theme of Christian forgiveness that runs throughout King's thought was deeply reassuring to a white America burdened (as it still is) by guilt and a near phobic fear of black anger and violence. King's emphasis on Christian charity and nonviolence promised a redemptive and peaceful healing to America's long-standing racial divide. Third, King's invocation of Gandhian philosophy added an exotic intellectual patina to his thought that many in the northern media (and northern intellectuals in general) found appealing. Finally, while singling out this or that theme in King's thought, it should be noted that the very variety of themes granted those in the media (and the general public) multiple points of ideological contact with the movement. Thus, secular liberals might be unmoved by King's reading of Christian theology but resonate with his application of democratic theory and so on.

3. *The signifying function of SCLC actions.* King and his SCLC lieutenants' genius as "master framers," however, extended beyond the ideational content of their formal pronouncements. In their planning and orchestration of major campaigns, the SCLC brain trust displayed what can only be described as a genius for strategic dramaturgy. That is, in the staging of demonstrations, King and his lieutenants were also engaged in signifying work—mindful of the messages and potent symbols encoded in the actions they took and hoped to induce their opponents to take.

Arguably the best example of SCLC's penchant for staging compelling and resonant dramas is their 1963 campaign in Birmingham. Like virtually all major cities in the Deep South, Birmingham in 1963 remained a wholly segregated city, with blacks and whites confined to their own restaurants, schools, churches, and even public restrooms. In April of that year, the SCLC launched a citywide campaign of civil disobedience aimed at desegregating Birmingham's public facilities; but why, among all southern cities, was Birmingham targeted? The answer bespeaks the SCLC's strategic and dramaturgic genius. As a major chronicler of the events in Birmingham notes, "King's Birmingham innovation was pre-eminently strategic. Its essence was . . . the selection of a target city which had as its Commissioner of Public Safety 'Bull' Connor, a notorious racist and hothead who could be depended on not to respond nonviolently" (Hubbard 1968, 5).

The view that King's choice of Birmingham was a conscious, strategic one is supported by the fact that Connor was a lame-duck official, having been defeated by a moderate in a runoff election in early April 1963. Had the SCLC waited to launch its campaign until after the moderate took office, there likely would have been considerably less violence and less press coverage as well. "The supposition has to be that . . . SCLC, in a shrewd . . . stratagem, knew a good enemy when they saw him . . . one who could be counted on in stupidity and natural viciousness to play into their hands, for full exploitation in the press as archfiend and villain" (Watters 1971, 266).

King and his lieutenants had learned their lessons well. After several days of uncharacteristic restraint, Connor trained fire hoses and unleashed attack dogs on peaceful demonstrators. The resulting scenes of demonstrators being slammed into storefronts by the force of the hoses and attacked by snarling police dogs were picked up and broadcast nationwide on the nightly news. Photographs of the same events appeared in newspapers and magazines throughout the nation and the world. The former Soviet Union used the pictures as anti-American propaganda at home and abroad. Thus, the media's coverage of the events in Birmingham succeeded in generating enormous sympathy for the demonstrators and putting increased pressure on a reluctant federal government to intervene on behalf of the movement.

In short, by successfully courting violence while restraining violence in his followers, King and the SCLC were able to frame the events in Birmingham as highly dramatic confrontations between a "good" movement and an "evil" system. Moreover, the movement's dominant religious ideology granted this interpretation all the more credibility and resonance. These were no longer demonstrators; rather, they were peaceful, Christian petitioners being martyred by an evil, oppressive system. The stark, highly dramatic nature of this ritualized confrontation between good and evil proved irresistible to the media and, in turn, to the American public.

Mobilizing Public Support

While favorable media coverage was the immediate goal of King and his lieutenants, it was never conceived of as an end in itself. Instead, the SCLC courted the media for the role that it might play in mobilizing greater public awareness of and support for the movement. That support, in turn, was seen as the key to breaking the strategic stalemate in which the SCLC and the broader movement found itself. With no chance of defeating the white supremacists in a direct confrontation, the SCLC knew that its prospects for initiating change would turn on its ability to prod a reluctant federal government into more supportive action on behalf of civil rights. Ironically, the election of John F. Kennedy as president in 1960 only intensified the government's longstanding aversion to "meddling" in southern race relations. The specific explanation for Kennedy's reluctance to intervene had to do with his narrow margin of victory in 1960 and the "strange bedfellows" that comprised his electoral coalition. Not only had Kennedy garnered the so-called black vote and the votes of northern liberals and labor, but he was also beholden to the "solid South." In rejecting the Republican Party as the party of Abraham Lincoln, white southerners had voted consistently Democratic since the late nineteenth century. Thus, Kennedy, no less than his party predecessors, counted racist southerners and civil rights advocates among his constituents. The electoral challenge for Kennedy, then, was to preserve his fragile coalition by not unduly antagonizing either white southerners or civil rights forces. More immediately, Kennedy knew that the success of his legislative agenda would depend, to a large extent, on the support of conservative southern congressmen whose long tenure granted them disproportionate power within both the House and the Senate. For both electoral and legislative reasons, then, Kennedy came to office determined to effect a stance of qualified neutrality on civil rights matters.

In this context, the SCLC saw its task as destroying the political calculus on which Kennedy's stance of neutrality rested. It had to make the political, and especially the electoral, benefits of supporting civil rights appear to out-weigh the costs of alienating southern white voters and their elected officials. This meant mobilizing the support of the general public, thereby broadening the electoral basis of civil rights advocacy. In concert with the other major civil rights groups, the SCLC was able to do just that. Between 1962 and 1965, the salience of the civil rights issue reached such proportions that it consistently came to be identified in public opinion surveys as the "most important" problem confronting the country. In six of the eleven national polls conducted by Gallup (1972) between January 1961 and January 1966, it was designated as the country's most pressing problem by survey respon-dents. In three other polls, it ranked second. Only twice did it rank as low as fourth. Moreover, the imprint of the SCLC's dramaturgic genius is clearly reflected in these data. The two highest percentages attached to the issue correspond to the SCLC's highly publicized campaigns in Birmingham (April to May 1963) and Selma (March 1965). Quite simply, the SCLC's ability to lure supremacists into well-publicized outbursts of racist violence kept the issue squarely before the public and ensured the growing support necessary to pressure Kennedy and Congress into more decisive action.

Constraining the Social Control Options of Segregationists

To this point, I have said very little about the effect of the SCLC's tactics on southern segregationists, but, in a very real sense, the success of the SCLC's politics of disruption depended not on the media or the general public but on the movement's opponents in the South. Had segregationists not responded to the SCLC's actions with the kind of violent disruptions of public order seen in Birmingham, the SCLC would have been denied the media coverage so critical to its overall strategy. Indeed, the SCLC's most celebrated failure turned on its inability to provoke precisely this response from segregationists. I am referring to the citywide campaign that the SCLC launched in Albany, Georgia, in November 1961. In all respects, the campaign was comparable to the organization's later efforts in Birmingham and Selma. However, while the campaigns themselves were similar, the opponents' response to them was anything but. What was absent in Albany were the celebrated atrocities and breakdown in public order characteristic of Birmingham and Selma. This difference owed to Albany Police Chief Laurie Pritchett's clear understanding of the SCLC's strategy and his firm resolve to deny them the villain that they so badly needed. While systematically denying demonstrators their rights, Pritchett nonetheless did so through mass arrests rather than the kind of reactive violence that proved so productive of sympathetic media coverage in Birmingham and Selma. . . .

Shaping Public Policy and State Action

. . . The ultimate goal of King and the SCLC was to prod the government into action and to reshape federal civil rights policy in the process. That they were able to do so is clear. . . . What is also clear is that the extent and pace of their achievements were inextricably linked to their success in orchestrating the politics of disruption described here. In particular, the movement's two most significant legislative victories—the Civil Rights Act of 1964 and the Voting Rights Act of 1965—owed, in large measure, to the Birmingham and Selma campaigns, respectively.

Birmingham, as we have seen, featured the brutality of Bull Connor and, in the waning days of the campaign, a Sunday morning bombing of a black church that claimed the lives of three little girls. As broadcast nightly into the living rooms of America, these atrocities mobilized public opinion like never before and, in turn, put enormous pressure on President Kennedy to act forcefully on behalf of civil rights. The ultimate result was administration sponsorship of the Civil Rights Act, which, even in a much weaker form, had earlier been described as politically too risky by Kennedy himself. Finally, there was Selma. One last time, King and the SCLC orchestrated the by-now familiar politics of disruption to perfection. Initiated in January 1965, the campaign reached its peak in March with a series of widely publicized atrocities by segregationists. . . .

In response to this consistent breakdown in public order and the public outrage that it aroused throughout the nation, the federal government was forced to once again intervene in support of black interests. On March 17, President Lyndon Johnson submitted to Congress a tough voting rights bill containing several provisions that movement leaders had earlier been told were politically too unpopular to be incorporated into legislative proposals. The bill passed by overwhelming margins in both the Senate and the House and was signed into law on August 6 of the same year.

However, Selma was to represent the high-water mark for King, the SCLC, and the movement as a whole. Never again was King able to successfully stage the politics of disruption at which he had become so skilled. The reason for this is simple: As the movement moved out of the American South and sought to confront the much more complicated forms of racism endemic to the North, King was deprived of the willing antagonists he had faced in the South. As King had learned, southern segregationists could be counted on, when sufficiently provoked, to respond with the violence so critical to media attention and the increased public and government support that sympathetic coverage inevitably produced. No such convenient foil was available to the movement outside the South. In fact, more often than not, after 1965 civil rights forces came to resemble a movement in search of an enemy. . . .

Even when the movement was able, as in the 1966 open housing marches in Cicero, Illinois, to provoke southern-style violence in the North, local authorities were unwilling to intervene because they feared the political consequences of doing so. They knew that while the general public was prepared to accept an end to Jim Crow segregation in the South, it was assuredly not ready to acquiesce in the dismantling of de facto segregation in the North. Thus, the absence of supportive public opinion in the North denied the movement the critical source of pressure that had helped compel federal action in the South. The ability to command public and, by extension, state attention and support had been lost. In no public opinion poll since 1965 has the American public ever accorded black civil rights the status of the number one problem confronting the country, nor since then has Congress passed, with the exception of the Civil Rights Act of 1968, any significant civil rights legislation.

References

Hubbard, Howard. 1968. "Five Long Hot Summers and How They Grew." *Public Interest* 12:3–24.

Snow, David A., Jr., E. Burke Rochford, Steven K. Worden, and Robert D. Benford. 1986. "Frame Alignment Processes, Micromobilization, and Movement Participation." *American Sociological Review* 51 (4):464–481.

Watters, Pat. 1971. *Down to Now: Reflections on the Southern Civil Rights Movement*. New York: Pantheon.

23

THE AL JAZEERA EFFECT: HOW THE NEW GLOBAL MEDIA ARE RESHAPING WORLD POLITICS

Philip Seib

Editor's Note

If we think of news media as microphones that expand the range of message senders' voices, the number of truly powerful microphones, like the *New York Times* or major broadcast networks, was severely limited in the past. Established Western influential individuals and groups, such as high-level government leaders and large corporations, captured most of the time and space on these microphones. That scenario has changed dramatically. Philip Seib calls it the "Al Jazeera effect," referring to the transformation of the global media landscape in the Internet age. New broadcast channels and new voices from previously invisible and inaudible people and places have come to the fore.

In the Middle East, the Al Jazeera news network is a prominent example. It broadcasts news about life in the Middle East from perspectives offered by a medley of local voices, giving people from all parts of the world a chance to see and hear them. Obviously, the Western media's near-monopoly over the news flow and its content has been broken. The power of the traditional media and their traditional clients has been greatly diminished. The news spotlight now illuminates new faces, places, and issues.

Philip Seib was a professor of journalism and public diplomacy at the University of Southern California when his book about the Al Jazeera effect was published. His many books about the media's role in international relations had made him a highly regarded pioneer in this underexplored research field.

Source: Excerpted from Philip Seib, *The Al Jazeera Effect: How the New Global Media Are Reshaping World Politics,* Washington, D.C.: Potomac Books, Inc., 2008. Chapter 8. Reprinted by permission of Potomac Books, Inc.

To varying degrees throughout the world, the connectivity of new media is superseding the traditional political connections that have brought identity and structure to global politics. This rewiring of the world's neural system is proceeding at remarkable speed, and its reach keeps extending ever farther. It changes the way states and citizens interact with each other and it gives the individual a chance at a new kind of autonomy, at least on an intellectual level, because of the greater availability of information.

This is the Al Jazeera effect. The Arab satellite channel itself is just the most visible player in a huge universe of new communications and information providers that are changing the relationship between those who govern and those who are governed. It is also assisting those with previously unachievable political agendas. The advent of television a half-century ago pales in comparison with new media's effects on global political life today.

Political actors respond to this in different ways. Some are quick to appreciate the enhancements of power enabled by new media. The use of the Internet by candidates in the 2008 U.S. presidential campaign illustrates this on one level. More common are the scrambling blogs and Web sites used by political activists in many countries who now have a fast and efficient way to disseminate information and mobilize supporters, often in the face of opposition—sometimes fierce—from the political establishment.

Printing a few leaflets on a basement press and distributing them on street corners has been replaced by creating an electronic product that can be seen by millions in moments. Governments felt confident that those handing out material on a street corner could fairly easily be chased away or arrested, and so their impact could be limited. Those using new media tools are far harder to deal with. In China and many other countries, the flood of new media is intrinsically democratic and governments can do only so much to stop it.

That is transformative progress. Satellite television ensures a new era of political diversity, as different kinds of discourse reach mass audiences. The Internet has even greater effect because it is truly a popular medium—accessible, inexpensive, and far-reaching. Almost anyone can use it to proselytize, recruit, mobilize, or whatever. Whether anyone else pays attention is another matter, but this, too, can be seen as a positive characteristic in that the competition for audience should inspire cyber-articulateness and creativity in order to make a message stand out in the crowded virtual marketplace. This is how elements of democracy can be nurtured.

Wider dissemination of information should be a good thing, but caveats exist. "Information" and truth are not necessarily the same, and the Internet has already proved to be a hospitable laboratory for fraud and other deception, ranging from scams aimed at individuals' bank accounts to hate-filled polemics targeting large audiences. The speed and reach of new media are wonderful when there is need to alert people about an approaching hurricane or such, but those same qualities can be poisonous when vicious rumor is presented as the "news" of the moment.

Political leaders and related organizations, scrupulous and unscrupulous alike, are confronted with media and political environments that have converged to an unprecedented extent. Few individuals or groups have as yet mastered this new realm, but some have shown skill at using parts of it to [their] advantage. Some of these are spokesmen for al Qaeda and its ilk, but on the other side are men and women who are trying to use these media to make the world more humane.

Stories That Need to Be Told

Beyond the world of high-powered activists putting communication to use are places invisible to most, where debate about political systems and esoteric issues is unknown. All that matters in these places is basic survival: finding water, medical care, refuge from violence. These are terrible places, where hope is usually nothing more than illusion. New media cannot solve these problems, but they might help.

First, the world needs to be awakened. New media are looked to because traditional journalism has devoted few resources to reporting about events such as the genocidal war in Sudan. According to an analysis of network newscasts by the American Progress Action Fund, during 2004 ABC, CBS, and NBC combined to air just twenty-six minutes of coverage of the conflict in Darfur on their principal nightly newscasts. By comparison, Martha Stewart's legal problems received 130 minutes of airtime. In June 2005 the big three devoted fifteen minutes to the Darfur genocide while airing 1,608 minutes of reports about Michael Jackson's trial. CNN, purportedly a serious news channel, spent forty-seven minutes that month covering events in Darfur and 878 minutes on Jackson.[1] Writing about this in the *New York Times*, Nicholas Kristof noted that the BBC had outperformed the American networks. That was not surprising, but Kristof pointed out that so too had mtvU, the MTV channel aimed at a college student audience.[2]

The content on mtvu.com is an example of what Web-based information sources can provide, and it also underscores its limitations. The site provides basic background material and links to other providers, such as Amnesty International's satellite imagery pages that show what has happened to selected Sudanese villages during the fighting. It also links to a video game, "Darfur Is Dying," in which players "must keep their refugee camp functioning in the face of possible attack by Janjaweed militias." The game involves tasks such as searching for water while avoiding hostile troops.

For those who have slight interest in conventional news offerings, this approach may have value in creating at least threshold awareness of what is taking place in Sudan. But despite such innovative Web products that call attention to the conflict, there is little evidence that policy has been affected. It is good that new media try to spur action, but in this case, as in most others, expecting the situation to be turned upside down is unrealistic.

Underreported as it is, the war in Darfur receives more attention than other stories that rival it in importance. The UN and Doctors Without Borders prepare lists each year of stories that, as the UN puts it, "the world should hear more about." From Haiti to Congo to Sri Lanka, the list underscores the gaps in most news coverage and perhaps stimulates passing interest in underreported stories of horror and misery. Humanitarian organizations use their Web sites to shine a light on these cases, but no matter how articulately anguished these reports might be, there is no evidence that they do much more than stir a few consciences and elicit some financial help. That's all to the good, but in practical terms even the substantial amount of information that these Web sites can provide has only a tiny fraction of the impact a two-minute story on ABC would have.

At least for now. Changing habits of information gathering may enhance the significance of online alarms about international crises. As more people rely more heavily on the Internet rather than traditional news formats, the structure of influence will also change. This will take a while, as reliance on the long-dominant players continues to diminish (evidenced by declines in newspaper circulation and broadcast news audience) and as some among the almost infinite number of Web sites develop sizable and faithful constituencies. Clearinghouse sites, such as YouTube and Technorati, can lead visitors to lesser known sites, as can new and traditional information providers that already have large audiences. This symbiosis of old and new media will continue indefinitely.

Amid the technology-related expansion of "newsworthiness" are some journalistic verities. Some stories must be covered and must be forced into the public's field of vision. Longtime *Nightline* executive producer Leroy Sievers wrote about covering Rwanda during the 1994 genocide: "Was it a story that needed telling? Absolutely. Did the world listen? I don't know. I fear that people just turned the channel, that the images were too painful." Sievers wrote that years later Elie Wiesel spoke to the *Nightline* staff. "He said that the role of the journalist is to speak for those who have no voice. That was it. That's what we were trying to do. That's what we had to do. There, and after Rwanda—because there was a dividing line, before Rwanda and after Rwanda—anywhere in the world where man was doing the worst that he was capable of."[3]

Despite the heroic efforts and good intentions of a few journalists and news organizations, the coverage of the Rwanda genocide was too little, too late, as was the military and political response by the international community. By the time big news organizations, such as *Nightline*'s ABC, got to Rwanda, the worst was done. A decade later, in Darfur, media in various forms are only inconsistently on the scene, and the public is more likely to hear about the crisis in Darfur from a movie star on a talk show than from a major news organization.

By mid-2007 youtube.com had a large roster of Darfur-related videos available, some of which had been viewed a few thousand times, some more than 100,000 times. Did this result in public anger and activism that influenced policymakers? Apparently not. The agony of the genocide continued. At some point, perhaps a critical mass of awareness can be attained and a political tipping point can be reached.

If that happens, the quantity of information that new media provide will be a contributing factor, although not a determinative one. Some encouragement can be found in the ways that responses to non-conflict-related humanitarian emergencies have changed because of information and communication technologies. Aid donors use new technologies to locate disaster victims and keep track of supplies that have been sent. An essential part of relief operations is the communications center, which allows aid workers to communicate with their organizations and governments, check security updates, and study satellite maps of the areas in which they are working.

To make this possible, among the first respondents on the ground may be volunteers from Télécoms sans Frontières, who keep communication flowing even under horrendous circumstances. Clearinghouse sites such as the UN's ReliefWeb provide constantly updated information about crises around the world. On any given day, the list might include reports about a cyclone in Pakistan, locust infestation in Yemen, landslides in Nepal, and many more. NetHope, a nonprofit consortium of international NGOs, helps relief groups with organization and finances. For their part, the people who are endangered by disasters have found mobile phones to be invaluable in contacting neighbors and the world during times of peril. Access is increasing; in sub-Saharan Africa, according to the World Bank, the number of mobile phone subscribers increased sevenfold between 2000 and 2006.[4]

In disaster relief as in politics, new technologies do not in themselves solve problems. But they can change the process, making things work better. If you are a victim of a tsunami or a war, that means something.

Satellite News Channels and More

Al Jazeera receives plenty of attention, not just from its audience of 35 million but also from observers intrigued by the station's influence. Without again getting into the debate about satellite channels' objectivity or lack thereof, it is important to consider their overall effect on the populations they serve. Ability to get lively and relatively independent content is a new and energizing phenomenon in areas such as the Arab Middle East, and it has profoundly changed politics there.

People who live in Western democracies take for granted the open exchange of political ideas and rarely ponder what their lives would be like without this. New media are allowing people who have never enjoyed this kind of freedom to revel in it. They learn more and they expect more, and although strong governments—such as those in Egypt and Saudi Arabia—show no inclination to embrace democracy, the pot is boiling and the lid has popped off.

Forces are at work that may be slowed down from time to time, but they will not—and cannot—be brought to a full halt. Eventually people will see a transformation of the structure of sociopolitical life, driven in part by the openness that is a by-product of the work of the hundreds of regional satellite channels and in part by other new communication technologies.

As one of the oldest forms of new media (these age terms are all relative), television has seen ups and downs in the attempts by its champions to prove that it is, in Edward R. Murrow's words, more than "merely wires and lights in a box." The liberating influence of many of the newest television channels gives heart to those who believe television remains, in essence, a worthwhile medium.

Beyond television, new media constitute an even more revolutionary force. "Citizen media," which at one level can be defined as a populist, participatory kind of journalism, allow individuals to play the role filled by traditional information providers such as the major news organizations. Blogs—written and video—create a community that can be energized by swift delivery of impressionistic interpretations of events. How much blog content is true conversation and how much is just self-indulgent ranting is open to debate, but unquestionably the blogosphere is at least a supplemental influence on the news agenda. Individuals peruse online information that they have not seen elsewhere, and the impact of these messages can be magnified when more conventional news media take information from blogs and disseminate it even more widely.

Plenty of noise is emerging from all this activity. Is it symphony or cacophony? It is probably more of the latter at the moment, but that is changing as certain blogs become regular stopping places for information consumers, much as the *New York Times* and the BBC have been for so long. As in other forms of media, dominant voices will emerge with a rowdy chorus in the background. Clearly, user-generated content is finding a place in the discourse of the global community. More broadly, if information is the fuel for engines of democracy, those engines should be able to run faster and in more places.

Sheer volume means something. Anyone who uses search engines to scan the blogosphere generally and blogs with political content in particular will find the numbers overwhelming. This means that it is impossible to look at everything, but it also means that some material will inevitably find its way to an audience, no matter how draconian the efforts to stop it. Governments that seized documents or jammed radio signals in the past now try to close the portals through which the Internet flows. But even if they succeed for a while, the technology and its users will eventually prevail.

In addition to activists, the quiet information consumer will also rely more on unmediated media. The Internet encourages independent exploration, and people will follow their curiosity along the strands of the Web. This will have ramifications in journalism and politics. Less dependence on traditional media will have economic impact on the already shaky news business. Why rely on a news organization that you already suspect of bias when you can get "news" on your own?

As for politics, why trust a politician whom you believe to be manipulative when you can check countless sources on your own to verify claims and investigate issues? For years, trust in the information provided by the news media and politicians has declined, but there were no alternatives. Now a new level of independence is possible, and millions of people who were passive recipients of information will seek new providers and then themselves will become secondary disseminators of various kinds of news products.

These changes in the information flow will affect the continuation of globalization. For those who fear that a globalized society will be characterized by uniformity as global standards take hold, this media revolution should provide reassurance about the staying power of diversity. Rather than finding bland conformity, information consumers will face the daunting task of deciding which among an unprecedented number of voices deserve attention. This is somewhat similar to the time when people in big cities had dozens of newspapers to choose from each day. Now, if they choose to do so, people living anywhere with Internet access can read dozens of newspapers from dozens of countries, watch hundreds of streaming television channels, and peruse an almost infinite number of additional Web sites, online newsletters, written and video blogs, podcasts, and so on.

Intellectual diversity is an elemental part of the Al Jazeera effect. Uniformity will be far less of a problem than finding time to plunge into all the information that is available. . . .

The Rise of Virtual Communities

One facet of the Al Jazeera effect can be seen in the strengthening of communities of interest that rely on new media to enhance, and in some instances create, cohesion. New media can link people who share cultural, religious, or political characteristics with unprecedented thoroughness. When more people throughout the world gain access to these media, communities that were once just imagined will become more tangible as they expand their populations and their "citizens" assert common interests.

The effect this will have on global politics is hard to predict. Some groups may choose to keep their virtual communities relatively closed, using their media tools for intracommunity purposes. Others may try to use the weight of their numbers to play a more active role on the world stage. Still others may create virtual states with violent intentions. Those who address the dangers of terrorism should consider the virtual state concept in this context because creating such a community can vastly expand the power of terrorist organizations. Communication is an essential element of any organization's unity and effectiveness, and ample documentation illustrates how al Qaeda—to cite just one example—has successfully used new media to proselytize, recruit, instruct, and command.

The virtual community is more than a network. Given the hard-edged purposefulness of many terrorist organizations, their cyber-communities may be more definitively formed than networks that are more loosely constructed. Furthermore, if a "war" on terrorism is to be conducted, and if it is—as is likely—to entail many years of conflict, then defining the enemy is important. Underestimating its organizational strengths and staying power and dismissing such groups as deranged fanatics operating out of remote caves is a gross strategic error. There is much more to al Qaeda and its brethren than that. Public support for that struggle can be weakened if the nature of the threat is understated, whether for political reasons or out of ignorance. Fighting a war against a state—even a virtual state—requires that the enemy be taken seriously and defined in terms that establish the political as well as military context for a long struggle. A case can be made that al Qaeda should be treated as this kind of state.

Virtual states/communities have spawned their own warrior class: Irhabi007, the name used by the young Moroccan Younis Tsouli, lamented in e-mails to colleagues that he was not engaged in traditional combat in Iraq, but from his home in Britain he became one of the best-known architects of cyber-jihad. As Webmaster for Iraq's al Qaeda leader, Abu Musab al-Zarqawi, and as an instructor of others who use the Internet to disseminate recruiting materials and training manuals about weapons and tactics, Irhabi007 was—until his arrest in 2005—a pioneer in building al Qaeda's electronic infrastructure. With thousands of Web sites in use and a stream of video products designed for its sizable audience, al Qaeda continues to expand its global presence. Although the physical territory it holds is minimal, it occupies as much cyber-territory as it needs.

Governments hostile to al Qaeda should recognize that the limited real estate along the Pakistan–Afghanistan border where some al Qaeda fighters are encamped is meaningless as a measure of al Qaeda's territory. Al Qaeda is, in truth, a criminally violent state that relies on media technologies to constitute its global "homeland." Bin Laden and his lieutenants understand that cyberspace is at least as good a terrain for war as are the mountains of Waziristan. This dark side of the Al Jazeera effect will influence global politics for the foreseeable future.

Notes

1. "Overview of Research and Methodology," BeAWitness.org, www.beawitness .org/methodology.
2. Nicholas Kristof, "All Ears for Tom Cruise, All Eyes on Brad Pitt," *New York Times,* July 26, 2005.
3. Leroy Sievers, "There Is Evil," *Los Angeles Times,* June 12, 2005.
4. "Flood, Famine, and Mobile Phones," *The Economist,* July 28, 2007, 61–62; ReliefWeb, www.reliefweb.int; NetHope: Wiring the Global Village, www.neth ope.org.

24

A SYMBIOTIC RELATIONSHIP: BLOGGERS AND JOURNALISTS

Richard Davis

Editor's Note

Blogs are promising new tools for political actors who want to control how their own messages and stories about them and their policies are reported. It is easy and relatively inexpensive to set up and use a blog. Political actors use them to broadcast information that is framed to their liking and to critique competing messages offered by mainstream media. Bloggers' framing of events and people may undermine or even negate rival frames offered by the mainstream media. Blogs may occasionally alter the course of politics.

Richard Davis is a political communication scholar who is well known for exploring the roles that political blogs play in the American political mosaic. Chapter 24 focuses on the symbiotic relationship between mainstream journalists and bloggers. They fight and compete, but they also support each other in submitting important, multifaceted news and opinions to the American public. When this book was published, Richard Davis was a professor of political science at Brigham Young University.

Blogs: The New Journalism?

One of the problems with blogs' relations with journalism is that . . . bloggers are uncertain what they really are. Some view themselves as journalists, even the "new journalists." They disseminate news to an audience, particularly information their readers may not get elsewhere. Those bloggers seek to abide by standards of fairness in reporting. They do investigative research.[1] They have been called participatory journalists because theirs is a journalism featuring interactivity and participation over spectating. These reportorial blogs also have been termed "black market journalism" because

Source: Excerpted from Richard Davis, *Typing Politics: The Role of Blogs in American Politics,* New York: Oxford University Press, 2009, Chapter 6. Copyright © 2009 by the Oxford University Press, Inc. Reprinted by permission of the Oxford University Press, Inc.

their product is outside of the journalism system dominated by large media conglomerates.[2]

One critical difference from traditional journalists is that these bloggers would not argue that they are unbiased in their news presentation. Rather, the news presentation reflects their own perceptions of events and issues. After all, they argue, traditional journalists are biased as well and shape news gathering accordingly.

Other bloggers view themselves primarily as commentators, not journalists. John Hinderaker of Power Line said that he is not a journalist or even a part-time journalist.[3] Eugene Volokh (Volokh Conspiracy) admitted that he is "an amateur pundit, which is to say someone whose hobby it is to opine on various matters that are in the news."[4] Still others admit that they are no substitute for journalists and do not claim to be. Instapundit's Glenn Reynolds urged his readers not to rely solely or primarily on his blog for news. "What you get here—as with any blog—is my idiosyncratic selection of things that interest me, as I have time to note them, with my own idiosyncratic comments."[5]

Others see themselves as activists. For Moulitsas [founder of the popular blog Daily Kos], a paramount goal is to help the Democratic Party win elections. He consults with candidates, raises money for them, and generally helps further the party.[6] Nor is activism true only on the left. The objective of the blog ConfirmThem was to help win confirmation of President George W. Bush's judicial appointments. Daily Kos is an activist blog where readers routinely are instructed to do something besides read the blog. Calling readers to action is common on some blogs. One study of four influential blogs found that 11 percent of the posts on Daily Kos called for readers to take some action. But such action is uncommon for the vast majority of blogs.[7]

Still others see themselves as journalists and commentators and even activists—all at the same time.[8] One scholar termed the blogosphere "activist media punditry."[9] According to Moulitsas, blogging has blended historical roles: "Traditionally it was easier for people to find the niche . . . you were either an activist or you were a writer or you were a pundit. . . . We're all of the above."[10]

Bloggers do not see a fundamental conflict between reporting on the news and commenting on it at the same time and also attempting to change policy. In the same post a blogger can report news, add commentary, and urge action on the part of the audience and policy makers. One journalist has summed up blogging as having "all the liberties of a traditional journalist but few of the obligations."[11] Bloggers emphasize the differences in their approach to journalism. Whereas traditional journalists value detachment from the story, an emphasis on description, neutrality in presenting conflicts within the story, the unidirectional nature of the communication, and the importance of structure, bloggers' traits include the importance of personal subjectivity, the honesty of opinion expression, a role for the audience in the communication process, and the absence of cohesion and organization.[12]

The journalistic style proposed by bloggers is not new. Over time traditional media have experienced the same angst over the nature of journalism. During the colonial era, printers of broadsheets agonized over their preferred role as commercial printers and the expected role of patriot, either in defense of the Crown or in the service of the Revolution. The same debate erupted during the framing of the U.S. Constitution as newspaper publishers sought to return to their old commercial role but were pressed into service as advocates or opponents. Debate over journalism's role continued throughout the 19th century as some elements of the press sought more independence from the clutches of partisan organizations and leaders, while others saw the press as a mouthpiece for party principles. Still another conflict came at the end of the 19th century over whether journalists should manufacture news to boost circulation or merely report news as presented by sources.[13]

Only in the 20th century did the practice of interweaving opinion and news begin to give way to a new standard of professionalism and objectivity.[14] Yet even that change seemed artificial. While many of the newspapers of the 18th and 19th centuries in the United States were proudly partisan and erected no barriers between news and commentary, even those of the 20th and early 21st century have contained both editorial opinion and news reporting, although on separate pages. Separating the news from the op-ed pages gave readers the impression that news stories were not affected by the editorial position of the paper and vice versa. By the end of the 20th century, however, explicit news analysis and commentary began to creep out of the editorial pages and into the news sections. Journalists also appeared to have freer rein in expressing opinions in the body of a news story, particularly a feature story.

Hence the role of the traditional media is hardly settled in American life. Public opinion about journalists has shifted in recent years. News audiences today are less likely than they were ten years ago to view the news they acquire from news organizations as credible.[15] Journalists themselves still debate the role of journalism. The appearance of the blogs, with their new standards of reporting, has accentuated that debate. For example, the blogosphere has altered somewhat the role of the journalist as gatekeeper. Readers now have access to original documents and other sources that blogs link them to. They also have news that journalists do not include because news professionals consider that information as not meeting the definition of newsworthiness.

Yet journalists still see themselves as performing the function of helping the average reader make sense of the surfeit of information before him or her. That comes in the form of filtering out what may not be important for the reader, listener, or viewer, and also placing that news in context for the reader.[16] For the vast majority of readers who are not interested in searching the Internet for additional information, that journalistic function is critical. If traditional journalism, with its over 200-year history in the United States, is still deliberating its role, it should be no surprise that the political blogosphere, with a life span in the single digits, would still be doing so.

Moreover, the roots of the blogosphere suggest no such role for bloggers. Although the blogosphere may be viewed by many as an alternative political information source and therefore in competition with the traditional media in their coverage of public policy and politics, blogs certainly did not start that way. It is easy to forget that early blogs were personal journals featuring individual expression, primarily by teenagers. Any political role was tangential at best. In fact, that description is still true of a blogosphere that is populated primarily by personal journals unread by all but a handful of other people.

But as a few of those blogs turned to national politics and attracted media circulation–size audiences, they morphed from introspective diaries to political news sources. Still featuring personal expressions by their authors (in the tradition of early blogs and the blogosphere generally), these blogs also disseminated news stories about political events, many of which were not covered (or perhaps were under-covered) by the traditional media. As they went from personal diaries to political news and information gatherers and disseminators, some bloggers envisioned themselves not as anonymous writers to family and friends but as the future of journalism. A new generation of media consumers would eschew the traditional media forms and supposed objectivity and gravitate to the partisan but far more interesting blog sources. . . .

Freeing Journalists

Blogging began as a public personal expression, much like writing a personal diary that is photocopied and handed out to perfect strangers. One survey of bloggers (both political and nonpolitical) found that the most common reason for blogging was to "document their personal experiences and share them with others." And the most common topic of blog writing, these bloggers said, was their "life and experiences."[17] That style carries over into political blogs. A-list [high-traffic] political bloggers broadcast their personal thoughts to hundreds of thousands of people. Joshua Micah Marshall lamented, "In a way I've lost my ability to have my own private reflections. I've gotten in the habit of just putting everything out there."[18]

Through most of the past century the professional norms of journalism were diametrically opposite to this personalized approach in news writing. As a vehement reaction to the partisan press of an earlier age, journalists were required to hide their personal feelings behind the mask of objectivity. Over the past several decades, the preeminence of objectivity has been eroded by successive challenges from the "new journalism" movement, advocacy journalism, and public journalism. Moreover, public opinion about the news media has become more critical of journalists' assertions that they maintain objectivity. Most Americans perceive at least a fair amount of political bias in the news they get.[19] Blogs are the most recent addition to the anti-objectivity trends of the past half-century.

But blogs are different from these previous movements because they come from outside of journalism. They offer journalists an alternative method of writing that combines the elements of previous movements, such as critical analysis and advocacy journalism, with an emphasis on the human nature of the reporter over the model of the journalist as an interchangeable professional. One blogger explained that blogs "tend to be impressionistic, telegraphic, raw, honest, individualistic, highly opinionated and passionate, often striking an emotional chord."[20] By adopting blog writing, journalists have been freed from the constraints of objective journalism. When blogging they are more likely to express personal views, make unsubstantiated assertions, and abandon their reliance on sources to make points. . . .

A Symbiotic Relationship

Bloggers often describe their relationship with journalists as a competitive one. Some bloggers have suggested that the blogosphere will replace traditional media. They envision a future where traditional media no longer serve a useful function. As blogs bypass traditional media filters and news consumers get their own direct information, there will no longer be a need for traditional news media sources, some bloggers predict.[21] For their part, journalists often criticize bloggers as wannabe journalists who lack the professionalism requisite for the title. Bloggers have even been called parasitic, accused of drawing on the media's work but making no original contribution in news generation.[22] Some journalists respond with silence, suggesting the blogosphere is not worthy of reply. They may pretend political blogs do not exist, or they acknowledge their existence but insist that blogs have no relationship to journalism.

Certainly competitive elements exist in the relationship. They compete because they are alike in many ways. They both gather and disseminate news. Bloggers want to be first with the story, as do journalists. Bloggers and journalists tussle over the media's agenda. Bloggers want media coverage to reflect more bloggers' priorities. Journalists, however, naturally seek to maintain control over that agenda. They compete because they overlap in the nature of their content. Both deal with straight news reporting and commentary. A-list political blogs often report current events as well as comment on them. The degree to which they do so varies significantly. For example, The Huffington Post features hard news coverage with lengthy late-breaking wire service stories, while others, such as Hugh Hewitt and Eschaton, typically ignore the latest breaking news. Similarly, traditional media have included commentary and analysis in the news presentation. Newspapers editorialize on their editorial pages and allow others, both columnists and readers, to express opinions on the same pages. And broadcast news programs have included commentary at times in segregated segments either during the news hour or at other times.

The overlap between the two media, therefore, is hardly complete. That is common sense. If blogs had duplicated journalism, there would have been no appeal. It is precisely because they did not that they have acquired an audience. They offer a facet of news that is underplayed in news reporting by journalists. Blogs emphasize commentary with some straight news, while news organizations offer straight news with some commentary. That is why competition is too narrow an explanation of the relationship between journalists and bloggers.

What has developed is a symbiotic relationship. That symbiotic relationship defines and predicts the relationship between journalists and bloggers. Such relationships form because both parts receive mutual benefits, but they also entail particular costs. Both bloggers and journalists have developed a dependency on one another. Blogs have become integrated into the news reporting process. Journalists pay attention to them; they read blogs and occasionally they even use blogs as news sources. . . .

. . . [Blogs have the] ability to broadcast a perspective emanating from outside traditional journalism. Reaction to news now is filtered through journalists interviewing journalists. Journalists can be accused of being too insular when they turn to each other for reaction to events. But theoretically bloggers allow journalists to see reaction from outside the journalistic community. Because bloggers spend little time in news rooms or briefing rooms or press galleries, their reaction becomes another perspective, one that may be seen as the public's reaction or at least a response by people who are more like the public than journalists are. Of course, as we have seen, that assumption is flawed because some of the influential bloggers are affiliated with traditional media or at one time themselves were journalists. Even those who were not journalists look far more like elites than they do the general public.

The act of gauging that reaction also is a profoundly subjective one. The two broad camps of the blogosphere—as well as the range within it—allow journalists potentially to pick and choose which blogs they seek to use in order to frame the story. Bloggers potentially become another source for the journalist using sources to say what the journalist cannot. Moreover, the blog analysis appears faster than editorials. Newspaper editorials appear once a day, whereas blog commentary can be nearly instantaneous. Within minutes of the announcement of Harriet Miers's nomination [as a U.S Supreme Court justice], blogs were commenting on it—typically unfavorably. For journalists on a twenty-four-hour cycle with constant deadlines, the blogs offer reaction much faster than other news sources. Of course, the instant analysis can lead to questions about whether the reaction is thoughtful and reasoned. But that is not the real question; in fact, one might argue that the more emotional the reaction, the more newsworthy the blog post. . . .

The image of bloggers linking to major stories in the traditional media and then commenting on them is more characteristic of some political blogs than others. Typically bloggers who do so use the press as a foil. One example is a post on Little Green Footballs that addressed a front-page *Washington Post* story of the same day. The story, which discussed the tendency of some conservative Muslims in the United States to isolate themselves from the larger society, was the topic of a Little Green Footballs post at 8:53 that morning. The post called the piece "today's episode of the *Washington Post*'s amazing public relations campaign to help us stop worrying and learn to love Islam." The blog then quoted some of the story and linked to the rest.

Repeating and commenting on the news media's daily product does not necessarily maintain an audience. Bloggers need a value-added component to make their product appealing. That means providing news and commentary that is not already available to their audience. . . . [B]loggers often turn to sources that may not be readily apparent to their blog audience in order to set their own agendas. These include other news stories that they may feel are under-covered by the traditional media. The blog posts include news stories, but they tend to be those that are shorter, less obvious news items that bloggers want to point their audience to, just in case they missed them. Additionally, sources may be news media that their audience may not already frequent, such as regional newspapers or specialized media. Blog posts cited the *Rocky Mountain News* (Denver), the *Daily Mail* (London), the *New York Observer*, the *Knoxville (Tennessee) News Sentinel*, and the *Australia Herald-Sun*, to name a few of the media that the vast majority of readers do not routinely read.

A blogger who concentrates on the media's agenda acknowledges the media's role in agenda setting. Finding what the press does not cover, or at least does not emphasize, does not acknowledge the news media's agenda-setting role. Instead, it challenges that role and asserts the blogosphere's role as a new agenda setter.

In summary, the blogosphere slightly overlaps with and draws from the news media's agenda; however, it does not merely replicate it. Conversely, the traditional media are even less likely to follow the lead of the blogosphere. The major stories in traditional media can make it into the blogosphere, but

. . . big stories in the blogosphere rarely make it into the important stories of the traditional media. That does not mean the blogosphere may not affect content in other ways. It could be the blogosphere's role is as a gauge of what is going on without particular mention of blogs. Information on blogs may find its way into print, but only after another source also has the story; that source becomes the direct agenda setter and the explicit source in the story, not the blog. This is easier to do in cases where the blog itself cites an original source. The blog then becomes a transmitter of information about possible sources rather than the actual source.

The blogosphere may not play an agenda-setting role yet because journalists are unsure about whether political blogs can be trusted. If the blogosphere ever gains that trust, it will be because it acquires a sense of legitimacy that equates with news media expectations for reliable sources. This transformation may be achieved by the blogosphere becoming professionalized, including establishing a code of ethics for gathering and reporting news, credentialing by government, and adhering to established standards of accuracy. The blogosphere may not be expected to abandon partisan bias. Opinion magazines long have been known for partisanship. Newspaper editorial pages are one-sided. And broadcast media in recent years have become associated with partisan leanings. However, blogs may be expected to establish a firewall between the news dissemination and opinion expression functions to enhance the credibility of their news presentation. . . .

Notes

1. See Michelle Dammon Loyalka, "Blog Alert: Battalion of Citizen Investigative Reporters Cannot Be Ignored by Mainstream Media," *IRE Journal,* July/August 2005, p. 19; Alexandra Starr, "Open-Source Reporting," *New York Times Magazine,* December 11, 2005, p. 82; Suzanne Perry, "Seeking Online Exposure," The Sunlight Foundation, January 10, 2008, at http://www.sunlightfoundation.com/node/4354; David D. Perlmutter, *Blogwars,* New York: Oxford University Press, 2008, pp. 124–125.

2. Melissa Wall, "'Blogs of War': Weblogs as News," *Journalism,* 6 (2005), pp. 157–158.

3. Interview with John Hinderaker, *Frontline,* PBS, August 26, 2006, at http://www.pbs.org/wgbh/pages/frontline/newswar.

4. Quoted in Daniel W. Drezner and Henry Farrell, "The Power and Politics of Blogs," paper presented at the annual meeting of the American Political Science Association, Chicago, September 2–5, 2004.

5. Quoted in Drezner and Farrell, "The Power and Politics of Blogs."

6. Matthew Klam, "Fear and Laptops on the Campaign Trail," *New York Times Magazine,* September 26, 2004, p. 43.

7. D. Travers Scott, "Pundits in Muckracker's Clothing: Political Blogs and the 2004 U.S. Presidential Election," in *Blogging, Citizenship, and the Future of Media,* ed. Mark Tremayne, New York: Routledge, 2007, p. 54.

8. Interview with Joshua Micah Marshall; Interview with Markos Moulitsas, *Frontline,* PBS, August 13, 2006, at http://www.pbs.org/wgbh/pages/frontline/news war.

9. Scott, "Pundits in Muckracker's Clothing," p. 54.

10. Interview with Markos Moulitsas.

11. Michael Skube, "Blogs: All the Noise That Fits," *Los Angeles Times,* August 19, 2007, p. M5.

12. Wall, "'Blogs of War,'" pp. 153–172.

13. See Bernard Bailyn and John B. Hench, eds., *The Press and the American Revolution,* Worcester, Mass.: American Antiquarian Society, 1980; John Byrne Cooke, *Reporting the War: Freedom of the Press from the American Revolution to the War on Terrorism,* New York: Palgrave Macmillan, 2007; Culver Smith, *The Press, Politics, and Patronage: The American Government's Use of Newspapers, 1789–1875,* Athens: University of Georgia Press, 1977.

14. See Michael Schudson, *Discovering the News,* New York: Basic Books, 1980.

15. "News Audiences Increasingly Polarized: Online News Audience Larger, More Diverse," Pew Research Center for the People and the Press, June 8, 2004, at http://people-press.org/reports/pdf/215.pdf.

16. Jane B. Singer, "Still Guarding the Gate? The Newspaper Journalist's Role in an On-line World," *Convergence,* 3 (1997), pp. 72–89.

17. Amanda Lenhart and Susannah Fox, "Bloggers: A Portrait of the Internet's New Storytellers," Pew Internet and American Life Project, July 19, 2006, at http://www.pewinternet.org/PPF/r/l86/report_display.asp.

18. "Blogger: Joshua Micah Marshall, 34, Editor, Talking Points Memo," *Washington Post,* December 21, 2003, p. M3.

19. "Internet's Broader Role in Campaign 2008: Social Networking and Online Videos Take Off," Pew Research Center, January 11, 2008, at http://people-press .org/reports/pdf/384.pdf; "Internet News Audience Highly Critical of News Organizations," Pew Research Center, August 9, 2007, at http://people-press .org/reports/pdf/348.pdf.

20. Lasica, "Weblogs: A New Source of News."

21. J. D. Lasica, "Blogging as a Form of Journalism," *USC Annenberg Online Journalism Review,* April 29, 2001, at http://www.ojr.org/ojr/lasica/1019166956 .php.

22. Paul McLeary, "Franklin Foer on the Blogosphere's War on the Media," *Columbia Journalism Review,* January 6, 2006, at http://www.cjr.org/the_water_cooler/ franklin_foer_on_the_blogosphe.php.

Part V

GUIDING PUBLIC POLICIES

Doris Graber

News stories affect public policies in many ways. Publicity may engender governmental action when none might otherwise have taken place. Media attention may narrow or foreclose the policy choices available to public officials. Mobilizing hostile public or interest group opinions may force a halt to ongoing policies. American journalists usually disclaim any motivation to influence public policies through their news stories, but like all human beings, they know that total objectivity is impossible to achieve. Irrespective of their intentions, journalists' control over story selection involves choices that inevitably favor some stakeholders and harm others. Additionally journalists' control over story selection is limited by the unequal power of news providers to frame stories attractively and bring them to journalists' attention. Part V contains examples of policy impact studies that involve a variety of situations in both domestic and foreign policy domains.

The opening selection shows how news media can be lured into providing favorable coverage for public policies that benefit special interest groups and harm the general public. Christopher Loomis tells the tale of a talented lobbyist who framed appealing stories that supported his clients' interests. He offered his stories to small media enterprises free of charge. They accepted them and published them as regular news because the stories were well written and seemed to cover matters of wide public interest. Consequently, the concerns of special interest groups appeared on the public's and politicians' agenda as items that required action. Ultimately, the realization that news was subject to manipulation by paid lobbyists undermined the public's faith in the objectivity of the press.

In the next selection, Robert M. Entman tracks the actual influence of news media in specific foreign policy situations. He points out that influence over policy requires control over its framing, making battles over framing common. When policy outcomes are analyzed, it is extraordinarily difficult to assign precise weights to the influence exercised by various stakeholders during the framing process. Entman's research suggests that government officials and journalists usually dominate framing. The public's influence is difficult to gauge because public opinions are articulated by the very elites, including journalists, who have been active, partisan opinion shapers. When the media report about public opinions, they may merely reflect the views that elites project onto public opinion rather than genuine grassroots views.

Doubts about the nature and merits of publicized opinions grow when evidence casts doubts on the factual accuracy of many news media reports. Sean Aday's essay sheds further light on the problem of conveying truth. In addition to all of the difficulties that journalists face in identifying important events, getting all the facts right, and condensing them into appealing stories, they must also weigh the likely consequences of news. Particularly in times of crisis, an exposé can harm the actors in the story, the people who hear and watch it, and the government policies designed to cope with the impact of crisis events. Aday uses the display on television of the bodies of dead and wounded soldiers in wartime as an example of stories that are extraordinarily difficult to report. He concludes that journalists have been conditioned by their training, their sensibilities, and their sense of patriotism to conceal the ugly "truth" of battlefront carnage from impressionable audiences.

Besides demonstrating that news media coverage plays a crucial role in the formation and adoption of public policies at the national level, it is important to analyze comparable situations at the state level. Yue Tan and David Weaver do that in chapter 28. Their study explores the relationships among local newspaper coverage, state-level public opinion, and state legislative policies. The research encompasses multiple states and ranges over a fourteen-year period. While the specific findings vary geographically and over time, collectively they demonstrate that news coverage, and the opinions it generates, definitely affect legislative policies.

Chapter 29 deals with the news media's role in the implementation of public policies that require large-scale public cooperation. Five health communication specialists—May G. Kennedy, Ann O'Leary, Vicki Beck, Katrina Pollard, and Penny Simpson—report on government efforts to enlist the media's help to publicize information about AIDS prevention and treatment. Their essay confirms that properly designed and attractively packaged health messages, embedded in news or entertainment programs, can stimulate sizeable numbers of readers, viewers, and listeners to act in line with a health policy's goals. Collaboration between public officials and the media works when it is carefully designed and executed.

Part V ends with a reminder about the traditional media's ebbing power to dominate how public policies are framed. In the foreign policy field, for example, national governments could previously exercise substantial control over the thrust of media coverage by releasing or withholding information that was not available elsewhere. Monopoly power has vanished. The rise of satellites and the spread of the Internet now enable transnational information flows that have brought many new voices into play. A broad array of policy recommendations is surfacing and generates lively discussions. The new technologies have even made it possible for governments in one country to address populations in another country over the objections of the national sovereign. The ability to discuss public policies on a global scale, across national boundaries, may have limits, but they are not yet well developed or understood.

25

THE POLITICS OF UNCERTAINTY: LOBBYISTS AND PROPAGANDA IN EARLY TWENTIETH-CENTURY AMERICA

Christopher M. Loomis

Editor's Note

Advocating for or against public policies is at the heart of the political process, especially in democracies. Because it is so important, it has become increasingly professionalized, propelled by technological advances. Trained lobbyists still contact individual legislators directly or via members of the legislators' personal networks. But lobbyists also go public, using the news media to gain audiences in the halls of power and among the general public.

   Christopher Loomis tracks the career of super-lobbyist James Arnold, who worked on behalf of conservative business interests in the opening decades of the twentieth century. Arnold, motivated by a mixture of greed, cunning, and idealism, composed news stories that favored his clients' interests. He put them on readily printable "plates" that he distributed to news media free of charge. Small publications gobbled up this bonanza of free, smoothly written copy of slanted stories and distributed it to their readers. The essay demonstrates the interface of policy proponents with media to promote a wide range of purposes of varying merits. When this essay was written, Christopher Loomis was a doctoral candidate in the Corcoran Department of History at the University of Virginia. He was completing his dissertation, "Rechanneling Democracy: Public Television in America, 1950–1980."

   . . . In practicing the art of propaganda, James Arnold exemplified the transformation of lobbying during the early twentieth century. Arnold sought to mold public opinion through newspaper articles, direct canvassing,

Source: Excerpted from Christopher M. Loomis, "The politics of uncertainty: Lobbyists and propaganda in early twentieth-century America," in *Journal of Policy History,* 21:2 (April 2009): 187–213. Copyright © 2009 by Donald Critchlow and Cambridge University Press. Reprinted with the permission of Cambridge University Press.

and later, the radio—a process he referred to as "developing sentiment."[1] While politicians and journalists were only beginning to connect developing sentiment with lobbying when Arnold began his career at the turn of the century, by the 1930s such techniques were widely regarded as an essential part of a lobbyist's repertoire. Arnold's ability to mobilize constituents played a significant role in what he claimed as his principal success: securing higher rates for southern agricultural products in the Fordney-McCumber Tariff of 1922, but even when he advocated for losing causes—including challenges to southern Democrats during the 1920s and the New Deal in the 1930s—his opponents did not regard his talents lightly. . . .

Arnold's case, however, also shows how lobbyists' use of propaganda infused new uncertainties into the democratic process. While Arnold successfully rallied supporters to his causes, he often did so by spreading false or misleading information. Evidence also indicates that Arnold used his skills to reap pecuniary, as well as political, benefits. The issue, however, was not simply whether Arnold was a legitimate petitioner or a corrupt lobbyist, or whether the opinions he activated were based on good or bad information, but that legislators and other elites had a hard time telling the difference. Indeed, lawmakers' encounters with Arnold and other lobbyists during these years demonstrated that the answers to these questions could be highly ambiguous. If there was a modicum of sincerity behind Arnold's more unsavory activities, then perhaps there was a bit of Arnold in even the most earnest lobbyist.[2] In sum, James Arnold's story reveals the ironies of early interest-group politics, as well as the roots of our continued ambivalence toward lobbying. Even as Arnold and his cohorts employed propaganda to assert a more prominent role in the policymaking process, these same tactics called into question their profession's legitimacy. Similarly, while lobbyists aspired to amplify their constituents' power and influence, the methods they employed cast doubt on the ordinary citizen's capacity to participate in democratic politics.

The Usual Arnold Publicity

James Arnold was born in Illinois in 1869 and began his career as a white-collar worker, serving as a clerk and a stenographer for railroads throughout the Midwest. By 1906, Arnold had established himself in Beaumont, Texas, where he became involved in the local chamber of commerce, as well as a statewide booster club called the Texas Business Men's Association (also known as the Commercial Secretaries' Association).

Rising quickly through the ranks at the TBMA, Arnold soon helped to steer the association toward politics. In 1912, the TBMA set up a joint venture with the populist Farmers' Union known as the Farm Life Commission, ostensibly to aid embattled Texas farmers. But as state investigators would later allege, Arnold and the association operated the commission as a clandestine publicity bureau designed to turn public opinion against progressive reforms within the state, most notably prohibition. Arnold wrote pro-business articles for the commission, then had them signed by Farmers' Union officials, whom he bribed using secret corporate contributions. He subsequently distributed the articles for free on ready-to-use "boiler" plates to hundreds of rural newspapers, many of which needed the copy to fill their pages. Local subscribers reading these pieces saw no evidence of the commission's corporate backers—only the imprimatur of the Farmers' Union—and Arnold hoped this purloined endorsement would sway citizens against reform.[3] . . .

. . . Arnold [was] determined to try the same strategy again—this time at the national level. He rapidly established a second plate service, announcing that the organization would "promote and protect the interests of the men who feed and clothe the world."[4] In order to put some weight behind this declaration, the new publicity bureau also claimed affiliation with the Farmers' Union and its 6 million members. All of this was a pretense that Arnold fabricated. Much like the earlier publicity bureau, Arnold's real patrons were railroads and breweries, and he continued to pay Farmers' Union officials for their support. The new press bureau operated until 1917, sending out articles opposing prohibition, women's suffrage, and business regulation—none of which revealed their true sponsors. At one point, Arnold's plates were circulated to an estimated six thousand newspapers around the country.[5] . . .

. . . The *New Republic* . . . castigated Arnold's tactics in a 1915 exposé. As the editors opined:

> It is when the propaganda is not avowed, when it crops up unexpectedly and half hidden, to be traced with difficulty to its source, that it assumes a sinister aspect. When, under the guise of a series of educational articles, readers of rural newspapers are misinformed, and business motives put on the finery of morality and sentiment; when appeals bear the name of a respected organization which is in reality the tool of business; when the authority of that name is used to brace a brittle and dangerous contention—then it is that public opinion is being poisoned.[6]

While the journal did not object to brewers and other businesses openly advocating for their political interests, Arnold's machinations menaced unsuspecting citizens by actively concealing the source of biased information. Only the belated discovery of the plot offered some solace to the outraged editors, who speculated that the episode might indirectly strengthen support for the progressive causes that Arnold's publicity targeted.[7] . . .

. . . [L]arge segments of the body politic, including farmers, labor, women, and professionals, had begun to form extrapartisan political organizations around the turn of the century, and many hired professionals to represent their demands to policymakers at the state and national levels.[8] Just 256 such groups appeared before congressional committees between 1890 and 1899; 1,301 would offer testimony between 1910 and 1917.[9] The new style of interest-group politics changed not only who lobbyists represented but also the nature of their work. In order to exert influence, interest groups generally required large blocs of voters, and their agents relied on various media, including editorials, newsletters, and pamphlets, to mobilize their constituents. As the *Washington Post* noted in 1912, these shifts fundamentally changed the source of lobbyists' power. "The old-fashioned lobbyist went out when the publicity agent came in. Practically all the lobbying done now is conducted by press agents, working away from Washington," the editors mused. "The new method is not to bribe statesmen, but to create a public sentiment in their districts which will impel or compel them to vote this way or that."[10] In other words, the new brand of lobbyist looked a lot like James Arnold.

While the development of interest-group politics may have softened fears of bribery and other overt acts of corruption, Arnold's case also contributed to a whole new set of anxieties—with these misgivings focused on lobbyists' efforts to affect public opinion. Anyone with a cause, a skilled copywriter, and the requisite cash might reach a large audience through the newspapers, and it seemed as though there was little to stop them from distorting, manipulating, or concealing the truth. Muckraking journalists reported that public utilities, life insurance companies, Standard Oil, and the railroads all retained publicity bureaus during these years. Similar to Arnold's operation, these corporate-funded news agencies produced stories friendly to their patrons, then supplied the articles to newspapers, which either received advertising fees or, if they needed the copy badly enough, took the stories for free. The newspapers ran the articles as straight news or editorials without any mention of their sponsor.[11] The threat of exposure always made this strategy a dicey proposition, and many business interests hewed to more conventional approaches to public opinion, retaining public relations agents and sponsoring clearly labeled advertisements.[12] On the other hand, publicity bureaus could also yield impressive results. In a 1906 article for *McClure's*, Ray Stannard Baker reported that in the space of just eleven weeks, corporate-funded news bureaus transformed local newspaper coverage of the railroads in Nebraska from almost unanimously hostile to nearly wholly positive.[13]

Lawmakers were keenly aware of these media campaigns, as well as the pressure they generated. Congress did require clear labeling of printed advertisements in its 1912 appropriation to the post office, but the measure apparently lacked teeth. By the following year, Illinois Representative Clyde H. Tavenner was complaining on the floor of the House that newspapers were being "filled with paid advertisements calculated to create an artificial public opinion against certain items on the tariff bill."[14] Such opinion, however, was not always entirely "artificial," and as Baker's account noted, the railroads supplemented their publicity by organizing telegram and letter-writing campaigns to legislators and bringing delegations to testify before Congress.[15]

The public relations schemes described by Baker and other journalists, however, would soon seem amateurish in comparison to the U.S. government's propaganda efforts during World War I. Under the leadership of George Creel, the Committee on Public Information (CPI) used stump speakers, print advertising, and movies in what was widely viewed as a successful effort to rally the public around the flag. The CPI was unique in its utilization of the new medium of motion pictures, as well as in its ability to disseminate information on an unprecedented scale. The committee's 75,000 "Four-Minute Men" alone, for example, gave speeches to an estimated 400 million Americans.[16] At the same time, the CPI's centralized coordination of a national propaganda campaign seemed to underscore the modern media's ability to persuade and further amplified misgivings that such instruments might fall into the wrong hands.

Thus, when the Senate Judiciary Committee convened its investigation of propaganda in 1919, it had initially sought to determine whether foreign governments or subversive elements might employ the same strategies to influence American public opinion. In stumbling upon Arnold, however, they found a home-grown propagandist. If German spies and Bolshevik agents posed a clear threat to the republic, then Arnold presented a more ambiguous dilemma, and one that would grow more complex in the years that followed. As lobbyists adopted Arnold's tactics as standard operating procedure during the 1920s, it would become nearly impossible to distinguish Arnold from any other petitioner, and yet more difficult for politicians to judge the meaning of their constituents' opinions. . . .

. . . If Arnold was a con man, then he also may well have been a crusader. . . . [H]e also appears to have had very real political objectives, goals that he made a concerted—and sometimes effective—effort to achieve. . . .

During the early 1920s, Arnold and the STA [Southern Tariff Association] played an important role in the passage of the Fordney-McCumber Tariff. The STA was originally constituted in 1920 under John H. Kirby, a Texas lumber and oil magnate who claimed that a high tariff was the best way to protect southern farmers.[17] Kirby had probably met Arnold through the TBMA, of which he had also been a member, and immediately brought the lobbyist on to run the STA's Washington office.[18] From the capital, Arnold set about the ambitious task of reversing southern Democrats' long-standing opposition to protectionism. He managed a public relations campaign in the press, organized conferences, brought delegations to meet with elected officials, built alliances with other farm organizations, and developed contacts with legislators, tariff commission officers, and even President Harding's private secretary.[19] A later study of roll-call votes on the Fordney-McCumber bill showed that the STA may have successfully persuaded a small group of southern senators to break away from the Democratic bloc, thereby helping to push through the bill's high duties.[20] . . .

Arnold's tactics mirrored those employed by nearly every other interest group during the 1920s. Of these strategies, none was more important than what Arnold variously termed "developing sentiment" and "educational work." Political scientist Peter Odegard put these same methods at the center of his 1928 analysis of the Anti-Saloon League, by his accounts one of the largest and most influential interest groups of the early twentieth century. As Odegard showed, the league launched a "deluge" of publicity during the 1910s, and the organization even went so far as to establish its own publishing company in order to get out its message. The league's eight presses pumped out more than thirty state newsletters and a host of other journals, all aimed at activating public opinion against the nation's saloons. In total, the organization produced more than 150 million books, pamphlets, leaflets, and other documents between 1909 and 1923, and at their peak the league's journals boasted a total circulation of more than 550,000.[21] "That such a gigantic outpouring should have profoundly modified the behavior of the American people toward the liquor traffic is not surprising," Odegard concluded.[22] Other pressure groups differed in scale from the Anti-Saloon League, but all relied on similar tactics. As Odegard later argued, "The pressure which these groups are able to exert depends in the final analysis upon the efficiency of their propaganda."[23] . . .

The propaganda problem, however, raised questions about just how citizens would obtain dependable information untainted by pressure groups or other sources. Columnist Walter Lippmann, himself a former officer with the Committee on Public Information, questioned whether even leading citizens were capable of deciphering complex public issues. In his 1925 book, *The Phantom Public,* he wrote:

> They [public affairs] are managed, if they are managed at all, at distant centers, from behind the scenes, by unnamed powers. As a private person he does not know for certain what is going on, or who is doing it, or where he is being carried. No newspaper reports his environment so that he can grasp it; no school has taught him how to imagine it; his ideals, often, do not fit with it; listening to speeches, uttering opinions and voting do not, he finds, enable him to govern it. He lives in a world which he cannot see, does not understand and is unable to direct.[24]

Striking a more optimistic tone, John Dewey argued that while the average voter would never embody Lippmann's "sovereign and omnicompetent citizen," they might yet be capable of choosing intelligently among options provided by objective experts.[25] Still, both Dewey's and Lippmann's voter remained dependent on others for political information about the world beyond their town or neighborhood. . . .

Notes

1. U.S. Senate, Subcommittee of the Committee on the Judiciary, *Lobby Investigation,* 71st Cong., 2nd sess., 1929–30, 797 (hereafter *Lobby Investigation, 1929–30*).
2. Although scholars have written extensively about what lobbyists do, their effectiveness remains largely unclear. This holds true for historical accounts, as well as more recent political science, which has yet to systematically measure and explain lobbyists' influence on the policymaking process. . . .
3. "Looney Brings Suit to Dissolve Business Men's Association," *Dallas Morning News,* 28 June 1914, 1; "B. F. Looney Opens Campaign," *Dallas Morning News,* 21 May 1916, 7; "Brewing Propaganda," *New Republic,* 21 August 1915, 62–64. For a broader overview of the Texas prohibition battle, see Peter H. Odegard, *Pressure Politics: The Story of the Anti-Saloon League* (New York, 1928), 249–56.
4. "Brewing Propaganda," 62–64; U.S. Senate, Committee on the Judiciary, *Brewing and Liquor Interests and German and Bolshevik Propaganda,* vol. 2, 65th Cong., 3rd sess., 1918–19, 2525–26 (hereafter *Brewing and Liquor Interests*).
5. According to Arnold, various brewers contributed somewhere between $29,000 and $41,000 between 1914 and 1916 (some of these funds may have gone to the Farm Life Commission). Eight to ten railroads—including the Santa Fe, Southern Pacific, Union Pacific, and the Missouri, Kansas, and Texas—gave $40,000 to $50,000. Arnold put his own salary at $500 a month, although it is unclear if he was always able to draw the full amount. "Brewing Propaganda," 62–64; *Brewing and Liquor Interests,* 2524–615.
6. "Brewing Propaganda," 62.
7. Ibid., 64.
8. Elizabeth S. Clemens, *The People's Lobby: Organizational Innovation and the Rise of Interest Group Politics in the United States, 1890–1925.* (Chicago, 1997).
9. In both periods, the vast majority of these groups were making their first appearance before Congress. Daniel J. Tichenor and Richard A. Harris, "Organized Interests and American Political Development," *Political Science Quarterly* 117 (Winter 2002–3): 587–612, 598.
10. "Where Are Those Lobbyists?" *Washington Post,* 22 March 1912, 6.
11. The rise of professional journalism likely amplified the shock of these exposés. Whereas the predominantly partisan press of the late nineteenth century provided an unabashedly slanted interpretation of the news, by the first decade of the twentieth century Arnold's articles would have likely been published in independent newspapers and consumed by readers who expected their news to be presented objectively. Ray Stannard Baker, "Railroads on Trial, V: How Railroads Make Public Opinion," *McClure's,* March 1906, 535; "Tainted News as Seen in

the Making," *Bookman,* December 1906, 396; William Kittle, "The Making of Public Opinion," *Arena,* July 1909, 433; Michael McGerr, *The Decline of Popular Politics: The American North, 1865–1928* (New York, 1986), 107–37.

12. Corporate interests also employed more ham-fisted tactics, such as undercutting hostile papers' advertising revenue, or simply buying the publications outright. Baker, "Railroads on Trial"; Sherman Morse, "An Awakening in Wall Street," *American Magazine,* September 1906, 2; "Publicity Campaigning," *Independent,* 29 July 1909, 224.

13. Baker, "Railroads on Trial."

14. Tavenner, *Congressional Record* 50, pt. 3 (27 June 1913), 2247. On the post office, see J. Michael Sproule, *Propaganda and Democracy: The American Experience of Media and Mass Persuasion (*New York, 1997), 25.

15. Baker, "Railroads on Trial"; Gabriel Kolko, *Railroads and Regulation, 1877–1916* (Princeton, 1965), 103–5, 131.

16. Sproule, *Propaganda and Democracy,* 9–16; Brett Gary, *The Nervous Liberals: Propaganda Anxieties from World War I to the Cold War* (New York, 1999), 18–23.

17. George Brown Tindall, *The Emergence of the New South, 1913–1945: A History of the South,* vol. 10 (Baton Rouge, 1967), 135.

18. "Five Million Club," *Dallas Morning News,* 26 October 1906, 10. "Texas Economic League Is Organized," *Dallas Morning News,* 15 December 1915, 8.

19. According to Charles M. Dollar, Kirby handled the fundraising at this stage. Dollar, "The South and the Fordney-McCumber Tariff of 1922: A Study in Regional Politics," *Journal of Southern History* 39, no. 1 (1973): 53–55.

20. Ibid., 48–51.

21. Odegard, *Pressure Politics,* 12, 75–76.

22. Ibid., 76.

23. Peter H. Odegard, *The American Public Mind* (New York, 1930), 178.

24. Walter Lippmann, *The Phantom Public* (New York, 1925), 13–14.

25. For further discussion of this debate, see Michael Schudson, *The Good Citizen: A History of American Civic Life* (New York, 1998), 212–19.

26

MEDIATING THE PUBLIC'S INFLUENCE ON FOREIGN POLICY

Robert M. Entman

Editor's Note

Foreign policy results from the interplay of many factors. Robert M. Entman disentangles these factors, using a series of case studies to discover the role played by public opinion. He demonstrates that the interactions produced by the publicity efforts of official and nonofficial elites, the images held by the public, and the objectives of journalists are so complex, and the actors so interdependent, that no firm conclusions are possible about how much weight each factor receives in a particular decision.

However, the evidence clearly shows that the nature of news frames is crucial and that framing is dominated by elites, including journalists. The influence of the citizenry is less clear, partly because public opinion reflects the information disseminated by elites and partly because using different yardsticks for measuring public opinion yields drastically different conclusions.

Entman was a professor of communication and political science at North Carolina State University when *Projections of Power* was published. He has authored many books, articles, and book chapters on media, politics, and public policy. His research has won numerous awards, including prizes sponsored by the American Political Science Association, the National Communication Association, and Harvard University's John F. Kennedy School of Government.

. . . Prior research into the impact of public opinion on public policy offers surprisingly little insight into exactly how elites figure out what the public is thinking. Most treatments simply assume that political motivations lead officials more or less accurately to detect and respond to public opinion. This chapter opens up this critical path of political communication to reveal the complex interplay of news frames with the thinking of elites and citizens. Three insights . . . are especially pertinent here:

1. The public's actual opinions arise from framed information, from selected highlights of events, issues, and problems rather than from direct contact with the realities of foreign affairs.
2. Elites for their part cannot know the full reality of public thinking and feeling, but must rely on selective interpretations that draw heavily on news frames.
3. Policymakers relentlessly contend to influence the very news frames that influence them.

   In this process, officials must take account of several facets of public opinion, not just the standard measure of majority preferences. Despite their importance to leaders, these distinct faces of public opinion are rarely tested apart in empirical research. . . .

Framing Is Inescapable

. . . For foreign affairs, few people have direct data, and most information originates in media reports even if it is passed along selectively (or framed) in conversation with informants who themselves saw the news. Answers to questions on how much the United States should spend on defense, for instance (the case discussed below), respond to media threat signals—few citizens have anywhere else to get their information on enemies' military intentions and capabilities.[1] At least for foreign policy, there are few if any cases where a pure, unmediated public opinion emerges directly from reality. That does not mean everyone responds to the media's frames identically, but it does mean that most people's opinions will be influenced by their reactions to the frames. . . .

. . . The real issue, and the important role for media and public opinion in the political process, is determining which problem definition, cause, and policy response gain widespread adherence. These interpretations are rarely automatically deduced from the event itself. . . .

[Public Opinion about] National Defense

. . . That observation brings us to the first case study in this chapter, on defense spending. An important article by Hartley and Russett[2] on the impact of public opinion on defense policy connects normative democratic theory with empirical data to ask "Who governs military spending in the United States?" It serves as a good basis for anchoring the analysis of the inescapability of framing in studying public opinion, and helps to clarify the often-neglected influences of news media on representation. Reflecting a view common in recent political science, the article concludes that "public opinion" significantly helps "govern." However, if much of the public opinion this study identifies is actually polling opinion, and thus has been influenced by media frames, that conclusion demands further scrutiny.

The study finds that between 1965 and 1990, "changes in public opinion consistently exert an effect on changes in military spending."[3] It measures public opinion by responses to a standard survey question: whether government is spending too little, too much, or about the right amount on defense. Employing pooled estimates from six different polling organizations to generate unusually reliable estimates, Hartley and Russett find that changes in the levels of "too little" (or "too much") responses significantly predict alteration in the total defense obligations Congress approved (spending figures in constant 1982 dollars).[4] On this basis the authors argue that, judging by the case of defense spending, Congress responded to public opinion, fulfilling its representative duties according to at least one reasonable version of democracy.

Of particular interest for our purposes here is the period encompassing the Carter and Reagan administrations (1977–89), which saw the widest swings in public sentiment and provided the best opportunity for congressional responsiveness, although similar arguments could be made for the Johnson and Nixon years. Surveys showed a large shift toward favoring more spending during the years 1978–81, and Congress did approve sharp increases in defense spending thereafter.

Yet Congress failed to respond to several other strains of what polls suggest were majority sentiments during the period. Congress did not mandate that Reagan approach nuclear negotiations seriously in his first term,[5] nor did it approve a nuclear freeze, though surveys showed majorities favoring such action, often by upwards of 75 percent. If one used the survey data only on the nuclear freeze while ignoring the data on defense spending, one could well conclude Congress was entirely unresponsive to the public on defense policy. Of course it may be that the public was conflicted on the nuclear freeze or that survey questions on it gave misleading impressions of the actual underlying individual preferences and priorities of citizens. But this only reinforces the point that public opinion is usually a product of selective interpretation or framing.

. . . Bartels notes, the same polls recording increases in public desires for higher spending on defense simultaneously recorded demands for "social programs, tax reduction, and fiscal responsibility," which "manifestly limited the ability of Congress to respond to each of them separately."[6] In this sense it would appear nearly arbitrary to pick one dimension where opinion and congressional action seemed to coincide while neglecting others where they did not, and then drawing general conclusions on government responsiveness.

Looking more carefully at defense spending data raises additional questions about representation. As Figure 26–1 suggests,[7] there was a noticeable

Figure 26–1   Increased Defense Spending Despite Drop in Public Support, 1980–1990

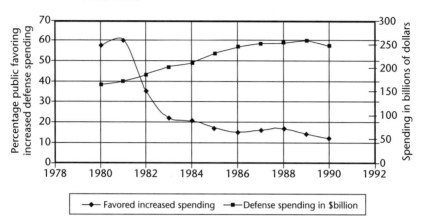

lack of representation from 1982 to 1985, when Congress continued to raise defense spending despite the sharp dovish turn in polling opinion. Those favoring an increase rose from 40 percent in 1979 to 58 percent in 1980 and 60 percent in 1981. But the next year saw this proportion plummet to 35 percent, then to 22 percent in 1983, and even lower after that. Surveyed sentiment shifted even more sharply *away* from defense spending during this time than it had turned *toward* support between 1977 and 1981, so if Congress was responding to altered public sentiment it should have cut defense—or at least slowed the rate of increase—by 1983 or 1984. Yet defense spending began declining in real terms only in *fiscal 1990*. Defense allocations kept growing as public support declined. The *rate* of growth in spending began slowing notably in fiscal 1987, which might signify a response to public opinion.[8] But here we had decisions to raise defense budgets that persisted for eight years (1982–89) against a sharp and persistent dovish trend in opinion, a trend that soon reduced the proportion of citizens favoring those increases to a small minority. Classifying such policies as responsive would seem to mark a striking redefinition of democratic representation.[9]

Now it might be that officials interpreted the 1983 surge in negative media symbols spurred by the KAL incident [Korean Airlines plane shot down by Soviet fighter plane] as signaling that public opinion favored even more spending hikes, despite polls showing it did not. Such a possibility would be consistent with . . . research . . . indicating that officials infer elements of public opinion—perceived and anticipated majorities, and priorities—from media content. Perhaps elites anticipated that majorities would prefer more defense spending once they digested the heightened threat, and would weigh defense as a high enough priority to punish softness come election time. In addition, public opinion was frequently depicted in the media as highly supportive of the unabashedly hawkish Reagan. Even though Reagan's average approval ratings were actually quite low in his first term, news reports tended to laud his popularity.[10] And indeed, by his second term Reagan's average approval was relatively high. From the perceived majority support in his first term and actual polling opinion in his second, officials might well have inferred a low priority for the public's apparent desires to cut defense spending—and maybe they were correct. This could explain, in part, the lack of congressional responsiveness to the clear turn of surveyed majorities against higher defense budgets starting in 1982.

But another major reason for continued budget growth during this period was that long-term commitments to weapons systems had been made at the outset. Once weapons programs begin they are difficult to stop. Spending momentum is reinforced by electoral incentives in specific congressional districts where military spending is vital to the economy; their representatives often exert disproportionate influence over defense budgets. And an enormous military-industrial complex—very much including the Pentagon itself—has compelling incentives and vast resources to lobby Congress and engage in public relations initiatives to keep the defense contracts coming. These points further underscore the complexity of generalizing about government responsiveness to public opinion. . . .

. . . [T]he survey data on raising or cutting defense spending cannot tell us whether the public ever wanted the *magnitude* of increase approved by Congress during the 1980s. A much smaller increase might have been enough to satisfy most Americans even at their most hawkish. This seems especially likely in view of many other poll findings, some from the very surveys on "more" or "less" government spending that the authors use, of large majorities desiring higher budgets for crime fighting, education, health care, or other domestic priorities.[11] . . .

Furthermore, probing defense spending attitudes during the 1990s, after military budgets were reduced, Kull and Ramsay still found substantial willingness to support further cuts, so long as opinions were probed in detail and in larger context rather than simply asking the one question on spending more or less. Their data also showed elites tending to overestimate public support for high defense spending. . . . [T]o conclude from some poll evidence that the public really preferred to raise defense spending as much as Congress did over alternative uses of the money, scholars and Congress members themselves had to select some polling data and disregard the kinds of polls just cited. Include all the information at once and guidance from public opinion . . . becomes, at the least, murky. . . .

Acknowledging this process suggests limited expectations for democratic responsiveness. Public opinion includes a variety of individual preferences and intensities, contradictions and harmonies, which are imperfectly susceptible to measurement and aggregation whether by public officials or by scholars.[12] As for measuring government response, aside from whatever Congress as a whole decided, the degree to which individual legislators were responding to mass opinion also varied from member to member.

. . . [T]he degree of Soviet threat represented in the mass media corresponds closely to the movement of polling opinion on defense spending. The data in Figure 26–2 were compiled by searching for all *Washington Post* stories since 1977 (the first year the *Post*'s archives were computerized) in which the words "Russia" or "Soviet" occurred within twenty-five words of "aggression," "buildup," or "threat." Each story was checked to ensure the passages containing the terms did refer to the USSR's actions or intentions.[13]

The relationship graphs nicely; Figure 26–2 shows how the two moved in tandem. The number of threat references peaked in 1980, and public backing of higher defense budgets peaked the following year. (The sharp upward movement in mediated threats during 1983 resulted from Reagan's "evil empire" speech in March of that year and, especially, the autumn crisis over the Soviets' destruction of Korean Airlines Flight 007, after which the trend continued downward.) The correlation is quite high for this kind of research (Pearson's $r = .69$, $p < .01$), and the measure is not even very refined. With enough searching and fine-tuning one could probably match up media content with the movement of public opinion even more precisely.

Indeed, if the media measure were entered into the Hartley-Russett calculations while omitting the survey data, one might conclude that Congress

Figure 26–2   Support for More Defense Spending and Media References to Soviet Threat

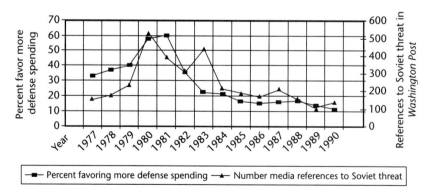

responds attentively to *media* rather than to public opinion. That is *not* the argument here. These data do not allow us to infer that alterations in the news caused policy changes; for one thing, again, defense spending did not drop significantly until 1990 despite the decline in mediated threats. Nor can the data prove that the changes in these symbols of threat were significant causes of the shifts in polling opinion. The point is quite different: namely, that it is difficult even conceptually to disentangle these relationships. Entering both the polling and media data together into an equation to explain variation in defense spending would not be appropriate to the complexity of the underlying relationships. Perceived and actual public sentiments influence and are influenced by elites and policy; all of these influence and are influenced by media; and obtainable measures of elite and mass opinion, of policy itself and of media content, are all deeply problematic.

. . . [L]ooking at all these forces at play, it appears the media played a role in shaping outcomes, along with leaders' talk, actions, and perceptions of public opinion, and the public's actual sentiments. In this jumbled spiral, this double helix, of reciprocal influences, movements, and resistances among elites and the public, evidence for the independent influence of public opinion on policy, or for genuinely democratic control of government by the public, is likely to remain incomplete.[14]

The dramatic divergence between surveyed opinion and defense spending during most of the 1980s suggests the need to develop more inclusive models that can explain the many spells of clear unresponsiveness as well as periods that seem to indicate responsiveness, that can distinguish the episodes where polling opinion changes independent of elite information blitzes from those where any shift arises from the White House's management of the news. Public opinion—whether framed as polling opinion, perceived and anticipated majorities, or priorities—appears to be a sporadic constraint,[15] not a controlling force on which government depends to guide its choices. Although media frames do serve as a kind of transmission belt, communicating the public's thinking up to elites as well as moving information in the reverse direction, so many complexities and imperfections mark this process that optimistic conclusions about public control appear unfounded. . . .

The Frozen Out Public

When we turn to public opinion articulated in a more active and precise form than merely answering survey questions, evidence suggests that far from being eager to respond, journalists and elites may in some instances not even favor much public input into foreign policy. Scholars have long recognized that, however accounted and described, public opinion surveys send imprecise signals.[16] Perhaps a more efficient vehicle for the expression of public opinion than surveys are social movements. A paper written jointly with Andrew Rojecki[17] explored the media's unfavorable framing of the "nuclear freeze" movement. This section summarizes its findings and draws lessons for the questions raised in this chapter.

Two factors make the freeze particularly noteworthy as a test of media frames' ability to influence perceptions of public opinion and, . . . perhaps affect government responses. First, poll after poll revealed a stable and large majority in favor of the movement's basic proposal: freezing the nuclear arsenals of the United States and its prime adversary, the Soviet Union, at the levels of overkill prevailing in the early 1980s, and then negotiating strategic arms limitations. If Congress were consistently responsive to public opinion (or in the terms of this chapter, to polling opinion), we would expect to see passage of legislation supporting this stable majority. Second, the freeze was a policy option actively pressed on government by a large, organized, and determinedly mainstream political movement in the best tradition of grassroots activism. Unlike many prior movements, most notably the groups protesting the Vietnam War, freeze advocates and leaders were at pains to portray the movement in ways that would reassure rather than alienate the average, moderate American.[18]

For a movement with national ambitions, grassroots networks can help spread activation, but the media will be crucial for getting the word out to the mass of potential supporters. . . . [U]nfavorable media assessments can seriously weaken a group's recruitment efforts. Apart from this, the news helps determine whether elites feel pressure to support the movement's policy goals. Since elites use news treatment as surrogates for public opinion, positive coverage can convey to them that citizens favor the policy and that the issue merits a high and favorable place on the agenda.[19]

Unfavorable media framing of the movement discouraged involvement by those ordinary citizens who supported the remedy but remained outside the group's activities; these potential recruits may not have been able to tell that they were actually part of a vast majority. The power of the media's framing was to inhibit ordinary Americans—and their leaders—from making mental associations between the freeze and such legitimizing concepts as "democracy" and "public opinion." Instead news frames tended to make delegitimizing associations, at least within media texts, and perhaps influenced audiences' minds. For example, stories frequently alluded to the frivolous hippies or the even more unpopular antiwar dissidents of the 1960s. The dearth of favorable publicity diminished any sense among the movement's inactive supporters that the freeze idea might legitimately demand a place on the agenda and a positive, concrete government response—or that perhaps they should vote against officials who failed to respond. In this way negative media treatment might have lowered the pressure elites felt to act favorably on the proposal— . . . reducing the *priority* of this particular policy preference—thereby providing political cover for an unresponsive government.

Conclusion

Public opinion cannot be divorced from the political discourse and media frames that surround it. The apparent impact of the public on government policy often arises from a circular process in which government officials respond to the polling opinions, anticipated or perceived majorities, and priorities that many of them helped create. Arguably that was the case with defense spending. And when it came to the nuclear freeze proposal, government disregarded and journalists on balance derogated an immense and stable majority of poll respondents. Just as Destler and others have suggested, there is some evidence in this that, rhetorical endorsements of democracy notwithstanding, foreign policy elites (and journalists) would just as soon keep the public out of the loop.[20] In any case, governing elites at best respond to selected interpretations of public opinion, and that almost certainly gives media frames a central role in the process of representation. For these and other reasons discussed above, any match between the majority positions registered by surveys and government decisions supplies imperfect evidence for the extent of democracy in the foreign policymaking process. . . .

Notes

1. This is not to deny that personal ideology plays a major role too. Many Americans, elites and citizens alike, regularly see imminent threats from the communists, terrorists, or other enemies no matter what the media are reporting.
2. Hartley and Russett 1992; also see Wlezien 1996.
3. Hartley and Russett 1992, 905.
4. Ibid., 907.
5. See Talbott 1984, on Reagan's negotiating approach.
6. Bartels 1991, 466.
7. The public opinion figures are the same as those used by Hartley and Russett. The spending figures are actual defense expenditures (not as in Hartley and Russett, defense authorizations), in constant 1982 dollars, taken from the *Budget of the United States Government, Fiscal 1992, 69–70.* . . .
8. Cf. Wlezien 1996, 87.
9. According to Erikson, MacKuen, and Stimson 2002, 359, it takes about eight years for policy (measured as major domestic policy laws passed by Congress) to catch up with and match opinion changes, which they view as appropriate to the Madisonian structure (checks and balances) of the U.S. government. So the findings here do accord with Erikson et al.'s model, since defense spending

was finally cut in 1990, about eight years after polls indicated the public wanted reductions. . . . What the finding in this chapter and the findings of the far more complicated and exhaustive study by Erikson et al. reveal, of course, is that there is no objective basis for concluding a system is doing a good enough job of responding to public desires. . . .

10. This provides another example of the frequent disjunctions between perceived majorities as depicted in the news and actual polling opinion as measured by surveys. See King and Schudson 1991.
11. Page and Shapiro 1992, chaps. 2 and 4.
12. Cf. Herbst 1993, 1998; see Page and Shapiro 1992, 263–74 on the twists and turns in public and elite opinion about foreign policy, and Page 2002 on the many complexities of measuring public opinion and its impacts on policy.
13. Spending opinion data from Hartley and Russett 1992, 909.
14. Page 2002 provides a detailed analysis of these matters. Manza and Cook (2002, 21) write: "Quantitative studies have established a case for . . . policy responsiveness to public opinion. But because these studies tend to include few other covariates they may miss factors that mediate or precede the relationship between opinion and policy." They also note: "[B]ecause foreign and defense policies are often event- and crisis-driven, there are sharp problems of causal inference. When a foreign crisis changes the context within which the public views a question, rapid changes in public attitudes are possible, which may, in turn, appear to be associated with later changes in policy. But in such cases, it appears likely that the same factors that move public opinion also move elites and the overall direction of policy making" (30 n. 7).
15. Cf. Sobel 2001; Jacobs and Shapiro 2000; Powlick and Katz 1998.
16. E.g., cf. Herbst 1993; Verba and Nie 1987.
17. Entman and Rojecki 1993; cf. Rojecki 1999. Also see Meyer 1995.
18. Cf. Gitlin 1980; Rojecki 1999.
19. Cf. Bennett 1993; Lipsky 1968.
20. Destler 2001; Powlick and Katz 1998. Adherents of the realist school (Keohane 1986; cf. Foyle 1999) would defend this elitist position of trying to maintain public quiescence (cf. Edelman 1988; Jacobs and Shapiro 2000) to allow officials maximum freedom of action so they can best pursue the national interest in the anarchic international system.

References

Bartels, Larry M. 1991. Constituency Opinion and Congressional Policymaking: The Reagan Defense Buildup. *American Political Science Review* 85: 457–75.

Bennett, W. Lance. 1993. Constructing Publics and Their Opinions. *Political Communication* 10, no. 2: 101–20.

Destler, I. M. 2001. The Reasonable Public and the Polarized Policy Process. In *The Real and the Ideal: Essays on International Relations in Honor of Richard H. Ullman,* ed. Anthony Lake and David Ochmanek, 75–90. Lanham, Md.: Rowman and Littlefield.

Edelman, Murray. 1988. *Constructing the Political Spectacle*. Chicago: University of Chicago Press.

Entman, Robert M., and Andrew Rojecki. 1993. Freezing out the Public: Elite and Media Framing of the U.S. Anti-Nuclear Movement. *Political Communication* 10, no. 2: 151–67.

Erikson, Robert S., Michael B. MacKuen, and James A. Stimson. 2002. *The Macro-Polity*. New York: Cambridge University Press.

Foyle, Douglas. 1999. *Counting the Public In: Presidents, Public Opinion, and Foreign Policy*. New York: Columbia University Press.

Gitlin, Todd. 1980. *The Whole World Is Watching: News Media in the Making and Unmaking of the New Left*. Berkeley: University of California Press.

Hartley, Thomas, and Bruce Russett. 1992. Public Opinion and the Common Defense. *American Political Science Review* 86: 905–15.

Herbst, Susan. 1993. *Numbered Voices: How Opinion Polling Has Shaped American Politics*. Chicago: University of Chicago Press.

———. 1998. *Reading Public Opinion: How Political Actors View the Democratic Process*. Chicago: University of Chicago Press.

Jacobs, Lawrence, and Robert Y. Shapiro. 2000. *Politicians Don't Pander: Political Manipulation and the Loss of Democratic Responsiveness*. Chicago: University of Chicago Press.

Keohane, Robert. 1986. *Neo-realism and Its Critics*. New York: Columbia University Press.

King, Elliot, and Michael Schudson. 1991. The Myth of the Great Communicator. *Columbia Journalism Review* 26 (November/December): 37–39.

Lipsky, Michael. 1968. Protest as a Political Resource. *American Political Science Review* 62, no. 4: 1144–58.

Manza, Jeff, and Fay Lomax Cook. 2002. The Impact of Public Opinion on Public Policy: The State of the Debate. In *Navigating Public Opinion,* ed. Jeff Manza, Fay Lomax Cook, and Benjamin I. Page, 17–32. New York: Oxford University Press.

Manza, Jeff, Fay Lomax Cook, and Benjamin I. Page, eds. 2002. *Navigating Public Opinion: Polls, Policy, and the Future of American Democracy*. New York: Oxford University Press.

Meyer, D. S. 1995. Framing National Security: Elite Public Discourse on Nuclear Weapons during the Cold War. *Political Communication* 12, no. 2: 173–92.

Page, Benjamin I. 2002. The Semisovereign Public. In *Navigating Public Opinion: Polls, Policy and the Future of American Democracy,* ed. Jeff Manza, Fay Lomax Cook, and Benjamin I. Page, 325–44. New York: Oxford University Press.

Page, Benjamin I., and Robert Y. Shapiro. 1992. *The Rational Public*. Chicago: University of Chicago Press.

Powlick, Philip J., and Andrew Z. Katz. 1998. Defining the American Public Opinion/ Foreign Policy Nexus. *International Studies Quarterly* 42, no. 1 (Supp. 1): 29–63.

Rojecki, Andrew. 1999. *Silencing the Opposition: Anti-Nuclear Movements and the Media in the Cold War*. Urbana: University of Illinois Press.

Sobel, Richard. 2001. *The Impact of Public Opinion on U.S. Foreign Policy since Vietnam: Constraining the Colossus.* New York: Oxford University Press.

Talbott, Strobe. 1984. *Deadly Gambits.* New York: Knopf.

Verba, Sidney, and Norman Nie. 1987. *Participation in America: Political Democracy and Social Equality.* Chicago: University of Chicago Press.

Wlezien, Christopher. 1996. Dynamics of representation: The Case of U.S. Spending on Defence. *British Journal of Political Science* 26, no. 1: 81–103.

27

THE REAL WAR WILL NEVER GET ON TELEVISION: AN ANALYSIS OF CASUALTY IMAGERY

Sean Aday

Editor's Note

The ideal of a free press that reports reality as journalists experience it is most difficult to achieve in times of war. Journalists must wrestle with patriotic desires to show their country at its best, with the difficulty of gaining access to war zones, and with the pressure to publicize their government's propaganda messages. If they gain access to the fields of battle, the gruesome situations that they witness may seem unsuitable for exposure to audiences unaccustomed to such carnage.

Yet if journalists sanitize the truth, do they serve the public well when the nation must adopt sound policies during critical times? Sean Aday documents the dilemmas of wartime coverage that trouble journalists everywhere. These dilemmas often result in lack of candor that leads to skewed, misleading coverage. The consequences can be monumental.

At the time of writing, Sean Aday was an assistant professor of media and public affairs at George Washington University. His keen insights into the problems facing journalists spring from his newspaper reporting days. On the academic side, Aday had already contributed essays about the mass media and public opinion to major political science and communication journals.

In 1862, photographer Alexander Gardner visited the battlefield at Antietam and shot several dozen pictures for the New York gallery run by his employer, Mathew Brady. Most of the images he captured were landscapes and group portraits, reflecting the tastes of the limited but enthusiastic contemporary market for photographs, which had only begun to be in mass

Source: Sean Aday, "The Real War Will Never Get on Television: An Analysis of Casualty Imagery in American Television Coverage of the Iraq War," in *Media and Conflict in the Twenty-First Century*, ed. Philip Seib, New York: Palgrave Macmillan, 2005, 141–155. Copyright © 2005 by Philip Seib. Reproduced with permission of Palgrave Macmillan.

circulation for about two decades. About a third of his exposures, however, were of dead Confederate soldiers who had not yet been removed from the field.[1] At the time, Gardner had no reason to think these shots would be of any commercial interest; they were, after all, the first images of battlefield death scenes circulated in America. As it turned out, the pictures were a sensation, stimulating a highly profitable frenzy of interest in similar scenes from other battles. When Gardner went to Gettysburg a year later, having set off on his own business, three-quarters of his pictures were graphic depictions of the dead, albeit often rearranged into romanticized poses.[2]

Today, our historical memory of the gruesomeness (and romanticism) of the Civil War is illustrated by the pictures of dead soldiers taken by Gardner, Brady, and others. Several factors made it possible to capture these images, notably the wet plate processing method that made outdoor photography easier, and the proximity of many important battles like Antietam and Gettysburg to population centers and roads, especially in the north. Despite these factors, though, the rapid mobility of the armies and the still cumbersome technical requirements of the medium meant that only six battles yielded pictures of dead soldiers. In all, probably no more than 100 such photographs were taken during the entire war.

Yet the history of war photography in the Civil War offers several interesting points of departure for understanding the images transmitted through television coverage of the recent Iraq war. First, as in the 1860s, important technological advances in the visual medium, most notably mobile satellite video, allowed reporters to get closer to the fighting and, if they chose to, show the gory reality of modern warfare to their audiences back home. Second, changes in military policy allowed journalists to be embedded with military units and have even better battlefield access than their Civil War counterparts. Indeed, journalists covering the last several American military engagements before Iraq were intentionally kept from the front by the military. The question is whether American journalists chose to take advantage of these technological advances and increased battlefield access to show audiences not only the exciting whiz bang nature of American military power, but also the grim ramifications of its use.

This chapter begins to answer this question through a detailed and comprehensive content analysis of battle and casualty coverage of the Iraq war on CNN, Fox News Channel (FNC), and ABC.[3] At its most basic level, this study asks: given that broadcast news had the ability to generate a complete portrait of the war, did it do so? Or did it instead reduce the war to a video game and shield viewers from the dead and wounded? . . .

Visualizing War

For millennia, war has been depicted through imagery, be it on a canvas, a plate, or a broadcast signal. Before photography, these images were invariably captured after the fact (often years later) by artists who were nowhere near the action being depicted, and were heavily romanticized even when they were quite graphic.[4] . . . Importantly, the recording of these events has historically been done in a way that glorifies the protagonists (typically the victors, but more generally the countrymen of the artists or culturally similar participants). Hence, these images are more artful in every sense of the word than they are literal. One might even refer to them as propagandistic. At the least, they have often been driven by and reflected marketplace demands, be it from sponsors in the case of pre-twentieth-century painters or collectors and readers of illustrated weeklies in the case of Civil War era photography and woodcuts.[5]

In other words, the imagery of war and battle has historically been intended to do two things: rally the public consciousness around the righteousness of the conflict (even, and perhaps especially, as the event itself drifts back in time and memory), and please a commercial audience.

Critiques of contemporary war coverage in the American press, particularly in broadcast news, often make the same case against the media, with coverage of the 1991 Persian Gulf War being a prime example. In that conflict, the Pentagon enforced strict censorship of the press and instituted a system of pool reporting that virtually eliminated the potential for independent journalistic observers and allowed the military to exercise near total control of the portrait of the war fed to American audiences. Although media organizations and reporters complained about the restrictions, at the same time they dutifully saturated their coverage with Pentagon press briefings that included dramatic visuals of bombs mounted with cameras striking targets in Iraq, and effusive claims of technical wizardry and precision, many of which turned out to be gross exaggerations at best and outright falsehoods at worst.

The result was imagery that made the war look, to use a popular metaphor, like a video game.[6] Daniel Hallin wrote that coverage defined the Persian Gulf conflict as "patriotic celebration and technological triumph."[7] He also showed how coverage mirrored that during the early years of the Vietnam War in many ways, with the war seen as: (1) a national endeavor, complete with use of the first person plural, such as "our troops," a trait of some Iraq war coverage, too;[8] (2) an American tradition, signified by references to World War II and other iconic moments and images in American history; and (3) necessitating a win at all costs commitment.[9] Others showed how these tendencies were particularly pronounced at CNN, whose need to fill a 24-hour news cycle led them to be less analytical and more focused on event-driven, flashy imagery than the network newscast.[10]

In addition to a focus on the alleged technical perfection of the American war effort and the Pentagon-produced images purporting to demonstrate it, a key component of the media's sanitization (and indeed romanticization) of the Persian Gulf War was their near total lack of casualty visuals. Hallin's analysis showed that American audiences were shown an essentially "clean" war,[11] despite the loss of an estimated 100,000 Iraqi soldiers and perhaps the same number of civilians (not to mention more than 100 American troops). Although much of the explanation for the lack of casualty visuals can be explained by the fact that reporters were kept from the front lines and Baghdad where casualties would occur, others have pointed out that press norms and even ideology were also at play. . . .

That the press largely followed the lead of official Washington in the Persian Gulf War is in many ways to be expected. Between Vietnam and the recent Iraq war, the main finding of scholars looking at war and foreign policy coverage is that the news tends to privilege official sources, especially those from the White House. Most notably, Bennett has shown that news coverage of war and foreign policy is indexed to the limited range of elite opinions, at least in the short run.[12] Dickson, for example, found that government sources defined the range of debate in *New York Times* coverage of the U.S. invasion of Panama.[13] Entman and Page found similar results in coverage leading up to the beginning of the Persian Gulf War, showing that dissenters received less coverage than did officials who exercised some control over war policy, and that even when the press did air criticisms of the administration's policy, those critiques were procedural rather than fundamental in nature.[14]

Although Althaus[15] has recently questioned these assumptions by showing various ways in which dissenting opinions appeared in the press during the Persian Gulf War period, the prevailing finding of scholars to date is that officials exercise a great deal of control over the content and framing of international news, even in the contemporary era of technological advances in news gathering that might theoretically allow for more media independence.[16]

The tendency of modern war reportage, especially on television, to reflect establishment sentiment could be seen as extending to the hesitancy to show images of casualties. As mentioned above, broadcast coverage of the Persian Gulf War fit well with the administration's view that it was waging a moral and relatively painless war. . . .

At the same time, coverage of the Persian Gulf War in other countries, especially Arab ones, showed the gory results of American "smart" bombs, further suggesting that American coverage reflected the biases of its indigenous culture and official point of view in the same way foreign coverage did.[17] Although this chapter reports the results of the first thorough examination of the scale and nature of casualty imagery in American broadcast coverage of the Iraq war, an earlier study looking just at the nightly news across five U.S. networks and two Arabian-based news channels (Al Jazeera and Egypt's

Esc-1) also found cultural differences in the overall tone of coverage and in the depiction of casualties.[18] In addition, an exhaustive analysis of British Broadcasting Company coverage of the Iraq war by Cardiff University found casualty coverage largely absent.[19] In that case, researchers noted that British laws forbidding the airing of graphic imagery prevented the press from showing them, but they expressed apprehension that the resulting bloodless war shown on television might inure citizens from the grave consequences of military action.

The Iraq War

American broadcast reporters often candidly admit that the norms of their medium prevent them from showing the same shots of bodily carnage aired in other parts of the world. Discussing his time covering the recent Iraq war as a reporter embedded with the Second Light Armored Recognizance Battalion, CBS's John Roberts said bluntly, "In terms of what kind of images we could air, there are certain pictures that you just can't show on television. *We saw plenty of those,* so you had to sanitize your coverage to some degree."[20]

Other reporters embedded in Iraq pointed out that most of the casualties were inflicted at long range, limiting their ability to capture them on film. But they also implied that even if they did shoot the gore, their superiors at the network back in America often edited the images out of the final story. . . .

Yet especially since the terrorist attacks on September 11, many, including several prominent journalists, have argued that to show casualties, especially civilians, is unpatriotic. Indeed, everything from whether anchors should wear patriotic lapel pins to how much a network should show civilian casualties has been at issue,[21] with some suggesting that there is no place for detachment in wartime.[22] As FNC lead anchor Brit Hume said in defending his network's reluctance to show images of civilian casualties during the U.S.–Afghanistan war in 2001–02: "Look, neutrality as a general principle is an appropriate concept for journalists who are covering institutions of some comparable quality. This is a conflict between the United States and murdering barbarians."[23]

This raises the question of what effect showing, or ignoring, casualty imagery might have on shaping public opinion about a given war. Several scholars have explored the role of media coverage in general on generating support or opposition to war. But while these studies might reference trends in casualty coverage as an explanation for their findings, they do not parse its specific effects or can only infer them imprecisely from time series analyses.[24] . . .

If the central critique of recent war coverage has been that it sanitized conflicts and reduced them visually and emotionally to the level of a video game, the war in Iraq offered the press an opportunity to provide a more

comprehensive portrait of battle. The Pentagon's policy of embedding reporters with military units gave the media access to the front lines they hadn't had
during an American war since Vietnam. Granted, the killing still occurred at
long range, but the human aftereffects of that combat were seen in the hours
and days that followed as forces moved past the remnants of vanquished Iraqi
units and toward Baghdad. First-person accounts of embedded reporters after
the war describing the carnage they saw make this clear. Second, unlike in the
Persian Gulf War, all American networks had correspondents based in Baghdad, where much of the civilian casualties were inflicted. Finally, advances
in technology theoretically made it possible for reporters to show viewers
exactly what they saw, even live. If a legitimate defense of the press coverage
of the first Gulf War was that they were preventing from seeing, much less airing images of casualties, the war in Iraq rendered that excuse moot.

Conclusions

Following the Persian Gulf War, the press came under considerable attack
both from outside and inside its ranks for presenting a sanitized version of
events to American audiences. Many, again outside and inside the media,
blamed the Pentagon for its heavy-handed policy of precensorship, the
implication being that freed from their kennels the press would be aggressive
and reliable watchdogs.

In 2003, the Pentagon loosened censorship restrictions and embedded
reporters with coalition units at the front lines of the Iraq war. Yet the resulting imagery broadcast by American networks did not differ discernibly from
those 12 years earlier. Television transformed a war with hundreds of coalition and tens of thousands of Iraqi civilian and military casualties into something closer to a defense contractor's training video: a lot of action, but no
consequences, as if shells simply disappeared into the air and an invisible
enemy magically ceased to exist.

That those shells end up tearing apart people is clear to anyone who gives
it some thought, and certainly to the soldiers embroiled in the fighting. But
more to the point, it is obvious to the reporters covering the war because
they see it right in front of them. As CBS's John Roberts described of his
experience embedded in Iraq:

> It was pretty horrible to see all those guys lying around. There was this one
> guy whose feet were facing me; he's lying out of the back, his feet were
> facing me, he was sort of spread-eagled on the ground. As I walked up, his
> body was in perfect shape, but when I got right up on top of him, his head
> was missing, like it had been removed. Then there was another guy whose
> head was blown into three pieces and part of his body had been ripped off
> by a shell.[25]

Reading the accounts of reporters in Iraq, this was not an uncommon sight. And yet, as this study shows, they rarely turned on their camera and showed even a relatively less gruesome angle to their audiences. The proportion of firefight to casualty images was overwhelmingly in favor of the former, and the dead were rarely shown at all, even by reporters embedded on the front lines who saw hundreds if not thousands of corpses. As Walt Whitman wrote of the Civil War, "The real war will never get in the books."

Indeed, a great irony can be found in comparing the defining images from the Persian Gulf and Iraq wars—the smart bomb hitting its target in the former and artillery firing in the latter: the dominant image of war actually became *more* distanced in Iraq as reporters got closer to the front.

Critics of past war coverage, especially in the Gulf War, worry that such a sanitized portrait dehumanizes an enemy and its citizenry, helps perpetuate (or, if one is so inclined, manufacture) consent for war and any policies an administration might try and link to it, and risks numbing the moral revulsion that leads societies to see war as a last resort. When Roberts saw the broken bodies of the Iraqi soldiers described above, his reaction was compassion: "I said to myself, 'Gosh, this is tragic. These poor people,' regardless of the fact that they're enemy soldiers. You have to have some sort of human pity for them."[26] Pity does not, of course, have to lead journalists to stop doing their job objectively, or even to change their personal opinion on the validity of the war. As Savidge commented:

You have to realize that people die in war. I'm not saying all wars are bad. I am saying all wars are awful. There is no such thing as a pleasant war. I've been in enough of them to know that. War can be justified. There could be reasons why, as a last resort, you go to war. You must know that once it starts, it's a horrible, terrible thing. People die gruesome, terrible deaths. But in America we'll edit that down. Especially anything that deals with U.S. service personnel.[27]

What is remarkable given the data presented in this study is that war correspondents think this way precisely *because* they have seen the gruesome reality of war, and yet they, or at least their network superiors (themselves often veteran reporters), insist on shielding audiences from that same knowledge.

Reporters—and policymakers—have typically justified this self-censorship by arguing that viewers would be repelled by a more accurate portrait of war. Presumably, the fear here is at one level a commercial one: they might lose their audience to a network presenting a more upbeat story. And indeed, there is research suggesting that they may be right.[28] There is also the perception that such imagery might damage public support for a just war, that

Americans don't have the stomach for casualties. Although these are considered part of conventional wisdom, in fact they are testable hypotheses that scholars should spend more time exploring.

Also worth investigating further is the role of new technologies in press–government relations. Livingston and Bennett have shown that contrary to what one might expect, the dominance of news norms privileging official sources overwhelms the potential of these new technologies to create a more independent press in international coverage.[29] Cameras may be mobile, but the news it seems is still tethered to bureaucrats and policymakers.

Finally, it is interesting to note that in the time since the birth of realistic visual media in the form of photography, American popular images of war have become less, not more, authentic. For all the posing and aesthetic manipulations of the dead in photographs of the Civil War, the fact remains that people were able to see contemporary pictures of the true cost of war. Historian John Keegan makes the point that the paradox of modern warfare is that as Western society has become more humane—mostly banning the death penalty, making remarkable advances in medicine and healing, and expressing great concern for the sick and dying—it has simultaneously become increasingly innovative in devising weaponry that destroys human beings in progressively more creative ways.[30] He might have added that this societal cognitive dissonance—or hypocrisy, in his words—is amplified through the images of war we see on television.

Notes

1. Granted, the audiences for their work were northerners and all the dead pictured were Confederates. But this was due to the requisite delays in reaching the battlefield and setting up the camera. By the time that had happened, Union soldiers had already buried their own dead (always the priority) and the only bodies left on the field were those of the enemy.

2. Earl Hess, "A Terrible Fascination: The Portrayal of Combat in the Civil War Media" in P. A. Cimbala and R. M. Miller, eds., *An Uncommon Time: The Civil War and the Northern Home Front* (New York: Fordham, 2002), pp. 1–26.

3. Only network news on ABC was analyzed, not news on its local affiliate. "Network" news included *Good Morning America, World News Tonight,* and, when it occurred, national break-ins and extended coverage at other times of day that fell during our sample period.

4. H. Bruce Franklin, "From Realism to Virtual Reality: Images of America's Wars," in L. Rabinovitz and S. Jeffords, eds., *Seeing Through the Media: The Persian Gulf War* (New Brunswick, NJ: Rutgers, 1991), pp. 25–44; Francis Haskell, *History and Its Images: Art and the Interpretation of the Past* (New Haven: Yale, 1993).

5. Haskell, *History and Its Images;* Hess, "A Terrible Fascination."

6. Franklin, "From Realism to Virtual Reality"; G. Cheney, "We're Talking War: Symbols, Strategies, and Images," in Bradley S. Greenberg and Walter Gantz,

eds., *Desert Storm and the Mass Media* (Cresskill, NJ: Hampton Press, 1993), pp. 61–73.

7. Daniel C. Hallin, "Images of the Vietnam and the Persian Gulf Wars in U.S. Television," in L. Rabinovitz and S. Jeffords, eds., *Seeing Through the Media: The Persian Gulf War* (New Brunswick, NJ: Rutgers, 1991).

8. Sean Aday, Steve Livingston, and Maeve Hebert, "Embedding the Truth: A Cross-Cultural Analysis of Objectivity and Television Coverage of the Iraq War." Paper presented at the annual meeting of the International Communication Association in New Orleans (May 29, 2004).

9. Hallin, "Images," pp. 53–54.

10. R. H. Wicks and D. C. Walker, "Differences Between CNN and the Broadcast Networks in Live War Coverage," in Bradley S. Greenberg and Walter Gantz, eds., *Desert Storm and the Mass Media* (Cresskill, NJ: Hampton Press, 1993), pp. 99–112.

11. Hallin, "Images," p. 55.

12. W. Lance Bennett, "The News About Foreign Policy," in W. L. Bennett and D. L. Paletz, eds., *Taken by Storm: The Media, Public Opinion, and U.S. Foreign Policy in the Gulf War* (Chicago: The University of Chicago Press, 1994), pp. 12–42.

13. Sandra H. Dickson, "Understanding Media Bias: The Press and the U.S. Invasion of Panama," *Journalism Quarterly,* Vol. 71, No. 4 (1995), pp. 809–819.

14. Robert M. Entman and Benjamin I. Page, "The News Before the Storm: The Iraq War Debate and the Limits to Media Independence," in W. L. Bennett and D. L. Paletz, eds., *Taken by Storm: The Media, Public Opinion, and U.S. Foreign Policy in the Gulf War* (Chicago: The University of Chicago Press, 1994), pp. 82–104.

15. Scott L. Althaus, "When News Norms Collide, Follow the Lead: New Evidence for Press Independence," *Political Communication,* Vol. 20, No. 4 (2003), pp. 381–414.

16. Steven Livingston and W. Lance Bennett, "Gatekeeping, Indexing, and Live-Event News: Is Technology Altering the Construction of News?" *Political Communication* (October–December, 2003), pp. 363–380.

17. David L. Swanson and Larry D. Smith, "War in the Global Village: A Seven-Country Comparison of Television News Coverage of the Beginning of the Gulf War," in R. E. Denton, Jr., ed., *The Media and the Persian Gulf War* (Westport, CT: Praeger, 1993).

18. Aday, Livingston, and Hebert, "Embedding the Truth."

19. Cardiff School of Journalism, Media and Cultural Studies, "The Role of Embedded Reporting During the 2003 Iraq War." Report commissioned by the British Broadcasting Company (2003).

20. Bill Katovsky and Timothy Carlson, *Embedded: The Media at War in Iraq* (Guilford, CT: The Lyons Press, 2003), p. 173 (emphasis added).

21. Bill Carter and Felicity Barringer, "At U.S. Request, Networks Agree to Edit Future bin Laden Tapes," *New York Times,* October 11, 2001; Paul Farhi, "For Broadcast Media, Patriotism Pays," *Washington Post* (March 28, 2003, p. C1);

Howard Kurtz, "CNN Chief Orders 'Balance' in War News," *Washington Post* (October 31, 2001, p. C1).

22. Tim Graham, "No Honest Eyewitnesses: There's Little Truth Coming Out of Baghdad," *National Review Online* (April 4, 2003); Morton Kondracke, "Memo to U.S. Media: Stop Spreading Negativism Over War," *Roll Call* (November 8, 2001); Dorothy Rabinowitz, "Neutral in the Newsroom," Opinionjournal.com (November 6, 2001).

23. Jim Rutenberg and Bill Carter, "Network Coverage a Target of Fire from Conservatives," *New York Times* (November 7, 2001), p. B2.

24. John Mueller, *War, Presidents, and Public Opinion* (New York: John Wiley and Sons, 1973); M. B. Oliver, M. Mares, and J. Cantor, "New Viewing, Authoritarianism, and Attitudes Toward the Gulf War," in R. E. Denton, Jr., ed., *The Media and the Persian Gulf War* (Westport, CT: Praeger, 1993); Scott S. Gartner and Gary M. Segura, "War, Casualties, and Public Opinion," *Journal of Conflict Resolution,* Vol. 42, No. 3 (1998), pp. 278–300.

25. Katovsky and Carlson, *Embedded,* p. 173.

26. Ibid., p. 174.

27. Ibid., p. 277.

28. Oliver et al., *The Media and the Persian Gulf War.*

29. Livingston and Bennett, "Gatekeeping, Indexing, and Live-Event-News," pp. 363–380.

30. John Keegan, *The Face of Battle* (New York: Penguin Books, 1976).

28

LOCAL MEDIA, PUBLIC OPINION, AND STATE LEGISLATIVE POLICIES: AGENDA SETTING AT THE STATE LEVEL

Yue Tan and David H. Weaver

Editor's Note

Studies of the impact of news media stories on public policies in the United States have primarily examined the situation at the national level. The essay presented in chapter 28 is therefore pathbreaking because it focuses on agenda-setting relationships at state and local levels and because it does so over a fourteen-year period. Yue Tan and David Weaver analyzed stories reported by local newspapers and then tracked their impact on state-level policy making. Their research covers fourteen states. The findings reveal that news coverage definitely stimulates legislative action as well as strongly influences the public's attention to specific policies.

When this essay was written, Yue Tan had just finished her doctoral work at Indiana University's School of Journalism, earning a PhD in 2008. The essay springs from her dissertation research. David H. Weaver was the Roy W. Howard Research Professor in the School of Journalism at Indiana University. His writings about American journalists, media agenda setting, and voter learning from the news media are widely known and highly praised. Unlike most news media scholars, Weaver had extensive experience as a practicing journalist.

This study . . . examines the relationships among media coverage of local newspapers, state-level public opinion, and state legislative policies to better understand mass media's role in state policy making. . . .

Source: Excerpted from Yue Tan and David H. Weaver, "Local media, public opinion, and state legislative policies: agenda setting at the state level," *The International Journal of Press/Politics,* 14:4 (October 2009): 454–476. Copyright © 2009 by SAGE Publications. Reprinted by Permission of SAGE Publications, Inc.

This study is important because it touches two understudied areas of agenda-setting research: policy agenda setting and state-level policy making. Even though the entire agenda-setting process is composed of the media agenda, the public agenda, and the policy agenda, few studies have considered them together. One obstacle to this type of research is the complexity of subjects, which often involves collective political behavior with both visible and invisible participants (including the president, interest groups, lobbyists, nongovernmental organizations (NGOs), the public, congressional caucuses, the media, and other administrative branches).

Examining relationships among mass media, the public, and policy makers concurrently maps political communications at the societal level more completely and probably more accurately than considering these collective actors separately. These interactions indicate the media's role in the formation of public opinion and public policy and the degree to which public policy follows or leads public opinion. Therefore, this framework allows reflections on the wider implications these relationships have for democratic theory and institutional development (Soroka 2002).

The policy agenda is of key importance because it represents the resolution of problems that were issues on the media agenda and the public agenda; and the policy institutionalization of responses to public issues is how governments grow (Dearing and Rogers 1996). Nevertheless, in the literature there are fewer studies and less coherent literature of policy agenda setting than for media and public agenda setting (McCombs 2004).

In a similar manner, there are fewer studies examining the policy-making process at the state level than at the national level (Cooper 2002). For the past two decades, responsibility for some policies, such as welfare and economic development, has been transferred from the national to the state government (J. E. Cohen 2006). At the state level, some intervening factors that mediate the relationships among the media agenda, the public agenda, and the policy agenda can be tested cross-sectionally. On one hand, the fifty states possess the same Madisonian political culture and structure composed of checks and balances and separation of powers. On the other hand, the states vary in terms of fundamental structures (e.g., term limits), institutional characteristics (e.g., legislative professionalism), and organizational characteristics (e.g., party control of state house) (Squire and Hamm 2005). Some of those variables may lead to different agenda-setting processes between the national and the state levels and among different states.

Even though researchers (J. M. McLeod et al. 1999; Moy et al. 2004) found that attention to local news enhances political knowledge and promotes political participation, research on local media effects often is overshadowed by a concern with the effects of national media (Friedland and McLeod 1999). Previous agenda-setting studies have mainly focused on national media (Ridout and Mellen 2007). This article examines state-level agenda setting because previous research suggests that all three agendas (the media agenda, the public agenda, and the policy agenda) may be different at the national level and at the state level. Because of different agendas, the state-level agenda-setting effects may differ from the national ones. However, this variation has remained largely untested in the literature. This study aims to fill this gap by empirically examining state-level agenda setting. . . .

Findings

. . . The sample for analyzing the agenda-setting effects between newspaper coverage and state public opinion includes five states. Those states were chosen because the states' public responses to MIP [Most Important Problem] are available on the Web site of Odum Institute for Research in Social Science and the states' most popular newspapers' archives are available at the newspapers' own Web sites. The dates of the data range from 1984 to 1997. . . .

The mean of the correlations among the newspaper agenda and the public agenda is .432 (SD = .167), ranging from .126 to .857, with a median value of .447. Of the twenty-four cases, all the states for all the years yield positive values. However, only nine positive correlations are statistically significant. Therefore, data provide partial support for [predicting] . . . a positive relationship between the public agenda and the newspaper agenda at the state level.

In the analysis of the agenda-setting effects between newspaper coverage and state house policies, fourteen states are selected because their most popular newspapers' archives are available at Lexis-Nexis academic and their general assemblies' bill archives are available on the state house Web sites. The dates of the data range from 1989 to 2006. Table 28–1 shows the findings. Of the thirty cases, twenty-two cases have reached the significance level of .05. The mean correlation is .688 (SD = .209), and the median is .692. . . . [T]here is a positive relationship between the newspaper agenda and the policy agenda at the state level.

South Carolina was chosen to examine the agenda-setting effects between public opinion and state house policies because it is the only state whose MIP data as well as the state house's bill archives are available online and for which the corresponding years (1989 and 1990) match each other. The mean of the two correlations is .434, which is not significant. Even though the null hypothesis . . . is not rejected because of the small N value, there is a substantial positive relationship between the public agenda and the policy agenda at the state level. . . .

In sum, at the state level, positive correlations exist among the newspaper agenda, the public agenda, and the policy agenda. That is, agenda-setting effects exist among newspaper coverage, public opinion, and legislative policies at the state level. In addition, the relationship between the newspaper agenda and the policy agenda is stronger than the public agenda's relationship with the media agenda and with the policy agenda. . . .

Table 28-1   States and Years That Are Randomly Selected to Compare the Newspaper Agenda and the Policy Agenda at the State Level

ID State Name	Year	Most Popular Newspaper	Spearman's Rho (n = 9)
1 Alaska	2000	*Anchorage Daily News*	.678*
2	2005		.767*
3 Colorado	1996	*Denver Post*	.683*
4	2002		.833**
5 Florida	1998	*Miami Herald*	.633
6	1999		.750*
7 Louisiana	2003	*Times-Picayune*	.700*
8	2006		.083
9 Massachusetts	2005	*Boston Globe*	.683*
10	2006		.683*
11 Minnesota	2002	*Star Tribune*	.867**
12	2005		.667*
13 Nevada	2001	*Las Vegas Review Journal*	.333
14	2003		.583
15	2005		.250
16 New Mexico	2003	*Albuquerque Journal*	.917**
17	2004		.767*
18 Oregon	1999	*Oregonian*	.767*
19	2005		.667*
20 Texas	1997	*Houston Chronicle*	.917**
21	2001		.667*
22 Utah	1998	*Salt Lake Tribune*	.600
23	2001		.750*
24 Virginia	1999	*Richmond Times-Dispatch*	.617
25	2005		.767*
26 Washington	1993	*Seattle Times*	.900**
27	1994		.900**
28 Wisconsin	1995	*Milwaukee Journal Sentinel*	.600
29	1997		.833**
30	1999		.767*
M			.688

*p < .05. **p < .01.

Conclusions
Summary of the Findings

To sum up, consistent with previous findings, there is a moderate and positive relationship between the newspaper agenda and the public agenda in five U.S. states across fourteen years (1984–1997). Second, there is a strong positive relationship between the newspaper agenda and the policy agenda in fifteen U.S. states at the state level dating from 1989 to 2006. Finally, there is a substantial positive relationship between the public agenda and the policy agenda in South Carolina in 1989 and 1990. The nonsignificance of the positive correlations primarily results from the small numbers of issue categories ($n = 9$). . . .

Generally speaking, the agenda-setting effect between newspaper coverage and state house bills is stronger than public opinion's relationship with newspaper coverage and with state house policies. This finding is consistent with findings at the national level (Tan and Weaver 2007). However, interpretation of this finding should be cautious because the newspaper agendas of the three agenda-setting effects are measured with different methods. More specifically, the newspaper agenda in the public–media comparison is searched with newspapers' online archives, while in the policy–media comparison it is searched with the Lexis-Nexis academic archives. Beside different searching functions, the Lexis-Nexis academic usually archives wire stories, while newspapers' online archives often do not.

In this study, the agenda-setting effects among the newspaper agenda, the public agenda, and the policy agenda at the state level are as strong as the findings for national-level agenda setting of previous studies. . . .

Using the time unit of one year, this study has provided some new findings that have been understudied by others. Within one year, many short-term effects cancel out each other, while many subtle but consistent impacts are accumulated. Thus, long-term effects provide a new perspective on the relationships among the media, the public, and the legislative branch. Covering a geographic scope of eighteen U.S. states at the state level, this study provides a comprehensive view of the first-level agenda-setting effects among the newspaper agenda, the public agenda, and the legislative agenda. Long-term and cumulative media effects are as important as short-term effects because they contribute to the public's reality construction and decision making. . . .

References

Cohen, Jeffrey E. 2006. "Introduction: Studying Public Opinion in the American States." In *Public Opinion in State Politics,* ed. Jeffrey E. Cohen. Stanford, CA: Stanford University Press.

Cooper, Christopher A. 2002. "Media Tactics in the State Legislature." *State Politics and Policy Quarterly* 2(4):353–71.

Dearing, James W., and Everett M. Rogers. 1996. *Agenda-setting.* Thousand Oaks, CA: Sage.

Friedland, Lewis A., and Jack M. McLeod. 1999. "Community Integration and Mass Media: A Reconsideration." In *Mass Media, Social Control, and Social Change,* ed. David P. Demers and K. Viswanath. Ames: Iowa State University Press.

McCombs, Maxwell. 2004. *Setting the Agenda: The Mass Media and Public Opinion.* Cambridge, UK: Polity.

McLeod, Jack M., Dietram A. Scheufele, and Patricia Moy. 1999. "Community, Communication, and Participation: The Role of Mass Media and Interpersonal Discussion in Local Political Participation." *Political Communication* 16(3):315–36.

Moy, Patricia, Michael R. McCluskey, Kelley McCoy, and Margaret A. Spratt. 2004. "Political Correlates of Local News Media Use." *Journal of Communication* 54(3):532–46.

Ridout, Travis N., and Rob Mellen, Jr. 2007. "Does the Media Agenda Reflect the Candidates' Agenda?" *Press/Politics* 12(2):44–62.

Soroka, Stuart N. 2002. "Issue Attributes and Agenda-setting by Media, the Public, and Policymakers in Canada." *International Journal of Public Opinion Research* 14(3):264–85.

Squire, Peverill, and Keith E. Hamm. 2005. *101 Chambers: Congress, State Legislatures and the Future of Legislative Studies.* Columbus: Ohio State University Press.

Tan, Yue, and David H. Weaver. 2007. "Agenda-setting effects among the Media, the Public, and Congress, 1946–2004." *Journalism and Mass Communication Quarterly* 84(4):729–44.

29

THE SOAP OPERA PATH TO HEALTH POLICY GOALS

May G. Kennedy, Ann O'Leary, Vicki Beck,
Katrina Pollard, and Penny Simpson

Editor's Note

Successful implementation of policies often requires the cooperation of millions of citizens. They must learn that the policies exist and which actions they are supposed to take. Mass media are the logical message carriers because of their broad reach and wide appeal. Research indicates that dramatic presentations on entertainment media are uniquely suited to attract the audience's attention to policies dealing with social problems and teach them how citizens can support these policies.

This essay demonstrates that people can be encouraged to acquire information about HIV/AIDS policies and to take steps to avoid infections or treat them. Unlike most research on media effects, studies of the impact of health messages provide strong rather than weak evidence that mediated messages can cause major behavioral changes that affect large numbers of citizens.

When this essay was written, May G. Kennedy was a communication analyst for the Centers for Disease Control and Prevention (CDC). Her research interests include social marketing, health risk communication strategies, and social and health policy applications of social science. Ann O'Leary was a senior behavioral scientist at the Division of HIV/AIDS at the CDC and the author of several books on the subject. Vicki Beck was the director of Hollywood, Health & Society at the USC Annenberg's Norman Lear Center. She oversaw outreach and research activity, including studies of the content and effects of health storylines on television. Katrina Pollard was a health communications specialist for the CDC's National Center for Environmental Health. Penny Simpson was a research analyst for the American Social Health Association.

Source: Excerpted from May G. Kennedy, Ann O'Leary, Vicki Beck, Katrina Pollard, and Penny Simpson, "Increases in Calls to the CDC National STD and AIDS Hotline Following AIDS-Related Episodes in a Soap Opera," in *Journal of Communication* 54:2 (June 2004): 287–301. Reprinted by permission of John Wiley and Sons.

. . . Mass media are efficient and promising communication channels for prevention messages (Jason, 1998), and nationally televised broadcasts reach millions of Americans. Television broadcasts have been shown to increase knowledge of health issues (Brodie et al., 2001; CDC, 1992), promote attitudes and norms that support prevention (Kalichman, 1994; Siska, Jason, Murdoch, Yang, & Donovan, 1992), model prevention behaviors (Basil, 1996), and elicit prevention behaviors (Andrews, McLeese, & Curran, 1995; Brodie et al., 2001; Fan, 1993; Myhre & Flora, 2000).

Compared with other broadcast formats (e.g., free-standing public service announcements [PSAs], news shows, and evening dramas), daytime television dramas or "soap operas" may offer several advantages for the dissemination of HIV prevention messages to high-risk women. The first advantage is that soap operas are relatively efficient in reaching minority women. African American and Hispanic households watch more daytime television than other audiences. . . . Among respondents to the 1999 Healthstyles survey, 31% of African Americans, 25% of Hispanics, and 17% of whites reported that they were regular soap opera viewers (i.e., that they watched at least twice a week; Beck, Pollard, & Greenberg, 2000). The second advantage is that soap operas may be viewed as a more credible source of health information by minority women than by other racial and ethnic groups. Of women who reported regular soap opera viewing, 53% of all women, 56% of Hispanic women, and 69% of African American women said that they had learned something about diseases or how to prevent them from soap operas in the last year (Beck et al., 2000). Finally, regardless of viewer race or ethnicity, the expectation that daytime soap operas would be an unusually effective channel of HIV-relevant communication is consistent with several theories and with the findings of related bodies of research.

Theoretical and Empirical Support

Miguel Sabido pioneered the dissemination of educational messages through broadcasts of serialized novellas, a format analogous to U.S. soap operas but usually less long-running. His approach has come to be known as Entertainment-Education (Singhal & Rogers, 1999). Used predominantly in developing countries to date, Entertainment-Education employs an entertaining format to engage a large audience, eventually weaving in educational messages designed to inform audiences, influence their attitudes about the educational issue, and persuade them to adopt pertinent behaviors (Papa et al., 2000). Some characters perform a recommended behavior and are rewarded with prosperity and happiness, while other characters do not adopt the behavior and meet disastrous ends. A third type of character, constructed to inspire audience identification, observes all of this, strives to overcome various obstacles to performing the behavior, ultimately succeeds, and is rewarded in a manner valued by the target audience.

These elements of Entertainment-Education were intentionally based on Albert Bandura's social cognitive theory (Bandura, 1986, 1994). Social cognitive theory postulates that learning occurs when an individual observes someone else performing a behavior and experiencing the consequences of that behavior. This observational learning influences the learner to perform a behavior by creating a positive outcome expectancy, the expectation that a certain action will result in a positive outcome, and by enhancing self-efficacy, the belief that one is able to perform a behavior. Self-efficacy is thought to be enhanced when the learner identifies with the role model—the individual who performed the behavior and experienced its consequences directly. The learner is considered most likely to engage in repeated attempts to perform the new behavior when two conditions hold. First, the behavioral role model achieves a behavioral goal through effortful mastery, defined as success following persistence in the face of barriers. Second, the reward for succeeding is something the learner values.

Other relevant theoretical models (e.g., McGuire, 1989; Prochaska, DiClemente, & Norcross, 1992) have maintained that individuals who are presented with behavioral recommendations go through a series of information processing and assessment steps before actually performing the behavior. Although an individual can travel recursively through these steps, the route is usually described as a unidirectional linear progression (Papa et al., 2000). Typically, the message recipient (a) becomes aware of and actively attends to a message, (b) comprehends and remembers the message, (c) considers the message, (d) decides to follow the recommendation, and (e) takes prerequisite or preliminary action before (f) actually exhibiting behavior in line with the message.

Taking the first step—becoming aware of the message—is facilitated by sending messages through channels to which a target audience attends; the point that soap operas are efficient channels for reaching high-risk women has already been made. Attention and persuasion are encouraged when messages are delivered dramatically by a character that viewers care about (O'Brien & Albrecht, 1992; Papa et al., 2000); soap operas are very dramatic, and soap opera viewers are often deeply involved with the characters on their favorite shows (Dines & Humez, 1995). In fact, some viewers use soap opera websites to advocate for particular plot developments (see www .cbs.com/daytime/bb for examples). A serialized format presents the opportunity to repeat and develop prevention themes, strategies that have been shown to enhance both comprehension and retention (Waugh & Norman,

1965). Moreover, recall of prevention messages may be enhanced if the messages are presented in the context of a storyline that viewers follow over time (Brinson & Brown, 1997).

... Papa and his colleagues (Papa et al., 2000) point out that many media messages are processed in a social context. Conversations and other social interactions stimulated by the media can create new impetus (e.g., collective efficacy) and opportunities for behavior change. Also, Entertainment-Education sparks parasocial interaction (e.g., forming a "relationship" with a fictional character or talking to the television; Papa et al., 2000; Pfau, 1990), which may enhance identification and efficacy. Parasocial interaction fosters active message processing (Papa et al., 2000), a goal-oriented activity that involves a decision to pay attention and the exertion of mental effort to evaluate arguments and seek information (Green, Lightfoot, Bandy, & Buchanan, 1985; Park & Smith, 1989). Active processing improves retention (Larson, 1991) and may lead to more behavior change than does passive processing (Parrott, 1995).

When a health message is easy to follow, self-efficacy and skill modeling are less relevant than they are for complex behaviors. The health belief model (Becker, 1974) has been shown to predict behaviors that require little skill, such as asking for health information (Aiken, West, Woodward, & Reno, 1994; Champion & Miller, 1996; Graham, 2002; Jacobs, 2002). According to the health belief model, health behavior is driven primarily by the perceived seriousness of a disease and one's perceived vulnerability to the disease. Once these factors obtain, an individual is motivated to attempt to reduce the health threat in response to cues to action. Having fewer constructs, this theory may provide a simpler explanation for the influence of serialized dramas on health-relevant behavior than social cognitive theory does. However, predictions based on either the health belief model or social cognitive theory would often be consistent because perceived vulnerability can be construed as an outcome expectancy.

There is not only theoretical support for the Entertainment-Education approach, but also empirical evidence that it can be effective. Relatively weak designs from at least a dozen studies in developing countries suggest that exposure to this kind of serialized novella increases levels of target behaviors (Papa et al., 2000), and there is now confirming evidence from a carefully controlled field experiment. A radio soap opera employed the Entertainment-Education approach to promote HIV risk avoidance in the relatively uncrowded media environment of Tanzania. Compared with respondents in a comparison district in which the soap opera was not broadcast, respondents in the district in which the program was aired reported significant increases in attitudes and behaviors that are consistent with HIV prevention (Rogers et al., 1999). . . .

A Domestic Entertainment-Education Program

There has been much less study of the potential of Entertainment-Education in the United States, where no nationally broadcast soap opera has employed the full approach. However, some Hollywood writers and producers have been willing to collaborate with public health professionals to embed accurate, timely prevention messages and scenarios into major network programming. Several of these collaborations have grown out of a broad entertainment industry outreach program initiated by CDC [the federal Centers for Disease Control and Prevention]. CDC now works in partnership with the Norman Lear Center of the University of Southern California (see www.cdc.gov/communication/entertainment_education.htm) to engage producers and writers by means of regular mailings of health-related resource materials, face-to-face meetings to discuss potential storylines that could address health issues, and an award program called "The Sentinel for Health Award for Daytime Drama." This award is given to the soap opera with the storyline that does the best job of informing viewers and motivating them to make healthy choices.

After collaboration with CDC scientists, a long-running, televised, day-time soap opera, *The Bold and the Beautiful (B&B)*, introduced a subplot about HIV. The Nielson rating for *B&B* during the week of July 30, 2001, through August 3, 2001, was 4.4 (4.4% of the 102.2 million U.S. house-holds with televisions, or 4,496,000 households). The rating indicates that millions of *B&B* viewers saw an attractive young Hispanic man get tested for HIV and learn that his HIV serostatus was positive. He told his doc-tor he had used condoms consistently with recent sexual partners (all of whom were women), disclosed his positive HIV serostatus to them, and encouraged them to be tested for HIV. He also disclosed his serostatus to the woman that he would eventually marry. He then proceeded to overcome emotional and interpersonal obstacles to living a full, satisfying life. Clearly, the storyline embodied several key elements of the Entertainment-Education approach.

The Present Study

The director of the American Diabetic Association (Graham, 2001) wrote a letter to CDC reporting a large surge in the volume of callers to a helpline after a character from a topically pertinent soap opera episode displayed the helpline number. CDC officials had noted such surges in the past. Documenting this kind of association formally was seen as a feasible way to begin an empirical examination of the impact of disseminating health messages through collaborations between public health agencies and private entertainment media partners.

This study examined data on the number of calls made to the CDC National STD [sexuality transmitted diseases] and AIDS Hotline's English Service (hereinafter referred to as "the Hotline") following *B&B* episodes with powerful AIDS-relevant themes. Calling the Hotline is an important health information-seeking behavior. Based on the theory, empirical findings, and anecdotal evidence reviewed above, we made three directional hypotheses:

H1: Presenting the Hotline number immediately after *B&B* episodes with an HIV theme would be associated with an increase in the number of calls to the Hotline during that time slot relative to other time slots on that same day.

H2: Presenting the Hotline number immediately after *B&B* episodes with an HIV theme would be associated with an increase in the number of calls to the Hotline relative to the number of calls during that time slot on other days.

H3: The number of calls made on the 2 days when the Hotline number was presented during *B&B* episodes with HIV themes would be greater than the number of calls made on days when other kinds of shows were presented.

There was also interest in the kinds of topics callers brought up during calls. A final, qualitative, exploratory research question was this:

RQ1: When Hotline callers say they called because of the *B&B* episode or a PSA on *B&B*, what kinds of issues will they bring up?

Method

Participants

During 2001, all calls to the Hotline originating within the United States were tallied by the Federal Technology Service 2000 system and AT&T. These calls were counted whether or not the callers actually reached the Hotline or spoke with Hotline staff. Participants in this study were the individuals who attempted to call the Hotline.

There were 12–15 trained Hotline staff members answering calls during the period that the show aired. When there was high caller volume, some callers heard a taped message asking them to stay on the line until a staff member was available. When the hold queue was full, callers were asked to call back at a later time. It was not possible to distinguish repeat callers from those who called once in the call attempt data presented in this paper.

Design and Procedure

On August 3, 2001, the *B&B* episode included a male character's diagnosis of HIV. On August 13, 2001, the character disclosed his positive

HIV serostatus to his fiancée. During the last 5 minutes of each of these two episodes, a PSA was aired. It displayed the toll-free number of the Hotline (800-342-2437) while the actor who played the HIV-positive character invited viewers to call the Hotline for answers to questions about HIV or AIDS. Hotline staff members were notified of the issues to be addressed in the *B&B* HIV storyline and of the days when the PSA would be aired. The episodes were broadcast at 1:30 p.m. Eastern Daylight Time (EDT) and at 12:30 p.m. Central, Mountain, and Pacific time. Calls were tallied by EDT because the Hotline is physically located on the East Coast.

Following the Hotline's standard procedure, both active and passive survey data were collected from a random sample of callers. One in 15 "productive" calls (those that result in service provision) was selected for the sample by a computer program. The staff member asked the selected caller for permission to be interviewed; no data were recorded if the request was not granted. No identifying information was requested or recorded. The standard part of the interview included questions about caller demographics, whether the caller had ever called before, and where the caller had heard about the Hotline. Passive data recorded after these calls included the first question asked or topic discussed during the call, the nature of the service rendered (e.g., referral), and any STD history that the caller mentioned. During August 2001, with approval from the Office of Management and Budget, interviewed callers who said that they heard about the Hotline through a television show were asked which show, how frequently they watched, whether they intended to make any changes or take any action as a result of seeing the show, and what kind of action they intended to take.

Results

Call Attempts

. . . [On] the 2 days on which the PSA was displayed, very large increases, or spikes, in numbers of originating call attempts were observed in the time slot during and immediately after the *B&B* broadcast. Whether or not the number of calls per hour was assumed to be normally distributed, the spikes were found to be significantly higher than call levels at other times of day ($z = 14.63$, $p < .0001$; rank test, $p = .04$). This result constituted support for H1.

On August 3, the Hotline received 1,426 calls originating between 1 p.m. and 2 p.m.; 37% of the calls that day were made in the *B&B* time slot. The day before, there had been only 88 call attempts during that time slot. On August 4, between 1 p.m. and 2 p.m., there were 108 call attempts. There was an even higher spike on August 13; 1,840 calls originated during and shortly after the *B&B* episode. On the previous day, only 94 calls had been made between 1 p.m. and 2 p.m., and on August 14, 234 calls were made during that hour. The number of calls in the spikes were averaged and compared with the average number of calls during that time period on comparison days in a one-tailed statistical test. There were significantly fewer calls in the *B&B* time slot on comparison days . . . so H2 was supported.

There was a possibility that these spikes were a function of time of the month or month of the year, so we examined call attempt patterns on July 2, 3, 4, 12, 13, and 14, 2001, and the same days in August 2000. For the non-*B&B* HIV episode days, numbers of call attempts per daytime time slot fluctuated, but the highest call level during any daytime period was no more than 200 calls higher than the next highest level for that day. . . . In contrast, the call levels for the *B&B* time slots on August 3 and 13, 2001, were more than 1,000 calls higher than the next highest levels for those days. . . . The spike in call attempts during the *B&B* time slot is evident even in the monthly data from 2001. . . .

Active Interviews

On the 2 days that the Hotline number was broadcast, caller volume was so high during and immediately after the *B&B* time slot that the capacity of the Hotline was overwhelmed. Attempted calls were tallied electronically as described above, but only a small fraction of them could be serviced by a health information specialist. Consequently, the number of active interviews with individuals who saw the show is a misleadingly low figure. Of the 1,904 callers who were selected for interviews during August 2001, 1,430 provided active interviews. Of these, only 28 callers indicated that they had heard about the Hotline from a PSA on *B&B* or on the soap opera itself. In all, 194 of the callers surveyed that month said they got the Hotline number from a TV PSA or program. More callers (just under 30%) said they got the number from the telephone book than from any other single source—a typical finding of routine interviews of Hotline callers.

Thirty-six percent of the callers who mentioned *B&B* identified themselves as African American. The majority of the callers reported being first-time callers, female, and prompted to call by the topic of positive HIV serostatus disclosure in the show. Fifty-seven percent said that they intended to make a change or take action after seeing the show; of those, 44% said that they intended to "get tested" and 28% said that they intended to "use condoms." The number of callers was too small to provide a satisfying answer to RQ1.

Discussion

After the Hotline number was displayed at the end of two August 2001 episodes of *B&B* that dealt with AIDS themes, Hotline call volume rose dramatically, as predicted. It is reasonable to conclude that many members of the American public can be motivated to seek health information by a dramatic, televised storyline that addresses health issues.

The increase in calls did not appear to be a regular temporal phenomenon. Similar spikes in call attempts were not observed during the analogous time slots on the same days the previous month, July 2001, or on the same days in August the previous year.

Compared with call spikes associated with other kinds of television broadcasts in 2001 that contained AIDS-relevant information, the *B&B* spikes were higher. Of course, it was not possible to vary comparison shows systematically, and some of the other broadcasts that dealt with HIV/AIDS during 2001 (e.g., *60 Minutes*) did not include the Hotline number. Although most respondents to routine Hotline surveys report getting the number from the telephone book, viewers of broadcasts that did not provide the number may have been unaware of its existence. Even if they knew there was a Hotline, finding its number in a phone book is an extra information-seeking step that would probably depress call numbers. Nonetheless, the demonstrated advantage of the soap opera context is striking, if not definitive.

As a group, these outcomes provide support for the elements of the Entertainment-Education approach in the HIV storyline on *B&B* and are consistent with several information-processing models and social cognitive theory. Moreover, social cognitive theory could be used to explain why the second *B&B* spike was higher than the first. In the second *B&B* episode, the female fiancée character may have sparked deeper identification among the predominantly female audience members than did the male and professional characters depicted in the first episode. She may have prompted more self-efficacy as she vowed to find out all there was to know about HIV and AIDS.

Although this study was a "natural experiment" not designed to test particular theoretical mechanisms of behavior change, the present findings seem to fit the health belief model better than social cognitive theory. A likely effect of exposure to the heterosexual transmission of HIV in the storyline would be to enhance perceptions of personal vulnerability, a key element of the health belief model. Furthermore, the placement of the Hotline number clearly served as a "cue to action." Calling a telephone number does not require a great deal of skill, and it is the more complex behaviors for which notions of skill modeling and self-efficacy enhancement are important. Because the health belief model contains fewer and arguably simpler constructs than social cognitive theory, a storyline guided by the health belief model would consume less air time and require fewer constraints on character and plot development. These efficiencies could be salient to writers of shows in the United States who find the full Entertainment-Education approach too demanding or restrictive either initially or over time.

Another possible limitation of these results is that repeat callers cannot be distinguished in the call attempt data, so there probably were fewer individual callers than the tally indicates. Nonetheless, repeat callers were persistent in health information-seeking, and such persistence is important to encourage.

Unfortunately, during and immediately after the *B&B* episodes, the incoming call volume far exceeded the Hotline's surge capacity. A few survey respondents that month said that they had heard about the Hotline from a soap opera. They were demographically similar to soap opera viewers, and most were making their first call to the Hotline. A substantial percentage of these callers reported either an intention to get an HIV test or to start using condoms, the key HIV risk reduction behaviors for sexually active women. Anecdotal evidence to support the contention that the *B&B* storyline encouraged preventive behavior was presented by the director of *B&B* when the CDC awarded the 2002 Sentinel for Health award to the show. At the ceremony, he described calls and letters stating that viewers had gotten HIV tests because of the storyline. . . .

. . . [B]ecause some of the television programming produced in the United States is broadcast around the world, it is important to understand how health messages in these programs affect international audiences (Blakley, 2001). *B&B* may be the most watched television show in the world, reaching an estimated 300,000,000 viewers in 110 countries daily (Tobin, 2002). The *B&B* HIV storyline emphasized HIV testing and expensive combination drug therapy, and we need to know what viewers in developing countries with limited healthcare resources took away from these broadcasts.

Continued collaboration with entertainment industry partners will be necessary. . . . Such a partnership is important not only to leverage the extensive resources and audience access of the private entertainment industry, but also to benefit from its deep expertise in engaging and communicating with the public.

References

Aiken, L. S., West, S. G., Woodward, C. K., & Reno, R. R. (1994). Health beliefs and compliance with mammography-screening recommendations in asymptomatic women. *Health Psychology*, 13, 122–129.

Andrews, A. B., McLeese, D. G., & Curran, S. (1995). The impact of a media campaign on public action to help maltreated children in addictive families. *Child Abuse & Neglect*, 19, 921–932.

Bandura, A. (1986). *Social foundations of thought and action: A social cognitive theory.* Englewood Cliffs, NJ: Prentice Hall.

Bandura, A. (1994). Social cognitive theory of mass communication. In J. Bryant & D. Zillman (Eds.), *Media effects: Advances in theory and research* (pp. 61–90). Hillsdale, NJ: Erlbaum.

Basil, M. D. (1996). Identification as a mediator of celebrity effects. *Journal of the Broadcasting Electronic Media*, 40, 478–495.

Beck, V., Pollard, W., & Greenberg, B. (November 15, 2000). Tune in for health: Working with television entertainment shows and partners to deliver health information for at-risk audiences. Paper presented at the annual meeting of the American Public Health Association, Boston, MA. (Data available at www.cdc.gov/communication/healthsoap.htm.)

Becker, M. H. (1974). *The health belief model and personal health behavior.* Thorofare, NJ: Slack.

Blakley, J. (2001). Entertainment goes global: Mass culture in a transforming world (Research Reports and Occasional Papers, No. 2). Los Angeles: University of Southern California, Norman Lear Center.

Brinson, S. L., & Brown, M. H. (1997). The AIDS risk narrative in the 1994 CDC campaign. *Journal of Health Communication, 2,* 101–112.

Brodie, M., Foehr, U., Rideout, V., Baer, N., Miller, C., Flournoy, R., & Altman, D. (2001). Communicating health information through the entertainment media. *Health Affairs, 20,* 192–199.

CDC. (1992). Community awareness and use of HIV/AIDS-prevention services among minority populations—Connecticut, 1991. *Mortality and Morbidity Weekly Review,* 30(41), 825–829.

Champion, V. L., & Miller, T. (1996). Predicting mammography utilization through model generation. *Psychology, Health & Medicine, 1,* 273–283.

Dines, G., & Humez, J. (Eds.). (1995). *Gender, race, and class in media: A test reader.* Thousand Oaks, CA: Sage.

Fan, D. P. (1993). Quantitative estimates for the effects of AIDS public education on HIV infections. *International Journal of Biomedical Computation, 33,* 157–177.

Graham, J. (June 13, 2001). Personal letter from the chief executive officer of the American Diabetes Association to Vicki Beck, director of CDC's Entertainment-Education activity.

Graham, M. E. (2002). Health beliefs and self breast examination in black women. *Journal of Cultural Diversity,* 9(2): 49–54.

Green, S. K., Lightfoot, M. A., Bandy, C., & Buchanan, D. R. (1985). A general model of the attribution process. *Basic and Applied Social Psychology, 6,* 159–179.

Jacobs, L. A. (2002). Health beliefs of first-degree relatives of individuals with colorectal cancer and participation in health maintenance visits: A population-based survey. *Cancer Nursing, 25,* 251–265.

Jason, L. A. (1998). Tobacco, drug, and HIV preventive media interventions. *American Journal of Community Psychology, 26,* 151–187.

Kalichman, S. C. (1994). Magic Johnson and public attitudes toward AIDS: A review of empirical findings. *AIDS Education and Prevention, 6,* 542–557.

Larson, M. S. (1991). Health-related messages embedded in prime-time television entertainment. *Health Communication, 3,* 175–184.

McGuire, W. J. (1989). Theoretical foundations of campaigns. In: R. E. Rice & C. K. Atkin (Eds.), *Public communication campaigns* (pp. 43–65). Thousand Oaks, CA: Sage.

Myhre, S. L., & Flora, J. A. (2000). HIV/AIDS communication campaigns: Progress and prospects. *Journal of Health Communication, 5* (Supplement), 29–45.

O'Brien, E. J., & Albrecht, J. E. (1992). Comprehension strategies in the development of a mental model. *Journal of Experimental Psychology: Learning, Memory & Cognition, 4,* 777–784.

Papa, M. J., Singhal, A., Law, S., Pant, S., Sood, S., Rogers, E. M., et al. (2000). Entertainment-Education and social change: An analysis of parasocial interaction, social learning, collective efficacy, and paradoxical communication. *Journal of Communication, 50,* 31–55.

Park, C. W., & Smith, D. C. (1989). Product-level choice: A top-down or bottom-up process? *Journal of Consumer Research, 16,* 289–299.

Parrott, R. L. (1995). Motivation to attend to health messages. In E. Maibach & R. L. Parrott (Eds.), *Designing health messages: Approaches from communication theory and public health practice* (pp. 7–23). Thousand Oaks, CA: Sage.

Pfau, M. (1990). A channel approach to television influence. *Journal of Broadcasting and Electronic Media, 34,* 195–214.

Prochaska, J. O., DiClemente, C. C., & Norcross, J. C. (1992). In search of how people change: Applications to addictive behaviors. *American Psychologist, 47,* 1102–1114.

Rogers, E. M., Vaughn, P. W., Swalehe, R. M., Rao, N., Svenkernd, P., & Sood, S. (1999). Effects of an entertainment-education radio soap opera on family planning behavior in Tanzania. *Studies in Family Planning, 30,* 193–211.

Singhal, A., & Rogers, E. M. (1999). *Entertainment-Education: A communication strategy for social change.* Mahwah, NJ: Erlbaum.

Siska, M., Jason, J., Murdoch, P., Yang, W. S., & Donovan, R. J. (1992). Recall of AIDS public service announcements and their impact on the ranking of AIDS as a national problem. *American Journal of Public Health, 82,* 1029–1032.

Tobin, F. (2002). *Report to Frank Tobin Public Relations from Bell-Phillip Television Productions,* Los Angeles, CA.

Waugh, N. C., & Norman, D. A. (1965). Primary memory. *Psychological Review, 72,* 92–93.

30

END OF TELEVISION AND FOREIGN POLICY

Monroe E. Price

Editor's Note

In the past, battles over gaining favorable attention for foreign and domestic public policy issues amounted to fights over access to supportive news media coverage. Short of communicating via the limited number of established news channels, public- and private-sector stakeholders lacked routes to reach nationwide audiences. New, more powerful and versatile technologies have vastly changed the situation. They have spawned inexpensive and readily available opportunities for all kinds of stakeholders to join the public policy debate.

In this environment, groups of citizens in the United States and elsewhere have been able to generate actions that reflect their own priorities and to contest policies favored by established institutions. Consequently, the strength of established political and media institutions has ebbed. Still the battle over control of public policy debates continues, and no decisive victories are in sight. The old warriors have slowed their decline by adding the new technologies to their arsenal.

In chapter 30, Monroe Price bares the shrinking ability of states to control public policy debates by framing the messages and dominating news media coverage. Monroe E. Price was the director of the Center for Global Communication Studies at the Annenberg School for Communication, University of Pennsylvania, when this essay was written. He also held leading positions at the Stanhope Centre for Communications Policy Research in London and at the Center for Media and Communication Studies at the Central European University in Budapest.

Source: Excerpted from Monroe E. Price, "End of television and foreign policy," in *The Annals of the American Academy of Political and Social Science,* 625:1 (September 2009): 196-204. Copyright © 2009 by the American Academy of Political and Social Science. Reprinted by Permission of SAGE Publications, Inc.

Should a specific kind of foreign policy be (more or less) identified with the classic era in broadcast television? If such a media-influenced foreign policy existed, has its content and approach been modified or altered because of transformations in communications technologies and distribution systems? Two questions when thinking about foreign policy and the media are (1) Do modern technological developments cause foreign policy to be increasingly affected by media concerns? and (2) Is there what might be called a foreign policy of media structures, namely, an interest by one state (or the international community) in the mode by which media are developed through an interdependent set of nations? The answer to both questions is yes, and the issues are interconnected.

Think of the cold war—or elements of it—mapped against the 1950s and 1960s structure of radio and television broadcasting. A claim might be that the cold war was only possible in a period of (almost) hermetically sealed borders with strong and centralized spheres of influence. In this telling, the effectiveness of the Berlin Wall depended on the very conditions that yielded to the increased information permeability of borders by media, the images of freedom projected through transporter media. International broadcasting (the Voice of America, Radio Free Europe/Radio Liberty, and the BBC World Service among others), relying on short-wave facilities, helped to crack information monopolies, but the dam broke with the rise of satellite and the increase in spillover broadcasts from neighboring states. In parallel, one might argue, the system of scarce broadcasting with heavy licensing or state-connected public broadcasting systems in Western Europe and the United States allowed for the reinforcement of a national consensus against the Soviet threat.

A second, more general, claim, easier to substantiate, would be that any intelligent foreign policy involved in relations with publics abroad (and maintaining support at home) would have a necessary relationship with changing structures of the media (for a general introduction, see Nye 2004). National identities—and interactions between states—are consequences, in part, of media and communications systems. The concept of an effective national identity, associated with a state, presupposes a kind of information system that produces it. That information system may have, as part of its composition, narratives about the place of the state in the world. As information systems alter, indeed alter substantially, it might be assumed that there are knock-on effects for national identities and for the states with which such identities are politically central. Television is only a small part of an information system or set of systems that are used to produce national identities. But even so, reorganizations in the mode of making, distributing, and controlling television images yield consequences for those fashioning attitudes toward the greater world.

To understand how the "end of television" in its classic sense may have implications for diplomacy and public diplomacy, a few initial words about these terms are in order. The historic element of foreign policy is the diplomatic interaction between officials of two or more states; "public diplomacy" seeks to bypass the state and reach directly to audiences. How the balance between the two has changed with altered television technology is implicated in the "CNN effect." The term was first used during the Gulf War of 1990. With the rise of CNN and its twenty-four-hour style of reporting, it was argued, leaders learned more from television than from their own officials about what was going on in the battlefield (and in the diplomatic sphere). Leaders could conduct diplomacy in real time, and in the fishbowl of a global news service, they could directly reach past official and autocratic gatekeepers to broad civil publics. Steven Livingston (1997) has listed three potential shifts because of this phenomenon: media as (1) an enhanced agenda setter (where the media trump the agenda-setting effort of the government), (2) an impediment to policy making (where the existence of the media effect narrows or forecloses options open to the government), and (3) an accelerant to policy decision making (where the impact of media coverage forces the government to take an action it might otherwise not have been inclined to). . . .

There has been much controversy over the extent of the CNN effect and its transformation of the diplomatic sphere. . . .

The CNN phenomenon tended to locate the broadcaster as the independent variable and the leaders, governments, and publics as the dependent variables. We now see a broader interplay between leaders, governments, and publics than was identified in connection with the CNN effect, but the examination of a foreign policy of the media sphere demonstrates how almost all aspects are interdependent. James Hoge (1994) has argued that the impact of the media is greatest during a humanitarian crisis, when domestic communities mobilize to press their officials to take action. Hoge sees a special impact as well where a broadcast shows, to a government's domestic audience, a sustained set of images that, through its tragic and dramatic force, undermines the narrative of success that officials have proclaimed. Here such a broadcast narrative can impede or accelerate government action or alter the agenda. The issue can be put differently. The ubiquity of media and their capacity to provide unfiltered access to harsh global events increases emotional impact (and an emotional impact not constructed or controlled by the government or its gatekeepers). This is not to say that foreign policy has always been based entirely on reason and conducted in an environment wholly immunized from public opinion. But at certain times, and subject to the varying skills of international players, media can foreshorten time for reflection and raise spectacularly the way the stakes are perceived and governments are measured.

As significant, perhaps, is the impact that changed broadcasting technology and structure have had on public diplomacy. There are elements of the conduct of foreign policy where public opinion plays little if any role. But the proportion of foreign policy initiatives that involve influencing the public (to influence leaders) seems to have increased. There is a new imperative for reaching out to publics, changing hearts and minds, and engaging in soft power. New technologies enable and, as a result of competition, virtually require that states have a strategy to deal with foreign audiences (Dizard 2004).

For decades, states have invested in persistent and large-scale "international broadcasting" efforts to subsidize radio (and later television) that would alter the flow of ideas in a target society. The Voice of America and Deutsche Welle emerged during World War II; Radio Free Europe/Radio Liberty and the BBC World Service were established during the cold war. But the process of developing government-subsidized efforts for radio and television that reach a global audience has altered greatly with technological and political change.

The strongest of these international services, like the U.S.-funded Voice of America, Radio Free Europe/Radio Liberty (established as "surrogate radios" in the cold war, ostensibly to provide information-deprived populations with access to news and information about their own society), and the BBC World Service, financed by the United Kingdom's Foreign and Commonwealth Office, had extensive ambitions that were tied to foreign policy goals (sometimes only the goal of greater access to information, but sometimes more). In the early-twenty-first century, the U.S. foreign policy question was which of these services to maintain and at what level or, put differently, whether, given scarce resources, international broadcasting efforts to reach, inform, and persuade should be redirected from the former Soviet Union toward target publics elsewhere, such as in the Middle East. . . .

Shifts in broadcasting technologies and distribution systems have had limited impact on these elements of foreign policy, the foreign policy of broadcasting structures, and the transformations of international broadcasting. Undoubtedly, institutions like the BBC World Service and the Voice of America will change substantially because of the Internet and satellite, but the existing relationships, the confidence in the existing method of reaching audiences, and institutional inertia have meant less change than might have been expected. For some target societies, the "end of TV" in the classic sense of broadcasting has not yet occurred. . . .

The end of TV is marked by the decline of state control over information space. As that occurs, voluntary negotiations between states (or between states and media conglomerates) concerning the flow of certain categories of information (for example, hate speech, pornography, and information related to national security) increase—as do new means for states to reinstate their authority. Historically, states have had a tacit agreement that the media of one state would not persistently permeate the boundaries of another. The International Telecommunication Union was, in a sense, created to help police the allocation of spectrum so that, for the most part, radio (and then television) signals would be contained within national boundaries. Short-wave efforts designed at first to reach subjects around a colonial world were an exception to this general rule. While there were accepted and less accepted violations of the general principle, it was only with the arrival of the satellite (and to a lesser extent cable) that the general understanding disintegrated. Even then, the UN and other organizations attempted to transfer to the satellite regime the state-protective elements of terrestrial radio and television.

The 1982 UN resolution concerning direct television broadcasting sought to encourage consultation between broadcasting states and receiving states (UN General Assembly 1982). The Television without Frontiers Directive of 1989 (and the subsequent revisions of 1997 and 2007), governing members of the European Union, is an example of a more successful operative effort to establish a regime that mediates information crossing the relevant boundaries. Article 22 requires bilateral consultations where a member state hosts programs that significantly impair the moral development of children in a receiving member state, thus imposing a limit (though only an extremely narrow one) on the circumstances in which one member state can allow signals to flow, without objection, into the territory of another (Craufurd Smith 1997).

In addition to bilateral and multilateral negotiations between states, other unofficial (and often much less transparent) forms of negotiation between states and between states and broadcasting entities or distributors limit or affect the impact of transborder information flow.

This hidden "foreign policy" of the media reflects changes in media technologies. New competitors are much more dependent on agreements with states or with gatekeeper broadcast entities within states than is realized. Domestic structures are the pillars upon which global media systems are built. The television signals of CNN or BBC do not simply waft through the air, encountering no controllable gatekeeper before they invade the collective local consciousness. Today, to understand the actions of News Corporation or MTV, or the competition between CNN and BBC World, we must look at the domestic structures in the receiving countries, structures upon which dependence often still exists. We must see how shifts in those pillars are used to temper the entry of the global players. Indeed, "law," in the sense of officially developed norms that control behavior, may be less often the result of unilaterally declared statute or regulation than of negotiation.

These negotiations take place in the midst of two transitions: the transformation of scope and scale among the producers of channel services and

programming who seek to distribute signals transnationally and the transformation of the structure of receiving mechanisms that exist as gatekeepers
and filters within every country. For music video channels to gain entry
into certain markets, or to gain shelf space on cable or in a bouquet of
channels carried by a direct-to-home provider, the channel must negotiate
the program content with the provider. There is usually no explicit legal
standard at the base of such negotiations: channels may promise that they
will confine themselves to entertainment and not carry news, not as a result
of formal law but as an informal condition for entry. Another example is
to be found in negotiations between international broadcasters and local
transmission facilities. Formal or informal arrangements between states and
large-scale international news organizations will become more frequent,
implicating contractual ties with governments to operate terrestrial transmitters, to broadcast via the national system, or merely to gather information. Increasingly, states seek to regulate who has access to transponders or
uplink facilities.

An increasing number of such negotiations protects information space.
Some of the most well-known examples are between the receiving state and
the large multinational private broadcasting firms. In 1995, India agreed,
in an arrangement that soon fell apart, to permit CNN to broadcast on a
favored Doordarshan frequency if CNN agreed that the Indian broadcasting host would provide most of the news about its own domestic affairs
(Page and Crawley 2001). China agreed to more extensive entry for Star-TV
but, in apparent exchange, Star-TV's parent, News Corporation, agreed that
the BBC would not be carried. It is extremely likely that MTV, the popular
global music television service, negotiates to ensure that it is cognizant of
and, to the necessary extent, abides by local custom and preference in its
choice of music, music videos, and hosts. More confident post-Soviet Repub-
lics negotiated with Russia to admit Russian-language programming under
approved circumstances. Similarly, a meeting of information ministers of the
Gulf Cooperation Council (GCC) served, even before the war in Afghanistan, as the arena to mediate disputes between Qatar, the home of outspoken
satellite broadcaster Al-Jazeera, and the government of Bahrain, which considered Al-Jazeera's broadcasts deleterious and volatile of the public order
(BBC 1999).

Other efforts have focused not on the broadcaster itself but on the distribution channel. One example is the story of MED-TV, the satellite service
established in 1994 in the United Kingdom, which targeted Kurdish populations worldwide but particularly in Turkey, Iran, and Iraq. Turkey contended
that MED-TV was a "political organization" that supported the PKK, widely
characterized as a terrorist organization, and attempted to suppress MED-TV

unilaterally by policing the purchase and mounting of satellite dishes within Turkey's borders. Failing at this, Turkey was required to employ a bilateral strategy to stifle the MED-TV channel: officials mounted a campaign to pressure the British government to withdraw MED-TV's license and sought, in other European capitals, to deny MED-TV leasing rights on government-controlled transponders on Eutelsat.

International human rights norms, such as Article 19 of the Universal Declaration of Human Rights, which outlines the right to receive and impart information, can be said to be part of an international "foreign policy" of media structures. States have used Article 19 to press for a greater range of domestic voices, especially in societies that are thought to be authoritarian or oppressive of domestic minorities. The general proscription against hate speech and bilateral agreements to adjust media use in the interest of peace is another example. In the ill-fated Oslo Accords, part of the Middle East Peace Process, Israel and the Palestinian Authority mutually sought a media sphere that was more conducive to sustained amity. Increasingly, regional efforts, such as the Arab Satellite Broadcasting Charter adopted in February 2008, try (often in vain) to control the implications of new technologies for multilateral relations. The power of images will create novel ways, in the future, for foreign policy goals and the uses of media to intertwine.

Conclusion

From the perspective of foreign policies, there are implications of transformations in television systems. The major change is the seeming decline of national systems of broadcast regulation and the rise of transnational flows of information where local gatekeepers are not so salient. In the age of the state gatekeeper, there was at least the illusion (and often more) that the government could substantially control the flow of images within its borders. No foreign government's policy could reach local audiences in a massive and effective way. States could play with this system around the edges, through international broadcasting, cultural exchanges, and other devices. But the system was maintained, almost by common understanding among the powers.

The rise of satellites with regional footprints, the forest of dishes in major cities where diasporic groups live, and the spread of the Internet and Internet cafes give governments the ability, if they are clever enough (which few may actually be), to reach over the heads of the state and speak directly to populations. This process may have limits that are not yet well understood, as states intent on control regulate the use of dishes or the carrying of signals on transponders. States will have foreign policies about the meaning of the right to receive and impart information and the extent to which satellite signals can be regulated or channeled.

Finally, the transformation of television has—at least to the extent the CNN effect is alive—altered the capacity of the state to control the agenda for making war, convening peace, and otherwise exercising its foreign policy options. As broadcasters become more abundant, more diverse, and more partisan, the locus and substance of debate on global issues shifts. Oddly, states may opt for greater commercialization to counter this danger of lack of control or seek other means to restore systems to the status quo ante.

References

Baran, Paul A. 1957. *The political economy of growth.* New York: Monthly Review Press.

BBC Summary of World Broadcasts. 1999. GCC information ministers voice concern at activities of Al-Jazeera TV. October 15. *Al-Ra 'y,* Amman [in Arabic], October 10, 1999. [Al-Jazeera has also generated complaints from Algerian, Moroccan, Saudi Arabian, Kuwaiti, and Egyptian governments.]

Carlsson, Ulla. 2003. The rise and fall of NWICO—And then? Paper presented at EURICOM Colloquium on Information Society: Visions and Governance. http://www.bfsf.it/wsis/cosa%20dietro%20al%20nuovo%20ordine.pdf.

Craufurd Smith, Rachel. 1997. *Broadcasting law and fundamental rights.* Oxford, UK: Clarendon.

Dizard, W., Jr. 2004. *Inventing public diplomacy: The story of the U.S. Information Agency.* Boulder, CO: Lynne Rienner.

Dos Santos, Theotonio. 1970. The structure of dependence. *American Economic Review* 60 (2): 231–36.

Frank, Andre G. 1969. *Capitalism and underdevelopment in Latin America.* New York: Monthly Review Press.

Galtung, Johan. 1971. *Members of two worlds; a development study of three villages in western Sicily.* New York: Columbia University Press.

Giddens, Anthony. 1990. *The consequences of modernity.* Cambridge, UK: Polity.

Hamelink, C. 1979. *The new international economic order and the new international information order.* Mauve Paper 34. Paris: UNESCO, International Commission for the Study of Communication Problems.

Heil, Alan L., Jr. 2007. Rate of Arabic language TV start-ups shows no sign of abating. *Arab Media and Society.* http://www.arabmediasociety.com/?article=180.

Hoge, James F., Jr. 1994. Media pervasiveness. *Foreign Affairs* 73 (4): 136–44.

Lerner, Daniel. 1958. *The passing of traditional society: Modernizing the Middle East.* New York: Free Press.

Livingston, Steven. 1997. Beyond the "CNN effect": The media–foreign policy dynamic. In *Politics and the press: The news media and their influences,* ed. P. Norris, 291–318. Boulder, CO: Lynne Rienner.

McClelland, David. 1961. *The achieving society.* Princeton, NJ: Van Nostrand.

Nye, Joseph S. 2004. *Soft power: The means to success in world politics.* New York: Public Affairs.

Page, David, and William Crawley. 2001. *Satellites over South Asia: Broadcasting, culture, and the public interest.* New Delhi, India: Sage.

Rogers, Everett M. 1962. *Diffusion of innovations.* New York: Free Press.

Schramm, Wilber. 1964. *Mass media and national development.* Stanford, CA: Stanford University.

UN General Assembly Resolution. 1982. Principles governing the use by states of artificial earth satellites for international direct television broadcasting. A/RES/37/92. Adopted at 100th plenary meeting, December 10. http://www.un.org/documents/ga/res/37/a37r092.htm.

Part VI

REGULATING AND MANIPULATING MEDIA EFFECTS

Doris Graber

The scholarly community is continuing to debate the scope of media influence in the twenty-first century, as it did in previous centuries. Meanwhile, as has been customary, governments and people everywhere believe that the media are extremely powerful political forces and treat them accordingly. Governments use legislation and administrative rules along with less formal means to regulate media to ensure that news stories do not work at cross-purposes with major policies and do not endanger national interests. Government institutions in all branches and at all levels invest sizeable resources to manipulate the news so that stories favor their causes and generate supportive public opinions.

Part VI begins with a broad overview of regulatory policies in eighteen countries that have media regulation agencies in place. Just about everywhere, such agencies face onslaughts by numerous stakeholders seeking to influence the regulatory process because media publicity affects them profoundly. How do regulatory agencies know which pleas they should heed? In chapter 31, Irene Wu sets forth guidelines based on the fundamental principle that regulatory agencies must be independent enough so that they can resist undue external pressures. She distilled the guidelines by comparing seemingly successful decision-making procedures and practices in the countries included in her research.

The next essay focuses more narrowly on the politics of communication regulation in the United States. Chapter 32 examines the political forces that come into play in the United States when Congress wrestles with formulating and adopting laws for controlling media power. Since the First Amendment to the U.S. Constitution prohibits Congress from making any "law abridging the freedom of the press," many people wrongly believe that all U.S. media are free from government control. Print media do enjoy ample, although not unlimited, freedom to support or sabotage governmental policies and philosophies. They are free to grant or deny publicity to various interest groups and viewpoints. However, the situation is quite different for the broadcast media, although legislators and regulatory commissions explicitly deny any intent to control news content. Still, government regulations cover many essential aspects of broadcast media operations and, in the process, shape news content more or less directly.

Patricia Aufderheide traces the pressures brought to bear on Congress by various stakeholders when a major law, such as the comprehensive Telecommunications Act of 1996, takes shape. When laws finally pass, the strident claims of government and industry interests invariably trump the more muted claims made on behalf of the general public. Regulatory policies thus more often serve the interests of the regulated industries than the interests of ordinary citizens who presumably are the chief beneficiaries of the restraints placed on media.

In the next essay, the focus moves from government regulation of the media to curbs on government behavior *by* the media. A large portion of political news comes from government sources. Ideally, journalists are democracy's watchdogs who alert the public to flawed policies and official misbehaviors. Instead, they stand accused of primarily acting like docile lapdogs who crave and savor the news tidbits that government officials drop into their collective mouth. W. Lance Bennett and William Serrin appraise the reality of the situation. They delineate the crucial functions that watchdog journalism, at its best, can serve in keeping government performance in democracies transparent and reasonably honest. The authors record a number of brilliant successes. But they also bemoan colossal failures, usually due to inadequate resources for investigative journalism and a waning appetite for the time-consuming, meticulous, and often tedious hunts for information that investigative journalism requires.

Governments have learned that it is often far easier to sport velvet gloves than iron fists when controlling the news media's behavior. The history of censorship of news reports in times of war or during other crises provides many illustrations. Doris Graber's essay traces how the U.S. government has moved from heavy-handed wartime controls that included prepublication scrutiny and even imprisonment of government critics to a system of wooing the press through actually facilitating access to news stories. Still, the access privileges generally are quite limited, and the news flow is sharply constrained by swearing most government news sources to secrecy and by equating their self-censorship with patriotism. The end result is a press that remains shackled in times of crisis.

Efforts to manipulate news media coverage often are highly successful because public relations techniques have become very sophisticated. Jarol Manheim describes the tactics that news shapers use to gain entry into the news message flow for messages that are skillfully constructed to evoke images of a reality that suits news shapers' goals. Yet the myth remains intact that the news reflects journalists' perceptions of important political happenings, obscuring the disturbing fact that unseen self-serving movers and shakers are calling the political tunes.

Part VI ends on an optimistic note that emphasizes that the Internet has drastically changed the political scene. The Web provides a cheap route open to millions of people to send policy-relevant messages worldwide to anyone willing to listen. Helen Z. Margetts discusses the Internet as a political tool that disseminates transformative messages. She ponders potential major changes in government policy making made possible by the ease of cheap access to Internet messages. The Web, she predicts, will enhance trust, openness, and equity; it will foster innovations that promote needed social changes and democratic values. Governments must understand and master its technological, sociopolitical, and economic consequences.

31

WHAT MAKES A COMMUNICATIONS REGULATOR INDEPENDENT AND WHY IT MATTERS

Irene Wu

Editor's Note

In the twenty-first century, communication flows have become worldwide. Guide-lines for regulating communication networks are drawing global attention. Many countries are trying to create "independent" regulatory agencies to free regulators from pressures by stakeholders who want regulations that support their interests. In the past, there has been agreement in democratic nations that circulation of political information must be unimpeded. But there has been little specific agree-ment about the essential features of genuinely independent regulatory agencies.

Irene Wu's research addresses the issue, based on a survey of communication regulatory agencies in eighteen countries. The survey was designed to determine which practices have been widely adopted to ensure independence. Additionally, she studied relevant decision-making procedures in four countries. Wu concluded that regulatory agencies must deal with three main constituencies: other government institutions, the communications industry, and communication consumers. Independence requires that these agencies be protected from pressures by other government institutions and the communi-cations industry and be free to serve as advocates for consumer interests. Chapter 31 reports the essence of her findings.

When this essay was written, Irene Wu was the Yahoo! Fellow in Residence at the School of Foreign Service at Georgetown University. She had served as the director of research in the International Bureau of the Federal Communications Commission, where she guided studies on international trends in regulating telecommunications and the Internet.

Source: Excerpted from Irene Wu, "Who regulates phones, television, and the Internet? What makes a communications regulator independent and why it matters," in *Perspectives on Politics,* 6:4 (December 2008): 769-783. Copyright © 2008 by the American Political Science Association. Reprinted with the permission of Cambridge University Press.

The interconnective tissue of the body politic—news reports on national leaders, the messages between community activists, the symbolic assertions of power, the expressions of ideology, and the protests of the counter-culture—all rest on the telecom infrastructure, television networks, and Internet. . . . As the world moves from the industrial to the information age, governing the communications market will become more important. In the next five to ten years, countries all over the world will solidify the institutions responsible for policy and rules for communications services—telecommunications, Internet, and media—and define such institutions' relationships with other parts of government, industry, and consumers. This change is occurring now because of two major shifts, one conceptual and one technological.

First, governments accepted and implemented the idea that a competitive paradigm for communications markets was more economically beneficial than a monopoly model. With multiple players in the markets, more debates and conflicts occur that need to be resolved. One way to frame this challenge is to distinguish between *policy* and *regulation*. The policy maker is expected to broker agreement on broad objectives, and every brokered agreement could be unique from the next depending on political circumstances. The regulator that is independent from direct political pressure is expected in similar cases to reach similar conclusions. The challenge, however, becomes how to design a regulatory institution insulated from the vagaries of politics that is still consistent with democratic notions of accountability and majority rule.

Second, the shift from analog to digital technologies makes services that were once discrete—television programming and print publishing, for example—all physically reducible to data that can be sent over Internet protocol (IP) networks, sparking a redefinition of these services and the institutions that govern them. Regulators decide how such services are defined, who can offer them, who can use them, and assign any scarce resources such as radio spectrum that may be necessary to make the services available. This is a transformative moment in communications policy; researchers have an opportunity not only to contribute to the literature, but also to influence concrete institutional arrangements that govern telephones, televisions, radios, and Internet service worldwide.

The Advent of This Study

. . . What general characteristics or specific functions should regulatory institutions have? . . . The key goal that countries with new regulators aim for is an "independent" regulator, which reflects the current policy literature's suggestion that such regulators, insulated from political interference and pressure from industry players, are more likely to make good decisions that reflect the public interest. Many countries must establish independent regulators in order to fulfill World Trade Organization commitments.

. . . In 1990 there were only 14 communications regulatory agencies in the world. Since then, the number has roughly doubled every four to five years. As of 2007, there were no less than 148 such authorities.[1]

Globally, there has been a rise of regulatory agencies in a range of countries across a range of sectors—finance, electricity, water, gas, general competition policy. . . .

. . . I organized a survey of regulators for 18 countries chosen because they recently had significant improvement in their communications network development and FCC staff corresponded with them regularly. Where markets have separate regulators for telecommunications and broadcast, efforts were made to include both, although responses were not received in all cases. This survey was combined with a previous four-country study by Cathleen Hsu and me on ethics and decision-making processes, which drew on information collected in correspondence, materials, and interviews with regulatory officials.[2] The working strategy that shaped the construction of the survey was that among this group of good regulators, it might be possible to identify a useful set of characteristics, which could then be the basis of recommendations to other countries in the process of organizing their regulators. The survey questions reflected a mix of issues based on concerns raised in the literature and on practical regulatory experience.

The 18-country survey had three sets of questions related to regulatory independence. . . . The first related to the relationship between regulator and industry. The consensus among scholars and practitioners is if communications operators—telecommunications companies, television broadcasters, and Internet service providers—are still owned by the government, then the regulator is likely to be hostage to their concerns. The second set was on the relationship between regulator and other parts of government, such as the communications ministry, competition authority, and legislature. Unlike with privatization, among practicing regulators there is no consensus that separating regulation and policymaking enhances regulatory independence. The survey results suggest that among good regulators, this distinction is commonplace. A third set of questions related to regulator and consumers. The scholarly research focuses on what regulators should be independent *from*; there is very little work on what regulators should be independent *for* and accountable *to*. However, many of the most admired regulators are advocates of the long-term benefit of the consumer. . . .

Why Is It Important to Have an "Independent" Communications Regulator? What Makes a Regulatory Agency Independent?

Historically, communication services are run by monopolies, whether state-owned telecommunications operators or state-owned public broadcasters. As governments privatized and competitors entered these markets, regulators were established to set technical standards, settle disputes, allocate scarce resources, and other tasks. Theory suggests that governments establish *independent* regulators to make commitment to reforms easier and reduce investor risk, which should boost market growth.[3] Researchers have focused on whether the regulator is independent *from* industry players, usually the historic incumbent monopolist. . . .

There is less international consensus around additional characteristics that may improve a regulator's independence. . . . Research emphasizes the need to protect the regulator from political pressure from other state institutions.[4] For example, in an ideal world, a regulator faced with license applications from a number of different firms will use the same criteria to evaluate each application and not be influenced by the number of politicians calling in favors from the head of the regulatory agency. . . .

Stern and Holder's 1999 study identifies effective participation by interested parties in decisions and transparency in the regime to reduce the likelihood of unfairness and incompetence.[5] Not discussed in the literature, however, is the practical challenge of making transparent decision-making procedures work. The problem is not in the mechanics; publicizing notices and information is made easier every day with the Internet. Instead, the challenge is in transforming the culture of participation among firms and consumers who are affected by regulation. When regulators first begin asking comments from the public on proposed rule changes, frequently, parties are reluctant to participate. Why they are reluctant is fertile ground for further work—is it fear of retaliation, lack of resources, reluctance to share information, or lack of confidence in the process? This study includes a survey of four markets' decision-making process that can serve as a foundation for future comparative work.

Both Min and Stern and Holder identify the contestability of a regulator's decision as a characteristic of an independent regulator. In general many scholars argue that if a regulator's decision can be contested successfully, that is a demonstration of the independence of the regulatory regime. This makes sense because frequently regulators, thought of as "captured" by the industry they regulate, make decisions considered inordinately in favor of the incumbent operator. Therefore, the opportunity for small, innovative, or foreign operators to contest the decision successfully is considered a mark of a regulatory regime independent of the incumbent. However, if a regulatory decision were favorable to the competing operator and an incumbent operator were able to successfully contest such a decision, contestability appears no longer a mark of the regulator's independence, but instead a reflection of regulatory capture. For this reason, this study focuses on identifying whether the regulator has procedures in the decision-making process to enhance fairness and transparency as a basis for accountability, rather than the process of afterward contesting decisions.

What Is the Regulator's Relationship with Other State Organizations?

The 18-country survey shows that while many countries separate the policy-making organization from the regulatory organization, many do not. Three aspects of the survey are relevant to examining the regulatory relationship with other state institutions: the terms and conditions of the leadership, the scope of the regulatory authority to issue licenses, and the source of the regulator's budget. The first indicator of the relationship between the regulatory and other state institutions is how the leader of the regulatory organization is selected and dismissed. . . . The regulatory organization has greater independence if the leader's position is protected, by custom or by law, for a specified period of time or for life, no matter what decisions are taken. However, in some instances the leader can be dismissed if others in the state are dissatisfied with the decisions of the organization. Half of the countries surveyed have regulatory agencies with an independent leader. In these countries, having a predetermined term of office of between three and seven years often serves as a clear time frame that insulates the leader from pressures on day to day decisions. The one exception is Hong Kong, where a custom may be developing that the leader serves until he or she retires from civil service. If this custom is preserved, it serves as even greater source of independence than the common pre-set term of office.[6]

A second indicator is the clarity of the regulator's authority. . . . For example, one area where regulators typically have great influence is in issuing licenses for market entry. For wire line telecommunications licenses, where scarce resources are not usually at stake, many independent regulators have exclusive authority to issue licenses, whereas in other countries, the ministry that reports directly to the political leadership has an exclusive or partial control in the issuing of licenses. In 11 of the 18 countries examined, the regulator has the exclusive right to issue wire line licenses. Only in six countries did the ministry retain the whole or partial right to govern entry into the wireline market. The one exception in this set is New Zealand, since no licenses are required for firms to provide wireline service;

neither regulator nor ministry is involved. Licensing of wireline telecommunications service is only one of many areas of possible authority for regulatory organizations. If other areas were examined, a different range of responses on the relationship between the regulator and ministry's relationship might be uncovered.

A third indicator of the regulator's independence is the source of its budget. . . . Greater independence is possible if the regulatory organization has nearly complete control over how fees and funds are raised for its own operations. In other instances, the organization's budget is allocated and approved by institutions that may seek to use the budget process to influence regulatory decisions. Some organizations are funded both by their own fees and by a politically allocated budget. Seven of the surveyed bodies raise their entire budget from regulatory fees. In four countries, substantial funds are raised through fees, but also some portion of the budget must be allocated through the national budget process, which subjects them to political review. In Korea, the broadcast regulator's entire budget is raised from fees, but the telecom ministry has its funds allocated through the national budget.

At least based on these three indicators, four countries' regulators have very robust independence from other state institutions (in Brazil; Canada; Hong Kong, China; and Nigeria). Brazil, Canada, and Hong Kong do indeed have regulators with strong reputations for independence. Brazil and Hong Kong are especially known for their exceptionally vigorous regulatory efforts to break up and erode the market power of their respective incumbent telecommunications monopolist in the 1990s.[7] Nigeria's regulator is more recently established. Successful license auctions conducted in 2003 have established its reputation as independent and resourceful.[8]

What Is the Regulator's Relationship with Industry?

In the survey of eighteen countries, two sets of data were relevant to the regulator's relationship with industry: privatization of operators and regulator staff relationship with industry. The first indicator of the regulator's relationship with industry is if any state-owned incumbent operators were privatized. Greater independence is possible if the state responsibility is first to the consumer without any interest in the profitability of a state-owned operator. A second indicator is whether there is a revolving door for the staff to move between the regulator and the industry. Greater independence is possible if staff serve their entire careers in the regulatory organization; they are less likely to be influenced by other interests. In other instances, staff move frequently between the regulatory organization and industry or other parts of the state. However, a tradeoff is that regulators benefit from the market and technical knowledge of staff drawn from the industry. Frequent interchange of staff between industry and regulatory agency has its benefits, therefore, but it may have a dampening effect on the regulator's independence. . . .

. . . [F]or some of the surveyed countries, privatization is recent. This is true of Korea, which privatized Korea Telecom only in 2002. In other markets, such as Hong Kong, Spain, and the United States, the incumbent operators have been private for a long time. On the other hand, many countries listed as not having private incumbent operators have partially privatized. This is true, for example, for Australia, India, and Sweden.

Regulator's Relationship with Consumers

If a regulator is independent *from* industry interests and insulated *from* political vagaries, what is it *for*? One answer is that an independent regulator is an advocate for the long-term interests of the consumer, and the first step to acknowledging this objective is to have consumer interests represented within the regulatory agency. How this occurs varies widely among different states and the survey results reflect this diversity. In telecommunications, there are two major areas of consumer interest: handling of consumer complaints and concerns and universal service or universal access to services. These two areas are not equally important in all countries. . . .

In Brazil and the United States, overseers for universal service policy are organized inside the regulatory institution. In other instances, institutions other than the regulator are responsible. For example, in Australia, Hungary, and India, bodies other than the regulator handle consumer complaints.

The idea that an independent regulator should be *for* consumers, in addition to being independent *from* policymakers and industry, is a new contribution of this study. One critique of independent regulatory agencies is that they are too unaccountable to the public; this criticism is especially cogent in newly democratic states still in the midst of building political institutions responsive to the broader public rather than a privileged elite. If researchers investigate whether regulators that take long-term consumer welfare as their primary goal are more effective, some progress can be made in answering this critique.

In politics, representation is valuable. While in many countries there may be hundreds or even thousands of companies under the purview of a regulator, often there are easily millions of consumers. As a practical matter, customer-oriented interpersonal skills, a body of specially tailored information, and other expert techniques are necessary to handle direct interaction with consumers. The presence of these offices and representatives for consumer interests in these governments, therefore, reflects official recognition that consumers have interests distinct from other constituencies. If the political goal of regulating an industry is not to maximize its growth, but rather to improve the long-term quality of life of the citizens, then having an office devoted to their concerns—whether represented by a consumer office, a universal service office, or some other form—may serve as a useful indicator of whether its organizational resources are aligned with its objectives.

Transparency in Decision-Making Procedures

Beyond the organizational arrangements discussed here, the regulator's independence and credibility can be affected by the rules that govern its everyday interaction with others, whether state institutions, firms, or consumers. Transparent decision-making rules can increase confidence in a regulator's fairness. Clear ethics guidelines for regulatory staff can enhance the organization's integrity. In 2002, Cathleen Hsu and I undertook a study of the decision-making process and ethics rules in the communications regulators for Canada, Hong Kong, United Kingdom, and our own institution, the FCC in the U.S., regulators which all have strong reputations for integrity.[9] While these four markets have quite different styles of government, their communications regulator's decision-making procedures and ethics rules share remarkable similarities. . . .

All four regulators follow a basic three-stage rulemaking framework.[10] In the first stage, the regulator releases a consultation paper which identifies a problem, proposes new rules, and asks the public for opinions. In the second stage, the regulator receives comments on the consultation paper. While there is always at least one round of comments, often it is followed by additional rounds known as "reply comments," to allow the public to critique the initial comments. In the third stage, the regulator releases the final decision paper, which includes the new rules, a discussion of how they serve the public interest, and responses to public comments. For all four regulators, the consultation paper, comments and reply comments, and the final decision paper are available to the public at each stage, unless there are special arrangements requested to keep information confidential. This three-stage process guarantees basic transparency by ensuring the public are aware of possible regulatory changes, are given an opportunity to voice their views, and [are] informed of the final decision and the reasoning behind it. . . .

Ethics Rules for Integrity

An agency's transparency and impartiality in decision making could be jeopardized if its employees are influenced or are perceived to be influenced by gifts from outside sources, financial and personal conflict of interest, or post-employment prospects. Generally, there are four approaches to ensure ethical standards: (1) avoidance of activity, (2) disclosure of activities, and (3) divestment or resignation from positions that pose conflicts, or (4) recusal, or quarantine, from an area of the regulator's work.

Gifts

All four countries prohibit regulatory staff from receiving gifts that are improper or appear improper; in addition they all have criminal codes on bribery. The challenge in ethics rules related to gifts is in what exceptions can be made. Here, among the four countries, there are variations. . . .

Often there are support systems or specified procedures for staff who find themselves in a situation where a potential conflict or appearance of impropriety might arise. . . .

Conflict of Interest

The three main types of conflict of interest arise from pecuniary, personal affiliations, and family interests. Ethics rules come into effect when a regulatory employee participates in proceedings that involve close associates or family members, companies in which the employee holds stock, or companies about which the employee has gained confidential information through personal affiliations. The primary approach to prevent conflicts of interest is to require regulatory staff to disclose financial and personal interests in categories that could give rise to conflict. Often this leads to a requirement to divest of these interests if there is or appears to be a conflict. . . .

Post-Employment

Post-employment guidelines aim to prevent any suspicion that an official might be influenced by the hope or expectation of future employment with outside firms and the risk that a particular firm might gain an improper advantage over its competitors by employing someone who had access to information on the competitor through official capacities. . . .

. . . A regulator's independence *from* the policymaker and independen[ce] *from* industry is reflected not only in its organization arrangements, but also in the rules and procedures that govern its everyday interaction with these constituencies. The decision-making rules govern the regulator's everyday working relationship with firms, other stage institutions, consumer groups, and other interested parties. Ethics rules govern the regulatory staff's everyday working relationship with the employees of firms and other interested parties. . . .

Conclusions

There is tension between commitment and flexibility that all states face in creating and implementing communications policy and rules. *Policy* describes the decisions a state reaches by brokering the interests of various political groups. Once agreement is reached on a major policy, *rules* are needed for the state to implement the policy. The institutions that are responsible for developing these rules are often regulators. Given that the effectiveness of the regulatory institution depends largely on its independence—its ability to render similar decisions for similar cases—what indicators can be used to characterize a regulator as independent? In the main, these indicators reflect the regulatory institution's relationships with three other groups: other state institutions, industry, and consumers.

Relationship with Other State Institutions

While there should be some means to keep the regulator accountable to the public, an independent regulator has some measure of insulation from political winds. These can include:

- a leader who cannot be dismissed for unpopular decisions
- a leader with a guaranteed term of office
- scope of authority that is clearly distinct from the policy-maker
- funding which is independent of political review

Relationship with Industry

While industry can be a great source of market knowledge and technical data, the regulator must be independent from industry in order to be perceived as fair by other state institutions and consumers. Two markers of independence from industry include:

- privately owned incumbent telecommunications operator
- minimal exchange of staff between the regulator and regulated firms

Relationship with Consumers

Consumer interests are usually widely dispersed in the market and, therefore, their views are more easily overlooked both in the policy-making and rulemaking process. Regulators seeking to balance this against the strength of industry and other state institutions' views may make special efforts to collect and reflect consumer interests. Two indicators include a dedicated office to consumer affairs and a dedicated office to universal service, an important issue for consumers.

In addition to these indicators, there are systemic processes that regulators can use to mediate relationships with other state institutions, industry, and consumers, such as decision-making processes and ethics rules. In several well-established independent regulators, there are common elements in decision-making and ethics rules which help them manage their relationships with interest groups in a transparent manner. In decision-making, they had in common a three-step process which involved public notice of proposed rule changes, opportunity for all parties to provide written, public comments, followed by a written, public decision that includes the reasoning of the regulator.

In ethics rules, they had in common rules for gifts, conflicts of interest, and post-employment, which require regulatory employees to avoid certain activities, disclose other activities, divest or resign from positions that presented conflicts, and quarantine themselves from certain areas of regulatory work.

Table 31.1 summarizes how the surveyed regulators use these measures which can enhance their independence. The first three indicators, A–C, bear on the regulator's relationship with other state institutions; the next two, D and E, are relevant to its relationship with industry; F and G reflect its relationship with consumers, and the final columns, H through K, reflect its overall decision-making and ethics rules.

In no instance did any single regulator adopt the most independent option for all of the traits that were examined in this paper. However, nine of the countries have regulators that used most of the tools outlined in this paper: Australia, Brazil, Canada, Hong Kong, Hungary, Nigeria, Sri Lanka, Sweden, and the United States. Among the eighteen countries in the first survey, most had regulators with the sole authority to issue wireline licenses and offices that represented consumer interests. At least half had independent leadership and independent funding.

In democratic systems especially, demand for independent regulatory decisions must always be balanced against the need for all institutions to be accountable to the public. Which traits of independence are suitable for any one regulator to adopt will vary, depending on the state's institutional endowments and political culture. However, some combination of these traits is likely essential in establishing a regulatory institution perceived by all as independent. . . . These concerns affect not only economic growth, but also the evolution of political and social networks around the world that depend on the cell phone, television, the Internet, and other emerging technologies.

Table 31–1 Indicators of independent regulators: Summary of 18-country survey (A–G) and 4-country survey (H-K)

	Other State Institutions			Industry		Consumers		All Relationships			
	A. Independent Leader	B. License issued by regulator only	C. Independent Funding	D. Privatized incumbent telco	E. Little staff mov't between reg and industry	F. Consumer office	G. Universal service office	H. 3-step decision-making process	I. Gift rules	J. Conflict of interest rules	K. Post-employment rules
Australia	•	•				•		*These countries not surveyed*			
Brazil	•	•				•	•	*These countries not surveyed*			
Canada	•	•	•	•			•	•	•	•	•
Hong Kong	•	•	•	•				•	•	•	•
Hungary		•	•	•				*These countries not surveyed*			
India					•	•	•	*These countries not surveyed*			
Italy	•				•	•		*These countries not surveyed*			
Japan					•			*These countries not surveyed*			
Jordan						•		*These countries not surveyed*			
Korea		•	•	•	•	•		*These countries not surveyed*			
Malaysia		•	•	•	•			*These countries not surveyed*			
N. Zealand								*These countries not surveyed*			
Nigeria	•	•	•			•		*These countries not surveyed*			
Singapore				•				*These countries not surveyed*			
Spain	•		•	•				*These countries not surveyed*			
Sri Lanka	•	•	•	•	•	•		*These countries not surveyed*			
Sweden	•	•	•		•	•		•	•	•	•
U.S.	•	•				•	•	•	•	•	•
U.K.	*Not included in this survey*										

Notes

1. International Telecommunications Union 2007.
2. Wu and Hsu 2002.
3. Levy and Spiller 1994, North 1978.
4. Min 2000, 14–15.
5. Stern and Holder 1999.
6. Cowhey and McCubbins 1995, 17.
7. For more on Hong Kong, see Yan and Pitt 1999 and Ure 2000. For a discussion of Brazil, see Mariscal and Rivera 2005.
8. For more information, see Doyle and McShane 2003.
9. This section on decision-making and the following section on ethics rule draw heavily on Wu and Hsu 2002.
10. Please note that the CRTC has a separate rulemaking process for broadcasting issues. Unlike its rulemaking process for Telecom issues, if the broadcasting issue is a matter of great public importance, public hearings are held in place of the three-stage consultation process.

References

Cowhey, Peter, and Mathew McCubbins, eds. 1995. *Structure and Policy in Japan and the United States.* Cambridge: Cambridge University Press.

Doyle, Chris, and Paul McShane. 2003. On the design and implementation of the GSM auction in Nigeria—the world's first ascending clock spectrum auction. *Telecommunications Policy* 27: 383–405.

International Telecommunications Union. 2007. "Chairperson's Report for the Global Symposium of Regulators," http://www.itu.int/ITU-D/treg/Events/Seminars/GSR/GSR07/agenda-documents.html.

———. 2004. Trends in Telecommunications Reform 2004/2005. Geneva.

Levy, Brian, and Pablo Spiller. 1994. The institutional foundations of regulatory commitment: A comparative analysis of telecommunication regulation. *Journal of Law, Economics and Organization* 10 (2): 201–46.

Mariscal, Judith, and Eugenio Rivera. 2005. New trends in Latin American telecommunications market: Telefonica and Telmex. *Telecommunications Policy* 29: 757–77.

Min, Won-ki. May 26, 2000. "Telecommunications regulations: Institutional structures and relationships." Organisation for Economic Co-operation and Development. Working Party on Telecommunication and Information Services Policies.

North, Douglass. 1978. Structure and performance: The task of economic history. *Journal of Economic Literature* 16 (3): 963–78.

Stern, Jon, and Stuart Holder. 1999. Regulatory governance: Criteria for assessing the performance of regulatory systems: an application to infrastructure industries in the developing countries of Asia. *Utilities Policy* 8: 33–50.

Ure, John. 2000. The era of international simple resale: Not waving, but drowning? *Telecommunications Policy* 24: 9–30.

Wu, Irene, and Cathleen Hsu. August 2002. Decision-making procedures and ethics rules. Available at www.fcc.gov/globaloutreach.

Yan, Xu, and Douglas Pitt. 1999. One country, two systems: Contrasting approaches to telecommunications deregulation in Hong Kong and China. *Telecommunications Policy* 23: 245–60.

32

COMMUNICATIONS POLICY AND THE PUBLIC INTEREST

Patricia Aufderheide

Editor's Note

Why should governments regulate telecommunication, and what should be the main policy goals? With a focus on communication in the U.S. context, Patricia Aufderheide sets forth various rationales for a regulatory policy for U.S. telecommunication enterprises. She delineates the clashing interests of businesspeople, who oppose most restraints, and average citizens, who want government protection from messages they deem socially harmful. The Telecommunications Act of 1996 seeks to juggle these demands in an age characterized by an ever-expanding array of governmental and industry stakeholders in the telecommunications arena. Compared to these experienced and well-financed players in the pressure-group politics game, the civic sector is poorly represented, and its interests tend to be shortchanged.

At the time of writing Aufderheide was a professor in the School of Communication at American University in Washington, D.C., and the director of its Center for Social Media. She is a prolific cultural journalist, policy analyst, and editor on media and society. The excellence of her work has been recognized by numerous awards, including Fulbright and Guggenheim fellowships.

Telecommunications policy is a calculated government intervention in the structures of businesses that offer communications and media services. The public is endlessly invoked in communications policy, but rarely is it consulted or even defined. Policymakers claim that they do what they do

Source: Excerpted from Patricia Aufderheide, *Communications Policy and the Public Interest: the Telecommunications Act of 1996,* New York: The Guilford Press, 1999, chapters 1 and 5. Reproduced by permission of The Guilford Press.

in the name of and for the benefit of the people they represent, who may or may not be consumers of the service. Without this connection to the public, policymakers would have no grounds to intervene in these businesses.

Who is the public that U.S. policy represents, and what is its interest? . . . [E]arly communications and antitrust regulators took it to be coterminous with the economic health of a capitalist society, associated with social peace and prosperity. This is a definition that . . . effectively made government regulators the representatives of society's interests as well as of the large, stable businesses the government regulators helped to create and maintain. . . .

Another way to see the public is as an agglomeration of consumers, or potential consumers. . . . While opening the door to much broader (and more politically volatile) participation, this definition can lead to checkbook democracy on a grassroots level, where people participate in society to the extent that they are consumers, and to the extent that they exercise consumer choice. Not only does the definition measure social participation only by purchase, but it also conveniently ignores the social institutional structures within which we all live, and within which consumers make their small choices.

There is also much in communication policy that reaches past traditional economic concerns, whether at the macro- or microlevel, and that reaches into social welfare considerations. Government regulators act as allies of and sometimes protectors of the weak and vulnerable in society. Policies have been made to protect children, the disabled, rural dwellers, the poor; these policies ensure equality of access to a communications technology for everyone, no matter what's in their wallets or on their minds; and these policies further the political promise of free expression. Policies have even attempted to set cultural standards, such as public decency on the airwaves, and have attempted to create cultural spaces, as in the case of public broadcasting.

Each of these social welfare–oriented approaches has a slightly different take on the notion of the public and its relationship to government. Some approaches are blatantly paternalistic, and some respond to the squeaky-wheel version of American politics. But all of them go beyond economic concerns. They indicate, sometimes clumsily, the notion that the public is more than a mass of consumers or the inhabitants of a commercial society, but rather is a social institution important enough to address in nonmarketplace ways. These approaches can easily result in patch-up policies or can be accused of catering to special interests, however vulnerable or worthy those interests may be.

In recent decades, with the rise of deregulation, market liberals who are concerned with policy have basically asserted that the public is roughly the same thing, for the purposes of policymaking, as a vigorous marketplace. They have advocated deregulation, in order to promote an unfettered marketplace. However, in large infrastructure industries, deregulation does not necessarily lead to competition. Even then, these advocates would argue, so long as the sector is vigorous, growing, widely offering more jobs and a greater selection of products and choices, it acts in the public interest.

The equation of public interest with an unregulated marketplace, which has grown to be widely accepted, has resulted in disconnecting social consequences from the cultivation of the marketplace. But the booming electronic media and telecommunications marketplaces inevitably affect cultural habits and have social consequences. Dial-a-porn, Jerry Springer scandal shows, wrong credit rating data spread via the Internet are a few among many of the concerns that have mobilized activists to demand government action. Such concerns are marginalized into a fringe area of policy. A zone of cultural backlash grows, where antipornography, antiviolence, anticensorship, pro-privacy, and anti-hate crimes advocates all sullenly hunker down. Those pioneers of emerging social landscapes find uneasy alliances as often as they carve out new Balkan states of opinion. And inevitably, cultural advocates of all kinds return to policymakers.

This has been a pattern throughout the history of U.S. communications regulation, but it appears ever more boldly as deregulation unleashes new market behaviors and intensifies others. There is a bipolar quality to current communications policies. The passion for regulatory platforms that permit unregulated industries, unbounded by government constraints, vies with the passion for social control over the emerging networks and channels that we plug into each day.

The problem of designing policies appropriate to today's and tomorrow's communications technologies and business environments always comes back to the problem of the public. . . . Communications policy either encourages or discourages public life, whatever its intent. So, of course, do many other social policies, including electoral practices and educational regimes. But communications structures in many ways map our social connections, and our communications practices express our cultural habits and understandings.

Legal scholar Monroe Price (1995) shows that electronic media regulation has long danced around the question of culture. He argues for policies that recognize the importance of electronic media for establishing and maintaining public spaces. Simply endorsing the competitive marketplace, as if to do so were a value-neutral decision, merely displaces problems.

Within this notion of the public, then, policies make the political culture of a democracy a central priority. This argument accords well with those of political philosophers who argue, as does Sandel (1996), that the formative aspect of republican politics requires public spaces. . . . The global media and markets that shape our lives beckon us to a world beyond boundaries and belonging. But the civic resources we need to master these forces, or at least to contend with them, are still to be found in the places and stories, memories and meanings, incidents and identities, that situate [us] in the world and give our lives their moral particularity. (p. 349)

The revival of what Benjamin Barber (1984) contagiously called "strong democracy"—a more participatory and communitarian political system— requires "constructive civic uses of the new telecommunications technology" (p. 277).

But this approach to the public and the public interest has not been popular within the world of communications regulation. Over the years since the 1927 Radio Act, which was the precursor of the 1934 Communications Act, struggles over the notion of the public interest have inevitably, but often messily and uncomfortably, reflected the relationship between communications and culture. The very principles of economic intervention upon which regulation emerged as a social practice make it hard to see the connection between communication and culture. The First Amendment as it has evolved in the 20th century has also complicated any clear articulation. But tensions and conflicts in policy can often be seen as deriving from the thick and tangled relationship between communications businesses and services, on the one hand, and the expectations and habits of the societies they serve, on the other.

Rewriting the Rules

The creation of the Telecommunications Act of 1996, which President Bill Clinton signed into law on February 8, 1996, raised to public view issues that are often buried in regulatory procedures, and it showcased questions of the social impact of telecommunications policy.

The Act was designed to create a regulatory platform that would permit broad competition among different kinds of telecommunications service providers, encourage innovation, and recognize rapid technological change. The Act attempts to jump-start an era in which communications industries—and especially networked businesses that offer telephony and related network services—can operate as unregulated competitors rather than as monolithic utilities.

To accomplish this, the legislation rewrote the basic law that governs communications policy from top to bottom. That does not mean that the new law abolishes policies of the past or that it is even very foresightful, much less effective. In its amending of the 1934 Communications Act, the new law sketches out some regulatory principles, creates some possibilities, and proposes a controversial premise of interindustry competition. Its sketches may end up being far different from a workable, regulatory regime. But it is without a doubt the first step in a decisively different regulatory universe for communications.

The law lurched and stumbled into existence, driven forward by a combination of ideological and technological changes to the terms of an existing compact between big business and big government. For two decades before its passage, Congress attempted in a variety of ways to comprehend, foster, and get some social benefit from changing communications technologies. The ensuing law contains within it elements of previous regulatory regimes, and elements of a new one as well.

Its inelegance has a long history. The evolution of electronic communications policy has been a complex, and often ad hoc, process. This process has reflected, in part, the separate, independent development of several kinds of businesses. Each of those businesses, ranging from telephony to radio and television to computing, has evolved with its own logic. Government regulation evolved parochially with each industry, and typically with a powerful allegiance to incumbents (Winston, 1986).

But today, the technologies of telephony, mass media, and computing increasingly cross the borders of their traditional business arenas. Would-be entrepreneurs, within and without central industry positions, increasingly chafe at regulatory regimes designed for a former era and oppose opportunities for others. . . . Those regimes emerge from a welter of places. They include, at the federal level, Congress, the Federal Communications Commission, the Department of Justice, the Federal Trade Commission, and the Department of Commerce. At the state and local level, Public Service Commissions and Public Utility Commissions have powerful sway over telecommunications, while municipalities have plenty to negotiate with any user of their rights of way, such as cable companies.

This state will continue. Under the new law, multiple jurisdictions remain, and industry rivals go on making the most of leverage won by pitting courts, legislators, and regulators against each other. But industry frustration with lack of clarity about the legality and regulatory structure of emerging technology uses was a powerful push toward the rewrite as it finally emerged.

Technological Innovation

Changes in the technical possibilities of telecommunications have been dramatic in the last four decades, building on a hefty investment in communications research during and after World War II. Those innovations have also changed the shapes of the industries involved and have introduced new players (Cairncross, 1997).

Technical innovations have brought new services and also have challenged the value of monopoly. *More, bigger,* and *faster* were key words for these changes. These innovations also made increasingly artificial the crafted distinction between common-carriage networks and editor-based mass media. These innovations made it possible to imagine (and even experience) communications networks that had multiple purposes and to imagine spectrum with multiple or shared uses.

Key technical innovations included satellites and digitally based information processing. Satellites permitted, among other things, vastly more efficient, over-the-air, point-to-multipoint transmission of large amounts of information. Satellites turned cable from a small-time, mom-and-pop local business dedicated to improving the television viewer's reception of over-the-air signals into a highly centralized industry featuring local delivery of satellite-delivered signals. Satellites made it economically viable for newspapers to produce regional editions across the nation, using satellite-delivered copy. Satellites generated new mass media services and, indeed, eventually, a new video platform in direct broadcast satellite, or DBS. Satellite access also changed the economics of telephone networks, vastly shrinking the costs of connection and shrinking as well the difference between local and long-distance service.

Digital processing, which is the motor of growth in computing, has been another major disruptive force in the organization of communications industries. The encoding of signals in simple, binary code, allowing computers both to compute and to communicate with great accuracy and speed, has rocked the way we do business in everything from stock trading to shopping for swimsuits and has powerfully affected all telecommunications businesses. It has squeezed and reshaped spectrum, it has multiplied the uses to which we put phones, and it has hosted a new mode of communication, namely, the many-to-many environment of the Internet. It has provided a common electronic language on the spectrum, making the spectrum far more mutable, permitting machines to talk to machines, and blurring the distinction between content and infrastructure on any system.

Perhaps most important, digital processing has changed the very characteristics of communications networks. Rapidly evolving computing that is based on digital processing has made it possible to decentralize networks. Many of the decisions once made in large centralized switches are now made at intermediate stops or even within the consumer's telephone. Along with increased flexibility and the potential to reconfigure the very shape of networks and subnetworks, decentralized digital processing has dramatically increased the amount of intelligence—or the ability to respond to input and take action—in communications networks. This innovation provides a fundamental challenge to the notion of common carriage, or the restriction of network providers to transmission alone, because the clear lines between content and conduit have become muddied. Networks themselves have information, or content, built into them.

Related innovations have greatly, and suddenly, affected the variables of price, speed, and the cost of communication. Fiber optic wires, transmitting digital signals, vastly increased the capacity of wired networks. Compression techniques, ever in refinement, have permitted both increased speed of transmission and also new kinds of transmission. Wireless connections, in combination with wired networks, have permitted cheap, mobile communication in cellular phones as well as in data and even video transmission. Large businesses were the first beneficiaries of these innovations, and the incorporation of these innovations into business practice have driven further development, as well as the appetite for procompetitive policy (Harvey, 1992).

The elements of technological change that pushed toward rewriting the Communications Act were those that made it easy for telecommunications-based services to tap into existing networks and were those that potentially corroded the line between mass media and telecommunications. The first undercut the case for monopoly, and the second blurred regulatory categories. When a broadcaster was able to use part of available spectrum for non-broadcast services such as paging; when a phone company was tempted out of the common carrier box, maybe even to dream of offering cable service; when a cable network was able to offer phone service or Internet service to its customers, many different stakeholders appeared to redraw the rules. And when business—locally, internationally and virtually—had built telecommunications into its own infrastructures, all large users became invested in the prices and terms of provision of service.

The Political Process

The evolution of this rewrite legislation was, however, not primarily understandable as a result of technological innovation that was driving change, although technology transformation was important in it. As described by Robert Horwitz in his pathbreaking analysis *The Irony of Regulatory Reform* (1989), transformations in regulatory approach can best be seen as a political process. Summarizing the historical process of deregulation in infrastructure industries throughout the past three decades, he notes:

> The reasons are, as usual, a complex mosaic of regulatory, political, economic, legal, and ideological factors. In telecommunications and banking they include technological changes as well. But . . . deregulation is at bottom a *political* phenomenon. Deregulation is basically a story of political movement from regulatory activism to regulatory "reform."

Nonetheless, deregulation *could not have occurred* without these supporting, underlying factors. . . . As a result [of the interplay between economic trends, political organizing, and legal actions], by the mid-1970s regulation came to be held responsible for the fall of American economic productivity. That ideological shift was surprisingly important, especially because it underlay the changing terms in which various political elites conceptualized regulation. (p. 198; emphasis in original)

Thus, the very notion of what regulation is and should be was at stake. Progressive Era federal agencies grew up around antitrust concerns generated by the monopolistic behavior of large national corporations. Such regulation safeguarded interests of small producers from large corporations. New Deal era agencies such as the Federal Communications [Commission] were mandated to protect and nurture specific industries. Such agencies ostensibly safeguarded the interests of consumers by providing the context in which dependable, affordable services could grow. The stability of this system "of mutual compromises and benefits to major corporations, organized labor, and even consumers" (Horwitz, 1989, p. 17) was irrevocably undermined in the 1960s and 1970s, with dramatic new technological possibilities. That instability was accompanied and facilitated by ideological ferment, in which the basic notion of what regulation—and even government itself—does came under revision. . . .

The Public Interest Beyond the Act

The Telecommunications Act of 1996 ensures that some kind of competitive telecommunications environment will emerge. But it is still not clear what kind of environment that will be, or what its advantages will be for social equity, democratic relationships, and the civil culture of a pluralist society. The Act ratifies long-developing trends toward a competitive marketplace, vertically integrated corporations, and a minimalist regulatory stance. It does not create a policy framework that resolves conflicts arising from a competitive environment, as the universal service debate demonstrates. It also raises questions about the capacity of government regulators to monitor uncompetitive behavior among the giants who are now unleashed.

If the most basic objectives of the 1996 Act are accomplished, then defining and acting upon the public interest in telecommunications become even more complicated, more contentious, and more public than ever before. FCC chairman Reed Hundt recognized this. As he put it succinctly on the eve of his departure from the Commission,

The primary job of the FCC Chairman historically was to give licenses to the airwaves to a limited group of folk and to rig markets so none would

ever do poorly. The good reason was to permit the firms to do well economically; the bad effect was a closed, oligopolized market with little
diversity of viewpoint.

The primary job now ought to be the opposite: introduce risk and
reward to all sectors of the communications business.

The problem then is how to promote noncommercial purposes—
such as conducting civic debate about political issues or educating
kids—without simply relying on a cozy partnership between government and a tiny group of media magnates. (Hundt, 1997)

That last problem has no easy answers. The preceding six decades had
established no clear precedent about what noncommercial functions or social
objectives are appropriate for government attention in communications
policy. Instead, that history established that such concerns would be dealt
with after the fact, accommodated at the margins, or made the subject of
endless and ongoing debate. . . .

The emerging communications landscape is thus, unsurprisingly, impoverished in public sites or even noncommercial arenas of any kind. For instance,
in the Act, public TV is simply treated as another broadcaster, potentially
benefitting from digital spectrum (but not required to contribute to the
quality of public life in any way as a result). Cable access channels that
already exist are recognized but not encouraged or given a more general
mandate. Schools, libraries, and rural health care facilities are given modest
and oblique encouragement to build public relationships through a universal
service provision that facilitates their access to advanced communications
technologies. That provision sets aside nothing for equipment, teacher training, investment in community education, or civic activities that might make
use of such networks.

There are no subsidies here, of course, for programming, production, or
content creation associated with civic, community, or democratic behaviors
and relationships. And there are no likely sources elsewhere in cultural policy. Such subsidy is being stripped away throughout the society. The National
Endowments for the Humanities and Arts are both on the endangered species
lists. Even the Department of Commerce's grants for demonstration nonprof-
it-sector projects in distributed networking (the so-called TIIAP, or Telecommunications and Information Infrastructure Assistance Program, grants) are
held hostage to congressional whim. To the extent that there are economic
benefits to the society from the changing terms of communications businesses, the largesse is thus carefully protected from falling upon the ground
of daily political life. The notion of a protected electronic commons has been
quashed, by corporations aspiring to be at once the shapers of culture and
the delivery systems of it.

The sheer abundance of communications options is unlikely to lead, in itself, to formations of electronic commonses. The promise that burgeoning communications systems will create an abundance of access, making governmentally protected spaces and activities unnecessary, turns out to be hollow as the electronic universe expands. It is not merely that corporations that are developing new services are striving to develop proprietary gates and pathways through that electronic universe. In order to make use of any such common or public spaces, people have to have something to say, someone to talk to, and something that can happen. They need habits, knowledge, history, resources.

A minitest of the opportunities provided by open space was initiated when the FCC addressed the problem of using space set aside for noncommercial purposes on DBS. This was an issue raised in the 1992 Cable Act, then set aside because of legal action for several years. Finally, in 1997, there was, hypothetically, space for noncommercial and public purposes available on direct broadcast satellite services. Who, the FCC basically asked, wanted to use such space, and for what? Viable takers were few. The two entities with ready programming appropriate for the channel—a consortium of universities, and public TV—were long-time recipients of various kinds of public subsidy (Aufderheide, 1998).

At the same time, informational and communications abundance increases in the commercial sphere, often feeding social polarization. Broad discontent and unease does not stop, for lack of ways and places to resolve it. It gets expressed in clumsy policy. The bipolar approach to communications policy sets up a dynamic that pushes for new solutions. The deregulatory era may thus lead to renewed governmental intrusion. It may also create conditions for renewed civic activism around communications, as incoherent discontent is articulated and channeled. The quality of a new wave of regulatory reform will depend on the vitality, diversity, and vision of such civic activism.

Ironically, civic activism may be essential to the success of a much-vaunted competitive business environment. The principle of forbearance, so central to the regulatory logic of the Act, not only assumes the vitality of marketplace forces but implies a vital and active civic sector as a concomitant of functioning markets. And yet that sector is starved of resources.

Government will also continue to be a crucial tool of transition, as Gigi Sohn, executive director of Media Access Project, told an audience at the libertarian Cato Institute:

> Government can play a constructive role in making markets work better, thereby lessening the need for government involvement in the future, and, in particular, obviating intrusive content-based regulation. It can do so by

ensuring that all Americans have access to the tools that are becoming more and more central to education, the economy, social interaction, First Amendment values and democracy. And it can do so by making more competitive markets than are currently dominated by entrenched monopolies. (Sohn, 1997, Appendix G)

Predictable cries of outrage at media concentration were common after passage of the Act, especially from journalists (Hickey, 1997; Schechter, 1997) and academics (Barnouw et al., 1997; McChesney, 1997). The Media and Democracy Congresses of 1996 and 1997 featured vigorous denunciations of media fat cats by left-wing journalists, and at Cultural Environment Movement meetings speakers denounced commercialism in media as a kind of pollution.

But far harder for media activists, noted consultant David Bollier, was finding "a coherent, positive *vision* that can help mobilize and unify diverse nonprofit players," in comparison with the "intellectually respectable, highly marketable consumerist and entertainment-oriented vision of the new media" put forward in the corporate world. What was needed was a "sovereign citizen vision" of community and civic life supported crucially by a web of accessible electronic pathways and services. To do that, he argued, there needed to be more, larger, more committed and visible constituencies than civic advocates had been able to mobilize for anything other than consumer price issues (Bollier, 1997). . . .

Advocates of civil society, concerned with communications policy, will have their hands full in coming years. It will be crucial to assess the viability of the association between the public interest and a competitive environment in communications policy. Is competition truly developing? Does it strengthen the economy and workers' and consumers' options within it? Is that competition also fostering or permitting democratic behaviors, public life, and mutual respect? It will also be important to use, even if in demonstration projects, emerging communications to foster habits and relationships of civil society. Systems that have already become the lifeblood of global business surely have applications for vital democratic practices in the global community. Finally, it will be important to promote policies that pay for such experiments in public practice.

The passage and implementation of the legislation revising the platform for U.S. communications policy has demonstrated a continuing and even increased need for social participation on familiar issues of industry structure. It has demonstrated a continuing need for regulators to monitor performance by media corporations of their public obligations. Finally, it has shown the growing importance of the complicated fact that communications systems transmit not merely information but culture.

References

Aufderheide, P. (1998). The public interest in new communications services: The DBS debate. In A. Calabrese & J. C. Burgelman (Eds.), *Communication, citizenship and social policy: Re-thinking the limits of the welfare state.* Lanham, MD: Rowman & Littlefield.

Barber, B. (1984). *Strong democracy.* Berkeley: University of California Press.

Barnouw, E., et al. (1997). *Conglomerates and the media.* New York: New Press.

Bollier, D. (1997). *Reinventing democratic culture in an age of electronic networks.* Chicago: John D. and Catherine T. MacArthur Foundation.

Cairncross, F. (1997). *The death of distance: How the communications revolution will change our lives.* Boston: Harvard Business School Press.

Harvey, D. (1992). *The condition of postmodernity.* Cambridge: Blackwell.

Hickey, N. (1997, January/February). So big: The Telecommunications Act at Year One. *Columbia Journalism Review,* pp. 23–32.

Horwitz, R. B. (1989). *The irony of regulatory reform.* New York: Oxford University Press.

Hundt, R. (1997, September 23). Yale Law School 1997 Dean's Lecture Series. www.fcc.gov.

McChesney, R. (1997). *Corporate media and the threat to democracy.* New York: Seven Stories Press.

Price, M. (1995). *Television, the public sphere, and national identity.* New York: Oxford University Press.

Sandel, M. (1996). *Democracy's discontent: America in search of a public philosophy.* London: Belknap Press of Harvard University Press.

Schechter, D. (1997). *The more you watch the less you know.* New York: Seven Stories Press.

Sohn, G. (1997, September 12). *Why government is the solution, and not the problem* [Speech at Cato Institute]. Washington, DC: Media Access Project.

Winston, B. (1986). *Misunderstanding media.* Cambridge: Harvard University Press.

33

THE WATCHDOG ROLE OF THE PRESS

W. Lance Bennett and William Serrin

Editor's Note

Power corrupts. Keeping a democracy healthy, therefore, requires institutions that monitor the actions of political elites. The news media fill that watchdog role in the United States. Regrettably, as W. Lance Bennett and William Serrin point out, their performance record has been quite spotty. They have scored many important successes, exposing corruption and mismanagement, and corrective action has often followed. But failures have been more plentiful because investigative journalism is tedious, time consuming, and very costly. The authors suggest remedies for this troubling situation, but the obstacles to effective watchdog journalism currently are so enormous that the chances for success are slim.

When this essay was written, Bennett was the Ruddick C. Lawrence Professor of Communication and a professor of political science at the University of Washington. He had already authored numerous important books covering political communication issues. He is also the founder and director of the Center for Communication and Civic Engagement at the University of Washington, which sponsors communication research and policy initiatives that enhance the quality of citizens' political engagements.

Serrin was an associate professor of journalism and mass communication at New York University. He is also an author and a prize-winning journalist who has worked for the *New York Times,* the *Detroit Free Press,* and *Newsweek.* His essays have been published in the *Atlantic Monthly, American Heritage, The Nation, Columbia Journalism Review,* and the *Village Voice.*

Source: Excerpted from W. Lance Bennett and William Serrin, "The Watchdog Role of the Press," in *The Institutions of American Democracy: The Press,* ed. Geneva Overholser and Kathleen Hall Jamieson, New York: Oxford University Press, 2005, chapter 10. Copyright © 2005 by the Oxford University Press, Inc. Reprinted by permission of the Oxford University Press, Inc.

To begin with, *watchdog journalism* is defined here as: (1) independent scrutiny by the press of the activities of government, business, and other public institutions, with an aim toward (2) documenting, questioning, and investigating those activities, in order to (3) provide publics and officials with timely information on issues of public concern. Each of these elements—documenting, questioning, and investigating—can be found almost every day in reporting about some matters of importance for the working of American democracy. Yet there are also stunning gaps that, in retrospect, suggest the hesitancy or inability of news organizations to act systematically or routinely as watchdogs in covering other matters of high importance. In this chapter, we explore some of the factors contributing to the fragility of the watchdog role. . . .

. . . [T]he watchdog role of journalism may involve simply documenting the activities of government, business, and other public institutions in ways that expose little-publicized or hidden activities to public scrutiny. Much documentation of this sort does occur, yet journalists also often miss early-warning signs of important activities that later blow up as scandals that prove costly to the public. The energy crises and corporate accounting and fraud scandals of the early millennium come to mind here.

Another defining element of watchdog journalism involves clarifying the significance of documented activities by asking probing questions of public officials and authorities. Again, there are many cases of effective press interrogation of officials, as when high officers of the Catholic Church were challenged in the early 2000s about their knowledge of widespread child abuse at the hands of priests. Yet there are also puzzling lapses of critical questions, as when journalists initially reported administration claims about Iraqi links to the September 11 terror attacks and the presence of weapons of mass destruction in Iraq without giving similar space to the volume of challenging evidence to the contrary. When serious press challenges finally emerged, it was in response to questions raised by congressional leaders and public commissions. But those questions about the war came so late that the administration case for war was by then more a matter for historians to judge.

Also included in the above definition of watchdog journalism are the practices of enterprise or investigative reporting aimed at finding hidden evidence of social ills, official deception, and institutional corruption. Some instances of investigative reporting may point toward constructive reforms, or alert and mobilize publics to take action on pressing problems such as environmental hazards or health care abuses.[1] Other investigative reports may be aimed less at mobilizing broad publics than at finding failures that threaten the integrity of institutions themselves, such as the investigations of David Protess and Robert Warden that reversed the wrongful convictions of four black men accused in the brutal murder of a white couple in Illinois.[2]

Whether it involves merely documenting the behaviors of authorities and asking them challenging questions, or digging up evidence of corruption or deception, the idea of independent journalistic scrutiny of social, economic, and governmental institutions is commonly regarded as fundamental for keeping authorities in line with the values and norms that charter the institutions they manage. The watchdog function may also alert publics to issues that can affect their opinions and their modes of engagement in public life. Despite its prominence among the ideals that have come to define the press and its various professional responsibilities, the watchdog role has been rather weakly institutionalized in the daily routines and responsibilities of the press. In some instances, press performance provides exemplary service to the public interest, such as the disclosure of the My Lai massacre during the Vietnam War, coverage of the Watergate scandal in the 1970s, and the more recent widespread reporting on nursing home abuse and neglect of elderly patients. At the same time, there are examples of equally spectacular failures to challenge the claims of authorities, such as the gross imbalance between the high volume of reports and editorials publicizing Bush administration claims about links between the Iraq invasion and the war on terror, and the low volume of timely reports on available evidence that contradicted those claims.

. . . [New York Times ombudsman Daniel] Okrent's analysis suggests why watchdog journalism is often lost among the other considerations that drive news decisions: the "hunger for scoops" that lead news organizations to tolerate stories based on anonymous and often partisan sources; the "front-page syndrome" that leads reporters and editors to favor more dramatic and less qualified accounts; "hit-and-run journalism" that keeps news organizations from revisiting earlier headlines in light of later contradictory information; "coddling sources" to keep a story going at the price of granting them anonymity that disguises suspect motives and information; and "end-run editing" that leads editors to favor star reporter scoops, while discounting challenges by other reporters in the newsroom who may have different information from other sources.[3] . . .

Why Watchdog Journalism Matters

Journalism is the heart of democracy, the humorist Garrison Keillor once said. What he meant was that hard-edged reporting aimed at making the world a better place is central to democracy. "More crime, immorality and rascality is prevented by the fear of exposure in the newspapers than by all the laws, moral and statute, ever devised," said the publisher Joseph Pulitzer in 1878.[4] Without journalists acting as watchdogs, American democracy—at least in anything close to the form we know it today—would not exist. . . .

Communication scholars generally agree that democracy requires a public sphere where people can communicate about society and government at least somewhat independently of the authorities that convene and govern social institutions. In contemporary societies, the press and, more generally, the media make important contributions to the quality of this public sphere. Yet the mix of professional journalism norms, public tastes, political spin, and business imperatives that construct what we call news makes it difficult to imagine how to keep the public responsibilities of the press in step with a civic life that is also changing in terms of how citizens define their public roles and relations to government. In other words, it is not clear just how the press should facilitate the production of this public sphere. It is not even obvious how much scrutiny of public officials and their activities is the right amount. Too much press intrusion may become annoying and burdensome both to authorities and publics.[5] Too little critical reporting may produce poor-quality public policy debates and weaken the everyday accountability relations between authorities and publics. . . .

Uneven Practice of the Watchdog Role

. . . [I]t is easier to say that journalists should be watchdogs than to find agreement on precisely what this entails or how it might be achieved consistently. Perhaps this is why the mythic status of the watchdog press looms larger than the evidence for its universally accepted practice. . . .

The veteran journalist Murray Marder argues that the problematic standing of watchdog journalism is revealed most clearly in how reporters praise the ideal without having a firm sense of how to put it into practice. In an address on the subject at Harvard's Nieman Center, Marder noted that, all too often, the press appear not as watchdogs, but as a snarling, barking pack, substituting the spectacle or the posture of adversarialism for the sort of journalism that might better serve the public interest. Marder's prescription for restoring the watchdog role involves a simple recommendation to his colleagues:

> Disassociate ourselves wherever we can from crude, discourteous behavior whether by packs of elbowing news people lying in wait for Monica Lewinsky, or by shouting, snarling participants in a television encounter posing as news commentators. . . . That will not come easy. For in my view, watchdog journalism is by no means just occasional selective, hard-hitting investigative reporting. It starts with a state of mind, accepting responsibility as a surrogate for the public, asking penetrating questions at every level, from the town council to the state house to the White House, in corporate offices, in union halls and in professional offices and all points in between.[6]

What Marder implies here is that the press sometimes gets it right and sometimes does not, but that there is great inconsistency in being able to predict when either result might happen. What accounts for this inconsistency and its accompanying lack of institutional grounding? The most obvious and frequently discussed factor is that most news organizations in the United States are driven by business formulas that exert various limits on defining and elevating democratic press functions above other considerations. In the case of public service organizations, news decisions are made in the context of politically sensitive governmental, foundation, or corporate funding constraints. What seems puzzling is that, for all the criticism of the press, there is surprisingly little formal discussion among journalists of just what the watchdog role might look like in practical terms, and how it might be promoted more effectively. . . .

With little elaboration of a clear set of democratic reporting responsibilities, the news that we witness today has evolved as a strange hybrid of deference to authorities, and ritualistic displays of antagonism and feeding frenzy against those same authorities, interspersed with occasional displays of watchdog reporting. . . . [I]t is clear that reporters and news organizations are most drawn to stories that offer the greatest dramatic potential and hold the greatest promise of continuing plot development. Some of those stories end up being manufactured out of little more than spin, staging, and the efforts of the press pack to inject life into the political routine. . . .

When the Watchdog Barks

. . . [T]here are also many times when journalists raise challenges or discover hidden information that changes the thinking of publics or policy makers about important issues. Thomas Patterson has suggested that in its contemporary form, watchdog journalism may work best when in partnership with other institutions that are serving similar watchdog roles—parties and public-interest advocacy groups come to mind. Watchdog journalism may need these institutional partners in order to prosper—partners such as whistle-blowers . . . or political parties that are more concerned about principled opposition than strategic calculations. . . . More probing voices are likely to be introduced into the news for more extended periods when journalists find sources with prominent institutional standing who are already raising critical questions.[7] Hence, the same concerns that existed before the invasion of Iraq (about lack of Bush administration evidence for linking Iraq to the war on terror) were only given sustained voice after the commission investigating September 11 invited witnesses to raise them. By the same explanation, when journalists are the lone voices raising concerns—even documentable concerns—it is far more difficult for them to perform the watchdog function.

Ironically, the independent-press watchdog function may work least well when it is most needed.

* * *

Status of the Watchdog Role

What is the institutional status of investigative journalism today? What is the regard for this tradition among journalists and the public? What are the prospects for better integrating investigative and, more generally, watchdog reporting within the constraining matrix of corporate business imperatives, professional standards of the journalism profession, and the needs of citizens? At the opening of the twenty-first century, there was still a good deal of watchdog reporting going on, but it was scattered unevenly across the media. In the case of investigative reporting—defined as enterprise reporting on important public issues involving the discovery and documentation of previously hidden information—far more of it could be said to emerge from the print press than from television news organizations. A five-year study of TV news at the turn of the millennium found investigative reporting on television, particularly at the local level, in continuing decline. By self-report of news directors in 2002, less than 1 percent of all news was station-initiated investigation. By the research team's judgment, the ratio was more on the order of 1 out of 150 stories, down from 1 in 60 in 1998. Most of the reports that qualified as station-initiated and as containing information not already on the public record dealt with government malfeasance, consumer fraud, and health care scandals.[8]

Whether the subject is investigative reporting, or the companion activities of documenting the claims and activities of institutional authorities and raising probing questions about them, most observers agree that the present period is not a time of rich watchdog reporting in any media. Perhaps this reflects the absence of large numbers of citizens mobilized in reform movements eager for a sense of common inclusion and good information about their causes. Perhaps it reflects a time in which political culture—or at least the parties in government and the corporate culture that supports them—is bent away from government regulation and progressive public legislation. History suggests that these conditions may change and kindle more investigative activity. However, as the run of corporate scandals, environmental deterioration, military adventures, and rising levels of inequality in the 1990s and 2000s indicate, there is no lack of material to investigate. Yet reporting on the epidemic of illegal corporate accounting, disclosure, and finance did not hit the front pages until government investigations and whistle-blower reports had already begun. And the timidity with which mainstream journalism handled early evidence of Bush administration distortions in the campaign to go to war against Iraq suggests that news organizations are not eager to reframe heavily spun stories in the absence of voiced outrage from credible political-opposition voices.[9] In light of these patterns, two concerns seem to highlight the watchdog role of the press in the present era:

1. *The watchdog role has become overly stylized or ritualized.* The press has adopted a tone of cynicism and negativity often without offering original documentary material or constructive solutions to accompany that tone.[10] Television news magazines have appropriated a pseudo-investigative style, emphasizing consumer rip-offs and celebrity confessionals of little broad social consequence.

2. *When potentially significant investigative reports do surface, they are often not pursued or even echoed by other organizations cautiously following the collective lead.* . . . Even though such reports were surely read by many journalists, there was little concerted effort to follow them up or to shift general press coverage in a timely fashion—that is, before situations had grown so serious that officials inside government finally began formal investigations.[11]

Perhaps the good news is that neither publics nor journalists seem particularly happy with this state of affairs. Not surprisingly, the public has been less happy with the negative tone of journalism than reporters, who understandably perceive themselves as doing the best they can, often triumphing under challenging organizational conditions. Andrew Kohut summarized polling on the watchdog role by the Pew Research Center for the People and the Press in these terms:

The biggest gap between the people and the press is over the way news media play their watchdog role. Almost all journalists are sure that media scrutiny of politicians is worth the effort because it prevents wrongdoing. But the percentage of Americans thinking that press criticism impedes political leaders from doing their jobs has increased . . . while the number saying they value the press's watchdog role has fallen. . . . Many Americans see an ill-mannered watchdog that barks too often—one that is driven by its own interests rather than by a desire to protect the public interest.[12] . . .

The good news here is that both journalists and publics seem to recognize that the watchdog role has somehow gone off course, and that it may be time to think more seriously about how to bring it back in line with contemporary public values and concerns. Encouraging poll trends suggest strong public support for the watchdog ideal, if not for the way if is often bent in practice.

For example, a review of five national polls from the 1980s through the 1990s showed increases in public support for investigative reporting to a peak of 84 percent in 1997. However, there was also considerable objection to the practices often employed in what passes for investigative journalism today, and the emphasis on pseudo investigation and sensationalism.[13] All of this leads to the question of why watchdog journalism seems to have lost its bearing, and what can be done about it.

The Sleeping Watchdog?

Newsrooms are often organized in an old-fashioned way that dates to the founding of modern journalism in the 1840s. Because of this, many areas that should be important receive little or no watchdog coverage—advertising, the military (except for coverage of war), farming and food policy, taxes, and government regulatory and other so-called alphabet agencies. At the same time, many beats in journalism that should be important essentially are backwaters, among them religion, environment, education, labor, urban affairs, state governments, and road and sewer construction. It is sometimes said that mankind's greatest needs are food, clothing, and shelter: none of these areas are covered well. Beats that came out of the 1960s and 1970s, such as consumer beats, urban affairs beats, and coverage of the environment, had virtually disappeared by 2000.

Generally, rocking boats is not a way to get ahead in newsrooms. Publishers and editors often distrust reporters who they think have a point of view. It is OK to say you want to be a reporter covering sports, politics, or business, say, but if you want to cover the poor or labor or the environment, you are often regarded as a person with an agenda. You often won't be promoted, and you'll be watched with great suspicion.

Journalists have sold their souls for access to public officials. . . . This is not an attitude that makes for good journalism. . . . This is a particular problem in Washington, D.C. Reporters there want to cover the White House or Congress or the Pentagon, but most people do not want to cover the regulatory agencies, where things that affect people happen. Journalistic careers seldom flourish by covering the latter; star journalists are drawn to the glitter of the Georgetown social circuit and the White House. As a result, in the nation's capital, the press is often not the "fourth estate," it is part of government. And the same tendencies apply in the state house, at city hall, and at corporate headquarters.

It is also important to ask the question of who goes into journalism today. As Russell Baker has pointed out, as the news business has become more professionalized, many reporters and editors now come from upper-class and middle-class backgrounds. They are well bred, they have impressive educations, but the average American reporter has little or no knowledge of how people beyond his or her class think or act. "They belong to the culture for which the American political system works exceedingly well," Baker said, adding, "This is not a background likely to produce angry reporters and aggressive editors."[14] . . .

With conglomeration, and Wall Street's definition of what constitutes proper profits, media corporations are often run as if they were nothing more than any other kind of business. Newsrooms are deliberately kept under-staffed to save money. Reporters are pressured to do more stories in less time—again, to save money. Expense budgets for travel are cut. . . .

In all this, it must be remembered that watchdog reporting is particularly challenging. In the case of investigative reporting, the journalist is looking for things that people want to keep hidden. It is time-consuming and expensive. Simply documenting the background details of public activities and official claims takes time and work. Rarely can a reporter drop all other responsibilities to concentrate on one investigative story. Moreover, asking challenging questions of sources that must be covered on a regular basis may strain journalists' future relations with those sources. Reporters, beware the watchdog role: You will make enemies doing it.

* * *

Conclusion

In this essay several factors have been identified that affect when the watchdog role of the press is likely to work well, and when it is not. Not surprisingly, watchdog journalism functions best when reporters understand it and news organizations and their audience support it. The business climate of many news organizations today is not fully supportive; nor is the curriculum in most journalism schools; nor are publics who, perhaps rightly, see too much negativity and insider posturing in place of reporters simply asking hard questions about important subjects.

In addition, it may be time to rethink the curious professional norms of the objective or politically neutral press that remains a legacy of the Progressive Era. Such norms often seem to pit the journalistic commitment to balance and objectivity against the values of advocacy or probity. What the public receives as a result are confusing debates that seem impossible to resolve or make much sense of. What, for example, is the point of the construction of a two-sided debate about global warming when one side consists overwhelmingly of scientists who have little scholarly doubt or disagreement, and the other side consists primarily of politicians and business interests who have quite another agenda fueling their skepticism? What was the point of "balancing" the findings of the National Commission on Terrorist Attacks upon the United States (the 9/11 Commission), which stated that there was no evidence of Iraqi involvement, with continued face-value reporting of unsup-ported claims to the contrary from the president and vice president? How can journalists moderate such debates when their own current practices compel them to report them in ways that may create more confusion than clarity? The flip side of this normative dilemma is the problem of what watchdogs should do when one side of an issue is dominated by spin from a media-savvy source with high social standing, and opponents have failed for whatever reasons to mount an equally effective press relations campaign. All too often, the watchdog retreats, and what is reported as the public record goes unchal-lenged in the news.

. . . When today's press watchdog serves the public interest, it is generally in a partnership with other public watchdogs such as public interest or consumer advocacy organizations, courts, interest groups, and government itself.

During an era of a conservative turn away from public life and institu-tions, this somewhat limited watchdog function may be the best that can be hoped for from an embattled press. Yet there is also a prescription here for strengthening the watchdog role in these times:

1. Find new ways to define the democratic responsibilities of the press through journalism education, foundation support, and public discussion.
2. Strike a better balance between currently embattled professional norms and some broad and well-crafted notion of the public interest.
3. Expand beats and sources to give more voice to those who are currently left out of democratic debate, and who might subscribe to papers and watch the news if they saw themselves represented more frequently and more fairly there.
4. Stimulate debate in the profession about steering a clearer course between fear and favor in relations with the powerful sources who continue to dominate the news.
5. Explore new institutional means—including government support and regulation, public commissions, and new business models for news—to create better accountability relations between journalists and other demo-cratic stakeholders.

Mythology aside, perhaps it is the lack of clear democratic standing for the press as expressed in daily reporting practices that best explains why the watchdog sometimes barks when it should sleep, sometimes sleeps when it should bark, and too often barks at nothing.

Notes

1. See David L. Protess et al., *The Journalism of Outrage: Investigative Reporting and Agenda Building in America* (New York: Guilford, 1992).

2. David Protess and Robert Warden, *A Promise of Justice: The 14 Year Fight to Save Four Innocent Men* (New York: Hyperion, 1998).

3. *New York Times,* May 30, 2004.

4. As cited in Judith Serrin and William Serrin, eds., *Muckraking! The Journalism that Changed America* (New York: New Press, 2002).

5. See John Zaller, "A New Standard of News Quality: Burglar Alarms for the Monitorial Citizen," *Political Communication* 20, no. 2 (2003): 109–30.

6. Murray Marder, "This Is Watchdog Journalism" (2 parts), Nieman Reports 53, no. 4 (winter 1999), and 54, no. 1 (spring 2000), http://www.nieman.harvard .edu/reports/99–4_00–1NR/Marder_ThisIs.html.

7. W. Lance Bennett, "Toward a Theory of Press-State Relations in the United States," *Journal of Communication* 40 (spring 1990): 103–27.

8. Marion Just, Rosalind Levine, and Kathleen Regan, "Investigative Reporting Despite the Odds: Watchdog Reporting Continues to Decline," Local TV News Project, http://www.journalism.org/resources/research/reports/localTV/2002/investi gative.asp.

9. W. Lance Bennett, "Toward a Theory of Press-State Relations" and "The Perfect Storm? The American Media and Iraq," *OpenDemocracy,* August 28, 2003, http://www.opendemocracy.net/debates/article-8–92–1457.jsp.

10. Joseph N. Cappella and Kathleen Hall Jamieson, *Spiral of Cynicism: The Press and the Public Good* (New York: Oxford University Press, 1997); Thomas Patterson, "Doing Well and Doing Good: How Soft News and Critical Journalism Are Shrinking the News and Weakening Democracy—And What News Outlets Can Do about It" (working paper, Joan Shorenstein Center on Press, Politics and Public Policy, Kennedy School of Government, Harvard University, Cambridge, Mass., 2000).

11. See Robert M. Entman, *Projections of Power: Framing News, Public Opinion, and U.S. Foreign Policy* (Chicago: University of Chicago Press, 2004).

12. Andrew Kohut, "Public Support for the Watchdog Role Is Fading," *Columbia Journalism Review* (May/June 2001): 46.

13. Lars Willnat and David H. Weaver, "Public Opinion on Investigative Reporting in the 1990s: Has Anything Changed since the 1980s?" *Journalism and Mass Communication Quarterly* 75 (autumn 1998): 449–63.

14. *New York Review of Books,* December 18, 2003, http://www.nybooks.com/ articles/16863.

34

TERRORISM, CENSORSHIP, AND THE FIRST AMENDMENT

Doris A. Graber

Editor's Note

Although democracies tout the crucial importance of a free press, they routinely try to control the news in times of crisis, such as terrorist assaults and wars. They fear that news, especially if it is negative, will help enemies and harm efforts to maintain morale and cope with the crisis. Negative news is likely to undermine support for the government's policies and operations.

Accordingly, governments seek control over news by preventing journalists from covering potentially sensitive situations, by censoring journalists' news stories, and by appointing authorized spokespersons who have monopoly control over the news supply. The public generally supports censorship efforts, especially when news stories have argued that the country faces grave dangers and that the government is meeting them in the best possible way. The perils of indiscreet news coverage are real and serious, but so are the dangers of censorship, which may lead to a poorly informed public and to major cover-ups of government failures and misconduct.

Doris A. Graber is a professor of political science at the University of Illinois at Chicago. She has authored numerous books and articles dealing with political communication, information processing, and management of information in political organizations. *Media Power in Politics* was originally prepared as a supplement to her text *Mass Media and American Politics,* which is now in its eighth edition.

Source: Doris A. Graber, "Terrorism, Censorship and the 1st Amendment," in *Framing Terrorism: The News Media, the Government, and the Public,* ed. Pippa Norris, Montague Kern, and Marion Just, New York: Routledge, 2003, chapter 2. Copyright 2003 by TAYLOR & FRANCIS GROUP LLC - BOOKS. Reproduced with permission of TAYLOR & FRANCIS GROUP LLC - BOOKS in the format Textbook via Copyright Clearance Center.

When important values clash in democracies, policy makers and publics face a typical trade-off dilemma. Which should prevail? The dilemma is starkest when the clashing values are national security threatened by terrorism or war, endangering the survival of large numbers of citizens, if not the nation itself, and freedom of the press, which is an indispensable ingredient of democracy. Arguments about whether a free press is actually essential to democracy are beyond the scope of this chapter. Many observers believe that it is and that press freedom is particularly vital in crisis periods because decisions made at that time are apt to produce profound consequences for the nation and its people.

In the post–World War II era, national security risks have appeared in a number of guises. Formal declarations of war have become less common while military confrontations involving terrorism, counter-terrorism, guerilla warfare, peacekeeping operations, and similar so-called 'low intensity conflicts' have increased. Government deliberations, like congressional hearings on the Anti-Terrorism Act of 2001, make it clear that public officials equate the dangers posed by such low-intensity operations with the dangers posed by open warfare.

Many such military missions are comparatively brief with little advance planning and require complete secrecy to succeed. They would be compromised by premature disclosure, especially since reporters are now able to send messages, including pictures, from remote locations at lightening speed. Hence it seems reasonable to consider the history of press restraints during anticipated or actual war as precedent for press freedom policies during periods of anticipated and actual terrorism and subsequent military operations. Periods of ideological onslaught, like the Cold War following World War II, also belong in this category of extreme dangers that generate calls for the suspension or dilution of constitutional guarantees.

The Patterns of Past Solutions

There are basically three approaches to the dilemma of reconciling the conflicting aspects of press freedom and survival security. The *'formal censorship'* approach has been most common. It involves legislation that sets forth what may or may not be published. Such laws vary in the terms and scope of the censorship operations and often stipulate severe penalties for violations. The press may still be allowed to decide what is publishable within the government's guidelines. Alternatively, the decision about what may be published may be in the hands of official censors who use their discretion about the sensitivity of particular information at a specific time. In either case, freedom of the press is in abeyance, as American constitutional lawyers generally interpret it, including the traditional reluctance of American courts to permit prior censorship of potentially harmful news reports (Silverberg 1991).

The opposite *'free press'* approach leaves journalists free to decide what is or is not safe to publish under the circumstances, journalists may choose to follow guidelines provided by the government or respond to specific requests by public officials. But reporters make the ultimate decision free from formal pressure by public officials, although there are always ethical mandates to be risk-averse when national security is at stake.

The third approach, the *'informal censorship'* scheme, is an ingenious combination of the two: There are no censorship laws and the press is left officially free to decide what it does or does not wish to publish. But pronouncements by high-level government leaders constitute informal censorship because they create a coercive climate that forces the press into self-censorship in line with the wishes of public officials. Criticism of government policy is castigated as unpatriotic, flirting with treason. This form of pressure is often enhanced by a barrage of glowing reports about government progress in coping with the crisis. Self-censorship by the press is complemented by self-censorship by government officials who have been admonished by their leaders to keep their lips tightly sealed. Such "voluntary" constraints, as social scientists have documented, can be just as potent as official censorship laws (Aukofer and Lawrence 1995; Carter and Barringer 2001a).

In a 1987 speech at Hebrew University in Jerusalem, Associate U.S. Supreme Court Justice William J. Brennan Jr. reviewed what he called the "shabby treatment" that America's vaunted freedoms have received in times of war and threats to national security (Brennan 1987). He attributed these lapses to the crisis mentality that Americans develop when faced with danger intermittently, rather than living with it constantly. America's decision-makers have been inexperienced in assessing the severity of security threats and in devising measures to cope with them in ways that respect conflicting rights and liberties.

Brennan might also have added that the equally inexperienced American public has traditionally supported restraints on First Amendment rights and civil liberties when it has been polled during crises, especially if it feels militarily or ideologically threatened (Blendon et al. 2002; Kinsley 2002; Pew 2001). For example, 53 percent of the respondents to a Pew poll reported in the press on November 29, 2001, in the aftermath of the September terrorist attack on U.S. sites, agreed that the government should be able to censor news that "it deems a threat to national security" (Pew 2001). The pollsters asked which was more important: the government's ability to censor or the media's ability to report what seemed in the national interest. Four percent of respondents volunteered that both were equally important.

It is important to note that the vote in favor of government censorship hardly constitutes overwhelming agreement. Besides, a bare majority (52 percent) indicated that the media should dig hard for the news rather than accept government refusals to release it, and 54 percent agreed that media's criticism of leaders keeps them from misbehaving. On balance, however, trust in government trumped trust in the media. Sixty-one percent of respondents expressed a fair amount of confidence that the government was giving the public an accurate picture about its response to terrorism, and 70 percent thought that public safety and protection of American military forces were the main reasons for censorship.

The 'Shabby' Record of Protecting Press Freedom

In a nutshell, press freedom has routinely succumbed to national security concerns on the home front as well as on foreign battlefields. Customarily, in the United States and other democracies with strong traditions of press independence from government, this has been accomplished through legislation or orders by the chief executive or administrative agencies. A quick journey through some of the relevant events in U.S. history is instructive. In democracies where the government owns or otherwise controls the press, wartime situations are more amenable to routine press management procedures (Sajó and Price 1996).

On the verge of war with France in 1798, Congress enacted the Alien and Sedition Acts, claiming that home front censorship was essential to forestall enemy espionage and sabotage. The Sedition Act made it unlawful to "write, print, utter or publish . . . any false, scandalous and malicious writing" against government officials intending "to bring them . . . into contempt or disrepute" (1798, 1 Stat. 570). There were 25 arrests, 15 indictments, and 10 convictions under the act, mostly involving newspaper editors and politicians from the party in opposition to the government. Legal challenges to the act were unsuccessful at the time. But when party fortunes changed, the convicted were pardoned, most fines were returned, and it was widely acknowledged that the laws had been an unnecessary aberration. The dangers had been exaggerated.

Still, when the Civil War presented a major test in 1861, the story was quite similar. As soon as armed conflict started, President Lincoln took drastic measures to neutralize disaffected citizens and potential traitors in the name of national security. Through executive orders, he blocked the distribution of dissenting newspapers and, during the latter part of the war, seized control of the telegraph lines that transmitted war news. The most drastic step was the suspension of habeas corpus. Thousands of people were arrested on suspicion of disloyalty and held in military custody, often without charges. Trials were before military tribunals that lacked the procedural safeguards available in civilian courts. Such steps were bound to intimidate reporters. The public, by and large, approved these actions and condemned judges who questioned their constitutionality.

Another example of censorship legislation comes from the First World War. Congress enacted the Espionage Act, making it a crime to utter, print, write, or publish any "disloyal, profane, scurrilous, or abusive language" or any language intended to bring the U.S. form of government or the Constitution or the flag "into contempt, scorn, contumely, or disrepute" (1918, 40 Stat. 553). More than 2000 individuals, including journalists, were prosecuted under the act. Convictions were mostly for criticizing U.S. participation in the war. In *Abrams v. United States* (1919, 250 U.S. 616) the U.S. Supreme Court upheld such convictions. . . .

During the early years of the nation's history, when foreign policies were often highly controversial, the American government considered the media primarily as an obstacle to war that had to be kept under control through strict censorship legislation. That perception had changed by the time World War II started. Impressed by the successful use of propaganda by authoritarian governments, democratic governments had begun to appreciate the power of the press to rally mass publics. They now deemed it a potentially powerful ally in their struggle against the enemies of Western democracies.

The government wanted a policy that would yield ample favorable coverage of the war without risking adverse stories by roaming correspondents. This was to be accomplished by facilitating reporters' access to news about the war, including ongoing battles, but binding them to a gentleman's agreement that they would not reveal anything that might interfere with the military's mission. Instead of the harsh censorship laws of the past, there would be voluntary cooperation. Most reporters knew and complied with the unstated terms of the compact because it gave them broad access to war information; they censored themselves to live within the terms (Thompson 1991; Thrall 2000). This was easy because, unlike the situation in earlier wars, the objectives of World War II were never controversial in the United States.

In addition to these unwritten understandings, there were more formal arrangements as well to provide guidance to reporters about the limits of safe reporting. . . . Compliance with these guidelines was excellent (Aukofer and Lawrence 1995; Thompson 1991). Military authorities in the war zones were authorized to conduct their own censorship operations, which tended to be more restrictive than the civilian censorship at home.

With the Korean War, which began in 1950, the country moved back to the conditions of earlier years when foreign policies had been controversial and civilian and military government leaders feared that hostile reporters might undermine the war effort. The controversial nature of the war made it difficult for the press to keep their stories supportive of the military action while also reflecting the political controversy. Military commanders complained that the system of voluntary self-censorship allowed news sources to publish stories that endangered the war effort. They therefore urged the

Defense Department to provide compulsory guidelines. An official censorship code for war correspondents was issued shortly thereafter, in December 1950. Leaders from the journalism community and the military had agreed, following extensive discussions, that all future reports from Korea should first be cleared with Army headquarters. Stringent screening ensued that caused long delays in the transmission of news from the front and frustrated the press. As is usually the case, many provisions of the code were vague, such as the prohibition of stories that might "injure the morale" of American or Allied forces or stories that might 'embarrass' the United States, its Allies, or neutral countries. That made controversies over the administration of the codes inevitable.

By the time of the Vietnam War, the notion that news stories were likely to harm government efforts had regained full currency. Knowing that its policies in Vietnam would be highly controversial, the American government did not wish to alert the public to the extent of U.S. involvement or to the shortcomings of the South Vietnamese government, which it was supporting. Withholding of news so that it could not be published, exaggerating successes to make policies more palatable, and some outright falsifications of potentially damaging data, became accepted policy tools. News people and their reports would not be formally censored. Instead, correspondents would simply be kept in the dark or government sources would feed them carefully selected, and sometimes doctored, news morsels.

The government instructed the U.S. mission in Saigon to control information related to the war tightly by classifying documents and by keeping reporters away from military operations (Aukofer and Lawrence 1995; Thompson 1991). The U.S. mission also negotiated another code of voluntary restraint between the press and the military. Although the military favored a compulsory code in line with those used in earlier wars, none was instituted because of concerns that it might be unconstitutional absent a formal declaration of war. Overall, the self-censorship worked reasonably well; few serious security breeches occurred (Aukofer and Lawrence 1995; Thompson 1991). Of course, the codes did not prevent correspondents from reporting negative news.

To counterbalance unfavorable media stories, the Johnson administration engaged in large-scale press management. It supplied the press with favorable stories in hopes of gaining ample supportive news coverage. That approach backfired when military reverses presented a sharp contrast to earlier reports and appeared larger than they actually were because of the exaggerated optimism. Negative news provided by war correspondents was contradicted by positive reports from government sources, forcing home-front editors to choose between conflicting visions of the war. Initially, most stuck with the government's optimistic framing, but that changed later on. After the war, the military as well as many civilian analysts blamed negative news coverage for loss of public support for the war and the ultimate failure to accomplish U.S. objectives. That judgment poisoned subsequent relations between the military and the press.

During the mid-century Cold War years, Congress had passed laws to prevent spoken and written communications that might expose the country to the danger of a Communist takeover. These laws included the Smith Act, the Internal Security Act of 1950, and the Communist Control Act of 1954. The Smith Act, for example, made it a crime to advocate in a speech or in print the overthrow of the U.S. government by force (1940, 54 Stat. 671). There were many legal challenges to these laws at the time.

The clearest confrontation between the news media and the government's fight against communism occurred during and following a minor military venture in 1983 when the United States tried to avert a Marxist revolution in Grenada, a tiny Caribbean island nation. During the U.S. military invasion of the island, the media were at first kept out entirely and prevented from filing stories. When journalists were allowed to visit the island, military escorts accompanied them. It became clear after the fighting stopped that the operation had been seriously flawed and that the clumsy censorship had prevented disclosing mishaps to policy makers in the United States and to the American public. To avoid similar fiascoes, the chairman of the Joint Chiefs of Staff established a commission, headed by Major General Winant Sidle to study how relations between the press and the military could be handled better in the future. The commission was composed of experienced journalists as well as military and civilian press relations officers. The panel reported its recommendations in August of 1984. Unfortunately, its most novel recommendation—establishment of press pools for operations, which required limiting the number of reporters who cover the event—failed miserably in Panama in 1989 in a mission designed to oust Panamanian President Manuel Noriega.

Despite revisions, the pool concept did not work smoothly in the 1991 Gulf war. This brief conflict is a textbook example of government control over war news without resorting to formal censorship. The government took almost complete control of the war news supply. It used a handful of top-level military leaders to brief the press on all of the aspects of the war that it cared to disclose. When journalists were allowed to visit the front, military escorts accompanied them. The military also supplied excellent visuals of elegantly executed precision maneuvers for use by television reporters. A few journalists defied the constraints imposed by the military during the war and executives from major American media filed complaints with the Defense Department after the war about the efforts to control what reporters saw and about efforts to sanitize and delay the news. These complaints led to yet another revision of the pool system and new, albeit incomplete, rules designed to make it easier for reporters to cover the battlefronts without being leashed to officials.

The Statement of Principles—News Coverage of Combat—which was adopted in April 1992, failed to settle whose judgment prevails about what is publishable. Journalists and military personnel disagreed, and continue to disagree, about whether the military must have the final say on which stories must be submitted to it for security review and censorship. Multiple efforts to draft new ground rules have continued. But the problem may be insoluble (Department of Defense News 2001). The clashing objectives of the major players prevent permanent resolutions, despite a lot of good will and good faith on both sides.

During the conflict with Afghanistan that began in the winter of 2001, the familiar problems resurfaced. . . . The military initially restricted the media's access to the battle zones, claiming that complete secrecy was required to assure the success of the operation and the safety of the troops. Reporters were actually locked up in a warehouse to prevent coverage of one incident that involved injuries to U.S. troops from a U.S. bombing raid. The outburst of indignation that followed that episode led to a formal apology from the Defense Department and new rules to allow reporters greater access to the battlefronts. Access did improve subsequently, though many sites remained closed for a variety of hotly disputed reasons. As had been true in past wars, the courts sided with the military in censorship disputes brought before them. A federal district court, while agreeing that the First Amendment protects a limited right of access to foreign battle grounds, nonetheless refused to grant an injunction that would force the military to allow correspondents to accompany American troops in Afghanistan (*Flynt v. Rumsfeld*, 2002).

[Embedment Journalism] and Censorship

In anticipation of a second Gulf War, the Pentagon announced in February, 2003 that this would be the best-covered military engagement in American history. The new plan is designed to produce battle front coverage from an American perspective to match coverage by foreign news venues like al Jazeera. Pentagon officials selected and trained a representative pool of approximately 600 print and broadcast war correspondents, including some from foreign countries, to accompany troops from all branches of the military. These 'embedded' journalists received elementary military training so that they would be fit to accompany their assigned units at all times. The journalists were required to sign an agreement on ground rules of coverage that obligated them to submit stories that the military deems sensitive to scrutiny by military censors. However, the Defense Department promised that most stories would remain uncensored. Journalists outside the embedded group were not to be subject to restrictive ground rules. But, in line with past history, freelancers had only very limited access to front-line operations.

It is far too early to assess whether this new plan will, indeed, lead to more extensive and informed coverage or whether it will become merely another form of government news management. It seems questionable whether journalists who are buddies with military folk will be able to retain their objectivity and skepticism when they share the troops' hardships, including combat and casualties on a daily basis. Being 'embedded,' as the term suggests, simply may amount to being 'in bed' with the military.

Post–9-11-01 Home Front Censorship

In the crisis following the September 11, 2001, attack, the main censorship problems on the home front have again involved strenuous government efforts to withhold information from the press, claiming that disclosures would endanger national security. These claims have been coupled with well-publicized appeals for self-censorship as a patriotic duty, adding the pressures springing from publicity to the request. Prominent examples of official secrecy are refusals to discuss war-related matters with reporters, withholding all information about people detained by the government, limiting reports about military activities in Afghanistan to reports by the Secretary of Defense and a few generals, and failure to produce the records of what the government knew prior to the 2001 attack that might have forestalled it (Steinhauer 2002).

The Justice Department has contended, albeit without providing evidence, that press inquiries about the detainees rounded up after September 11 could be denied on national security grounds because "public disclosure would undermine counter-terrorism efforts and put the detainees at risk of attack from angry Americans as well as terrorists" (Sachs 2002). Government lawyers have argued in cases that challenged the refusal to disclose the names of the detainees and the charges against them, that national security interests outweigh any public right to know who was detained for what reasons and for what length of time (Sachs 2002).

To throttle the circulation of war-related information, the government has followed the Gulf War pattern of allowing only a few top-level military and civilian officials to report about ongoing events and plans. Secretary of Defense Donald Rumsfeld, for example, has been very accessible to the media but extraordinarily circumspect in giving facts and making claims (Kilian 2002). Reporters have to accept his messages because most of the military activities are conducted by small groups of special operations forces who can be neither accompanied by journalists nor interviewed.

The Bush administration has also urged all high-level government officials to be extraordinarily, and probably excessively, tight-lipped. For example, Attorney General John Ashcroft declined to confirm information about the

September 2001 terrorists that Prime Minister Tony Blair had given to the British House of Commons in open session. Ashcroft also issued a memorandum urging federal agencies to resist most Freedom of Information Act requests. As has been typical in these most recent examples of censorship, Ashcroft's request was framed as an act to protect cherished rights. Information disclosures, he argued, might endanger institutional, commercial and personal privacy interests. . . .

One effort to suppress information concerned satellite images. It particularly riled the press because it damaged its ability to report the news. The U.S. government had bought exclusive rights to all satellite images of the bombing of Afghanistan available from the civilian satellite Ikonos. That purchase barred the press from seeing and publicizing these privately owned high-resolution images of damage caused by U.S. attacks in Afghanistan. At the time, the Pentagon already had its own, far sharper satellite images. The decision to buy came shortly after reports of heavy civilian casualties near the town of Darunta in Afghanistan. Critics saw it as a stealthy maneuver to hide a disaster.

Government clampdowns on access to video footage were especially damaging for television journalism. News media beyond the borders of the United States were able to feature pictures of the bombing damage in Afghanistan released by the pro-Arab media and framed to reflect anti-American views. There was no matching footage from U.S. sources for friends of the United States, who therefore chose to rely on the interesting footage provided by al Jazeera, the Arab-language satellite television network. . . .

The government's policy of withholding news has been complemented by unusually strong appeals to the press for self-censorship. The debate about the propriety and scope of self-censorship escalated after National Security Advisor Condoleezza Rice phoned the chief executives of the major television networks on October 10, 2001, one month after the terrorist assault, asking them not to broadcast messages from Osama bin Laden, the alleged mastermind behind the terrorist assault on the United States. Rice warned that the taped broadcasts by bin Laden might contain encoded messages for terrorists. They could therefore stir up more violence against Americans and recruit more followers in countries like Malaysia where Muslims are in the majority. She urged broadcasters to edit bin Laden's messages before disseminating them.

. . . [J]ournalists faced strong pressures to comply with White House requests in the wake of the horrific September 11 attacks. . . . Journalists who might be inclined to dissent feared the wrath of their readers and their editors and publishers, possibly leading to loss of their job. Such social pressures transformed White House requests into commands. Predictably, the news executives promised compliance with Condoleezza Rice's request. . . .

It is not unusual for the news media to censor their coverage when they deem it essential for security interests, especially when they agree with the government's objectives and face condemnation and economic penalties for voicing dissent. But self-censorship generally happens quietly behind the scenes to avoid the impression that the media are yielding to compulsion by the government. For example, Leonard Downie, the executive editor of the *Washington Post*, acknowledged that 'a handful of times' in the weeks following the September 11 attacks, the *Post*'s reporting had prompted calls from administration officials who raised concerns that a specific story or more often that certain facts in a certain story, would compromise national security. In response, Downie said, "In some instances we have kept out of certain stories certain facts that we agreed could be detrimental to national security and not instrumental to our readers, such as methods of intelligence collection" (Carter and Barringer 2001b). Similarly, Clark Hoyt, the Washington editor of *Knight Ridder*, said that his organization had held back a report that "some small units of U.S. special operations forces had entered Afghanistan and were trying to locate bin Laden" within two weeks of the 9/11 attacks (Carter and Barringer 2001b). Other examples of self-censorship have been reported that were not directly linked to government requests but were instead produced by an opinion climate that seems hostile to criticism of the government during war. For example, domestic criticism of President Bush abated. . . .

Cloaking Censorship with a 1st Amendment Mantle

A review of recent censorship practices in the United States makes it clear that when push comes to shove in reconciling wartime security and press freedom, the First Amendment is still forced to yield. The review also shows that American public officials, as well as the public, manage to cover censorship laws and admonitions with a cloak of First Amendment covers. The excuses that officials and others gave for censorship in the wake of the September 11, 2001, terrorist attacks, transformed censorship into a defense of First Amendment rights. . . . This is quite typical behavior. America's wars have always been defended as a protection of essential democratic rights. The end—saving democracy—then justifies and hallows the means—self-censorship or censorship by government fiat. For example, a *St. Louis Post Dispatch* editorial on October 11, 2001, noted "Throughout our history, we [Americans] have been willing to trade freedom for safety during wartime."

In an address to the nation delivered on November 8, 2001, . . . President George W. Bush justified censorship measures as necessary to protect the values Americans share. He contrasted Americans with their enemies. . . .

At the same time, people who question whether First Amendment and other civil rights are actually protected by government information policies are condemned as interfering with the war effort. At best, they are accused of lacking in patriotism; at worst they are called traitors willing to help the enemy and harm their fellow citizens. For instance, Attorney General Ashcroft tried to silence critics of censorship policies by suggesting that their pursuit of "phantoms of lost liberty" was unpatriotic, "giving ammunition to America's enemies and pause to America's friends" (*San Francisco Chronicle* 2001). All the while, Ashcroft continued to proclaim full support for civil liberties, saying that the United States had always met security challenges "in ways that preserved our fundamental freedoms and liberties." . . . Censorship was a weapon to preserve treasured freedoms, not an assault on them. . . .

The recount of past and ongoing current events makes it clear that national security concerns have always trumped first amendment protections in periods of crisis. It also makes it clear that decisions made while the crisis mentality prevailed were later regretted when it became clear that curtailments of first amendment and other civil rights were excessive. Obviously, sound ground-rules for appropriate behavior under crisis conditions are best forged in times of calm. . . .

As for the ultimate trade-off, in situations when national security values and press freedom confront each other directly, history suggests that democracies are best served by balancing the scales in favor of a responsible free press. As the *Baltimore Sun* editorialized on October 15, 2001, about the War on Terrorism:

> The United States is fighting this war in part to preserve democracy and freedom, neither of which can truly be achieved without an informed public. We need to keep the information flowing and work with each other to sort out what's true and what's not. . . . [T]here may be other instances in the next few months in which good judgment should inspire editors to hold back on information that could put the nation's troops or civilians in danger. *But editors, not government, must be the arbiters of what's fit to air or print.* [Italics added.] For a free society that's fighting to retain its freedom and procure it for others around the world, no other alternative is acceptable.

References

Abrams v. U.S., 1919, 250 U.S. 616.

Administration's Draft Anti-Terrorism Act of 2001, Hearing Before the Committee on the Judiciary, House of Representatives. September 24, 2001. Serial No. 39. http://www.house.gov/judiciary.

Aukofer, Frank and William P. Lawrence. 1995. *America's Team: The Odd Couple, A Report on the Relationship Between the Media and the Military.* http://www .freedomforum.org/publications/first/media and the military.

Baltimore Sun Editorial. 2001. 'A High-tech Information War.' 10-15-2001.

Blendon, Robert J., Stephen R. Pelletier, and Marcus Rosenbaum. 2002. 'Extraordinary Measures: Who Wants Military Tribunals and Who Wants to Listen in when Suspects Consult their Lawyers?' May 17, 2002. Paper presented at the annual meeting of the American Association of Public Opinion Research, St. Petersburg, FL.

Brennan, William J., Jr. 1987. 'The Quest to Develop a Jurisprudence of Civil Liberties in Times of Security Crises.' Speech, December 22, 1987, at the Law School of Hebrew University, Jerusalem, Israel.

Carter, Bill and Felicity Barringer. 2001a. 'In Patriotic Time, Dissent Is Muted.' *New York Times,* 9-28-2001.

Carter, Bill and Felicity Barringer. 2001b. 'Networks Agree to U.S. Request to Edit Future bin Laden Tapes.' *New York Times,* 10-11-2001.

Department of Defense. 2001. 'Seminar on Coverage of the War on Terrorism.' http://www.defenselink.mil/news/Nov2001/t11182001-t1108br.html. Statement by the *New York Daily News* reporter Tom DeFrank during the seminar, co-sponsored in November 2001 by the Department of Defense and the Brookings Institution.

Espionage Act, 1918, 40 Stat. 553, 1918.

Flynt v. Rumsfeld. Civ. No. 01=2399, DDC, Jan. 8, 2002.

Kilian, Michael. 2002. 'The Pentagon Puzzle.' *Chicago Tribune,* 1-7-02.

Kinsley, Michael. 2002. 'Listening to Our Inner Ashcrofts.' *Washington Post,* 1-4-02.

Office of Censorship, 1941. EO 8985, 12-19-1941, established under First War Powers Act, 55 Stat. 840, 12-18-1941.

Pew Research Center for the People and the Press, 2001. 'Terror Coverage Boosts News Media's Images But Military Censorship Backed.' http://people-press.org/reports/print.php3?PageID=14.

Sachs, Susan. 2002. 'U.S. Defends Withholding Immigrants' Names.' *New York Times,* 5-21-02.

Sajó, András and Monroe Price, eds. 1996. *Rights of Access to the Media.* The Hague: Kluwer Law International.

San Francisco Chronicle Editorial. 2001. 'On Civil Liberties; Under Cloak of Security,' 12-9-2001.

Sedition Act, 1798. 1 Stat. 570, 1798.

Silverberg, Marshall. 1991. 'Constitutional Concerns in Denying the Press Access to Military Operations.' pp. 165–175. In *Defense Beat: The Dilemmas of Defense Coverage,* Loren B. Thompson, Ed. New York: Lexington Books.

Smith Act, 1940, 54 Stat. 671.

St. Louis Post Dispatch, Editorial. 2001. 'The Power of Information.' 10-11-01.

Steinhauer, Jennifer. 2002. 'Records of 9/11 Response not for Public, City Says.' *New York Times,* July 23, 2002.

Thompson, Loren B. 1991. 'The Media Versus the Military: A Brief History of War Coverage in the United States.' pp. 3–56 in *Defense Beat: The Dilemmas of Defense Coverage,* Loren B. Thompson, ed. New York: Lexington Books, 1991.

Thrall, A. Trevor. 2000. *War in the Media Age.* Cresskill, NJ: Hampton.

35

THE NEWS SHAPERS: STRATEGIC COMMUNICATION AS A THIRD FORCE IN NEWSMAKING

Jarol B. Manheim

Editor's Note

Efforts to manipulate news media coverage often are highly successful because astute public relations practitioners know how to produce audience-pleasing news stories that are well attuned to the media's needs. Journalists find it difficult to reject them, especially when they are offered free of charge to cost-conscious enterprises. Much of the news reaching the public has therefore become a manufactured product, concocted by political strategists who strive to shape public opinion by controlling the public's news supply.

In chapter 35, Manheim describes the tactics through which news shapers usurp the mission of a free press. These mostly unseen elites manage to create the political reality that the public experiences, all the while perpetuating the myth that the news reflects journalists' perceptions of important political happenings. In essence, the press has abandoned its journalistic standards by yielding its power to freely select, frame, and feature news for publication to large, unseen, self-serving elites. As the idiom puts it, it is selling its soul for a mess of pottage.

At the time of writing Jarol B. Manheim was a professor of media and public affairs and political science at George Washington University. He was the founding director of its famed School of Media and Public Affairs. Manheim had written extensively about the profound political influence that private-sector interest groups enjoy in the public domain thanks to their massive strategic communication campaigns that allow them to dominate the thrust of the news.

Source: Excerpted from Jarol B. Manheim, "The news shapers: Strategic communication as a third force in newsmaking," in *The Politics of News: The News of Politics,* 2nd ed., ed. Doris A. Graber, Denis McQuail, and Pippa Norris, Washington, D.C.: CQ Press, 2008, chapter 5. Reprinted by permission of CQ Press, a division of SAGE Publications.

. . . [T]he assumed natural occurrence of news is closest to the heart of journalism's mythology, for the only reality that can exist under the myth of objectivity is the one true reality that can be observed.

Journalism's dependence on the observation of this one true naturally occurring reality—shaped by the individual and institutional norms of the profession—has left journalists, and the public that depends upon them for its understanding of political reality, susceptible to manipulation. The reason is that news is not necessarily a naturally occurring phenomenon; rather, some news is purposefully formulated and shaped with skill and effectiveness to take advantage of the needs and interests of reporters and news organizations, even as they serve the interests of other parties altogether. It is not the reporters or the news organizations that do the shaping. It is the news sources themselves, or more correctly, the strategic advisers whose recommendations guide and form their public actions. These strategic communicators . . . strive systematically to ensure, insofar as is possible, that the work product of journalism reflects events and an environment, and creates a reality, which they, not the journalists, define. Their purpose is not to question or undermine the credibility or esteem that our society attaches to journalism. To the contrary, their purpose is to capture and exploit it for their own benefit.

That newsmakers should have an interest in influencing stories relating to them or their interests is hardly a new idea. What is new is the sophistication with which they are now able to affect the news, the considerable and growing extent of their success, and the expanding body of newsmaker types who are employing such methods. The breadth and depth of this trend—and, as a result, the gap between the myth and the reality of news—are now sufficient to constitute a genuine threat to the viability of journalism as we have come to know it. Table 35–1 summarizes some dimensions of the myth-reality gap. . . .

Table 35–1 Journalism: Myth and reality

The myth	The reality
News occurs naturally.	News is manufactured.
News is a form of inquiry and explication.	News is a form of storytelling.
News organizations seek to find and expose the truth.	News organizations seek to maximize profits.
Journalists are independent-thinking professionals.	Journalists are bureaucrats whose job is to fill time or space in a cost-effective, audience-pleasing manner.
Journalists are deep-earth miners who will move mountains to find the truth.	Journalists are hunter-gatherers who skim the surface for the most readily available material.
News content is a product of objective observation.	News content is a product of manipulation.

Strategy and Tactics

In fact, the development of a social technology of influence has been well and widely documented.[1] Its adoption in the form of "strategic political communication" is quite advanced.[2] Elsewhere, I have defined this form of communication as "the use of sophisticated knowledge of such attributes of human behavior as attitude and preference structures, cultural tendencies, and media use patterns—and such relevant organizational behaviors as how news organizations make decisions regarding news content and how congressional committees schedule and structure hearings—to shape and target messages so as to maximize their desired impact while minimizing undesired collateral effects."[3] It is, in sum, an applied science of persuasive political communication. Among the common elements of this science are the identification of stakeholders and their respective interests and points of susceptibility to influence, the creation of positions, the forging of alliances, and the definition and promulgation of a persuasive and goal-supporting political reality.

Identifying Stakeholders

Every political institution and every political issue is associated with a set of stakeholders—individuals, groups, or organizations with some interest in its advancement. Typically, the principal stakeholders of a policy or agency are the beneficiaries of its implementation or actions or those whose positions could be put at risk through the same. For example, the stakeholders in health care policy would include health care providers, health care workers, insurers, employers who offer health care benefits to their workers, the public, and various levels of governments. Stakeholders in the Environmental Protection Agency would include the regulated industries, private contractors who work on EPA projects, and environmental interest groups, among others. Each of these stakeholders has a set of interests, and each has ways in which it is susceptible to influence. The strategic communicator typically initiates a persuasive effort by inventorying the range of stakeholders involved in a particular policy or agency, specifying insofar as possible the nature of their respective interests, delineating their respective susceptibilities to influence, and identifying those points around which some form of common interest or alliance might be established that could bring about the desired objective. The idea is not to get any stakeholder to act against its own interests, but to cause it to act selectively in its own interest in ways that help advance the goals of the communicator.

Building Positions

With this cluster of targets in mind, the strategic communicator next begins to develop, test, refine, and roll out issue positions in such a way that two objectives are achieved. First, the positions must serve—either explicitly or indirectly—the communicator's underlying goals. Second, the positions must be framed so as to maximize the chances of building a sufficiently powerful alliance to make their achievement likely. There are many ways to build such positions, ranging from selecting particular aspects of a given issue to highlight or obscure, to choosing specific language and visual images through which to portray them. Typically, when making these choices, strategists employ social science research—surveys, focus groups, content analysis, and even physiological experimentation—to evaluate specific formulations with representative audiences.[4] Then, as selections are made and implemented, they are tested through further research until the optimal strategy becomes clear.

Building Alliances

Having identified the relevant stakeholders and designed and tested the themes to be used to influence them, the communication strategist builds political alliances. Alliance building can have several purposes. The most obvious is to enhance the likelihood of obtaining the desired outcome. But other, less obvious, purposes can be at least as important. For example, a group that knows itself to be politically unpopular can, through strategic communication, generate an alliance of other groups without itself joining or even being identified with that alliance. It thereby stands to benefit, not merely from the achievements of the alliance it has fostered, but from the greater popularity of the participants.

Defining Realities

With a message and an alliance in place or in prospect, the communication strategist next sets out to exercise political influence—to advance the substantive cause. This is the point at which the greatest incentive exists to manage—manipulate—news outcomes.

For any individual or group or institution, reality is a social construct.[5] It is the product of (1) judgments made about the meaning of (2) the information that is available at any given time. The judgments themselves are driven by many well-entrenched internal dynamics—psychological, sociological, and other factors. The judgments are generally not highly susceptible to influence, but the same cannot be said of the flow of information upon which these judgments are to be based. In greater or lesser measure, that flow can be conditioned through political action in ways that will bend perceptions of reality in one direction or another. In politics and public policy, even in the age of blogs, Blackberries, and instant messaging, the principal form in which information flows is as news. Therefore, through effective management of the news, "reality" can be shaped and influence achieved.

News management can take many forms. Knowing, for example, the pre-dilection of editors for particular types of stories, such as those with distinct elements of human pathos, communication strategists can literally create stories of those types, then bring them to the attention of editors. Similarly, knowing the preference of television editors, in particular, for stories that incorporate graphic video imagery, stories can be crafted to incorporate such imagery, then "shopped" to those most likely to pursue them. Knowing that reporters like to document their stories with quotations from authorities, strategists can provide to those reporters lists of authorities whom they know (but the reporter may not) will support their view, or they can even deliver the quotations themselves. Knowing that the media gravitate toward simple language and visual imagery to represent complex stories, communication strategists can devise a verbal and visual lexicon that at once meets the jour-nalists' needs and benefits their own positions. Through these and many other devices, news can be—is—managed with some effect.[6]

The Players: Who Would Do Such a Thing?

Such behaviors might seem to lie beyond the pale in the context of a normative discussion of democratic practice, but they are, in fact, commonplace. Their existence is an empirical fact. Strategic communication is employed by an astonishingly wide range of players in the U.S. political system, and its use continues to grow.

Political Parties and Candidates

Not surprisingly, the techniques of influence I have described were first developed in the electoral arena, where today they are not only assumed to operate, but are actually afforded some measure of legitimacy. After all, people expect their politicians to attempt to influence them, and are not surprised when others . . . try to sway their votes. . . . Though perhaps the most prolific, these electoral efforts at persuasion are in many ways the least interesting and the least significant in the political system for the simple reason that they are widely recognized, a factor that automatically minimizes their effectiveness. Strategic communication is most effective when it is least visible, and least effective when it is revealed.[7]

Policy Interests in Nonelectoral Settings

By 1981, when Ronald Reagan became president, strategic communica-tion was a fully integrated component of the policy-making process. Reagan's advisers knew that the centerpiece of his legislative agenda, a massive tax cut, would be dead-on-arrival in the Democratic Congress, so they set out to resuscitate it through an orchestrated campaign of grassroots organizing, coalition building, issue framing, and media managing. By the time they had finished, they had not only made adoption of a relatively radical policy inevitable, but they had also demonstrated for all to see the potency of strategic communication.[8] In the major public policy battles that followed—perhaps most notably in the battle over health care policy in the first Clinton administration and in the contest to shape public understanding of the U.S. role in Iraq after the overthrow of Saddam Hussein—communication strategists have been employed by industry, interest groups, and others to create and generate support for versions of reality supporting their respective goals.

Foreign Governments

One area where journalists and news organizations are especially susceptible to manipulation is foreign policy making. With the exception of the occasional high profile crisis or conflict, and even in the wake of the September 11, 2001, attacks, the American public has relatively little knowledge of, or interest in, foreign affairs and makes few demands on the news media for extensive and informed coverage. . . . The combination of low interest and limited information translates into news organizations and citizens being vulnerable to manipulation. Over the years a number of governments have worked to exploit that vulnerability. One study has shown that by the mid-1980s more than five hundred foreign governments, political entities, and companies had hired American "agents" to assist them in the United States, and that number was growing. Many of these "agents" monitored and shaped media coverage expressly to influence U.S. foreign policy.[9]

Corporations

Corporations expend vast amounts of money every year for the purpose of shaping their images. The most obvious elements of this effort include advertising and public relations. . . .

The mechanics of marketing or other corporate activities often take forms similar to those characterized here as strategic political communication, especially with respect to a company's efforts to manage its portrayal in the news, which can affect everything from its stock price to its ability to attract customers. It is only natural, then, that when a corporation sees that a political interest is at stake, it employs the same methods of influence in that arena as it does elsewhere. . . .

Labor Unions

For labor unions, particularly since the mid-1990s, strategic communication has supplanted the strike as a weapon of choice in dealing with the managements of unionized companies and has played a primary role in efforts to organize workers at nonunion companies. The unions use "corporate campaigns," which are primarily strategic communication campaigns—generally negative in character—that are designed to attack the reputation and essential stakeholder relationships of a company to pressure management to accede to a union demand. These campaigns incorporate all of the principal elements identified earlier—stakeholder identification, message development and targeting, image framing, and media manipulation. The unions have become sophisticated practitioners of this approach, which they have directed at a growing number of companies.[10] In 1995, when John Sweeney was elected president of the AFL-CIO, then the nation's premier labor federation, he publicly committed the federation to increased corporate campaign activity and pledged tens of millions of dollars to the effort.[11] . . .

Social Interests

The core elements of corporate campaigns were first identified, not by the labor movement, but by New Left political activists in the 1960s. These activists, and their successors who now constitute the contemporary Progressive Left, did not lead in the full-scale development of this form of activism. But they have rediscovered it, particularly as an element of the environmental, human rights, and similar social movements. The result is a growing number of campaigns, primarily directed against corporations, but also against governments, that seek to mobilize stakeholders as a force for change. One of the most interesting and potentially far-reaching of these efforts is the social responsibility investment movement, which, in concert with union and public employee pension funds and other allies, has been working to leverage the influence of institutional shareholders (banks, pension funds, mutual funds, insurance companies, and the like, which hold millions of shares in publicly traded companies) to change corporate governance structures and social policies.[12]

Litigants

"Litigation journalism"—the systematic manipulation of the media by parties to a lawsuit—is another application of these techniques that came of age in the 1980s.[13] The objective of litigation journalism is to shape public opinion, either at large or among a specified pool of prospective jurors, in such a way that one side in a trial or the other defines the reality of the case. For example, it was only in the context of a civil trial alleging harm from the use of a cellular telephone that the public "learned" that the use of cell phones may be associated with an increased incidence of certain brain cancers.[14] There is some reason to doubt that association, but the fact that it entered the public discourse as an assertion of fact at a critical time in the litigation framed the trial in a whole new way.[15] In a similar way, it is now commonplace for corporations, other organizations, and even individual litigants to engage in media framing when they are involved in major litigation.

Outcomes

The presence of so many players in the game of strategic political communication seems to suggest pluralism at work. After all, if corporations and unions, governments and social activists, litigants and others are all playing the same game, is it not likely that a reasonable balance of some sort will emerge? That is the obvious question, but it misses the point.

To begin with, the ability of so many different kinds of political interests to manipulate the communication system to their respective advantage hardly constitutes a ringing endorsement of the system itself. To the contrary, it suggests that the information being distributed through news organizations and other channels is, in some broadly systemic sense, not what it appears. Moreover, because the information in question has, as a central feature of the strategic communication process, been systematically reduced to its lowest common denominator of audience appeal, the apparent quality of the information provided by the aforementioned political actors and through the news media is a mere façade.[16] In point of fact, much of that information has been stripped of its substantive content and packaged in verbal and visual symbols.

Added to that is an essential fact of strategic communication: negatives trump positives. For a variety of reasons ranging from their inherent appeal to journalists to their prurient appeal to the public and their memorability, negative messages carry more weight than positive messages, and those on the attack generally have the advantage over those on the defensive. Therefore, the labor union attacking a company's reputation in a corporate campaign holds the advantage, as does the litigant making broad damage claims against another, and so forth. The likely consequences of this rising tide of negativism are greater public cynicism and less public confidence in social institutions. Both trends can be observed in the United States today.

Finally, the pluralist presumption of offsetting interests carries an implicit assumption that all of the interests in question—or some set of relevant competing clusters or alliance structures—share equally in the skills, experience, and resources that can be brought to the contest. When one considers the range of players now employing these techniques, the pairs in which they might compete, and the constraints under which they operate, that assumption is not on its face valid.

For the society subjected to the substantial and growing degree of this strategizing and implementing, the net outcome is a diminution of the quality of political dialogue in direct proportion to the degree and effectiveness of the manipulation that occurs. To the extent that political dialogue guides and limits policy making and other political behaviors, and that such guides and limitations preserve the values of the society, the political life of that society is impaired. . . .

Notes

1. Gary Mauser, *Political Marketing: An Approach to Campaign Strategy* (New York: Praeger, 1983); Nicholas J. O'Shaughnessy, *The Phenomenon of Political Marketing* (New York: St. Martin's, 1990); and Philippe J. Maarek, *Political Marketing and Communication* (London: John Libbey, 1995).
2. Jarol B. Manheim, *All of the People, All the Time: Strategic Communication in American Politics* (Armonk, N.Y.: M. E. Sharpe, 1991); and W. Lance Bennett and Jarol B. Manheim, "The Big Spin: Strategic Communication and the Transformation of Pluralism Democracy," in *Mediated Politics: Communication in the Future of Democracy*, ed. W. Lance Bennett and Robert M. Entman (New York: Cambridge University Press, 2001).
3. Jarol B. Manheim, *Strategic Public Diplomacy and American Foreign Policy: The Evolution of Influence* (New York: Oxford University Press, 1994), 7.
4. For an example, see Liana Winett, "Advocates Guide to Developing Framing Memos," in *Do the Media Govern?* ed. Shanto Iyengar and Richard Reeves (Thousand Oaks, Calif.: Sage, 1997), 420–427.
5. For the definitive statement of this notion, see Peter L. Berger and Thomas Luckman, *The Social Construction of Reality: A Treatise in the Sociology of Knowledge* (New York: Doubleday, 1966).
6. For an example of this sort of analysis as applied by so-called "progressive activists," see Michael Pertschuk, "Putting Media Effects Research to Work: Lessons for Community Groups Who Would Be Heard," in *Do the Media Govern*, 391–400. To see why the term "progressive activists" is itself a demonstration of the art, see Jarol B. Manheim, *Biz-War and the Out-of-Power Elite: Anti-Corporate Activism and the Attack on the Corporation* (Mahwah, N.J.: Lawrence Erlbaum Associates, 2004), 82–88.
7. Manheim, *Strategic Public Diplomacy*, 139–142.
8. Manheim, *All of the People*, 69–73.
9. Manheim, *Strategic Public Diplomacy*, 160–162.
10. Jarol B. Manheim, *The Death of a Thousand Cuts: Corporate Campaigns and the Attack on the Corporation* (Mahwah, N.J.: Lawrence Erlbaum Associates, 2001). An annotated list of approximately two hundred such efforts from their inception through 1999 is found on pages 311–339.
11. James Worsham, "Labor's New Assault," *Nation's Business* (June 1997): 16.
12. See Manheim, *Biz-War*, esp. 169–173; and Jarol B. Manheim, *Power Failure, Power Surge: Union Pension Fund Activism and the Publicly Held Corporation* (Washington, D.C.: HR Policy Association, 2005).
13. Carole Gorney, "Litigation Journalism Is a Scourge," *New York Times*, February 15, 1993, A15.

14. Carla Lazzareschi, "Suit over Cellular Radiation Raises Hazard Questions," *Los Angeles Times,* January 23, 1993, D1.

15. As recently as June 2006, scientists, who were still unable to resolve this question, joined with tumor victims for a conference sponsored by the National Brain Tumor Foundation. See "Brain Cancer and the Environment: What's the Connection? First-Ever Conference to Take Place in San Francisco," *PR Newswire,* June 21, 2006.

16. Manheim, *All of the People.*

36

THE INTERNET AND PUBLIC POLICY

Helen Z. Margetts

Editor's Note

Manipulating media effects means more than merely trying to steer news media behavior. It also encompasses making use of the unique capacities of a particular medium to accomplish hitherto improbable tasks. In chapter 36, Helen Margetts spins out visions of changes in government policy making made possible through the technological capacities of the Internet and the fact that access to this message channel is open inexpensively to nearly everyone. The chapter focuses on the changing role played by governments in political communication networks and the impact of new capabilities on the power to govern and sustain cultural values. On balance, the picture that emerges is reasonably bright, albeit still quite hazy.

When this essay was written, Helen Z. Margetts was a professor at the Oxford Internet Institute, University of Oxford, United Kingdom. She was also the editor-in-chief of a new journal, *Policy and Internet*. The journal is dedicated to analyzing the role of the Internet in public policy making and the consequences that ensue and affect societal patterns. This was the opening essay in the first issue and intended to articulate the journal's mission and scope.

Policymaking in the twenty-first century takes place in a changed environment. A significant proportion of social, economic and political activity across the world takes place on the Internet. The Internet is intertwined with financial markets, with government and public services, with social life and social problems, and with the criminal world. Increasingly the major challenges that face public policy—from climate change to crime to public health—are tackled with technological innovations that involve the Internet. The Internet is embedded in interactions between citizens, firms, governments and NGOs, bringing with it new practices, norms and structures. These developments require—and facilitate—a policy response. . . .

This article sets out the agenda, pointing across the cornucopia of issues. . . . First, it considers societal trends that relate to the Internet and their implications for policymaking. Second, it looks at how these trends might affect each of the four 'tools' of government policy: nodality, authority, treasure and organizational capacity, in terms of sustaining the operations of government and driving innovation. Third, it asks what 'values' we might expect the Internet to bring to policymaking. . . .

Internet-Fuelled Social, Economic and Political Change—Requiring a Policy Response

For many people across the world, large chunks of their social, economic and political life have moved online. By 2009 there were an estimated 1.7 billion users of the Internet worldwide, a quarter of the world's population. Internet penetration has reached nearly 100 per cent in some Scandinavian countries, three quarters of the population in North America, half of the European population and nearly one fifth in Asia, where it continues to grow at a dramatic rate. Asian users already represent over 40 per cent of the total number of Internet users worldwide and over 380 million of them are using the Internet in Chinese (www.internetworldstats.com). For those who have access, the Internet is the first port of call for information on almost any subject, radically lowering the transaction costs of information seeking and exchange. People are . . . doing new things, particularly with the growth of so-called Web 2.0 applications, where users can easily produce as well as consume content themselves. Examples include social networking sites, used by around a third of Internet users; photo and video-sharing sites such as Flickr and YouTube; blogs and social media such as Twitter; and peer-produced information goods such as the online user-generated encyclopedia Wikipedia, the English language version of which has over 3 million articles and 11 million registered users. The huge growth in social networking and social media sites means that a significant proportion of Internet users now produces as well as consumes content on the Internet. . . .

Perhaps more than any other area, the economic world has moved online. From the first online bank in 1994 and the launch of Amazon.com in 1995, U.S. e-commerce and online retail sales reached over $200 billion in 2008. Internet-based networks such as intranets and extranets span the whole value chain of all but the smallest of businesses in the developed world. By 2009, over 80 per cent of Internet users in the UK had bought or searched for product information online. The Internet and related technologies have brought major changes to global financial markets, particularly in terms of reduced transaction costs, cross-border money flows and spiraling complexity. New 'peer-to-peer' markets have developed, where consumers sell to each other, including Internet auction 'houses' such as e-Bay where people buy from anonymous sellers and more personalized markets within social networking sites where people buy from people in their friendship networks.

Political and interest group mobilization has also shifted onto the Internet. There has been a rise in global political activism, with Internet-based mass demonstrations against corporate globalization. New globally oriented interest groups have formed almost entirely online, such as the civic campaigning organization Avaaz, with its mission to 'ensure that the views and values of the world's people inform global decision making' and a claim of more than three million members from every country in the world (www.avaaz .org), and the online NGO Kiva, the 'world's first person-to-person micro-lending website,' which matches potential entrepreneurs in developing countries with potential donors. . . . In 2003, millions of people were mobilized rapidly across the world to demonstrate against their state's involvement in the Iraq war. In 2006, millions of U.S. citizens protested against changes to U.S. immigration policy, including 500,000 in Los Angeles alone. Mass demonstrations took place in Iran in protest at allegedly rigged election results in 2009, both organized and broadcast across the world through Internet-based communications. Even more traditional groups operate through online networks and undertake a whole range of online activities, while running down their 'offline' activities. It is a topic of debate whether political parties may not be transforming themselves into mass membership organizations online (see Gibson and Ward, 2009; Margetts, 2006a), but in any case, the Internet has had a dramatic effect on how they interact with supporters, donors and potential voters.

Basically, then, the people, firms, interest groups and political organizations with whom governments interact and make policy 'about' are using the Internet in their lives and business in a huge variety of ways, with potentially profound policy effects. A taxation agency must take account of the virtualization and flows of capital across national boundaries. An employment agency must realise that job search has moved online and must enter a highly competitive market if it wishes to provide job seeking services. Education agencies must incorporate the Internet into teaching curricula and consider the possibilities of e-learning, health professionals must understand the proliferation of online health information, police agencies must contend with cybercrime, foreign offices deal with globally linked diaspora and protest movements. The list is endless.

Although these developments are much discussed as social and economic phenomena, the policy responses that they necessitate are less often analysed. The governance of the Internet is a hugely debated issue, perhaps ironically given the techno-utopian dream of the earliest users, who saw it as the ultimate ungovernable space (Barlow, 1996; Hofmann, 2010). The more diffuse yet pervasive implications for public policy of social, economic and political changes across sectors of society, the economy and government, has been less coherently explored. . . .

The Internet and the Tools of Public Policy: Shifting the Mix?

To consider what the implications of the Internet for policymaking might be, we need an analytical device to provide some structure to the diffuse range of possible policy effects. One such device is the 'tools of government' approach conceived by Hood (1983) and developed by Hood and Margetts (2007) for the digital era. When making policy, governments are trying to influence social behaviour and shape the world outside; these authors argue that to undertake this task, governments have four basic types of tool in their toolkit. First, *nodality* denotes the property of being 'nodal' to information and social networks and having the capacity to disseminate and collect information. Second, *authority* denotes the possession of legal or official power to demand, forbid, guarantee or adjudicate. Third, *treasure* denotes the possession of money or that which can be freely exchanged. Fourth, *organizational capacity* denotes the possession of a stock of people and skills, land, buildings, materials, computers and equipment, somehow arranged.

Any public policy will involve some mixture of these four basic resources. So for example, a governmental campaign to reduce levels of smoking in a population could involve a public information and advertising campaign (nodality), regulation of advertising and the banning of smoking in public places (authority), incentivization to give up smoking through the provision of free nicotine alternatives (treasure), and the provision of professional help to give up, such as a help-line or trained counselling (organizational capacity). A government planning such a campaign would be looking at some menu of these basic possibilities. . . .

. . . [W]hat important trends in policymaking might result from the shift of so much of societal life onto the Internet?

Nodality: Rising Competition in a Heterogenous Information Environment

First, with respect to nodality, the Internet has brought change to the whole information environment within which governments (and indeed all organizations) operate. In a fundamental shift in information seeking behaviour, the Internet is becoming the first port of call for any information seeking task; over half of UK citizens now say they would go to the Internet first to find out the 'name of their MP if they didn't know it,' for example, and the figures for travel or product information are much higher (Dutton et al., 2009). As citizens go to the Internet first to find things out, what they find will depend on their search strategy and the algorithm of search engines as well as the capacity of organizations to make sure they appear in the top ten search engine results (beyond which most citizens do not stray, Petricek et al., 2005). So the nodality of government will depend upon government's ability to compete successfully in the online space, something that many governments find challenging. Nodality will also be crucially affected by the decisions of the most popular search engines (Google in the UK), which become important new actors on the policymaking stage. And a whole range of social media will have further implications; as information flows through viral networks on applications such as Facebook and Twitter, the nodality of any organization depends not just on its own Web space but on its ability to operate within these networks. Traditional media outlets such as television channels and newspapers struggle to reinvent themselves in this environment, with many (particularly local newspapers) failing during the late 2000s. With the proliferation of information channels online, it can become more difficult for government to disseminate information; the potential audience is increasingly fragmented.

An 'Arms Race' for Authority

For authority, the Internet does not change the basic resource—something that government possesses by virtue of being government. But it does vastly influence government's ability to wield that authority, both in terms of how citizens use the Internet to challenge or circumvent authority, and how governments use the Internet and related technologies to respond. The network architecture chosen for the early Internet allowed a freedom of content exchange that led early Internet users to believe it to be an anarchic, ungovernable space (Hofmann, 2010). Indeed one of the pioneers famously proclaimed in his 'Declaration of the Independence of Cyberspace' to 'Governments of the Industrial World': 'I declare the global social space we are building to be naturally independent of the tyrannies you seek to impose on us' (John Perry Barlow, 1996). From this time, the Internet itself has been a highly contested policy object itself, with intense debate over the susceptibility of the Internet to regulation, particularly with the growth in e-commerce (Lessig, 2006). And those arrangements that have developed for governing the Internet have implications for how we understand governance *per se*. . . .

The intertwining of the Internet with authority could lead to a reshaping of state-citizen relationships across regimes of all kinds. In authoritarian states, opposition movements shift online and develop new forms of political mobilization, as in the Iranian demonstrations of 2009; many regimes respond by operating sophisticated Internet filtering regimes (Deibert et al., 2008) and targeting cyber-activists. In more democratic regimes, criminal justice agencies use the Internet to mine personal information held by government and to target authority at suspect groups or key areas (crime 'hotspots') in what some have come to label the 'surveillance state' (Lyon, 2003), raising issues of 'privacy' and 'identity' which have become key areas of concern for many Internet researchers. Internet technologies also present possibilities of 'techno-regulation,' both in terms of policing the Internet itself (through automatic censoring of child abuse images, for example) and new ways of directing authority within the state, for example, for regulating health professionals, and in the use of Internet-based systems as a means to limit state corruption in developing countries. Nearly all states face spiralling cybercrime of an increasingly professionalised kind (Hofmann, 2010) and some have even experienced 'cyber war,' requiring government agencies to participate in an 'arms race' of technological sophistication in their handling of authority.

Targeting Treasure: Conditionality in Public Policy

Third, treasure was perhaps the earliest resource to move online; firms and governments moved their financial systems online from the 1950s onwards and e-commerce boomed, busted and boomed again in the early days of widespread Internet use. Changes in the way that governments and firms process treasure range from macro to micro; it is uncontroversial to argue that the Internet has brought a 'virtualization of capital' (Castells, 2009) and a spiralling complexity of financial products that played such an important role in the worldwide banking crisis of 2008–9 and that pose major challenges to financial regulation and taxation policy. The Internet and related technologies greatly enhance government's ability to identify certain categories of citizens eligible for specific benefits and tax credits, bringing a general shift towards 'conditionality' in public policy (Henman, 2010). The Internet allows more fine-tuning of treasure in other areas, for example in labour markets, where it becomes possible for certain services (including governmental operations) to be located remotely in any part of the world. Forms of spot contracting of labour have also emerged, such as Amazon's micro-labour market Mechanical Turk, where users can work at home on their computers performing a range of tasks for micro-payments.

Organizational Capacity: Shifting Boundaries between Governments and Citizens

Widespread use of the Internet means that to some extent, the balance of government's organizational capacity relative to that of society has shifted, with the emergence of new 'para-organizational' forms, such as the rise of trans-national diaspora as coherent players in foreign policymaking

(Westcott, 2008). As noted in the introduction, social movements have leapt online, seemingly remodelling the 'logic' of collective action as the costs of mass mobilization reduce and real-time 'social information' can increase incentives to participate (Lupia and Sin, 2003; Margetts, John et al., 2009). Social media facilitate 'storms' of citizen-initiated policy activity that put pressure on policy-makers to change policies. The growing phenomenon of 'peer production' (Benkler, 2006) has led to the success of Wikipedia and a whole host of other freely available user-generated information goods. Government has lagged in making use of these models of production, weakening their capacity vis-à-vis society.

The Internet challenges one category of organizational capacity in particular: organizational expertise. That is, it facilitates deprofessionalization and a remodeling of 'principal-agent' relationships across public and private sectors. Changes in the scale and quality of information available to Internet users can in some contexts drastically shift information asymmetries between professionals and citizens, often in citizens' favour. Healthcare professionals regularly encounter patients that have used search to uncover large amounts of deeply specialised information, while university lecturers must face the fact that even while they speak, their students often have literally at their fingertips a huge range of knowledge and expertise which could challenge their pronouncements. . . .

As these trends develop, it has been argued that the Internet and related technologies could really transform government's organizational capacity, presenting a new paradigm for how government is organized, in what some have labelled Digital-Era Governance (DEG) (Dunleavy, Margetts et al., 2006) where digital technologies play a central role in public management reform. Under this view, government's organizational capacity is crucially affected by its capacity to use the Internet and related technologies internally and to interact with citizens, firms, voluntary organizations and other governments, in what is now widely known as 'e-government,' surely a topic for extensive analysis. . . . Under the DEG view, Internet-based technologies (particularly 'Web 2.0' applications) could allow a 'co-production' or even 'co-creation' of public services, where citizens enter the front office of government in a 'democratization of innovation' (von Hippel, 2005).

Each of the four 'tools' of government policy then is affected in distinct ways by widespread use of the Internet, which offers new solutions and new challenges to policy-makers. For nodality, we might expect to see growing competition for governments seeking to use nodality in public policy initiatives and an increasingly fragmented information environment, in which disseminating generalized messages to the world at large may become more difficult. For authority, we see challenges to governmental authority which can require (or are perceived to require) policy responses that ratchet up technological capability, which can become an 'arms race' between govern-ments and citizens. For treasure, the Internet makes new forms of group-targeted incentivization possible, making it potentially a more agile and flexible policy tool. Finally, for organizational capacity we see a blurring of boundaries between public and private sectors and shifts in information asymmetries between professionals and citizens.

A 'tools' approach can thereby lead to a more nuanced vision of the rela-tionship between the Internet and policy, rather than a general cry of 'all change' or 'no change' as was often the conclusion of early studies. Differen-tial changes to government's capacity to use the tools are important, because they can shift the 'mix' of policy tools that policymakers are likely to select. So the challenge to government's use of nodality, for example, might lead to more authoritarian or costly government through increased use of the other tools, which are more likely to be costly, in terms of effort, expense and staff-ing requirements and the bringing of 'trouble, vexation and oppression' to citizens (Smith, 1910; Hood and Margetts, 2007: 155).

Generalized Policy Effects: The Internet and Changing Values in Public Policy

As well as bringing changes to each of the 'tools' of government, the Internet might bring more generalized change to policymaking and to the norms, values and ethics of public policy. For all four tools discussed above, Hood and Margetts (2007) noted a development towards digitally enabled 'group targeting' with a move away from the 'general' or 'particular' ends of the spectrum noted above. Basically, technological developments tend to make easier policies geared at some particular group or category of people, while making highly particular and widely generalized applications proportionately more difficult and expensive, in what communications scholars would call narrowcasting. Government can target authority specifically at certain groups, for example, by 'fast-tracking' travellers entering the country, or conversely by restricting the movement of other categories, through electronic tagging of prisoners for example. Treasure, as noted above, can be targeted condi-tionally towards groups according to their particular circumstances. Even organizational capacity may be operated in a group-targeted way, for example as in those road barriers that retract into the ground when authorized vehicles (such as taxis and ambulances) drive up close. Group targeting can make public policy more targeted and more efficient—it can also have less desirable effects, such as rising inequities between those who end up being fast-tracked and those who are slow-tracked.

The Internet could also bring new 'values' to public policy. . . . The Inter-net has been much heralded for its capacity to facilitate innovation (in what Zittrain, 2006, 2008 has termed generativity); its freedom and openness; its capacity to engender trust in social and economic interactions; and the extent to which it lowers social boundaries and facilitates equity. If public policymaking and implementation is intertwined with the Internet and related technologies, could we expect some of these values to penetrate public policy trends as well?

The Internet as a platform for policy innovation: If this were the case, one such value would certainly be innovation. As Zittrain (2006) put it, the lack of any central controlling power means that the Internet should be conceptualized as a 'generative grid' including both PCs and networks, open to the creation and distribution of innovations. For the first time, digital technologies are being widely used by individuals and groups to innovate through interconnection with each other, in contrast to earlier information technologies which were largely internal to large firms and governments. As noted above, this proliferation of societal driven innovation requires a policy response across the policy tools. Quite simply, government has to innovate to preserve its nodality in the face of competition, to wield authority, to tax, to spend and to organize in the age of the Internet.

Openness in policymaking: Another value that the Internet might bring to public policy is openness, characterised by the freedom from control by any central agent in the design of the Internet; open access to information; and new possibilities for citizens to participate in policymaking. Openness is a value which contrasts strongly with the traditional perspective of governments and firms. The Internet has the potential to bring increased transparency (Hood and Heald, 2006), for example through open software which has even been hypothesised to lead to more effective democratic government (Camp, 2006), through reduced complexity of 'joined-up' government, greater accessibility of public information, moves towards freedom of information and 'open-book' government and more 'rule-like' government processes (Margetts, 2006b).

Trust in government?: Another potential value that the Internet could bring to public policy processes is trust, perhaps surprisingly given the traditional assumption that trust is something that evolves through face-to-face interaction. There is evidence to suggest that the Internet and the Web are 'experience technologies'; the more that people experience them the more they trust the applications and information that they provide (Dutton and Shepherd, 2006). . . . As electronic public services become ubiquitous, . . . [w]ill citizens trust government more online—because they feel that decisions have been made in an automated rules-based and impartial way—or less, because they perceive a ruthless automated dehumanised officialdom? And how can issues of privacy and online identity be resolved in ways that maintain trust in citizen-government and business-citizen relationships?

Equity—and inequity: Finally, equity was at the heart of the new forms of social organization heralded by the early techno-utopians who saw cyberspace as a place where traditional prejudices, social boundaries and inequities could be broken down. The anonymity that the Internet provides (encapsulated by the famous *New Yorker* cartoon of a dog sitting at a computer terminal with the caption 'On the Internet, no-one knows you are a dog,' 5th July 1993) can be one way that prejudices are reduced (although in the dog's case, they would re-emerge). In policy terms, however, it is clear that the Internet has also brought the potential for new inequities, particularly for those who lack Internet skills or access. Digital exclusion has been shown to be associated with social and economic exclusion (Helsper, 2008; Helsper and Galacz 2009) and such inequities between the digitally included and excluded could be exacerbated as electronic interaction becomes the norm, with the potential for 'residualization' of services for excluded groups, as offline channels are run down or even withdrawn altogether. Online equity is enhanced by the development of the non-English Internet, as huge new language populations move online, although other inequities could be on the way as the Web becomes increasingly segmented according to language.

There is of course nothing inevitable about the appearance of these values in public policy trends, but we can expect to see them raised by those analyzing the relationship between the Internet and policy. And if they do become prevalent in policymaking environments, then we might also expect particular counter-values in policymaking to arise. For example, as governments—traditionally viewed as poor innovators particularly where technology is involved—are forced into positions where they have to innovate, we might expect higher levels of risk in policymaking, and the attempt to counter risk by bringing robustness and resilience, at the heart of traditional perspectives on public administration, back in as counter-values (Hood, 1991). Likewise, if the values of openness and trust mean that public sector information becomes widely available and people more trusting of Internet-based applications, we might see security emerging as a key value of public policy and administration. Alternatively, as personal information becomes so freely available online, meaning that nothing is forgotten but remains available indefinitely, Mayer-Schöberger (2009) has argued that we need to bring specific policies geared at 'the virtue of forgetting,' such as mandatory expiry dates on documents that contain such information. And as openly produced and freely consumed goods have become widely available, such as encyclopaedias and news sources, we have seen the traditional producers of private goods, such as mainstream media, devise ways of returning such goods to the market; for example, various prominent media figures claim that most newspapers will soon be charging for content online (as the *Financial Times* already does). Finally, as noted above, the possibilities for equity facilitated by the Internet provoke new questions of inequity for those who do not have Internet access or skills, discussed under the banners of 'digital divides' and 'digital exclusion.' . . .

References

Barlow, J. P. 1996. *A Declaration of the Independence of Cyberspace.* 8 February. Available at: http://w2.eff.org/Censorship/Internet_censorship_bills/barlow_0296.declaration

Benkler, Y. 2006. *The Wealth of Networks: How Social Production Transforms Markets and Freedom,* Yale University Press.

Camp, L. J. 2006. 'Varieties of Software and their Implications for Effective Democratic Government,' in C. Hood and D. Heald (eds.), *Transparency: The Key to Better Governance?* Oxford University Press.

Castells, M. 2009. *Communication Power,* Oxford University Press.

Deibert, R., Palfrey, J., Rohozinkski, R., and Zittrain, J. 2008. *Access Denied: The Practice and Policy of Global Internet Filtering,* Cambridge: MIT Press.

Dunleavy, P., Margetts, H., Bastow, S., and Tinkler, J. 2006. *Digital-era Governance: IT Corporations, the State and e-Government,* Oxford University Press.

Dutton, W. H., and Shepherd, A. 2006. 'Trust in the Internet as an Experience Technology,' *Information, Communication and Society* 9 (4).

Dutton, W. H., Helsper, E., and Gerber, M. 2009. *The Internet in Britain: The Oxford Internet Survey (OxIS) 2009,* Oxford: Oxford Internet Institute.

Gibson, R., and Ward, S. 2009. 'Parties in the Digital Age—A Review Article,' *Representation* 45 (1): 87–100.

Helsper, E. J. 2008. *Digital Inclusion: An Analysis of Social Disadvantage and the Information Society,* Oxford: Oxford Internet Institute.

Helsper, E. J., and Galacz, A. 2009. Understanding Links between Digital Engagement and Social Inclusion in Europe, in A. Cheong and G. Cardoso (eds.), *World Wide Internet: Changing Societies, Economies and Cultures,* Macao University Printing House: Taipa, Macau.

Henman, P. 2010. *Governing Electronically,* Palgrave Macmillan.

Hofmann, J. 2010. 'Et in Arcadio Ego: From Techno-utopia to Cybercrime,' in Helen Margetts, Perri 6 and Christopher Hood (eds.), *Paradoxes of Modernization: Unintended Consequences of Public Policy Reform,* Oxford University Press.

Hood, C. 1991. 'A Public Management for all Seasons,' *Public Administration* 69 (1): 3–19.

Hood, C. 1983. *The Tools of Government,* London: Macmillan.

Hood, C., and Heald, D. (eds.) 2006. *Transparency: The Key to Better Governance?* Oxford University Press.

Hood, C., and Margetts, H. 2007. *The Tools of Government in the Digital Age,* London: Palgrave Macmillan.

Lessig, L. 2006. *Code and Other Laws of Cyberspace, Version 2.0,* New York: Basic Books.

Lupia, A., and Sin, G. 2003. 'Which Public Goods Are Endangered? How Evolving Communication Technologies Affect the Logic of Collective Action,' *Public Choice* 117: 315–331.

Lyon, D. 2003. *Surveillance as Social Sorting: Privacy, Risk and Digital Discrimination,* London: Routledge.

Margetts, H. 2006a. 'Cyber Parties,' *Handbook of Party Politics,* London: Sage.

Margetts, H. 2006b. 'Transparency in Digital Government,' in C. Hood and D. Heald (eds.), *Transparency: The Key to Better Governance?* Oxford University Press.

Margetts, H., John, P., Escher, T., and Reissfelder, S. 2009. 'Experiments for Web Science: Examining the Effect of the Internet on Collective Action,' Proceedings of the WebSci'09: Society On-Line Conference, 18–20 March 2009, Athens, Greece.

Mayer-Schönberger, V. 2009. *Delete: The Virtue of Forgetting in the Digital Age,* Princeton University Press.

Petricek, V., Escher, T., Cox, I. J., and Margetts, H. 2005. 'The Web Structure of E-Government—Developing a Methodology for Quantitative Evaluation,' in Proceedings of the 15th International World Wide Web Conference (WWW 2006).

Smith, A. 1910. *The Wealth of Nations,* London: Dent. First published 1776.

von Hippel, E. 2005. *Democratizing Innovation,* Cambridge: MIT Press.

Westcott, N. 2008. 'Digital Diplomacy: The Impact of the Internet on International Relations,' Oxford Internet Institute Working Paper, Number 16.

Zittrain, J. 2008. *The Future of the Internet, and How to Stop It,* London: Penguin Books.

Zittrain, J. 2006. 'The Generative Internet,' *Harvard Law Review* 119: 1974–2040.

INDEX

publicity bureaus and, 310–311
representation and responsiveness of,
    317–318, 319, 321, 322–323
strategic communications and, 253
subsidies and, 391
USA Patriot Act and, 238, 252,
    253–263
Connor, Theophilus Eugene ("Bull"),
    278–279, 281
Conservation and conservationists, 95
Conservative Party (UK), 21, 22, 26–27
Conservatives and conservatism,
    107, 176
Consumers, 375–376, 378, 384. *See also*
    Regulators and regulations
Cook, Timothy, 81–82, 101–111
Coopman, Ted, 251–266
Corporations, 426–428
CPI. *See* Committee on Public
    Information
Creel, George, 311
Crigler, Ann R., 116
Crime and punishment
    audience predisposition and, 82
    news stories of, 73, 129–139
    public opinions of (super-predator
        perspective), 129–139
    September 11, 2001 and, 142, 143,
        144, 145
Cronkite, Walter, 93
Cues, 351. *See also* Reporters and
    reporting; Voters and voting
Cultural Environment Movement, 393
Culture. *See* Social issues
Cunningham, Randal ("Duke";
    R-Calif.), 58
*Cycles of Spin: Strategic Communication
    in the U.S. Congress* (Sellers), 267

D

Daily Mail (UK), 21
Daily Star (UK), 22, 23, 25, 26
Dale, Iain, 212
Darfur (Sudan), 285–286, 287
Daschle, Tom (D-S.D.), 259, 267
Davis, Richard, 239, 293–301
DBS (direct broadcast satellite). *See*
    Technology—specific
Dean, Howard, 173–174, 206, 210

Debates. *See* Campaigns
Defense, Department of, 411–412,
    413–414
Defense spending issues, 316–321, 323
Definitions
    citizen empowerment, 208–209
    communication, 8
    democratic representation, 318
    foreign correspondent, 74
    framing, 72
    information, 8, 11
    information regimes, 11
    information revolutions, 11, 12
    interest groups, 12
    journalism, 71
    news, 71
    newsworthiness, 295
    political discourse, 8
    politics, 47
    the public, 384
    television and print services, 370
    watchdog journalism, 396
DEG. *See* Digital-Era Governance
DellaVigna, Stefano, 20
Democracy. *See also* First Amendment;
    Freedom of the Press
    audience fragmentation and,
        162–163, 205
    blogs and, 205, 289
    candidate sound bites and, 176
    checkbook and grassroots
        democracy, 384
    clashing values in, 408
    dependence on official sources and, 35
    e-democracy, 203–213
    elite influences on, 10, 28
    information and communication and,
        9, 10, 11, 13, 17, 288–289
    Jacksonian democratization, 11
    journalists and journalism and, 35, 61,
        397–398
    knowledge and, 7–8
    lobbying and, 308
    in the Middle East, 288
    news media and, 57–65, 68, 205
    the press and, 33–34, 43, 73n4,
        205, 410
    print media and, 179
    reporters and reporting and, 397, 399
    social networks and, 205